Franco Milicchio · Wolfgang A. Gehrke

Distributed Services with OpenAFS

for Enterprise and Education

With 67 Figures and 25 Tables

 Springer

Franco Milicchio
Wolfgang A. Gehrke

University Roma Tre
Department of Computer Science and Automation
Via della Vasca Navale, 79
00146 Roma
Italy
milicchio@dia.uniroma3.it
wgehrke@dia.uniroma3.it

ISBN 978-3-642-07172-0   e-ISBN 978-3-540-36634-8

Springer is a part of Springer Science+Business Media

springer.com

Cover design: KünkelLopka Werbeagentur, Heidelberg

Printed on acid-free paper   33/3100/YL - 5 4 3 2 1 0

Distributed Services with OpenAFS

To our families.

In memory of Giulio Balestreri.

Preface

This book provides a concise answer to how one should organize a robust enterprise IT infrastructure based on open-source software with mainstream hardware. It is a necessity for large organizations to build a central user authentication service, global user information storage, and to offer common access to personal files regardless of the location the user wishes to connect from. All these issues have been addressed with the help of well-established technologies such as the industry standard Kerberos for user authentication and the OpenAFS distributed file system, originally conceived at CMU and used at universities like MIT and Stanford and also at research institutions like CERN among many others.

Our presentation offers support for system architects and administrators, to decide and implement an enterprise IT infrastructure, and for advanced UNIX users wishing to look beyond isolated workstations, to experience the move from local to global administration and the resulting challenges. The presentation is a step-by-step guide, accompanied with a detailed explanation of the corresponding technical context that mirrors our own experience gained during the setup of an AFS cell at our computer science and engineering department. The main focus lies on the application of UNIX-based services, with particular attention to the underlying OpenAFS file system: therefore it can be seen as a companion to the excellent and currently only available book "Managing AFS: The Andrew File System" by Richard Campbell, which reflects the new state of today's implementation.

All services have been implemented with two primary goals: provide security and offer fault-tolerance. Our focus will be on the explanation of procedures to avoid insecure services, as well as provide reliability and redundancy. A key component in the realization is the OpenAFS file system, which provides a free and open-source solution, notable for its geographic scalability and data-recovery features like data replication and automated backup. With the advent of Gigabit Ethernet it can even be a low-cost NAS or SAN substitution. For implementing this architecture a solid operating system was needed, and our choice fell on the open-source Debian GNU/Linux distribution. This distribution is renowned as a free-of-charge, stable, UNIX-like operating system, equipped with an advanced package-management system for updating software, and furthermore offering all necessary packages without additional costs. Nevertheless the flexibility of OpenAFS permits a wide range of other UNIX versions as an underlying platform, too.

This book *confronts the problem* of client support with open network standards in an environment using different operating systems such as Linux, MacOS X, and Windows; *offers a general approach* consisting of the platform-independent combination of Kerberos, LDAP, and OpenAFS; *provides a solution* based on open-source server software on top of Debian GNU/Linux; and finally *goes operational* with the focus on configuration of the single components without the necessity of compilation. Because of the numerous cooperating technologies, not every aspect can be covered in detail. It has been compiled to the best of knowledge of both authors and required the consultation of many sources from the Internet.

The following implementation makes use of symmetric and asymmetric cryptography: you might have to examine the laws of your country in order to verify which use of cryptography is legitimate. All mentioned registered trademarks are the property of their respective owners.

Acknowledgments

We wish to thank our colleagues, in particular Prof. Alberto Paoluzzi, for encouraging us during the work on this complex topic. Furthermore we are deeply indebted to Prof. Jochen Pfalzgraf for establishing the initial contact with the publisher. Mr. Hermann Engesser from Springer actively supported our project and Ms. Dorothea Glaunsinger constantly kept in touch with us. The first author wishes to thank Prof. Vadim Shapiro, who very generously supported his studies while visiting the University of Wisconsin-Madison. The second author wishes to express his gratitude to Prof. Frank Pfenning for the invitation and hospitality during a stay as visiting scientist at the School of Computer Science at Carnegie Mellon University in 1994, which was also his first experience seeing AFS at work. Last but not least we have to acknowledge the work of the innumerable people and many companies contributing to the success of open-source software, in particular all developers of OpenAFS and Debian.

Contents

Part III Applications

List of Tables

1

The Beginning

> *The beginning of knowledge is the discovery of something we do not understand.*
> Frank Herbert

1.1 Outline

This book explores the distribution of fundamental network services in the UNIX world based on a client-server model. Historically the *Network Information System*, NIS, together with the *Network File System*, NFS, both developed by Sun Microsystems, have been employed frequently for this purpose. Here we will present a different approach, mainly characterized by the application of OpenAFS, which to some degree resembles the former Distributed Computing Environment, DCE, a software system developed in the 1990s by a consortium of software and hardware companies, including Apollo Computer (later part of the Hewlett-Packard Company), Digital Equipment Corporation (bought by Compaq which subsequently merged with Hewlett-Packard, too), and the International Business Machines Corporation.

This book is divided into three parts, providing a live description of services running on UNIX servers. The first part of the book describes the fundamental architecture of our software environment, from the basic services such as DNS and NTP, to the core consisting of Kerberos V, OpenLDAP, OpenAFS, and Samba as a gateway to the Windows world.

The second part includes additional services such as DHCP, TFTP, a Certificate Authority, and an emergency operating system which clients could boot directly from the network in case of system failures. On the top of the backbone services, the book will provide an overview of web and message services such as email, news, and mailing lists.

The third part is dedicated to the description of various application scenarios, including a basic cluster setup, a laboratory installation and additional collaborative services such as an instant messaging system and source version control services.

One comment should be added here about the realization of this book. All the services have been actually implemented on real machines connected to a network, and the output has been recorded live through the `script` UNIX command, which creates a complete typescript of a terminal session. Occasionally the other command `screendump` got used to record the screenshot of a given terminal.

Conventions

This book requires a basic knowledge of the functioning of a UNIX system and an essential networking background. Our exemplary domain will be named `example.edu`, referring to our hypothetical institution named *"Example Organization"*.

In the following occur many screenshots where the UNIX shell prompt will appear: the convention used in this book is to indicate with a dollar sign "$" a user prompt, and a `root` shell prompt with the pound "#". This convention is often adopted by the shell commands themselves. Command outputs may exceed the limits imposed by typographic margins, so to indicate that a particular line continues on the following, we will use the backslash "\" character. Not all the output will be reproduced in cases where considered not necessary.

Each chapter ends with a practical part suggesting exercises. These are just hints to reflect further the material presented, with the last one generally significantly more difficult.

1.2 Preparation

This section shows a really minimal Debian GNU/Linux installation, a rather server oriented distribution, started in 1993 by Ian Murdock, at the time a student at the Purdue University[1]. Its primary objective is to provide a free and open source operating system based on the UNIX tools released by the GNU Project, started by Richard Stallman in 1983.

Linux itself is essentially a kernel, and a complete UNIX-like operating system is obtainable in the form of *distributions* provided by independent vendors, either commercial as RedHat and Novell (former SuSE Linux), or by organizations developing the distribution free of charge such as the Debian GNU/Linux distribution. A notable non-commercial distribution is Slackware, started by Patrick Volkerding, which was one of the first distribution and today the oldest. We have been choosing the Debian GNU/Linux distribution because of its known stability and long-term support of packages, making it a suitable option for servers; moreover, it provides many integrated packages with an advanced management system that installs all dependent packages when needed. Several distributions have been choosing this software maintaining system, notably Ubuntu, an offspring of Debian and sponsored by

---

[1] The name "Debian" comes from the initials of Ian, and his girlfriend, and now wife, Debra.

Canonical Ltd. founded by Mark Shuttleworth with the objective of promoting the free software.

A minimal CD-ROM ISO image for a Debian system requires about 200 MB of free disk space, and provides a bootable CD-ROM image. The Debian installer guides the user through the setup process with a command-line based wizard, allowing an easy partitioning of hard drives with the choice of several file system types. A working network is vital during the installation of a Debian system, since all the needed packages will be downloaded from remote repositories: any ISP provides top-level network access to DNS services, and there are DNS services free of charge, too.

The installation process creates besides the administrative `root` user another one which we call `admin`. It is sufficient to configure the mail transport agent `exim` for local delivery only, redirecting mail for `root` to this second user `admin`. Anyway, the `exim` settings are not critical since they are going to be disabled in the following.

Debian Basics

We want to secure the freshly installed system as much as possible from the very beginning. Since by default Debian activates some services and opens some ports, we will manually correct this before we go on. To perform the following operation we need to gain `root` access. In general it is not desirable to run unnecessary processes on a server: they clearly consume resources, but more critically, open ports on a networked machine which might might provide an entry point of a possible break in, posing a security threat.

Before starting to close inessential services on our new host, we perform a basic update of the Debian system. The main tool used to handle package installation and removal is `apt-get`. The program provides an easy to use interface to manage the package repository, the database of all known software to the Debian system. It is common practice to synchronize the package list with the remote software sources, done via the **update** subcommand:

```
# apt-get update
```

Once the local package list is in sync with the remote repositories, with the **upgrade** subcommand it is possible to update all outdated packages to their new version:

```
# apt-get upgrade
```

The upgrade process should perform flawlessly, resolving all conflicts with different package versions and dependencies. The **dist-upgrade** subcommand is a shortcut to perform an upgrade, and handle package dependency conflicts automatically, giving higher priority to the most critical software if needed:

```
# apt-get dist-upgrade
```

As a detailed example for the installation of a package, let us install a useful command called `less`. The `less` command is a screen pager program for files, with displaying and searching capability. First we search the name of the package with the help of the `apt-cache` tool, retrieving all the packages with a "less" string in its name or description, using the `search` subcommand:

```
# apt-cache search less
3ddesktop - "Three-dimensional" desktop switcher
aircrack - wireless WEP cracker
...
smstools - SMS Server Tools for GSM modems
util-vserver - tools for Virtual private servers and context switching
```

The tool is shipped with the homonymous package, which can be inspected by the same tool with the `show` subcommand followed by the package name:

```
# apt-cache show less
Package: less
Priority: standard
Section: text
Installed-Size: 256
Maintainer: Thomas Schoepf <schoepf@debian.org>
Architecture: i386
Version: 382-1
Depends: libc6 (>= 2.3.2.ds1-4), libncurses5 (>= 5.4-1), debianutils (>= 1.8)
Filename: pool/main/l/less/less_382-1_i386.deb
Size: 101816
MD5sum: 49c50edc45a6ba8faf231873fbfef6e0
Description: Pager program similar to more
 Less is a program similar to more(1), but which allows backward
 movement in the file as well as forward movement. Also, less does not
 have to read the entire input file before starting, so with large input
 files it starts up faster than text editors like vi(1).  Less uses
 termcap (or terminfo on some systems), so it can run on a variety of
 terminals.  There is even limited support for hardcopy terminals.
 .
 Homepage: http://www.greenwoodsoftware.com/less/
```

A package information includes the list of all prerequisite packages, the current available version, and a brief description. Installing the `less` package can be done via the `apt-get` tool with the `install` subcommand followed by the package name:

```
# apt-get install less
Reading Package Lists...
Building Dependency Tree...
The following NEW packages will be installed:
  less
0 upgraded, 1 newly installed, 0 to remove and 0 not upgraded.
Need to get 102kB of archives.
After unpacking 262kB of additional disk space will be used.
Get:1 http://mirror.switch.ch stable/main less 382-1 [102kB]
Fetched 102kB in 0s (204kB/s)
Selecting previously deselected package less.
(Reading database ... 13098 files and directories currently installed.)
```

```
Unpacking less (from .../archives/less_382-1_i386.deb) ...
Setting up less (382-1) ...
```

In case the `apt-get` command also installs any required package, eventually prompting for the user approval.

The default way of enabling and disabling services at boot time is the Debian tool `update-rc.d`, which handles the startup script links in the `rc` directories on a per run-level basis. Apart from the bare bones command line tool, we find a graphical utility more practical. For this we install the `rcconf` tool with the standard `apt-get` tool, feeding it with the `install` subcommand followed by the package name:

```
# apt-get install rcconf
```

Using this text-based graphical interface, we can start removing all the unnecessary services such as `exim4`, `inetd`, and `ppp` - a mail daemon, a super-server[2], and a point-to-point dial-up service, respectively. For the moment just `atd`, `cron`, `klogd`, `makedev`, and `sysklogd` are needed: a user-available job scheduler, a system-level command scheduler, the Linux kernel log handler, the device creating tool, and the system events logger. Any running services are not stopped by the `rcconf` interface, and need to be stopped manually, for instance the `exim4` and `inetd` server:

```
# /etc/init.d/exim4 stop
Stopping MTA: exim4.

# /etc/init.d/inetd stop
Stopping internet superserver: inetd.
```

Afterwards the `rcconf` tool shows all the boot-time services, similar to the following output:

```
----------]] rcconf - Debian Runlevel Configuration tool [[-----------
|                                                                      |
|    [ ] anacron                                        ^              |
|    [*] atd                                            #              |
|    [*] cron                                           |              |
|    [ ] exim4                                          |              |
|    [ ] gpm                                            |              |
|    [*] klogd                                          |              |
|    [*] makedev                                        |              |
|    [ ] inetd                                          |              |
|    [ ] ppp                                            |              |
|    [ ] ssh                                            |              |
|    [*] sysklogd                                       v              |
|                                                                      |
|                                                                      |
|                                                                      |
|                                                                      |
|              <Ok>                        <Cancel>                    |
```

---

[2] We will introduce and explain such a service in the Kerberos chapter.

Stopping services results in a decrease in the running process list, viewable with the standard UNIX command ps:

```
# ps auxg
USER       PID %CPU %MEM   VSZ   RSS TTY      STAT START   TIME COMMAND
root         1  0.0  0.0  1496   512 ?        S    10:51   0:00 init [2]
root         2  0.0  0.0     0     0 ?        S    10:51   0:00 [keventd]
root         3  0.0  0.0     0     0 ?        SN   10:51   0:00 [ksoftirqd_CPU0]
root         4  0.0  0.0     0     0 ?        S    10:51   0:00 [kswapd]
root         5  0.0  0.0     0     0 ?        S    10:51   0:00 [bdflush]
root         6  0.0  0.0     0     0 ?        S    10:51   0:00 [kupdated]
root        99  0.0  0.0     0     0 ?        S    10:51   0:00 [kjournald]
root       457  0.0  0.0     0     0 ?        S    10:51   0:00 [khubd]
root      1083  0.0  0.1  1544   616 ?        Ss   10:52   0:00 /sbin/syslogd
root      1086  0.0  0.2  2208  1380 ?        Ss   10:52   0:00 /sbin/klogd
daemon    1128  0.0  0.1  1672   636 ?        Ss   10:52   0:00 /usr/sbin/atd
root      1131  0.0  0.1  1748   724 ?        Ss   10:52   0:00 /usr/sbin/cron
root      1138  0.0  0.0  1484   476 tty2     Ss+  10:52   0:00 /sbin/getty 38400 tty2
root      1139  0.0  0.0  1484   476 tty3     Ss+  10:52   0:00 /sbin/getty 38400 tty3
root      2293  0.0  0.0  1484   476 tty4     Ss+  10:58   0:00 /sbin/getty 38400 tty4
root      2294  0.0  0.0  1484   476 tty5     Ss+  10:58   0:00 /sbin/getty 38400 tty5
root      2295  0.0  0.0  1484   476 tty6     Ss+  10:58   0:00 /sbin/getty 38400 tty6
root      2301  0.0  0.3  3000  1684 tty1     Ss   10:58   0:00 -bash
root      2468  0.0  0.1  2480   864 tty1     R+   12:26   0:00 ps auxg
```

The ps tool shows the process list on our system, while the netstat command prints on the console all the network connections, statistics, and routing information, and with the -a option it displays both listening and non-listening sockets:

```
# netstat -a
Active Internet connections (servers and established)
Proto Recv-Q Send-Q Local Address           Foreign Address         State
Active UNIX domain sockets (servers and established)
Proto RefCnt Flags       Type       State         I-Node Path
unix  3      [ ]         DGRAM                    939     /dev/log
unix  2      [ ]         DGRAM                    970
```

For a more extended check of connections, we want to use the lsof and nmap security tools, installable with the usual apt-get command:

```
# apt-get install lsof nmap
```

The nmap program is a network security scanner and exploration tool, allowing many options for displaying various information about open ports and their status, running services and operating system version. For instance, we can use nmap to check all the open ports on the local machine both TCP and UDP with the -sT and -sU switches, respectively:

```
# nmap -sT -sU localhost
```

On UNIX systems all network connections are usually handled by files (e.g. sockets or pipes), and the `lsof` command is a practical tool to inspect all the open files in a system. It can be fed with the `-i` switch to show all the Internet connections, followed by the IP version number, i.e. 4 for IPv4 and 6 for the new IPv6 protocol:

```
# lsof -i4
```

Nothing should be shown open and that is the clean state we want to start out with.

Practice

Exercise 1. Test different file systems of your choice like `ext2`, `ext3`, and `xfs`. Use varying disk sizes too, for operations as creating the file system, checking it for inconsistencies, or producing and deleting big files. You should experience significant differences in speed.

Exercise 2. Reflect the choice of the Debian distribution in your case. Could the Ubuntu Server LTS (Long Term Support) version be an alternative? Damn Small Linux, KNOPPIX, or some Ubuntu LiveCD can give you a first impression of a Debian based distribution.

Exercise 3. To prepare for the next steps, review some available technical overview of AFS, DCE/DFS, and Microsoft's DFS. What do they have in common, and where do they differ?

Exercise 4. Examine whether you require further server hardening. Possible options may include a firewall for better service protection, SELinux for a stronger privilege separation between different services, the OpenBSD operating system as a safer choice for critical core services. All of these require significant technical skill.

Part I

Core Services

2

Foundations

Time is the most valuable thing a man can spend.
Theophrastus

2.1 Network Time Protocol

It is well known that time is an extremely important resource. In network environments time is fundamental for security reasons, just think about the log files which contain the exact time an event happened. This adjective *"exact"* can not be eliminated. All clients and servers should have their timers synchronized through a standard protocol called *Network Time Protocol*, or with the acronym NTP.

NTP was designed by Dave Mills using the UDP port 123 and is one of the oldest protocols still in use on TCP/IP networks. This protocol used the algorithm invented by Keith Marzullo for his Ph.D. and it is specifically designed to use a selected pool of sources estimating the correct time from these potentially perturbed references. Note that this protocol uses timings in the *Coordinated Universal Time*, or UTC[1] and at its last version, NTPv4, the protocol can reach an accuracy of 200 microseconds over local networks and 10 milliseconds over the Internet. For more informations refer to the publicly available specification in the RFC 1305, which describes NTPv3, as the fourth version is under formalization.

NTP Client

The first operation before becoming a server is to install the NTP client shipped in the package `ntpdate` on the chosen host. Our environment will have a host named `ntp.example.edu` acting as the local time server, so after installing and configuring Debian as we have seen in the previous chapter, proceed installing the NTP client:

---

[1] The UTC timing replaced the old *Greenwich Mean Time*, GMT, on January 1st 1972.

```
# apt-get install ntpdate
```

The package contains a command with the same name which accepts as an input a server name or an IP address. One main external and publicly available time reference is the ntp.org pool of time servers, and as the first operation we choose to synchronize the local clock with theirs:

```
# ntpdate pool.ntp.org
13 Apr 10:42:05 ntpdate[1992]: adjust time server 209.223.236.234 offset 0.022175 sec
```

The output shows the correct adjusted time and offset, and the IP address of the selected network resource. The ntpdate command uses the values contained in its default configuration file, located in /etc/default/, having the same name as the command. In this file we can specify a list of blank-separated network time servers and additional options. The option -u tells the command to use an unprivileged port, useful in some firewalled environments that filter privileged port communications, i.e. from 1 to 1023. The configuration file for our client looks like the following:

```
NTPSERVERS="pool.ntp.org"
NTPOPTIONS="-u"
```

For a list of public time servers refer to the Network Time Protocol Project, and to the Network Time Protocol Public Services Project.

NTP Server

Reliable time synchronization requires a local server providing the source for all hosts in the network. Contemporaneously our time server also synchronizes itself to an external source so that clocks can be considered accurate.

The Debian package that contains a time server is called ntp-server, so install it with the standard apt-get tool:

```
# apt-get install ntp-server
```

Debian starts the server immediately and adds the service to the default ones activated at boot time. Its configuration file is located in /etc/ with the file name ntp.conf, but before editing it we need to stop the server:

```
# /etc/init.d/ntp-server stop
Stopping NTP server: ntpd.
```

The configuration for our server needs small adjustments in order to work. Primarily, we have to specify the external source for the time synchronization with the server directive. We point the service to the pool.ntp.org servers: the server specification lines are not limited to only one, so you may add as many time pools as you assume necessary.

By default Debian enables the local host to have privileged access to the server, while other machines can interrogate the service but with fewer rights, specified in the `restrict` lines. All the other directives specify files necessary for the NTP server to work and Debian defaults are as follows:

```
driftfile /var/lib/ntp/ntp.drift
statsdir /var/log/ntpstats/

statistics loopstats peerstats clockstats
filegen loopstats file loopstats type day enable
filegen peerstats file peerstats type day enable
filegen clockstats file clockstats type day enable

server pool.ntp.org

restrict default kod notrap nomodify nopeer noquery

restrict 127.0.0.1 nomodify
```

Now that the NTP server configuration file has been modified, we can start the service:

```
# /etc/init.d/ntp-server start
Starting NTP server: ntpd.
```

The NTP server configuration provided by Debian as default uses the *syslog* facility to track every change, so its log is to be found in the `syslog` file located in the `/var/log/` directory. This is a typical NTP server output log:

```
13 Apr 11:03:42 ntp ntpd[27842]: ntpd 4.2.0a@1:4.2.0a Fri Aug 26 10:30:12 UTC 2005 (1)
13 Apr 11:03:42 ntp ntpd[27842]: signal_no_reset: signal 13 had flags 4000000
13 Apr 11:03:42 ntp ntpd[27842]: precision = 1.000 usec
13 Apr 11:03:42 ntp ntpd[27842]: Listening on interface wildcard, 0.0.0.0#123
13 Apr 11:03:42 ntp ntpd[27842]: Listening on interface lo, 127.0.0.1#123
13 Apr 11:03:42 ntp ntpd[27842]: Listening on interface eth0, 192.168.127.80#123
13 Apr 11:03:42 ntp ntpd[27842]: kernel time sync status 0040
```

The `restrict` lines may be modified to tighten access to the server, for example denying other hosts the ability to configure the time server, one may add a line that specifies the `nomodify` parameter to the local network:

```
restrict 192.168.127.0 mask 255.255.255.0 nomodify
```

NTP Test

To test the NTP server, we need a host with the `ntpdate` client command. The following two calls show a a communication failure and a successful time synchronization:

```
# ntpdate ntp.example.edu
13 Apr 11:00:39 ntpdate[7799]: no server suitable for synchronization found

# ntpdate ntp.example.edu
13 Apr 11:06:29 ntpdate[7800]: adjust time server 192.168.127.80 offset -0.276980 sec
```

Before the NTP server gets usable by clients, one might have to wait some minutes until it reaches an acceptable precision. On the server side we can notice that NTP opens its UDP port, using the nmap tool with the -sU switch for UDP port testing:

```
# nmap -sU localhost

Starting nmap 3.81 ( http://www.insecure.org/nmap/ ) at 2006-04-13 11:02 CEST
Interesting ports on localhost.localdomain (127.0.0.1):
(The 1477 ports scanned but not shown below are in state: closed)
PORT     STATE         SERVICE
123/udp  open|filtered ntp

Nmap finished: 1 IP address (1 host up) scanned in 1.433 seconds
```

In order to make a UDP scan you must be logged in as root. Later on we will add a secondary NTP server to increase the reliability of the time synchronization service, but first some more theory.

NTP Stratum

The NTP servers network is divided into categories called *strata*. Each *stratum* establishes accuracy and stability for the synchronization process and clock as defined by the standard ANSI/T1.101-1998 "*Synchronization Interface Standards for Digital Networks*", see Table 2.1 for reference.

Table 2.1. NTP stratum specification

Stratum	Accuracy	First Frame Slip
0		
1	$1 \cdot 10^{-11}$	72 days
2	$1 \cdot 10^{-8}$	7 days
3	$4.6 \cdot 10^{-6}$	6 minutes
4	$32 \cdot 10^{-8}$	*not specified*

The Stratum-0 devices are actual time devices, such as GPS, Radio and Loran-C clocks, attached via an RS-232 serial port or with an IRIG-B[2] device to a computer. Each host attached to a Stratum-0 device is a Stratum-1 server, and these are taken as the reference clocks for the following levels of accuracy. The Stratum-2 servers are connected to a number of higher-level servers that guarantee the necessary precision, established by the NTP algorithm, and discard any Stratum-1 host whose clock seems inaccurate with

---

[2] Inter-Range Instrumentation Group.

a certain probability. This layer of servers peer with each other to provide
the Stratum-3 hosts the best accuracy, robustness, and stability. The subsequent strata provide the same functionality as Stratum-2 servers, with lower
accuracy as we can see from the specification in Table 2.1.

At its start the ntpd daemon is assigned a high stratum, meaning that its
accuracy is yet to arrive at an acceptable level, and so the client gives up its
synchronization attempt. This fact can be seen adding the -d switch to show
all the ntpdate output for debugging:

```
# ntpdate -d
27 Apr 13:01:58 ntpdate[1155]: ntpdate 4.2.0a@1:4.2.0a Mon Mar 14 12:39:28 UTC 2005 (1)
transmit(192.168.127.80)
receive(192.168.127.80)
transmit(192.168.127.80)
receive(192.168.127.80)
transmit(192.168.127.80)
receive(192.168.127.80)
transmit(192.168.127.80)
receive(192.168.127.80)
transmit(192.168.127.80)
192.168.127.80: Server dropped: strata too high
server 192.168.127.80, port 123
stratum 16, precision -20, leap 11, trust 000
...

27 Apr 13:01:58 ntpdate[1155]: no server suitable for synchronization found
```

Within minutes the drift between our NTP service and the servers with
higher stratum becomes lower, and so it gains hierarchy levels until reaching
a Stratum-3 or even Stratum-2:

```
# ntpdate -d
27 Apr 13:13:51 ntpdate[7417]: ntpdate 4.2.0a@1:4.2.0a Mon Mar 14 12:39:28 UTC 2005 (1)
transmit(192.168.127.80)
receive(192.168.127.80)
transmit(192.168.127.80)
receive(192.168.127.80)
transmit(192.168.127.80)
receive(192.168.127.80)
transmit(192.168.127.80)
receive(192.168.127.80)
transmit(192.168.127.80)
server 192.168.127.80, port 123
stratum 2, precision -19, leap 00, trust 000
...

27 Apr 13:13:51 ntpdate[7417]: adjust time server 192.168.127.80 offset 0.025501 sec
```

2.2 Domain Name System

The whole Internet is based on the IP protocol which uses a unique number
assigned to every network card. Numbers are fast to be analyzed by machines,
and thus routing packets is one of the fastest operations on a network. Humans
are not machines though, and names are more familiar and easy to remember

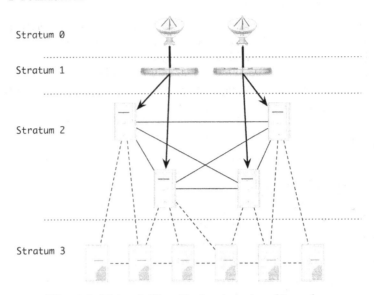

Stratum 0

Stratum 1

Stratum 2

Stratum 3

Fig. 2.1. Network Time Protocol stratum hierarchy

than numbers: the IP address 209.173.53.180 is hard to remember to des-
ignate the Internet Engineering Task Force, while the name www.ietf.org is
far easier. The original protocol was designed by Paul Mockapetris in 1983,
and became standard with RFC 882 and 883, obsoleted in 1987 with RFC
1034 and 1035, for the name resolution protocol on TCP/IP networks.

The standard protocol that converts names into IP addresses and vice versa
is called *Domain Name System* or DNS. The protocol uses both TCP and UDP
on port 53 to *resolve* a DNS query, from a name to a numeric address, and a
reverse DNS query, from an IP address to a name. The protocol divides the
name space into *zones*, for instance our fictitious organization seems to have
bought the domain example.edu, and belongs to the .edu zone. These zones
form a tree as we can see in Figure 2.2, and the name resolution relies on the
delegation of queries to the *authoritative* name server. This means that when
asking for the IP address of www.example.edu we have to traverse in reverse
order the tree, asking who is the authoritative server for the .edu zone to
the *Root Name Servers*, then asking to the .edu name server for the example
zone, and finally ask the example.edu DNS server the address of the host
called www. This is how it works in theory. On every client there is a cache for
DNS queries, so that it is not necessary to ask every time all servers starting
from the root.

The *root* zone is the one that holds every other one, in particular those
called *Top Level Domain* zones. These zones are divided into categories:

Infrastructure This category contains the arpa domains, used for infrastructure purposes, and inherits its name from the ancestor of Internet,

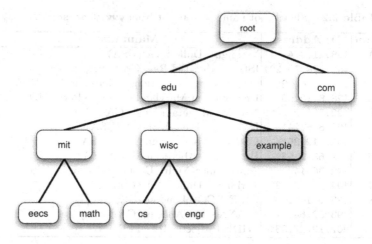

Fig. 2.2. Domain Name System zones with the `exmple.edu` network

ARPANET *Advanced Research Projects Agency Network*, built by the United States Department of Defense;

Country The *Country Code Top Level Domains*, ccTLD, are two-letters long character strings as `us` for the United States of America, `it` for Italy, and `de` for Germany, Deutschland in the German language;

Generic The *Generic Top Level Domains*, gTLD, are strings constituted by three or more characters, indicating a class of organizations independently of their nationality[3] as `com` for commercial and `edu` for educational organizations;

Sponsored The *Sponsored Top Level Domains*, sTLD, are proposed by independent agencies and are subject to their rules and approvals as `museum` for mueseums and `travel` for travel agencies.

The authoritative name servers for the root zones are known a priori in a system and are named with progressive letters. Currently there are 13 root servers belonging to the `root-servers.org` organization. All the root servers with their maintainers are shown in Table 2.2.

DNS Server

Debian includes one of the most used DNS daemons on the net: `bind`. Its story is long, and goes back to the historical 4.3BSD release, in fact, the name *bind* still retains his BSD ancestry being the acronym of *"Berkeley Internet Name Domain"*, nowadays supported by the Internet Systems Consortium. The version included in Debian is the ninth release of this historical service,

---

[3] For historic reasons the military `mil` and governmental `gov` gTLDs are reserved for the United States of America. The `edu` college-level organization is operated by the US and was originally meant to be used world-wide.

Table 2.2. Official root name servers list from `www.root-servers.org`

Letter	IP Address	Maintainer
A	198.41.0.4	VeriSign—Dulles, VA (USA)
B	192.228.79.201	ISI—Marina Del Rey, CA (USA)
C	192.33.4.12	Cogent Communications—Herndon, VA (USA)
D	128.8.10.90	University of Maryland—College Park, MD (USA)
E	192.203.230.10	NASA—Mountain View, CA (USA)
F	192.5.5.241	ISC, Inc.—Palo Alto, CA (USA)
G	192.112.36.4	US DoD NIC—Vienna, VA (USA)
H	128.63.2.53	US Army—Aberdeen MD (USA)
I	192.36.148.17	Autonomica-NORDUnet—Chicago, IL (USA)
J	192.58.128.30	VeriSign—Dulles, VA (USA)
K	193.0.14.129	RIPE-NCC—London (UK)
L	198.32.64.12	ICANN—Los Angeles, CA (USA)
M	202.12.27.33	WIDE Project—Tokyo (JP)

distributed by the package `bind9`. Our choice is to install it together with the corresponding client to query our DNS:

```
# apt-get install bind9 bind9-host
```

As in the majority of Debian's packages, the system starts `bind9` and adds it to the boot services, so before proceeding stop the daemon.

All the configuration files for `bind` are located in the directory `/etc/bind/`. The main file is called `named.conf`, and contains by default the zone databases used by the system, as we can see from its content:

```
include "/etc/bind/named.conf.options";

zone "." {
        type hint;
        file "/etc/bind/db.root";
};
zone "localhost" {
        type master;
        file "/etc/bind/db.local";
};
zone "127.in-addr.arpa" {
        type master;
        file "/etc/bind/db.127";
};
zone "0.in-addr.arpa" {
        type master;
        file "/etc/bind/db.0";
};
zone "255.in-addr.arpa" {
        type master;
        file "/etc/bind/db.255";
};
include "/etc/bind/named.conf.local";
```

We can notice that some zones are configured by default, for instance the root zone servers are known by default and are present with their database and their specific type hint. The file contains two inclusions, one directive for the daemon options, and the other for the local configuration. The named.conf.local is the file that is meant to be modified to handle our zone example.edu.

As we have already mentioned, the DNS resolves direct and reverse queries, so our configuration will contain a database of name-address entries, as well as the reverse address-name. Remember that DNS queries are made bottom-to-the-top, resolving a name like www.example.edu asking first to the root, then to the edu top level domain servers and so on. This aspect is reflected in the named.conf.local configuration file, where the reverse address mapping has inverted IP maps: the subnet 192.168.127.0 is described with 127.168.192 followed by the standard arpa:

```
zone "example.edu" {
        type master;
        notify no;
        file "/etc/bind/example.edu.zone";
};
zone "127.168.192.in-addr.arpa" {
        type master;
        notify no;
        file "/etc/bind/example.edu.zone.reverse";
};
```

The syntax is self-explaining: we are building an authoritative DNS for the example.edu zone, that is type master, which does not notify any other DNS server. The zone file databases are located in our example in the same directory as bind's configuration, but this is not a requirement.

Direct Database

First we start by creating our direct-query name database. Our DNS host has a name, dns.example.edu, and an administrator with e-mail address admin. The first item in our zone file is the zone configuration with its zone name origin set to null, and the cached record *time to live* in seconds, respectively $ORIGIN and $TTL. After this preamble, we have to begin our authority with the SOA, *Start Of Authority*. The SOA line contains in order the following parameters:

Zone The managed zone name, taking care of the $ORIGIN parameter if different from null, just a dot;
TTL The optional per-zone time to live parameter, the default $TTL applies if not specified;
Class The record class which the server handles, always[4] set to the standard Internet class IN;

---

[4] Besides the standard IN class, bind still handles historical *Hesiod* HS and *Chaos* CH classes, both coming from the MIT.

Server The *Primary Master* DNS server that respond authoritatively for the domain in case of a Dynamic DNS, or any valid DNS server, usually using the *Fully Qualified Domain Name* FQDN, that is the host name completed with the domain name, and it *must* end with a dot;

Mail The email address of the zone manager, substituting the @ with a dot, and it *should* end with a dot.

The SOA record has five mandatory parameters which are specified by parentheses, meant to define server-side parameters, these are in order:

1. Serial number of the database, updated each time an entry is modified: an unsigned 32-bits integer, although the common practice is to specify the date in the standard UNIX format YYYYmmDDss for year, month, day, sequence number for multiple updates in a single day;
2. The refresh time in seconds when a slave needs to update its database from the master DNS;
3. The retry delay time in case a slave fails to contact its master during an update process;
4. The expiration time in seconds when the zone database is considered obsolete and hence no longer authoritative: this affects slave DNS servers that do not resolve any other query until contacting the master again;
5. Negative cached entry time to live in seconds, with maximum value of 10800 or three hours—refer to RFC 2308 as this parameter has been redefined.

The start of authority stanza looks like the following, including the default origin and time to live values:

```
$ORIGIN .
$TTL    900
example.edu    IN    SOA    dns.example.edu admin.example.edu. (
                2006041301
                900
                300
                864000
                1800 )
```

Attention: this stanza is the most critical of all in the bind configuration, and must be written with *extreme* care. It is mandatory that the opening parenthesis in this stanza is located on the same line of the SOA string. To ease time value specifications bind supports short time-frame strings, using for instance 3h instead of 10800, and 15M for 900. For more informations refer to the daemon configuration manual.

The first entry in the zone file is the *resource record* item specifying the name server itself. This service is identified by a NS string followed by the name server host name. Actually, the NS entry is the second resource record in the configuration file, since the first one was the SOA entry.

All the entries that bind names to IP addresses are expressed with *address records*: lines containing the host name string followed by the record key A, and the IP address. Since we do not want to specify FQDNs, we use the $ORIGIN directive again in this section to add the example.edu, then our direct zone mapping file could be like the following:

```
$ORIGIN .
$TTL    900
example.edu     IN      SOA     dns.example.edu admin.example.edu. (
                                2006041301
                                900
                                300
                                864000
                                1800 )

                NS      dns.

$ORIGIN example.edu.

localhost       A       127.0.0.1
dns             A       192.168.127.154
ntp             A       192.168.127.80
```

Observe the dot at the end of NS and $ORIGIN entries. Right now we have specified just two host names, our name server itself and the time server.

Reverse Database

The other task of a name server is to map IP addresses back to names, reading the entries from the reverse database we have decided in the bind configuration file.

This database is symmetric to the direct one, having its preamble and SOA resource record. The IP addresses to host names maps are described by *pointer records*, PTR entries, similar to the address A ones, with the exception that the host names are followed by a dot. Our example.edu.zone.reverse looks like this:

```
$ORIGIN .
$TTL    900
127.168.192.in-addr.arpa IN     SOA     dns.example.edu admin.example.edu. (
                                2006041301
                                900
                                300
                                864000
                                1800 )

                NS      dns.

$ORIGIN 127.168.192.in-addr.arpa.

154             PTR     dns.example.edu.
80              PTR     ntp.example.edu.
```

As shown the $ORIGIN matches the SOA entry and ends with a dot. A minimal configuration for our bind-based DNS server is now complete and we may proceed in testing it.

DNS Security

The named daemon started from /etc/init.d/bind9 is controlled by the command rndc, which can also be used for remote control. The default installation of Debian is backward compatible with the previous version of bind so that old configuration files can be reused.

Without further configuration named and rndc, being on the same host, look in the file /etc/bind/rndc.key for a shared secret. The command rndc-confgen can be used to create a different configuration in the file /etc/bind/rndc.conf. In that case one has to use controls and key statements in named.conf.

Testing the DNS

During the server setup we have already installed a DNS client that allows us to make queries to our name server, direct and reverse interrogations. We test the DNS locally using the server itself to be sure that the daemon is working correctly. To enable our client to query the right DNS, we first have to edit the /etc/resolv.conf file that specifies the name servers, and optionally the default search domain, such that we can ask for ntp instead of the FQDN ntp.example.edu:

```
search example.edu
nameserver 127.0.0.1
```

The command that queries a DNS server is host, and we make use of the -v switch that enables verbose outputs. First we query our DNS for the host name dns with the host command:

```
# host -v dns
Trying "dns.example.edu"
;; ->>HEADER<<- opcode: QUERY, status: NOERROR, id: 18708
;; flags: qr aa rd ra; QUERY: 1, ANSWER: 1, AUTHORITY: 1, ADDITIONAL: 1

;; QUESTION SECTION:
;dns.example.edu.              IN      A

;; ANSWER SECTION:
dns.example.edu.       900     IN      A       192.168.127.154

;; AUTHORITY SECTION:
example.edu.           900     IN      NS      dns.

;; ADDITIONAL SECTION:
localhost.             604800  IN      A       127.0.0.1

Received 88 bytes from 127.0.0.1#53 in 2 ms
```

Since the first direct query worked, we can try to ask the daemon for the only other IP address known to the DNS, our ntp host:

```
# host -v ntp
Trying "ntp.example.edu"
;; ->>HEADER<<- opcode: QUERY, status: NOERROR, id: 35957
;; flags: qr aa rd ra; QUERY: 1, ANSWER: 2, AUTHORITY: 1, ADDITIONAL: 1

;; QUESTION SECTION:
;ntp.example.edu.              IN      A

;; ANSWER SECTION:
ntp.example.edu.       900    IN      A       192.168.127.80

;; AUTHORITY SECTION:
example.edu.           900    IN      NS      dns.

;; ADDITIONAL SECTION:
localhost.             604800 IN      A       127.0.0.1

Received 88 bytes from 127.0.0.1#53 in 2 ms
```

The last test is of course a reverse interrogation, this time we explicitly query the DNS by specifying its IP address as the last parameter of the host command:

```
# host -v 192.168.127.154 192.168.127.154
Trying "154.127.168.192.in-addr.arpa"
Using domain server:
Name: 192.168.127.154
Address: 192.168.127.154#53
Aliases:

;; ->>HEADER<<- opcode: QUERY, status: NOERROR, id: 61984
;; flags: qr aa rd ra; QUERY: 1, ANSWER: 1, AUTHORITY: 1, ADDITIONAL: 1

;; QUESTION SECTION:
;154.127.168.192.in-addr.arpa.  IN      PTR

;; ANSWER SECTION:
154.127.168.192.in-addr.arpa. 900 IN   PTR     dns.example.edu.

;; AUTHORITY SECTION:
127.168.192.in-addr.arpa. 900  IN      NS      dns.

;; ADDITIONAL SECTION:
localhost.              604800 IN      A       127.0.0.1

Received 107 bytes from 192.168.127.154#53 in 2 ms
```

2.3 Redundant Services

Our goal is to provide reliable and redundant network services, and this task involves the creation of more servers doing the same job, so that upon any machine failure we can promptly and fully automatically provide a backup.

In the previous sections we have built two services, a time and a name server. Adding secondary DNS and NTP machines is fundamental for our entire network, so we decide to create two NTP machines and two DNS servers. These machines can be called ntp1 and ntp2 for the time servers, and dns1 and **dns2** for the name service hosts. This habit of naming progressively is just a choice led by taste, and will become common in our growing network, since we want provide backups for all the critical services. Having changed the name of our primary DNS affects the master configuration files, by adding the corresponding names and reverse mappings in the zone files:

```
dns1            A       192.168.127.154
dns2            A       192.168.127.230
ntp1            A       192.168.127.80
ntp2            A       192.168.127.93

80              PTR     ntp1.example.edu.
93              PTR     ntp2.example.edu.
154             PTR     dns1.example.edu.
230             PRT     dns2.example.edu.
```

This imposes a change to the SOA entries on both files: a start of authority record *must* contain the primary name server, so the **dns1** host. The direct and reverse zone files have a start of authority record like the following:

```
example.edu      IN      SOA     dns1.example.edu admin.example.edu. (
                         2006041302
                         900
                         300
                         864000
                         1800 )

127.168.192.in-addr.arpa IN      SOA     dns1.example.edu admin.example.edu. (
                         2006041302
                         900
                         300
                         864000
                         1800 )
```

Having modified the primary DNS we can proceed in installing the secondary machines.

2.3.1 Secondary NTP Server

The instructions for a new network time server are exactly the same as for the primary. We know that NTP servers work with a pool of peering hosts, each of them synchronizing their clocks with the neighbors. In order to create a redundant time service, it is sufficient to follow the same steps described to build the primary NTP server, obtaining the same successful results:

```
# ntpdate -d ntp2.example.edu
27 Apr 12:22:32 ntpdate[7417]: ntpdate 4.2.0a@1:4.2.0a Fri Aug 26 10:30:13 UTC 2005 (1)
transmit(192.168.127.93)
receive(192.168.127.93)
transmit(192.168.127.93)
receive(192.168.127.93)
transmit(192.168.127.93)
receive(192.168.127.93)
transmit(192.168.127.93)
receive(192.168.127.93)
```

```
transmit(192.168.127.93)
server 192.168.127.93, port 123
stratum 2, precision -19, leap 00, trust 000
refid [192.168.127.230], delay 0.02574, dispersion 0.00000
transmitted 4, in filter 4
reference time:    c7fb1870.23af20ea  Thu, Apr 27 2006 12:16:16.139
originate timestamp: c7fb19e8.8a49b1fa  Thu, Apr 27 2006 12:22:32.540
transmit timestamp:  c7fb19e8.83bd8be7  Thu, Apr 27 2006 12:22:32.514
filter delay:  0.02591  0.02574  0.02574  0.02574
        0.00000  0.00000  0.00000  0.00000
filter offset: 0.025563 0.025501 0.025501 0.025501
        0.000000 0.000000 0.000000 0.000000
delay 0.02574, dispersion 0.00000
offset 0.025501

27 Apr 12:22:32 ntpdate[7417]: adjust time server 192.168.127.93 offset 0.025501 sec
```

You might have to wait again several minutes before your server is promoted to an acceptable stratum.

2.3.2 Secondary DNS Server

A secondary DNS server is subordinated to the master DNS, and fetches all the changes such that a consistent database is maintained across the network.

Master Configuration

The installation of a secondary DNS must be planned in advance on the master by allowing it to notify all its slave servers. This is easily configurable by editing the `notify` directive in the local zone configuration file `named.conf.local`:

```
zone "example.edu" {
      type master;
      notify yes;
      file "/etc/bind/example.edu.zone";
};
zone "127.168.192.in-addr.arpa" {
      type master;
      notify yes;
      file "/etc/bind/example.edu.zone.reverse";
};
```

The notification happens when the *serial* entry in the start of authority stanza is modified, and the changes are propagated automatically to the slave servers as specified by the NS records.

The direct zone description file does not only contain the new entries that match IP addresses to names, but also includes the new NS resource record for the secondary DNS:

```
example.edu    IN    SOA    dns1.example.edu admin.example.edu. (
                      2006041303
                      900
                      300
```

```
                          864000
                          1800 )

              NS      dns1.
              NS      dns2.

$ORIGIN example.edu.

localhost     A       127.0.0.1
dns1          A       192.168.127.154
dns2          A       192.168.127.230
ntp1          A       192.168.127.80
ntp2          A       192.168.127.93
```

The reverse zone file also reflects all needed changes so that it matches the direct database:

```
127.168.192.in-addr.arpa IN      SOA       dns1.example.edu admin.example.edu. (
                          2006041303
                          900
                          300
                          864000
                          1800 )

              NS      dns1.
              NS      dns2.

$ORIGIN 127.168.192.in-addr.arpa.

80            PTR     ntp1.example.edu.
93            PTR     ntp2.example.edu.
154           PTR     dns1.example.edu.
230           PRT     dns2.example.edu.
```

You notice two changes in these files. First of all, the serial number has changed, since we have modified the databases; second consideration, we respect a "good practice" for the A and PTR resources, having the direct zone in alphabetical order—except for the localhost entry which is the first—and ordering by numerical IP addresses the reverse: our choice is not to follow the strict lexical order here since for instance the IP addresses .1, .15, .102, and .203 would be ordered as .1, .102, .15, and .203.

Slave Configuration

On the slave machine we proceed exactly as we did for the master host. After installing the packages, we start configuring the slave database location by editing the named.conf.options file located in /etc/bind/. This file, previously unedited, contains the default location for the zone files in case these strings do not qualify as an *absolute path*:

```
options {
        directory "/var/cache/bind";
        auth-nxdomain no;
};
```

The **auth-nxdomain** is set to **no** in order to conform to RFC 1035, by not answering as an authoritative DNS if the server is not configured to be one. The default location is set to **/var/cache/bind/**, and it is a good idea not to interfere with the system **/etc/** directory.

The local zone configuration file **named.conf.local** on the slave is similar to the master, with the obvious exception of the **type**. Another modification is the specification of the master DNS servers where it fetches informations from, defined with the **masters** directive:

```
zone "example.edu" {
        type slave;
        file "example.edu.zone";
        masters {192.168.127.154; };
};
zone "127.168.192.in-addr.arpa" {
        type slave;
        file "example.edu.zone.reverse";
        masters {192.168.127.154; };
};
```

Observe that we specified a *relative path* for our zone databases. At this point we are ready to restart both DNS servers so that all the changes can take effect, as a matter of fact **bind** does not read dynamically its configuration files. On the secondary DNS, we can see that the **/etc/bind/** directory does not contain any database:

```
# ls /etc/bind
db.0    db.255   db.local  named.conf        named.conf.options  zones.rfc1918
db.127  db.empty db.root   named.conf.local  rndc.key
```

But in **/var/cache/bind/** we see that all the databases have been created by the notification process:

```
# ls /var/cache/bind/
example.edu.zone  example.edu.zone.reverse
```

The last step of this procedure is the test of the secondary DNS server, achieved simply by querying **localhost**, being logged in on it, for a direct and reverse address interrogation:

```
# host dns1.example.edu localhost
Using domain server:
Name: localhost
Address: 127.0.0.1#53
Aliases:

dns1.example.edu has address 192.168.127.154

# host 192.168.127.230 localhost
Using domain server:
Name: localhost
Address: 127.0.0.1#53
Aliases:

230.127.168.192.in-addr.arpa domain name pointer dns2.example.edu.
```

If the test ends successfully we are ready to make our secondary DNS server present in all `resolv.conf` files across the network:

```
search example.edu
nameserver 192.168.127.154
nameserver 192.168.127.230
```

Stealth DNS

Master and slave DNS servers are displayed publicly since we have used the standard NS resource records. We may want to have redundant services which are not known outside our network but only to the internal clients. These hidden DNS servers are known as *stealth DNS*, and are defined by an `also-notify` line in the zone configuration file of the master:

```
zone "example.edu" {
        type master;
        file "example.edu.zone";
        also-notify {192.168.127.200; };
};
```

Stealth servers are configured and work exactly as normal slaves, with the exception of not being included in the NS list. Publicly nobody can know about the DNS server 192.168.127.200, but for our internal purposes these are perfectly legal backups for name services.

2.4 Other DNS Uses

The DNS service may provide more than a simple database for IP addresses and host names. Domain name systems are used to serve aliases for hosts, provide service discovery and a trivial load balancing. The following sections will briefly describe the use and configuration for these.

2.4.1 Host Aliases

A domain name system can provide an alias record for any *canonical name*, that is the "real" name of a machine, meaning that the specified name cannot be an alias or an IP address.

This record is known as the *canonical name* record, declared with the same syntax of an address A record, by the statement CNAME. For example, if we want our main NTP server ntp1 to be known also as `time.example.edu`, all we have to add is a CNAME line like the following:

```
ntp1        A       192.168.127.80
ntp2        A       192.168.127.93
time        CNAME   ntp1
```

Aliases inherit all the properties of the original host they refer to, and a query shows that the specified name is an alias, followed by the real IP address:

```
# host time.example.edu
time.example.edu is an alias for ntp1.example.edu.
ntp1.example.edu has address 192.168.127.80
```

2.4.2 Service Records

Networks provide several services, such as web, email, instant messaging, and authentication servers, and for large institutions it may be difficult to discover what services are available without asking the network administration. The DNS protocol provides a way of specifying available services along with other informations with SRV records, *service records*. These entries are completely optional in a network and it is up to the client to make use or not of such a facility.

A service record is constituted by six entries divided into two categories: the service protocol, that precedes the SRV string, and the host specification. The service protocol is a dot-separated string constituted by three items, in order the **service**, the **protocol**, and the **domain**, where the first two strings are preceded by an underscore, and the domain ends with a dot. In our organization such an entry might look like the following:

```
_service._protocol.example.edu.
```

The **service** field specifies the service announced by the DNS as specified by the RFC 2782 "*Service Types*". The **protocol** string specifies the protocol involved in the service specification, which is usually _tcp or _udp. All valid protocol strings are available by the IANA Official Protocol Names Specification, described in the RFC 952. The SRV string that follows this entry may be preceded by the class string, which is usually of type IN.

The second half of the record is the host specification, a sequence of strings in the following order:

1. The priority of the specified host, a number in the range 0-65535, with the lowest number indicating a higher priority;
2. The weight of the service machine used to rank same-priority hosts, it has the same syntax as the priority field;
3. The port used by the service. It is not a requirement that services do actually match the usual port, for example a web server may be configured to work on the 8080 port instead of the usual 80;
4. The host that provides the service.

The domain field appears in both the first and last part of the SRV record. The reason for this is that we are specifying our services *before* we set the

$ORIGIN to our domain name example.edu. These fields can be left blank in case the current zone is already set.

As an example, we want to announce that an NTP service is available via DNS. The service string for the network time protocol is ntp, using the udp protocol. Our domain has two time servers, and we want a higher priority to be given to ntp1, both of them communicating on the standard port 123. The entry in our database could be like this:

```
_ntp._udp.example.edu.        SRV     0 0 123 ntp1.example.edu.
_ntp._udp.example.edu.        SRV     3 0 123 ntp2.example.edu.
```

There are dots at the end of the domain name, indicating that we are describing these services before setting $ORIGIN to the example.edu. string.

A useful and widely used service record is the one regarding the mailing system. This specification is about the incoming mail, and is specified by a record similar to the NS one, called MX. This entry specifies the server that handles all the incoming mail for our domain:

```
example.edu.    MX      0 smtp.example.edu.
```

It specifies the domain name, the record type MX, the priority of the server, similarly as we have already described, and the server name which handles incoming emails. This field is *mandatory* if the network is to handle emails, as we will see in a subsequent chapter.

Services Not Available

The absence of a SRV record does not mean that a service is not present in a networked environment. This record though may declare explicitly that a service is not available, with a similar syntax as the previous specification. The difference between the two is that non-present services have priority, weight, and port set to zero, and the host name set to null.

For instance our network provides NTP servers as we described above, and we want to announce to anyone that we do not provide any Gopher[5] server:

```
_gopher._tcp.example.edu.     SRV     0 0 0   .
```

2.4.3 Trivial Load Balancing

When we described the use of A records, we did not specify any constraint, except for the obvious fact that an IP address record must not specify a host name. Since there are no restrictions about the *uniqueness* of IP addresses, we safely may assign multiple IP addresses to a name.

---

[5] Gopher was a distributed document search-and-retrieve protocol used on the Internet, replaced nowadays by the world wide web.

When requesting a name to IP address query, the DNS protocol may respond with a *list of addresses*, and not a single one. Actually this fact is clear when investigating the POSIX call `gethostbyname()` that does this request, a standard UNIX function returning a list of IP addresses: it is up to the client whether to use them or not, and in which order. For example a client may ignore the list and use just the first returned entry, or use the following items if the connection with the first one fails. Anyway, this behavior is totally delegated to the client.

Multiple IP addresses are returned by the DNS in a randomly distributed order, and this provides us with a trivial load balancing that works out of the box. For example, if we use two IP addresses for a machine called `tmp`, our DNS database entries contain lines like the following:

```
tmp            A       192.168.127.145
tmp            A       192.168.127.237
```

If we ask the DNS to resolve the name `tmp` several times, we see that the returned order changes:

```
# host tmp
tmp.example.edu has address 192.168.127.145
tmp.example.edu has address 192.168.127.237

# host tmp
tmp.example.edu has address 192.168.127.237
tmp.example.edu has address 192.168.127.145

# host tmp
tmp.example.edu has address 192.168.127.237
tmp.example.edu has address 192.168.127.145

# host tmp
tmp.example.edu has address 192.168.127.145
tmp.example.edu has address 192.168.127.237

# host tmp
tmp.example.edu has address 192.168.127.237
tmp.example.edu has address 192.168.127.145
```

We recommend to carefully plan the use of this feature, since DNS provides only a randomization of IP addresses, without any knowledge of priorities or machine loads. When deploying highly-loaded servers, you should think of using a *real* load balancer.

2.4.4 Other DNS Records

There are several other DNS records which can be specified in a name server configuration, but many of them are either purely informational or experimental. We briefly describe some of these entries with their current or future use for information purposes:

AAAA This record is the IPv6, the successor of IPv4, equivalent of the A record;

HINFO A non functional, informational record, used to describe the computer
and the operating system of a particular host, it may follow the A record;

LOC Is a purely informational record describing latitude, longitude, altitude,
and dimensions of a host, it usually follows the host address record;

RP Indicates the person responsible for the DNS domain, the record is not
functional;

TXT Provides a textual information about some details regarding the domain,
it may be present multiple times and its use is purely informational;

WKS It is the experimental counterpart for the MX record, used to indicate any
well known service, like POP, HTTP, or IMAP, and its adoption is almost
zero on the Internet.

Practice

Exercise 5. Decide the organization of time servers in your environment. Of
course one can opt for some radio transmitted time signal: there exist special
hardware cards for this purpose.

Exercise 6. Invent a naming and numbering scheme for your computers,
defining IP ranges for servers and clients. Sometimes it is convenient to reference a group of hosts with a single combination of one IP address and one
netmask.

Exercise 7. Judge your needs for redundancy. How many time servers are
necessary and what is the best way to organize your DNS? Can SRV records
be helpful?

Exercise 8. Redundancy and security do not depend alone on your hosts.
Think about problems related to network hardware, power supply, and heat
production: each of those have a wide range of possible options to support
reliability.

3

Kerberos V

Identity would seem to be the garment with which one covers the nakedness of the self.
James Arthur Baldwin

3.1 Kerberos Network Authentication Protocol

Trust is an important issue in security, and part of the problem is related to *authentication*. This is not to be confused with *authorization*, and although these two terms are always coupled, they have different meanings and purposes. Authentication comes from the Greek $\alpha\upsilon\theta\varepsilon\nu\tau\iota\kappa\acute{o}\varsigma$ meaning *"genuine"*, *"real"*, and its purpose is to establish the identity of an individual or another previously untrusted interlocutor. The authorization on the other hand is the decision of allowing an individual a certain action: the authorization is thus subordinated to authentication. Giving an every-day metaphor, traveling abroad requires a passport and a visa; at the border we are asked for our passport, that *authenticates* us since we trust the document, and the issued visa *authorizes* us to enter the foreign country upon a successful passport check.

Kerberos is the answer to the authentication problem over networks. It was developed at the MIT for the *Project Athena* to ensure a secure and reliable identity check of individuals communicating over an insecure network, and was named after the mythological Greek dog Cerberus, or Kerberos, guard of the Hades, whose job was allowing only dead people to enter the underworld, and ensure that none of them would leave the place. The current version of Kerberos is the fifth, known as Kerberos V, usually with the Roman numeral, described in the official document RFC 4120, and by the subsequent IETF specifications RFC 3961, 3962, and 4121. The protocol is based on the Needham-Schroeder algorithm, and its first public version, Kerberos IV, was designed primarily by Steve Miller and Clifford Neuman at the MIT in the late 1980s.

A comprehensive description of Kerberos is beyond the objectives of this book, and in the following paragraphs we will explain from a systemic point of view the processes in act with the authentication service simplifying the actual protocol.

A client in need of a Kerberos-aware service first contacts a commonly trusted server called *Key Distribution Center* or KDC, which holds secret keys of all users and services, collectively known as *principals*. On this request the KDC sends to the client a package, encrypted with the client's secret key, made of two distinct parts: a freshly generated secret key and another encrypted data destined for the service, as depicted in Fig. 3.1. The secret key, called *Session Key*, is used for secure communication between the client and the service; the encrypted data contains the same session key encrypted with the service's secret key.

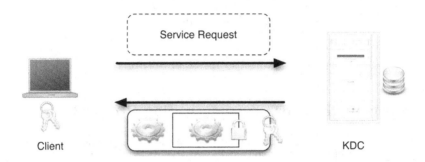

Fig. 3.1. A client requesting a service obtains a session key from the KDC

Decrypting the package from the KDC, the client obtains the session key, but is unable to decrypt the data for the service. At this point it forwards the encrypted data to the service, together with a service acknowledge request encrypted with the session key, as we can see in Fig. 3.2. Now the service can decrypt the data from the KDC forwarded by the client obtaining the session key. At this point it can decrypt the service acknowledge request and return a confirmation message to the client encrypting it with the session key which results in mutual authentication.

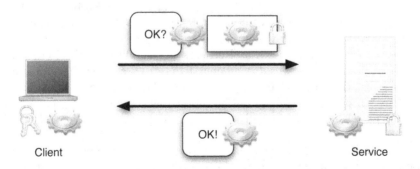

Fig. 3.2. A client uses the session key to contact the requested service

The encrypted data sent from the KDC to the client and intended for the requested service is called *ticket*. The encoded service acknowledge request is called *authenticator*. The secret key of a user is the password needed for decrypting the message from the KDC whereas a service has usually stored its secret key locally on the host where it is running.

In practice users do not have to type their passwords each time they request a service, since Kerberos provides a helper service called *Ticket Granting Service*. This service supply users a special ticket, the *Ticket Granting Ticket*, or briefly TGT, allowing to request tickets for other services without further passwords: having to provide the password just once is named *Single Sign-On*. A common synonym of the ticket granting ticket is *initial ticket*, since it is the first issued, and allows users to acquire new ones.

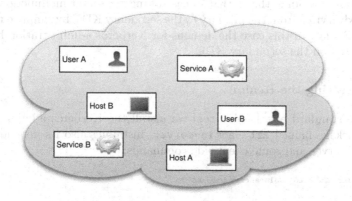

Fig. 3.3. A Kerberos Realm

Kerberos does not only authenticate users, but also machines and services, all called *principals*, and stores their passwords securely on the KDC. The set of all the machines, users and services that authenticate over Kerberos constitute a single entity called *realm* as show in Fig.3.3. In order to allow a secure authentication of non-interactive principals, like services and hosts, a system administrator stores the secret key for these principals on the machine itself, so that the system can verify the authenticity of the service. The keys are exported in a file called *Kerberos Key Table* or briefly *keytab*. Due to the nature of its client-server architecture and with the mechanism of keytabs, Kerberos does not rely on the locality of such principals: a user may authenticate to the KDC from outside the local network, and require trusted services being issued the corresponding ticket.

A concrete realization of the Kerberos protocol requires time-stamps and life-spans for every issued ticket in order to cope with replay attacks. Furthermore network addresses, and the identity of users and services are included in the tickets. The latest implementations of Kerberos permit pre-authentication where a first message from the client to the KDC is already encrypted with the user's secret key, and new types of symmetric cryptography beyond DES.

3.2 Master KDC

The plan is to install Kerberos in our network providing a reliable and redundant secure authentication service, and the first step is to create the first Key Distribution Center on a host called `kdc1.example.edu`. This machine will also act as the Kerberos administration server, where for example users can change their passwords.

For redundancy reasons, we create an alias to our primary KDC called `krb`. The purpose for doing this is that in case of master server malfunctioning we can quickly switch from the primary to the secondary KDC by simply changing the `CNAME` alias. In this case the demons for Kerberos administration have to be activated on the secondary KDC.

3.2.1 Creating the Realm

With the standard `apt` Debian tool we install the Kerberos administration server package named `krb5-admin-server`, installing also its dependencies, the KDC server and some client-side commands:

```
# apt-get install krb5-admin-server krb5-user
```

As usual, Debian configures the package asking us some information:

Realm The Kerberos realm name, usually is the same as the DNS domain name with uppercase letters: in our case this is `EXAMPLE.EDU`;

Kerberos IV We have to choose the level of compatibility with the old Kerberos IV, our choice is `nopreauth`: no pre-authentication is required; and not `full`

KDCs The list of Kerberos KDC servers, that is only our `kdc1.example.edu` host for the moment;

Administration The administrative server for our realm, since we have just one machine, we have no other choice than using `krb1`, or better its alias `krb` for reasons we have already described.

Unlike other services, after setting up the packages Debian does not start the daemons since they require further configuration.

At this point we are ready to create the Kerberos principal database, an encrypted database where all the principals are stored along with their secret keys. A principal name is a string in the form `name@REALM`, with the `name` indicating the *principal type*:

host/hostname Identifies a machine with its FQDN, our master KDC for
example has a principal called host/kdc1.example.edu@EXAMPLE.EDU;

service/hostname Identifies a service running on a machine (with its FQDN),
the service field is specific to the service, for example an LDAP daemon
requires a principal called ldap/hostname.example.edu@EXAMPLE.EDU;

username Identifies a user, a further subcategory is username/admin to indicate administrative principals.

To create the principal database, Debian provides the krb5_newrealm shell
script that creates the database and populates it with the necessary entries
with the Kerberos tool kdb5_util, and sets up a basic access control list for
the KDC administration. After setting up the necessary configuration, the
script starts both the KDC and administrative daemons:

```
# krb5_newrealm

This script should be run on the master KDC/admin server to initialize
a Kerberos realm.  It asks you to type in a master key password.
This password gets used to generate a key that is stored in
/etc/krb5kdc/stash.  You should try to remember this password, but it
is much more important that it be a strong password than that it be
remembered.  However, if you lose the password and /etc/krb5kdc/stash,
you cannot decrypt your Kerberos database.

Loading random data

Initializing database '/var/lib/krb5kdc/principal' for realm 'EXAMPLE.EDU',
master key name 'K/M@EXAMPLE.EDU'
You will be prompted for the database Master Password.
It is important that you NOT FORGET this password.

Enter KDC database master key:
Re-enter KDC database master key to verify:

Starting Kerberos KDC: krb5kdc krb524d.
Starting Kerberos Administration Servers: kadmind.

Now that your realm is set up you may wish to create an administrative
principal using the addprinc subcommand of the kadmin.local program.
Then, this principal can be added to /etc/krb5kdc/kadm5.acl so that
you can use the kadmin program on other computers.  Kerberos admin
principals usually belong to a single user and end in /admin.  For
example, if jruser is a Kerberos administrator, then in addition to
the normal jruser principal, a jruser/admin principal should be
created.

Don't forget to set up DNS information so your clients can find your
KDC and admin servers.  Doing so is documented in the administration
guide.
```

As we can see from the output, kdb5_util creates a principal called K/M
that is the Kerberos Master Key principal. The master key password, used to
encrypt the principal database, is stored not only in the K/M principal, but
also in a file located in the KDC configuration directory /etc/krb5kdc/:

```
# ls -l
total 12
-rw-r--r--  1 root root 340 2006-04-27 15:11 kadm5.acl
```

```
-rw-r--r--  1 root root 499 2006-04-27 15:02 kdc.conf
-rw-------  1 root root  30 2006-04-27 15:11 stash
```

The **stash** file contains the master key and is readable only by the **root** user. The password is not stored anywhere in clear text, both stash and master key principal are encrypted versions of the chosen password, so *do not forget it*, since it might put the database content in jeopardy in case of master key loss.

A port scan with **nmap** shows both UDP and TCP ports opened on a KDC for the Kerberos service:

```
# nmap -sU -sT localhost

Starting nmap 3.81 ( http://www.insecure.org/nmap/ ) at 2006-04-27 15:13 CEST
Interesting ports on localhost.localdomain (127.0.0.1):
(The 3134 ports scanned but not shown below are in state: closed)
PORT      STATE          SERVICE
464/udp   open           kpasswd5
749/tcp   open           kerberos-adm
4444/udp  open|filtered  krb524

Nmap finished: 1 IP address (1 host up) scanned in 0.215 seconds
```

Our KDC and administrative server has the **kpasswd5** password change daemon running along with the **kerberos-adm** administration service. The **krb524** process is the Kerberos V to Kerberos IV translator service, used in environments where both the new and the legacy authentication protocol are used. As we will see in the chapter about AFS, this service is needed by our distributed filesystem and has been the reason to set **nopreauth**.

3.2.2 Realm Configuration

We are now ready to start with the KDC configuration, modifying first the default values provided by Debian to suite our organization's needs. The basic and most important operation is to create some administrative principals used to modify remotely our Kerberos database. The file that maps principals to their respective access privilege is **kadm5.acl** located in the **/etc/krb5kdc/** directory. This file contains pairs of strings matching a principal to its ACL. For a list of all possible values, consult your Kerberos manual as it may change from one version to another; a sample list is reported in Table 3.1.

Our ACL specifications allows any operation to our system administrators, allowing all principals ending in **/admin** every operation, and the same for our first administrator, a principal that we choose to name **sysadmin**. The entries in our **kadm5.acl** file look like the following:

```
*/admin *
sysadmin *
```

The first line is necessary for Kerberos to work properly, as some default mandatory administrative principals present in a Kerberos database end with

Table 3.1. Kerberos administrative access control list values

Allow	Deny	Operation
a	A	Add principals or policies
d	D	Delete principals or policies
m	M	Modify principals or policies
c	C	Change passwords
i	I	Inquiry the database
l	L	List principals or policies
s	S	Set key for principals
* or x		Allow all privileges

the /admin string. We will see some of these special principals in the following paragraphs.

At this point we are ready to modify the Kerberos realm configuration file created by the Debian installer, the /etc/krb5.conf file. Initially this file contains additional realms, for instance the MIT realm ATHENA.MIT.EDU, along with a pre-generated configuration for our EXAMPLE.EDU Kerberos V realm:

```
[libdefaults]
        default_realm = EXAMPLE.EDU
        ccache_type = 4
        forwardable = true
        proxiable = true

[realms]
        EXAMPLE.EDU = {
            kdc = kdc1.example.edu
            admin_server = krb.example.edu
        }

[domain_realm]
        .example.edu = EXAMPLE.EDU
        example.edu = EXAMPLE.EDU
```

The [libdefaults] stanza specifies all the defaults for our Kerberos configuration, like the default realm, the credential cache type[1], and the ticket properties. The [realms] section specifies a list of all known realms, with their KDCs, domains, and administrative servers. The [domain_realm] stanza maps a DNS domain to a Kerberos realm as they are not requested to match. There are several other stanzas that could be used, such as the application specific stanza [appdefaults]: check with your Kerberos documentation for your specific software to obtain further information about this application-specific topic.

As we configured the realm, we are ready to create our first principals, and primarily, our sysadmin administrator. Right now we have no principals

---

[1] All the tickets for a principal are stored either in a file cache, as it is on almost every UNIX system, or in an OS-specific API cache as in Apple MacOS X and Microsoft Windows.

except for the private Kerberos ones, and we would never be able to connect to the administrative server remotely. Kerberos provides us a tool called `kadmin.local` which can be run by `root` on the administrative KDC in order to create the necessary entries in the database. The interface is shell-like with all the possible commands displayed with a brief description by issuing `help` or `?`:

```
# kadmin.local
Authenticating as principal root/admin@EXAMPLE.EDU with password.

kadmin.local:  ?
Available kadmin.local requests:

add_principal, addprinc, ank
                        Add principal
delete_principal, delprinc
                        Delete principal
modify_principal, modprinc
                        Modify principal
change_password, cpw    Change password
get_principal, getprinc  Get principal
list_principals, listprincs, get_principals, getprincs
                        List principals
add_policy, addpol      Add policy
modify_policy, modpol   Modify policy
delete_policy, delpol   Delete policy
get_policy, getpol      Get policy
list_policies, listpols, get_policies, getpols
                        List policies
get_privs, getprivs     Get privileges
ktadd, xst              Add entry(s) to a keytab
ktremove, ktrem         Remove entry(s) from a keytab
lock                    Lock database exclusively (use with extreme caution!)
unlock                  Release exclusive database lock
list_requests, lr, ?    List available requests.
quit, exit, q           Exit program.
kadmin.local:
```

As we can notice, the `root` user is mapped by `kadmin.local` to a special principal `root/admin@EXAMPLE.EDU` with all the administrative rights: in the `kadm5.acl` file we granted all privileges to `*/admin` principals.

3.2.3 Tuning Kerberos

Before creating the `sysadmin` principal we have to understand some key features of Kerberos. Each principal is an entry in the database, and gaining tickets deeply relies on the system clock, this means that a high clock skew between the ticket requester and the KDC results in a ticket denial. Our suggestion is that all the KDCs are synchronized with our NTP service via the `ntpd` daemon.

Another Kerberos aspect regards the issued tickets. A ticket is a piece of encrypted data given to the requester after providing valid credentials, and has some properties. The most important feature is that tickets have a lifetime, which by default is 10 hours, and can be *renewed* up to 7 days. These values affect the whole system, and should be carefully tweaked to suite your organization needs, since after a ticket has expired the user is no longer trusted by Kerberized services and is denied any operation.

By default, Kerberos has some principals which are there for Kerberos internal usage, viewable by issuing the listprincs command:

```
kadmin.local:  listprincs
K/M@EXAMPLE.EDU
kadmin/admin@EXAMPLE.EDU
kadmin/changepw@EXAMPLE.EDU
kadmin/history@EXAMPLE.EDU
krbtgt/EXAMPLE.EDU@EXAMPLE.EDU
```

We have already discussed the K/M principal as the database master key holder, and all the kadmin/* principals are managerial entries like administering the realm and changing password.

The last entry is the *Ticket Granting Ticket Service*: every Kerberos user gets issued upon a successful authentication a ticket granting ticket. All subsequent granted credentials are subject to the TGT default values and KDC configuration. We can retrieve all the information about a principal by issuing the getprinc command followed by the principal name:

```
kadmin.local:  getprinc krbtgt/EXAMPLE.EDU
Principal: krbtgt/EXAMPLE.EDU@EXAMPLE.EDU
Expiration date: [never]
Last password change: [never]
Password expiration date: [none]
Maximum ticket life: 0 days 10:00:00
Maximum renewable life: 7 days 00:00:00
Last modified: Thu Apr 27 15:11:13 CEST 2006 (db_creation@EXAMPLE.EDU)
Last successful authentication: [never]
Last failed authentication: [never]
Failed password attempts: 0
Number of keys: 3
Key: vno 1, Triple DES cbc mode with HMAC/sha1, no salt
Key: vno 1, DES cbc mode with CRC-32, no salt
Key: vno 1, DES cbc mode with RSA-MD5, no salt
Attributes: REQUIRES_PRE_AUTH
Policy: [none]
```

There is much information supplied by Kerberos, and most of it relate with time. We can see that the principal database stores information about the principal expiration date, password expiration and last change, the entry modification date, the date when the principal succeeded to authenticate, and the last time it failed along with a number of attempts. Of course the principal has a lifetime and maximum renewable time-window.

Kerberos principals may have more than one key. A key is an encrypted data with a checksum to guarantee its correctness, and so its authenticity. In our realm our TGT service has three keys, each of these is encrypted with an algorithm and supplied with a checksum. For instance the first one is encrypted with the Triple Data Encryption Standard algorithm with Cipher Block Chaining, also known as 3DES-CBC, whereas the second key uses a Single DES; the checksum used by the first encrypted key is the Hashed Message

Authentication Code using the Secure Hash Algorithm 1, or HMAC/SHA-1, considered highly reliable, while the second key uses a simple 32-bit Cyclic Redundancy Check, the CRC-32. The *Key Version Number*, indicated as VNO or KVNO, is a integer number assigned to each key and is incremented each time a modification happens to the key: typically starting with zero, the KVNO is incremented upon a principal creation, so our TGT principal has a KVNO equal to 1.

Our organization strongly depends on the default values we give to our TGT principal, especially its lifetime and renewal allowance. To modify a principal we have to call the `modprinc` instruction followed by the parameter we want to modify and the principal name; if we issue a command in the `kadmin.local` interface we can get a help about the optional and mandatory parameters:

```
kadmin.local:  modprinc
usage: modify_principal [options] principal
        options are:
                [-expire expdate] [-pwexpire pwexpdate] [-maxlife maxtixlife]
                [-kvno kvno] [-policy policy] [-clearpolicy]
                [-maxrenewlife maxrenewlife] [{+|-}attribute]
        attributes are:
                allow_postdated allow_forwardable allow_tgs_req allow_renewable
                allow_proxiable allow_dup_skey allow_tix requires_preauth
                requires_hwauth needchange allow_svr password_changing_service
```

On the one hand a user may require simple authentication for daily work, on the other hand the user might start complex batch jobs that require more than a single working day to complete. This is reflected by two values of our TGT service: lifetime and renewal time frames. In our case we set them respectively to 24 hours and 90 days: note that these values strongly depend on your company needs, you may opt for a strict lifetime such as few hours and a single working day for renewals, or you may need looser time frames allowing users to run longer jobs. In our case, we modify the TGT default values by issuing the `modprinc` command with the correct options:

```
kadmin.local:  modprinc -maxlife "1 day" -maxrenewlife "90 day" krbtgt/EXAMPLE.EDU
Principal "krbtgt/EXAMPLE.EDU@EXAMPLE.EDU" modified.
```

Kerberos can use human-readable dates such as `90 hours`, `tomorrow`, and `next year`: refer to your Kerberos implementation documentation for such usage. Any modification to a principal happens immediately, and a verification shows that the changes have been successfully happened:

```
kadmin.local:  getprinc krbtgt/EXAMPLE.EDU
Principal: krbtgt/EXAMPLE.EDU@EXAMPLE.EDU
Expiration date: [never]
Last password change: [never]
Password expiration date: [none]
Maximum ticket life: 1 day 00:00:00
Maximum renewable life: 90 days 00:00:00
Last modified: Thu Apr 27 15:38:29 CEST 2006 (root/admin@EXAMPLE.EDU)
```

```
Last successful authentication: [never]
Last failed authentication: [never]
Failed password attempts: 0
Number of keys: 3
Key: vno 1, Triple DES cbc mode with HMAC/sha1, no salt
Key: vno 1, DES cbc mode with CRC-32, no salt
Key: vno 1, DES cbc mode with RSA-MD5, no salt
Attributes: REQUIRES_PRE_AUTH
Policy: [none]
```

Notice that a change of lifetime properties do not affect the encryption keys, but the modification date has been updated along with the modifier name. This is not sufficient yet, since any other principal will be created based on the settings established in the kdc.conf file. Modify it to match the values you chose for your system, in our case it would be like the following:

```
[kdcdefaults]
        kdc_ports = 750,88

[realms]
EXAMPLE.EDU = {
                database_name = /var/lib/krb5kdc/principal
                admin_keytab = FILE:/etc/krb5kdc/kadm5.keytab
                acl_file = /etc/krb5kdc/kadm5.acl
                key_stash_file = /etc/krb5kdc/stash
                kdc_ports = 750,88
                max_life = 1d 0h 0m 0s
                max_renewable_life = 90d 0h 0m 0s
                master_key_type = des3-hmac-sha1
                supported_enctypes = des3-hmac-sha1:normal des-cbc-crc:normal
                                     des:normal des:v4 des:norealm des:onlyrealm
                                     des:afs3
                default_principal_flags = +preauth
        }
```

All is needed now to have our Kerberos system working with our new preferences, is to restart the servers. Notice that a change in the Kerberos database takes effect immediately, while a change in the configuration requires a daemon restart.

Our first task in our realm is to add our new system administrator, so that we can use Kerberos remotely from any client. So let us proceed adding our sysadmin principal:

```
kadmin.local:  addprinc sysadmin
WARNING: no policy specified for sysadmin@EXAMPLE.EDU; defaulting to no policy
Enter password for principal "sysadmin@EXAMPLE.EDU":
Re-enter password for principal "sysadmin@EXAMPLE.EDU":
Principal "sysadmin@EXAMPLE.EDU" created.
```

We can ignore about the warning: since we didn't specify any policy[2] for the principal, Kerberos uses a default non-restrictive one. After success-

---

[2] A Kerberos policy specifies restrictions to the principal password, such as lifetime, minimum length, character classes—numbers, uppercase and lowercase letters, and other characters—and the number of old passwords that the user cannot re-use.

ful creation, the principal shows our predefined ticket lifetime and renewable allowance values:

```
Principal: sysadmin@EXAMPLE.EDU
Expiration date: [never]
Last password change: Thu Apr 27 15:53:25 CEST 2006
Password expiration date: [none]
Maximum ticket life: 1 day 00:00:00
Maximum renewable life: 90 days 00:00:00
Last modified: Thu Apr 27 15:53:25 CEST 2006 (root/admin@EXAMPLE.EDU)
Last successful authentication: [never]
Last failed authentication: [never]
Failed password attempts: 0
Number of keys: 6
Key: vno 1, Triple DES cbc mode with HMAC/sha1, no salt
Key: vno 1, DES cbc mode with CRC-32, no salt
Key: vno 1, DES cbc mode with RSA-MD5, Version 4
Key: vno 1, DES cbc mode with RSA-MD5, Version 5 - No Realm
Key: vno 1, DES cbc mode with RSA-MD5, Version 5 - Realm Only
Key: vno 1, DES cbc mode with RSA-MD5, AFS version 3
Attributes: REQUIRES_PRE_AUTH
Policy: [none]
```

At this point, we can use Kerberos tools from any client with a valid installation, right now our KDC is the only server which happens to be also a Kerberos client. We can test our new KDC just by using the standard tools, such as the `kinit` program to obtain a valid ticket for a given principal name, so let us test it with our `sysadmin`:

```
# kinit sysadmin
Password for sysadmin@EXAMPLE.EDU:
```

We are prompted for a password, and following a common behavior nothing is shown on the screen, for two reasons: first, a UNIX command typically does not bother the user upon a successful run but only in case of failure, and second reason, showing the password length helps a malicious user to have a starting point for a brute-force attack. To list all the tickets we have, we can use the `klist` program:

```
# klist
Ticket cache: FILE:/tmp/krb5cc_0
Default principal: sysadmin@EXAMPLE.EDU

Valid starting       Expires            Service principal
04/27/06 15:56:29  04/28/06 01:56:26  krbtgt/EXAMPLE.EDU@EXAMPLE.EDU

Kerberos 4 ticket cache: /tmp/tkt0
klist: You have no tickets cached
```

As we can see from the output, we are authenticated as the principal `sysadmin` with only one ticket, the TGT, with its own validity period. Since `kinit` was called without any options it uses a hard coded life time of 10 hours. Discarding Kerberos credential is also possible, and we can do this operation by calling the `kdestroy` tool, knowing that it deletes *any* ticket, and that we are not prompted for any confirm:

```
# kdestroy

# klist
klist: No credentials cache found (ticket cache FILE:/tmp/krb5cc_0)


Kerberos 4 ticket cache: /tmp/tkt0
klist: You have no tickets cached
```

We do not use the `kadmin.local` tool again, instead we work with the standard remote `kadmin` interface. By default the tool tries to authenticate the current UNIX user—here it would be `root`—so we have to specify the principal to be used to administer the realm, provided that the ACLs permit it to do so:

```
# kadmin -p sysadmin
Authenticating as principal sysadmin with password.
Password for sysadmin@EXAMPLE.EDU:
kadmin:
```

3.3 Slave KDC

For redundancy reasons, we are going to create another KDC in our network whose name is `kdc2.example.edu`. This new server acts as a slave of our principal key distribution server and does not perform administrative tasks. This choice of course is arbitrary, but we must remember that the Kerberos database should be kept synchronized on all KDCs. We stress the fact that Kerberos relies heavily on time-stamps, and as we already pointed out for the master KDC, our recommendation is to make all key distribution centers NTP-enabled hosts.

3.3.1 Host Principals

Each Kerberos-enabled service needs some principal to be created and eventually exported in a keytab file, a file where the keys are stored. Let us create first the host principals for our KDCs. Each host principal has a name in the form `host/hostname`, where the host name is its fully qualified domain name. The fully qualified domain name must have a valid reverse DNS entry, so you cannot use any `CNAME` entry, but only plain `A` ones.

On the master KDC, connect as a Kerberos administrator with the `kdamin` tool and create the principal with the `addprinc` command. A machine cannot enter any password, so we create a random one using the `-randkey` switch:

```
kadmin:  addprinc -randkey host/kdc1.example.edu
WARNING: no policy specified for host/kdc1.example.edu@EXAMPLE.EDU; \
defaulting to no policy
Principal "host/kdc1.example.edu@EXAMPLE.EDU" created.
```

Having created the principal, all we have to do is to export its keys to a keytab file using the **ktadd** command, followed by the principal we intend to export. By default Kerberos puts all the exported keys in the **/etc/krb5.keytab** file, as we can see from the output:

```
kadmin:  ktadd host/kdc1.example.edu
Entry for principal host/kdc1.example.edu with kvno 3, encryption type \
Triple DES cbc mode with HMAC/sha1 added to keytab WRFILE:/etc/krb5.keytab.
Entry for principal host/kdc1.example.edu with kvno 3, encryption type \
DES cbc mode with CRC-32 added to keytab WRFILE:/etc/krb5.keytab.
```

We can analyze the contents of the keytab file using the standard **klist** command, with the parameters **-k** to view the default keytab content, and **-e** to show the encryption method:

```
# klist -ke
Keytab name: FILE:/etc/krb5.keytab
KVNO Principal
---- --------------------------------------------------------------------------
   3 host/kdc1.example.edu@EXAMPLE.EDU (Triple DES cbc mode with HMAC/sha1)
   3 host/kdc1.example.edu@EXAMPLE.EDU (DES cbc mode with CRC-32)
```

Now on the slave machine, after installing and configuring the system, we can install the **krb5-user** package, so that we can use the standard Kerberos tools we've used until now. Debian asks some information about the realm, administrative servers and KDCs: right now we have only one server, and the answers are obvious. After the installation process, all we need to modify is the [domain_realm] section to match DNS and realm. If Kerberos is configured, you can test it before proceeding by getting the initial ticket for a principal, in our case, the **sysadmin** one.

The secondary key distribution center needs a host principal and its relative keys to be exported into the default keytab file. This procedure can be achieved in the same way we acted for the master, so with the **kadmin** program, create and export the **host/kdc2.example.edu** principal with the **addprinc** and **ktadd** commands:

```
kadmin:  addprinc -randkey host/kdc2.example.edu
WARNING: no policy specified for host/kdc2.example.edu@EXAMPLE.EDU; \
defaulting to no policy
Principal "host/kdc2.example.edu@EXAMPLE.EDU" created.

kadmin:  ktadd host/kdc2.example.edu
Entry for principal host/kdc2.example.edu with kvno 3, encryption type \
Triple DES cbc mode with HMAC/sha1 added to keytab WRFILE:/etc/krb5.keytab.
Entry for principal host/kdc2.example.edu with kvno 3, encryption type \
DES cbc mode with CRC-32 added to keytab WRFILE:/etc/krb5.keytab.
```

At this point we are ready to install the KDC services on the slave machine, contained in the **krb5-kdc** package. As usual, Debian configures the software, asking questions like our chosen Kerberos IV compatibility, which we set as on the master to **nopreauth**.

3.3.2 The xinetd Daemon

Kerberos provides a way of propagating its database from the master to the slave KDCs with a daemon. Our choice is to use an on-demand service, started by a *"super-server"* that takes care of every aspect.

This meta-service is called *Extended Internet Daemon*, or xinetd, provided by the homonymous Debian package. This service replaces the old inetd shipped first with 4.3BSD in 1986, providing extended facilities such as access control lists, TCP wrapping, broad logging services, and mechanisms to protect the system against port scanners. Basically the xinetd server listens to ports specified by its configuration, and start the service when needed.

After installing the xinetd package, Debian starts the server but before proceeding we have to stop it:

```
# apt-get install xinetd

# /etc/init.d/xinetd stop
Stopping internet superserver: xinetd.
```

The default configuration file is xinetd.conf, which basically includes all the files located in the /etc/xinetd.d/ directory. The /etc/xinetd.d/ location contains all the xinetd-allowed services stored in individual files:

```
# cat /etc/xinetd.conf
defaults
{
}
includedir /etc/xinetd.d

# ls -l
total 16
-rw-r--r--  1 root root 798 2005-03-10 12:28 chargen
-rw-r--r--  1 root root 660 2005-03-10 12:28 daytime
-rw-r--r--  1 root root 580 2005-03-10 12:28 echo
-rw-r--r--  1 root root 726 2005-03-10 12:28 time
```

The xinetd service listens to the ports specified by the /etc/services file, which contains all the standard IANA service names and their relative TCP or UDP ports:

```
tcpmux          1/tcp                           # TCP port service multiplexer
echo            7/tcp
echo            7/udp
discard         9/tcp           sink null
discard         9/udp           sink null
systat          11/tcp          users
daytime         13/tcp
daytime         13/udp
netstat         15/tcp
qotd            17/tcp          quote
msp             18/tcp                          # message send protocol
msp             18/udp
...
```

We can see an example of a xinetd-enabled service in the following daytime[3] service specification:

```
service daytime
{
        disable         = yes
        type            = INTERNAL
        id              = daytime-stream
        socket_type     = stream
        protocol        = tcp
        user            = root
        wait            = no
}
service daytime
{
        disable         = yes
        type            = INTERNAL
        id              = daytime-dgram
        socket_type     = dgram
        protocol        = udp
        user            = root
        wait            = yes
}
```

Notice as the service description provides some information, other than the service name itself which identifies the relative port, such as the TCP and UDP versions, and the user that runs the service, commonly root.

3.3.3 Kerberos Database Propagation

Kerberos, as we already said, provides a service that propagates the database from the master KDC to its slaves. Such a service is supplied by a daemon called kpropd.

This simple service needs a configuration file that describes all the hosts that are allowed to the propagation, specified in the kpropd.acl file, located in the /etc/krb5kdc/ directory. This is a text file that contains one per line, all the principals entailed in the database propagation, and in our case looks like the following:

```
host/kdc1.example.edu@EXAMPLE.EDU
host/kdc2.example.edu@EXAMPLE.EDU
```

As we previewed in the previous section, the kpropd daemon is started on-demand by our xinetd super-server, so we need to create a file for our service in the /etc/xinetd.d/ directory, matching the service name as specified by /etc/services:

---

[3] The daytime protocol is defined by the RFC 867 on TCP/UDP ports 13, and it is used for tests and measurements by returning the host date and time as an ASCII string.

```
krb_prop        754/tcp         krb5_prop hprop # Kerberos slave propagation
```

The line tells us that we have to create a service file for the standard IANA name **krb_prop**:

```
service krb_prop
{
        disable         = no
        socket_type     = stream
        protocol        = tcp
        user            = root
        wait            = no
        server          = /usr/sbin/kpropd
}
```

Having prepared the **krb_prop** file, we can start the **xinetd** service. The TCP port 754 should be open, as we can see from the output of the **nmap** port scanner:

```
# nmap localhost

Starting nmap 3.81 ( http://www.insecure.org/nmap/ ) at 2006-05-18 14:55 CEST
Interesting ports on localhost.localdomain (127.0.0.1):
(The 1659 ports scanned but not shown below are in state: closed)
PORT    STATE SERVICE
754/tcp open  krb_prop

Nmap finished: 1 IP address (1 host up) scanned in 0.213 seconds
```

The propagation process happens in two steps: a complete database dump on the master, and its propagation to the slave KDCs. Dumping the database can be done via the Kerberos tool **kdb5_util**, specifying the dump action and the output file name:

```
# kdb5_util dump /var/lib/krb5kdc/slave_datatrans
```

If the file has been successfully created, in the **/var/lib/krb5kdc/** directory we can find files like the following:

```
# ls -l /var/lib/krb5kdc/
total 32
-rw-------  1 root root 16384 2006-04-27 17:03 principal
-rw-------  1 root root  8192 2006-04-27 15:11 principal.kadm5
-rw-------  1 root root     0 2006-04-27 15:11 principal.kadm5.lock
-rw-------  1 root root     0 2006-04-27 17:03 principal.ok
-rw-------  1 root root  3534 2006-05-18 14:58 slave_datatrans
-rw-------  1 root root     1 2006-05-18 14:58 slave_datatrans.dump_ok
```

The permissions for these files, the Kerberos database itself and the dumped file, are strictly related to the **root** user. Right now on the slave we have no files:

```
# ls -l /var/lib/krb5kdc/
total 0
```

We are ready to propagate our newly-created dump file using the kprop tool on the master. By default this program looks for a dump file in the directory /var/lib/krb5kdc/ named slave_datatrans:

```
# kprop kdc2.example.edu
Database propagation to kdc2.example.edu: SUCCEEDED
```

On the slave we can see that the database has been successfully populated:

```
# ls -l /var/lib/krb5kdc/
total 20
-rw-------  1 root root 3534 2006-05-18 15:04 from_master
-rw-------  1 root root 8192 2006-05-18 15:04 principal
-rw-------  1 root root 8192 2006-05-18 15:04 principal.kadm5
-rw-------  1 root root    0 2006-05-18 15:04 principal.kadm5.lock
-rw-------  1 root root    0 2006-05-18 15:04 principal.ok
```

Observe again the permission bits allowing reading and writing operations only to the root user. The database propagation must be done regularly to keep synchronized the master KDC with its slaves: how often this procedure happens depends on how fast your environment changes—passwords, users, and services—provided that all the KDCs have consistent databases. One simple solution could be to place a script in /etc/cron.hourly/ on the master.

The last step to make our slave KDC working is to create the stash file, containing the secret key that decrypts the database. This is easily done using the kdb5_util tool, supplying the same password we used on the master:

```
# kdb5_util stash
kdb5_util: Cannot find/read stored master key while reading master key
kdb5_util: Warning: proceeding without master key
Enter KDC database master key:
```

This last step could have been avoided copying directly the stash file from the master KDC to the slave with a secure method of our choice. The slave KDC is now ready to get started:

```
# /etc/init.d/krb5-kdc start
Starting Kerberos KDC: krb5kdc krb524d.
```

We can now add our new KDC to the Kerberos configuration file on each Kerberos-enabled client. Right now we have a master KDC kdc1 and a slave kdc2. We have already created an alias for our master key distribution center called krb.example.edu, so we can use this alias in the configuration file in order to have an easy way of handling failures:

```
EXAMPLE.EDU = {
        kdc = krb.example.edu
        kdc = kdc2.example.edu
        kdc = kdc1.example.edu
        admin_server = krb.example.edu
}
```

The first KDC a Kerberos client looks for is krb; if it fails, it would look for the second entry kdc2 and so on. We can thus easily switch from the failed master to the slave KDC just by changing the alias in the DNS database. In this case we have to activate the /etc/init.d/krb5-admin-server service on the slave since it became the master now, and re-establish the database propagation: the ACL we have previously shown enables propagation from both master and slave machines.

3.3.4 Service Discovery

Although not every service uses the DNS service discovery, it is a good practice to enter the necessary entries in the database to easily find KDCs, and administrative servers.

The DNS database can handle a TXT entry that identifies the realm name, and some SRV items to find all the servers. Our realm gets a stanza added in the DNS like the following:

```
_kerberos.example.edu.              TXT     "EXAMPLE.EDU"
_kerberos._udp.example.edu.         SRV     0 0  88 kdc1.example.edu
_kerberos._udp.example.edu.         SRV     0 0  88 kdc2.example.edu
_kerberos-master._udp.example.edu.  SRV     0 0  88 krb.example.edu
_kerberos-adm._tcp.example.edu.     SRV     0 0 749 krb.example.edu
_kpasswd._udp.example.edu.          SRV     0 0 464 krb.example.edu
```

3.4 Testing Kerberos

Our backbone system, constituted by Kerberos, LDAP, AFS, and Samba, will be tested and implemented incrementally. To do so, we create a user and a group on a computer, and step by step we replace all its information moving them to the proper location. Our first user is called testuser, and belongs to a group called testgroup. Here and in the following chapters, we show all the changes from a local user to a global user in our distributed environment.

3.4.1 Preparing the Test Environment

Local users authenticate to the standard local UNIX password file. Our aim is to remove this locality constraint and have Kerberos handle the authentication process. The first step is to create the test user and group on a computer, in our case, we use the master KDC to show the process. Our testing group is called `testgroup`, with GID 10000, so that we do not interfere with any pre-existing UNIX group:

```
# addgroup --gid 10000 testgroup
Adding group 'testgroup' (10000)...
Done.
```

Our `testuser` belongs to the GID 10000 as its primary group, and its UID is 10000:

```
# adduser --uid 10000 --ingroup testgroup testuser
Adding user 'testuser'...
Adding new user 'testuser' (10000) with group 'testgroup'.
Creating home directory '/home/testuser'.
Copying files from '/etc/skel'
Enter new UNIX password:
Retype new UNIX password:
passwd: password updated successfully
Changing the user information for testuser
Enter the new value, or press ENTER for the default
        Full Name []: Test User
        Room Number []: 001
        Work Phone []: 555-123
        Home Phone []: 1-123
        Other []: none
Is the information correct? [y/N] y
```

We can see from the `id` command, and from all the standard configuration files, that our user have been successfully created along with its information and home directory:

```
# id testuser
uid=10000(testuser) gid=10000(testgroup) groups=10000(testgroup)

# grep testuser /etc/passwd
testuser:x:10000:10000:Test User,001,555-123,1-123,none:/home/testuser:/bin/bash

# grep testuser /etc/shadow
testuser:$1$CoN658uK$6mKQ3PygWbmsnbB/PA8mF0:13321:0:99999:7:::

# grep testgroup /etc/group
testgroup:x:10000:
```

Our objective now is to let this user authenticate against Kerberos, discarding the existing UNIX authentication information. In order to do that, we need to create the principal for our user, so with the `kadmin` command let us create the `testuser` entry:

```
# kadmin -p sysadmin
Authenticating as principal sysadmin with password.
Password for sysadmin@EXAMPLE.EDU:

kadmin: add_principal testuser
WARNING: no policy specified for testuser@EXAMPLE.EDU; defaulting to no policy
Enter password for principal "testuser@EXAMPLE.EDU":
Re-enter password for principal "testuser@EXAMPLE.EDU":
Principal "testuser@EXAMPLE.EDU" created.
```

The successful creation of the new principal can be tested by getting a ticket granting ticket using the `kinit` command.

3.4.2 Pluggable Authentication Modules

Debian Linux has a comfortable way of authenticating users called *Pluggable Authentication Modules* or PAM. This software was developed by Sun Microsystems in the 1990s, and provides high-level APIs to build authentication modules as dynamic libraries.

Each service which wants to authenticate a user via PAM, provides a *service name*, and PAM looks in the directory `/etc/pam.d/` for a file with the specified name:

```
# ls /etc/pam.d/
chfn             common-password   cvs             other   ssh
chsh             common-session    gdm             passwd  su
common-account   cron              gdm-autologin   ppp     sudo
common-auth      cupsys            login           samba   xscreensaver
```

If PAM succeeds in opening the correct file for a requested service, it starts to execute the requested system calls to authenticate and open a working session using the specified libraries. As an example, the `login` service uses the following configuration:

```
auth       requisite  pam_securetty.so
auth       requisite  pam_nologin.so
auth       required   pam_env.so
@include common-auth

@include common-account
@include common-session

session    optional   pam_lastlog.so
session    optional   pam_motd.so
session    optional   pam_mail.so standard noenv

@include common-password
```

Lines starting with `auth` are used for authentication, so PAM would strictly require a secure console for `root` with `pam_securetty.so`, verify for non-root users the absence of the file `/etc/nologin`, require a specific environment with `pam_env.so`, and finally include the settings from a common authentication configuration file called `common-auth`. Upon a successful authentication, PAM opens a working session if the application requests so, for example `login` requires to open a working session on a console. The session configuration is driven by the lines beginning with `session`, and in our example we have a common session file and optional libraries that provide information about the user's last login using `pam_lastlog.so`, optionally print a message of the day by `pam_motd.so`, inform about unread emails with `pam_mail.so`. Here is a summary of the different types of module management groups:

account Possible restrictions not related to the authentication;
auth Authentication followed by granting of credentials;
password Modification of the authentication token;
session Actions before or after granting the service.

The type is followed by a control parameter. Afterwards there comes a module name and optionally some arguments. The Table 3.2 gives an overview of possible control parameters in the order of their strength.

Table 3.2. PAM control parameters

Control	On Failure	On Success
prerequisite	Immediate failure	Call next on stack
required	Failure but call next on stack	Call next on stack
sufficient	Call next on stack	Success if no previous failure
optional	Failure if the *only* module	Call next on stack

All the available modules are stored in the **/lib/security/** directory, for example we can have plenty of them used for many different purposes:

```
# ls /lib/security/
pam_access.so   pam_lastlog.so    pam_rhosts_auth.so   pam_unix_auth.so@
pam_debug.so    pam_limits.so     pam_rootok.so        pam_unix_passwd.so@
pam_deny.so     pam_listfile.so   pam_securetty.so     pam_unix_session.so@
pam_env.so      pam_mail.so       pam_shells.so        pam_unix.so
pam_filter.so   pam_mkhomedir.so  pam_stress.so        pam_userdb.so
pam_ftp.so      pam_motd.so       pam_tally.so         pam_warn.so
pam_group.so    pam_nologin.so    pam_time.so          pam_wheel.so
pam_issue.so    pam_permit.so     pam_unix_acct.so@
```

Since PAM is not a daemon, adding or removing a module, or modifying the configuration, does not require any restart and all the changes are always immediately active. The Kerberos module for PAM is called **pam_krb5.so** and is provided by the **libpam-krb5** package, so let us install it:

```
# apt-get install libpam-krb5
```

We want to enable **login** to use Kerberos as a valid authentication module. As we have seen, this service includes the **common-auth** file, so we have to modify it adding our Kerberos module as a means of authentication:

```
auth    sufficient    pam_unix.so
auth    sufficient    pam_krb5.so use_first_pass
auth    required      pam_deny.so
```

Let us analyze the authentication process. First the system authenticates the username and the given password against the common UNIX files as /etc/passwd and /etc/shadow, a successful authentication exits since we have specified the module as **sufficient**, a failure makes PAM try the next available one. If `pam_unix.so` fails, PAM tries to use the Kerberos module `pam_krb5.so` trying to use the password previously used for UNIX, specified by the `use_first_pass`[4] flag. In case it fails, the control passes over the last module `pam_deny.so` which always returns a failure to the calling service: the user is not authenticated when reaching this point. The entire process is visualized in Fig.3.4.

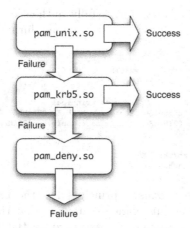

Fig. 3.4. Our authentication PAM stack

To test if the Kerberos login truly works, we have to remove all the passwords from the common UNIX password files. To delete the password we can use the `usermod` command, with the switch `-p` which lets us modify directly the encrypted password. If we specify ! for password we disable it, since the string ! can never be an encrypted version of a password:

```
# usermod -p '!' testuser

# grep testuser /etc/passwd
testuser:x:10000:10000:Test User,001,555-123,1-123,none:/home/testuser:/bin/bash

# grep testuser /etc/shadow
testuser:!:13321:0:99999:7:::
```

Now we are ready to test the login using a console:

```
Debian GNU/Linux 3.1 krb tty6

krb login: testuser
Password:
Last login: Tue Jun 20 17:58:57 2006 on tty6
```

---

[4] The specified `use_first_pass` flag uses a previous username and password; the `try_first_pass` does the same, but in case of failure it prompts the user for another password.

```
Linux krb 2.4.27-3-686 #1 Wed Feb 8 12:40:33 UTC 2006 i686 GNU/Linux

The programs included with the Debian GNU/Linux system are free software;
the exact distribution terms for each program are described in the
individual files in /usr/share/doc/*/copyright.

Debian GNU/Linux comes with ABSOLUTELY NO WARRANTY, to the extent
permitted by applicable law.
testuser@krb:~$
```

The user should have been successfully authenticated against Kerberos, and specifically, it shows all the tickets it gained during this process:

```
testuser@krb:~$ klist
Ticket cache: FILE:/tmp/krb5cc_10000_w2557X
Default principal: testuser@EXAMPLE.EDU

Valid starting     Expires            Service principal
06/20/06 17:59:30  06/21/06 03:59:30  krbtgt/EXAMPLE.EDU@EXAMPLE.EDU
06/20/06 17:59:30  06/21/06 03:59:30  host/kdc1.example.edu@EXAMPLE.EDU


Kerberos 4 ticket cache: /tmp/tkt10000
klist: You have no tickets cached
```

We notice that the **testuser** principal has the initial ticket, and also gained the host ticket: at this point we are sure that the machine is the one intended to use. Host principals are exported by the system administrator with **root** privileges, and are to ensure that this machine is a trusted host.

Practice

Exercise 9. Confront the Heimdal and MIT implementations of Kerberos. Do you prefer one over the other? Do you need to support both of them?

Exercise 10. Plan your Kerberos realm. What are your default ticket life-times? Do you have a password policy and how can it be enforced?

Exercise 11. Check available default modules for PAM located under the /lib/security/ directory. Search also all packets containing the string libpam. Remember that these can be combined with the help of the stacking mechanism.

Exercise 12. Test cross-realm authentication as described for example in the MIT Kerberos documentation. In both realms one has to create the following principal krbtgt/OTHER.REALM@EXAMPLE.EDU and also its counterpart krbtgt/EXAMPLE.EDU@OTHER.REALM.

4

LDAP

It is a very sad thing that nowadays there is so little useless information.
Oscar Wilde

4.1 Lightweight Directory Access Protocol

Information retrieval is a critical resource over distributed networks. A first example for its importance is a telephone directory: it grew over time to a considerable size and demanded a hierarchical organization so that information could be found with a reasonable effort. DNS was the answer to IP address and name lookup over a network, and *directory services* were the answer for other objects such as user names, telephone numbers, postal addresses, and so on.

One of the first directory services was the X.500 protocol publicized by the International Telecommunication Union, the ITU-T[1], used as a directory service for the electronic messaging protocol X.400 published in 1984: at that time email systems were almost everywhere implemented by in-house solutions, and X.500 was the official directory protocol for X.400. Another famous and still used directory service is NIS, the *Network Information Service*, developed by Sun Microsystems and formerly known as the *Yellow Pages* protocol. Sun had to change the name due to a trademark issue over the telephonic Yellow Pages owned by the British Telecom, but NIS commands still inherit the old YP-related names as ypcat or yppasswd.

LDAP is another directory service, originally intended to be a gateway for X.500-based networks, and it still inherits the tree-based structure. An LDAP database is based on a tree, as we can see from Fig. 4.1. The root of the LDAP tree defines what is called a *base* for information retrieval: this structure may be compared to the DNS, which is also a tree-based informative system as we have previously seen. Contrary to the strict information made available by the DNS, each LDAP entity possesses some attributes. As for the X.500 protocol, the attributes are defined by a *schema*, a description of all available attributes, their possible values, their priority. As a result, LDAP

---

[1] ITU-T was formerly known as the CCITT, the acronym for Comité Consultatif International Téléphonique et Télégraphique.

is a very flexible and customizable system capable of containing contents like the standard UNIX user information, as we can see in Fig. 4.1.

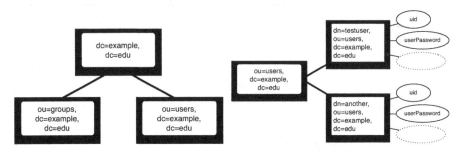

Fig. 4.1. LDAP tree with two *Organizational Units* and two *Posix Account* leaves

Our organization will have a base called `dc=example,dc=edu`, where `dc` stands for *Domain Component*. We organize entries hierarchically, creating some sub-trees called *Organizational Units*: for example our users belong to the ou named `ou=users,dc=example,dc=edu`. Entries have their own attributes and a key called *Distinguished Name*: a user for instance may be referred to as `uid=testuser,ou=users,dc=example,dc=edu`.

LDAP provides some advantages over NIS. It is basically a tree, and its hierarchy makes it possible to organize information in a more rational way, whereas NIS is a flat repository. LDAP may also delegate sub-trees to other servers, so it is a scalable solution from small to huge organizations. Of further importance is the fact that LDAP is a Kerberized service, allowing an already authenticated user to interact with the service employing its credentials. The first version of this protocol was developed by Tim Howes (University of Michigan), Steve Kille (ISODE), and Wengyik Yeong (Performance Systems International), circa 1993. The last LDAP protocol is LDAPv3 described in RFC 4510 and is maintained by the IETF.

4.2 Master LDAP

Our organization will employ two LDAP servers, a master and a slave. First we are going to install the master server on a machine called `ldap1.example.edu`, the slave host is named `ldap2.example.edu`: as we did for the Kerberos system, our choice is to have a `CNAME` alias in the DNS, called `ldap`, so that in case of failure we can easily switch master and slave hosts.

4.2.1 Installing LDAP

Debian provides an LDAP server which is a free and open-source implementation of the protocol, the OpenLDAP server, distributed as the `slapd` package.

As usual, when installing the package, the system tries to configure it, setting the search base to the DNS zone, in our case example.edu is transformed into the base dc=example,dc=edu. The system configures the LDAP server asking for an administrative password, and stores all this information in the database. Our suggestion is to support LDAPv2 only if you need it for legacy applications. After configuring the server, Debian starts the daemon, which incidentally is called slapd.

At this point, we need some administrative tools to query the database, so install the ldaputils package. In order to search a particular entry in LDAP, we may use a command called ldapsearch, which requires the specification of the LDAP search base, the server we want to contact, and the authentication method, respectively the -b, -h, and -x (for anonymous access) parameters:

```
# ldapsearch -x -h localhost -LLL -b "dc=example,dc=edu"

dn: dc=example,dc=edu
objectClass: top
objectClass: dcObject
objectClass: organization
o: Example Organization
dc: example

dn: cn=admin,dc=example,dc=edu
objectClass: simpleSecurityObject
objectClass: organizationalRole
cn: admin
description: LDAP administrator
```

As we can see from the output of the query, Debian created a tree for our LDAP database containing the root and the administrative user admin with the password we have specified in the installation process, although we had no choice about the name of this administrative entry.

The authentication we are using is called *simple*, allowing us to use even clear-text passwords. A -L switch tells the tool to display the information in the LDIFv1[2] format, duplicating the switch suppresses any comment supplied by the protocol. The last parameter we may supply to the command is the object to search: by leaving this option unspecified we query for all the LDAP database content. Let us inspect the produced LDIF to understand its meaning focusing on the first part of the output.

The entry beginning with dn is the unique key in the database, the *distinguished name* of the entry, in our case we are analyzing the root of our tree dn: dc=example,dc=edu. Lines beginning with objectClass specify the schemas used by the entry in the database. The root may thus have attributes taken from the top, dcObject, and organization schemas. These schemas define attributes and their values, for instance the o which specifies a textual description of our organization.

---

[2] LDIF stands for LDAP Data Interchange Format, a textual description of an interaction with the database, e.g. expressing outputs, additions, deletions, and modifications.

LDAP provides also credential-based attribute actions, for instance user passwords are not—by default—viewable to users except administrators and the user itself. This fact can be easily tested by using a simple authentication, and specifying some credential by a distinguished name with -D and a password with -w:

```
# ldapsearch -x -h localhost -b "dc=example,dc=edu" -D "cn=admin,dc=example,dc=edu" \
-w ldappass -LLL
dn: dc=example,dc=edu
objectClass: top
objectClass: dcObject
objectClass: organization
o: Example Organization
dc: example

dn: cn=admin,dc=example,dc=edu
objectClass: simpleSecurityObject
objectClass: organizationalRole
cn: admin
description: LDAP administrator
userPassword:: e2NyeXB0fWZSQ29pRk5GbHRaVi4=
```

The provided password is the same as the one defined during installation. Notice that the administrator has the right to view the hashed version of any password, included itself, as we can see from its description with the key cn=admin,dc=example,dc=edu where cn stands for *Common Name*.

The slapd daemon, that handles LDAP, has a major configuration file called slapd.conf, located in the /etc/ldap/ directory, and looks like the following:

```
include         /etc/ldap/schema/core.schema
include         /etc/ldap/schema/cosine.schema
include         /etc/ldap/schema/nis.schema
include         /etc/ldap/schema/inetorgperson.schema

schemacheck     on

pidfile         /var/run/slapd/slapd.pid
argsfile        /var/run/slapd.args
loglevel        0

modulepath      /usr/lib/ldap
moduleload      back_bdb

backend         bdb
checkpoint      512 30
database        bdb

suffix          "dc=example,dc=edu"

directory       "/var/lib/ldap"

index           objectClass eq

lastmod         on

access to attrs=userPassword
        by dn="cn=admin,dc=example,dc=edu" write
        by anonymous auth
```

```
        by self write
        by * none

access to dn.base="" by * read

access to *
        by dn="cn=admin,dc=example,dc=edu" write
        by * read
```

The configuration file specifies which schemas LDAP should use via the include directive and whether it has to validate them with schemacheck. LDAP has a default suffix and storage backend. The access directives specify the ACLs for each attribute, for example userPassword cannot be even viewed by anyone except by the user itself and the administrator. Since this file may contain administrative credentials, its permission bits are strictly root-related:

```
-rw------- 1 root root 3637 2006-05-30 10:51 slapd.conf
```

The entry "cn=admin,dc=example,dc=edu" has administrative rights because of the ACL defined above.

4.2.2 Removing the Administrator

We have already seen that Debian in its installation process created a tree and an administrator, but in our organization all the credentials are stored exclusively in the Kerberos database. Moreover, having passwords inside the LDAP database may be a security weakness, and our objective is to create secure services: LDAP will be used in our network to store *less* critical information, such as phone numbers, names, surnames, and mail addresses.

Before fully employing Kerberos, we have to remove the administrator from our LDAP tree, so as an intermediate step before proceeding, we have to stop the service and modify its configuration defining a new system administrator by rootdn with an explicit password in the rootpw parameter:

```
include        /etc/ldap/schema/core.schema
include        /etc/ldap/schema/cosine.schema
include        /etc/ldap/schema/nis.schema
include        /etc/ldap/schema/inetorgperson.schema

schemacheck    on

pidfile        /var/run/slapd/slapd.pid
argsfile       /var/run/slapd.args
loglevel       0

modulepath     /usr/lib/ldap
moduleload     back_bdb

backend        bdb
checkpoint     512 30
database       bdb
```

```
suffix          "dc=example,dc=edu"

rootdn  "cn=sysadmin,dc=example,dc=edu"
rootpw  ldappass

directory       "/var/lib/ldap"

index           objectClass eq

lastmod         on

access to attrs=userPassword
        by anonymous auth
        by self write
        by * none

access to dn.base="" by * read

access to *
        by * read
```

We chose to use the same name as the administrative Kerberos principal sysadmin but the choice is purely random: any valid common name can be used for this task. We have also altered the ACLs since the rootdn gets implicitly full access. Having modified the configuration, we have to restart the daemon in order to have the changes take effect:

```
# /etc/init.d/slapd start
Starting OpenLDAP: (db4.2_recover not found),  slapd.
```

We can test now our new system administrator by first searching all entries without any credential, and then re-issuing the same command authenticating ourselves as cn=sysadmin,dc=example,dc=edu. Note that the administrative password is sent in clear-text via the command line. The last command should show us the userPassword attribute:

```
# ldapsearch -x -h localhost -LLL -b "dc=example,dc=edu"
dn: dc=example,dc=edu
objectClass: top
objectClass: dcObject
objectClass: organization
o: Example Organization
dc: example

dn: cn=admin,dc=example,dc=edu
objectClass: simpleSecurityObject
objectClass: organizationalRole
cn: admin
description: LDAP administrator

# ldapsearch -x -h localhost -b "dc=example,dc=edu" -D "cn=sysadmin,dc=example,dc=edu" \
-w ldappass -LLL
dn: dc=example,dc=edu
objectClass: top
objectClass: dcObject
objectClass: organization
o: Example Organization
dc: example
```

```
dn: cn=admin,dc=example,dc=edu
objectClass: simpleSecurityObject
objectClass: organizationalRole
cn: admin
description: LDAP administrator
userPassword:: e2NyeXB0WZSQ29pRk5GbHRaVi4=
```

Now it is sure that the `syadmin` has full administrative privileges and it is not stored in the LDAP database. We are cleared to remove the old administrator using our credentials by calling the `ldapdelete` command, specifying the entry we want to erase. A successful deletion does not provide any output, as all common UNIX tools, but searching the database we can see as the distinguished name `cn=admin,dc=example,dc=edu` is no longer there:

```
# ldapdelete -x -h localhost -D "cn=sysadmin,dc=example,dc=edu" -w ldappass \
"cn=admin,dc=example,dc=edu"

# ldapsearch -x -h localhost -b "dc=example,dc=edu" -D "cn=sysadmin,dc=example,dc=edu" \
-w ldappass -LLL
dn: dc=example,dc=edu
objectClass: top
objectClass: dcObject
objectClass: organization
o: Example Organization
dc: example
```

Client-side Configuration

All the LDAP client-side tools were used until now specifying each time the root of our LDAP tree with the -b switch. To ease our interaction with the server, we can set the default search base by modifying the `ldap.conf` file in `/etc/ldap/`. This file contains directives that specify how client-side tools, like the `ldapsearch` command, behave by default. In our example, we set a default base and the default LDAP server:

```
BASE    dc=example, dc=edu
URI     ldap://ldap.example.edu
```

The URI directive, *Uniform Resource Identifier*[3], specifies the host to be contacted and the relative protocol to be used. We are familiar with URIs although we are not aware of this: for instance `http://www.ietf.org/` is a URI specifying that the protocol to use is HTTP, and that the server to contact is `www.ietf.org`, asking for the root path, the final /. The URI specification is suggested instead of using the deprecated HOST directive.

To test the default values, just query the LDAP server:

---

[3] URIs recognized by the IANA vary from emails to instant messaging, and specifically the LDAP protocol URIs are drafted in RFC 2255 and 4516.

```
# ldapsearch -x -h localhost -LLL
dn: dc=example,dc=edu
objectClass: top
objectClass: dcObject
objectClass: organization
o: Example Organization
dc: example
```

4.2.3 Building a Tree

Right now we have a tree constituted by just the root entry, and organizing an efficient tree depends on the future use. Our organization will principally employ LDAP to retrieve user information, groups of users, and mail aliases; but a directory service could store more than these.

Our decision is to create three sub-trees below the root: one for the users, one for groups, and one for mail aliases. Adding new *organizational units* is a simple task involving an input LDIF textual file that specifies at least the mandatory attributes for each entry. An organizational unit, for example `ou=users`, has three mandatory entries: the distinguished name as the key in the database, the schema and the unit's name. In our case, we create a text file that creates three items, and looks like the following:

```
dn: ou=users,dc=example,dc=edu
objectClass: organizationalUnit
ou: users

dn: ou=groups,dc=example,dc=edu
objectClass: organizationalUnit
ou: groups

dn: ou=aliases,dc=example,dc=edu
objectClass: organizationalUnit
ou: aliases
```

Observe that the **dn** begins with the **ou** entry matching the organization unit name specified in the attribute field **ou**. To add entries into the LDAP database we use the **ldapadd** tool, authenticating as **sysadmin**: only a system administrator can add new entries, since nothing else is specified in the **slapd.conf** ACLs section:

```
# ldapadd -x -D "cn=sysadmin,dc=example,dc=edu" -w ldappass -f create.ldif
adding new entry "ou=users,dc=example,dc=edu"

adding new entry "ou=groups,dc=example,dc=edu"

adding new entry "ou=aliases,dc=example,dc=edu"
```

This tool informs us of errors and also of successful operations as we can see from the produced output. Querying the server shows the newly-created organizational units along with the root:

```
# ldapsearch -x -LLL
dn: dc=example,dc=edu
objectClass: top
objectClass: dcObject
objectClass: organization
o: Example Organization
dc: example

dn: ou=users,dc=example,dc=edu
objectClass: organizationalUnit
ou: users

dn: ou=groups,dc=example,dc=edu
objectClass: organizationalUnit
ou: groups

dn: ou=aliases,dc=example,dc=edu
objectClass: organizationalUnit
ou: aliases
```

4.2.4 Kerberizing LDAP with GSSAPI

As we already previewed, one of the advantages of LDAP is its seamless integration in a Kerberos-based network. The OpenLDAP server can interact with various authentication methods based on an Application Programming Interface called GSSAPI, the *Generic Security Services Application Program Interface.*

The GSSAPI layer is a library allowing an abstraction level over security services: by itself GSSAPI does not provide any security facility. Vendors provide libraries that implement some generic functions that a standard GSSAPI should provide. For example instead of querying directly the Kerberos infrastructure via Kerberos native calls (as using functions like krb5_init_context() or krb5_auth_con_init()), employing GSSAPI a software may request the system to obtain credentials without caring about the involved protocol (for example using the gss_acquire_cred() call). The GSSAPI layer takes care of implementing the required calls, interacting on the network with the correct protocol and returning to the requester approval or denial. There are many security standards implemented by a GSSAPI library, as drafted by RFC 1508 for GSSAPIv1, and later RFC 2078 and 2743 for the second version. The Kerberos implementations (MIT or Heimdal) usually provide GSSAPI abstraction layers as described in RFC 1964.

GSSAPI often works coupled with SASL, the *Simple Authentication and Security Layer,* drafted in the RFC 4422 and the obsolete RFC 2222. This proposed IETF protocol provides a framework for various authentication protocols, among them we can mention:

- ANONYMOUS for anonymous and unauthenticated guests;
- CRAM-MD5 for challenge-response authentication with MD5 hash;
- EXTERNAL to be used in implicit authentication contexts (like IPsec);
- GSSAPI using a GSS-based Kerberos V authentication;

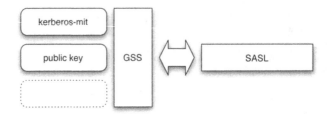

Fig. 4.2. The GSSAPI layer as gateway between SASL and Kerberos

- `PLAIN` for insecure clear-text passwords;
- `OTP` for one-time passwords.

LDAP uses SASL calls in order to authenticate a user by a trusted method, in our case, the MIT Kerberos via the GSSAPI abstraction layer as in Fig. 4.2, distributed as the `libsasl2-gssapi-mit` package, so install it before proceeding.

The GSSAPI layer needs a service key in order to authenticate the LDAP service, exported in a keytab file, as we have previously done for host authentication. The service principal must be in the form `ldap/FQDN`, and exported to a keytab file, our choice is to export the principal keys to the `ldap.keytab` file into `/etc/ldap/`:

```
# kadmin -p sysadmin
Authenticating as principal sysadmin with password.
Password for sysadmin@EXAMPLE.EDU:

kadmin:  addprinc -randkey ldap/dns.example.edu
WARNING: no policy specified for ldap/ldap.example.edu@EXAMPLE.EDU; \
defaulting to no policy
Principal "ldap/ldap1.example.edu@EXAMPLE.EDU" created.

kadmin:  ktadd -k /etc/ldap/ldap.keytab ldap/ldap1.example.edu
Entry for principal ldap/ldap1.example.edu with kvno 3, encryption type \
Triple DES cbc mode with HMAC/sha1 added to keytab WRFILE:/etc/ldap/ldap.keytab.
Entry for principal ldap/ldap1.example.edu with kvno 3, encryption type \
DES cbc mode with CRC-32 added to keytab WRFILE:/etc/ldap/ldap.keytab.
```

The Debian distribution usually makes use of files located in the directory `/etc/default/` in order to export default environment variables for various services. The LDAP server follows this behavior, and the keytab file should be listed in the `slapd` file with the `KRB5_KTNAME` environment variable:

```
SLAPD_CONF=
SLAPD_USER=
SLAPD_GROUP=
SLAPD_PIDFILE=
TRY_BDB_RECOVERY=yes
SLURPD_START=auto
SLAPD_OPTIONS=""
SLURPD_OPTIONS=""
```

```
KRB5_KTNAME="/etc/ldap/ldap.keytab"
export KRB5_KTNAME
```

To enable the LDAP-Kerberos link, we have to understand how GSSAPI works for our system. An authenticated user with a valid Kerberos ticket gets redirected to the GSSAPI mechanism by the SASL layer, with a distinguished name constituted by four parameters:

1. The principal name in the form `uid=principalname`;
2. The realm name `cn=realmname`;
3. A common name to the GSSAPI mechanism `cn=gssapi`;
4. The final call to the authentication `cn=auth`.

Thus, our principal called `sysadmin` is identified with a distinguished name `uid=sysadmin,cn=example.edu,cn=gssapi,cn=auth`. The key for making the whole Kerberized system work, is to map a GSSAPI-provided entry to an item for the LDAP database.

The map between GSSAPI and LDAP must be written explicitly in the `slapd.conf` file using regular expressions. We have to add the `sasl-regexp` stanza that translates every string to an entry in the users sub-tree in the database. After specifying the regular expression rule, SASL requires the FQDN for the host and the realm (`sasl-host` and `sasl-realm`):

```
sasl-regexp
        uid=(.*),cn=example.edu,cn=gssapi,cn=auth
        uid=$1,ou=users,dc=example,dc=edu

sasl-host ldap1.example.edu
sasl-realm EXAMPLE.EDU
```

The parentheses indicate a *named pattern* constituted by any number of characters (the dot followed by an asterisk): any string matching the rule is converted to an entry in the users sub-tree via the `$1` parameter.

As last step to fully Kerberize our LDAP server let us remove the hardwired administrative password from our configuration file, but leave the `sysadmin` user to administer the service. Hence it is sufficient to comment the provided password:

```
rootdn  "uid=sysadmin,ou=users,dc=example,dc=edu"
# rootpw  ldappass
```

Now the password is not specified anywhere in the LDAP configuration and `sysadmin` is not even in the database: the `rootdn` statement allows our Kerberos principal `sysadmin` to be a full administrator by means of the SASL regular expression matching.

We should now modify the client applications, such as `ldapsearch`, to make use of the SASL layer, specifying the authentication mechanism in the `ldap.conf` file as follows:

```
BASE      dc=example,dc=edu
URI       ldap://ldap.example.edu
SASL_MECH GSSAPI
```

Restarting the LDAP server `slapd` activates these changes which depend on the presence of the previously installed `libsasl2-gssapi-mit` for MIT Kerberos.

Testing the SASL Layer

After these changes a simple unauthenticated query should work as before:

```
# ldapsearch -x -LLL
dn: dc=example,dc=edu
objectClass: top
objectClass: dcObject
objectClass: organization
o: Example Organization
dc: example

dn: ou=users,dc=example,dc=edu
objectClass: organizationalUnit
ou: users

dn: ou=groups,dc=example,dc=edu
objectClass: organizationalUnit
ou: groups

dn: ou=aliases,dc=example,dc=edu
objectClass: organizationalUnit
ou: aliases
```

On the other hand, administrative privileges should be granted to the `sysadmin` user. If we try to query the LDAP server without specifying the simple authentication switch `-x`, the system tries to use our current Kerberos credential for the `root` user, resulting in a failure:

```
# ldapsearch -LLL
SASL/GSSAPI authentication started
ldap_sasl_interactive_bind_s: Local error (-2)
        additional info: SASL(-1): generic failure: GSSAPI Error: Miscellaneous failure \
(No credentials cache found)
```

In order to make use of our Kerberized server, we need a valid Kerberos credential. Let us obtain the initial ticket for the principal `sysadmin`:

```
# klist
klist: No credentials cache found (ticket cache FILE:/tmp/krb5cc_0)


Kerberos 4 ticket cache: /tmp/tkt0
klist: You have no tickets cached

# kinit sysadmin
Password for sysadmin@EXAMPLE.EDU:

# klist
```

```
Ticket cache: FILE:/tmp/krb5cc_0
Default principal: sysadmin@EXAMPLE.EDU

Valid starting       Expires               Service principal
05/30/06 12:49:12  05/30/06 22:49:01  krbtgt/EXAMPLE.EDU@EXAMPLE.EDU


Kerberos 4 ticket cache: /tmp/tkt0
klist: You have no tickets cached
```

Having a valid credential and starting a query, the SASL layer translates the principal name to a distinguished name as specified in the regular expression. Intentionally we have hard-wired the **sysadmin** distinguished name as the LDAP administrator: SASL uses the GSSAPI library provided by the MIT Kerberos to verify the identity, and then LDAP authorizes the user as we can see from the following successful output:

```
# ldapsearch -LLL
SASL/GSSAPI authentication started
SASL username: sysadmin@EXAMPLE.EDU
SASL SSF: 56
SASL installing layers
dn: dc=example,dc=edu
objectClass: top
objectClass: dcObject
objectClass: organization
o: Example Organization
dc: example

dn: ou=users,dc=example,dc=edu
objectClass: organizationalUnit
ou: users

dn: ou=groups,dc=example,dc=edu
objectClass: organizationalUnit
ou: groups

dn: ou=aliases,dc=example,dc=edu
objectClass: organizationalUnit
ou: aliases
```

The command **ldapwhoami** can help to verify if the translation process actually works.

4.2.5 Access Control Lists

LDAP has a broad selection of access control lists, expressed via the **access to** directive. The format for specifying access control lists is **access to ITEM** followed by the statements **by ENTITY PRIVILEGE**, as we can see from the example as in the configuration file after installation:

```
access to attrs=userPassword
        by dn="cn=admin,dc=example,dc=edu" write
        by anonymous auth
        by self write
        by * none
```

The ITEM specifies the object of the ACL, the item that is subject to the later defined rules of access. It can be one of the following:

* The wildcard * specifies any item in the tree;
attrs= A comma-sparated list of attributes specified by the keyword attrs as in the example above (although OpenLDAP should accept also the keyword attr);
dn= A distinguished name defined by a pattern or a regular expression.

The field ENTITY specifies the subject of the ACL, the entity entitled to a certain privileged access to the ITEM, specified by one of the following:

* The wildcard * specifies any entity;
self Specifies that the entry is accessible to an authenticated entity with that distinguished name;
users All authenticated users;
anonymous Any user, even non authenticated ones;
dn= Specifies a distinguished name, matching a string or a regular expression.

There are other entities that can be deloyed in the specification of an access control, such as IP matching, security access, and DNS domain. Consult your documentation for more information about such particular entity specifications.

The last parameter is the privilege granted to the preceding entity. The main levels of access are summarized in Table 4.1 from the lowest to the highest. A higher privilege implies any lower one.

Table 4.1. LDAP access control list levels

Level	Privilege Coding	Explanation
none	=0	No access at all
auth	=x	Permits authentication attempt
compare	=cx	Permits comparison
search	=scx	Permits search filter application
read	=rscx	Permits search result inspection
write	=wrscx	Permits modification or deletion

The actual implementation of the ACLs in OpenLDAP is utterly complex: making the simplest error can be extremely dangerous, so test thoroughly the privileges before deploying a new configuration.

Let us specify some examples that may be used in real situations. As the first example, let us note that passwords are sensible data, and should not be even displayed for obvious security reasons. In our system, LDAP would not even contain such sensible information. Since we are interested in *not* displaying or modifying such a field, the assigned ACL could look like the following:

```
access to attrs=userPassword
        by * none
```

Maybe the entire LDAP database should just be readable by any user, either internal or external, since it stores public and non-critical information in the LDAP tree. Such a choice allows clients to retrieve email addresses, web home pages, and any other detail usable by external clients (such as QUAL-COMM Eudora, Apple Mail, Microsoft Outlook or Mozilla Thunderbird):

```
access to * by * read
```

As last example we show how users can modify their home shell attribute which occurs in the schema posixAccount. This resembles some functionality of NIS. Of course every user should just be able to change the own (self) shell setting:

```
access to attrs=loginShell
        by self write
        by * read
```

4.3 Replication

Reliable services are mainly based on replication and distribution. At this point we have created a secure LDAP master server and in the following we are going to create, on another machine, a secondary server that replicates the service provided by the master. This machine is called ldap2.example.edu.

The OpenLDAP server provides two different methods for replicating the service. One is a master-slave replication. The other is a kind of automated mirror.

The master-slave replication is achieved via an additional process called slurpd, which basically synchronizes all the database entries with the slave servers. Every change of the database happens on the master. Afterwards it gets propagated automatically to the slaves.

We choose the second option: the mirroring service. A mirror LDAP server does not involve any further process and acts as a client querying the LDAP master server, updating its database locally. This operation is called *sync replication*. It is clear that a sync replication depends on the access privileges assigned to each item in the LDAP tree: since the slave queries the master, any non-readable information is not replicated on the slave. Our choice of not storing any critical data in LDAP is a key in our system. The replication receives in clear-text the database, allowing us to avoid encrypted channels such as SSL or TSL. Notice that this is true only because we have a fully Kerberized system, without password information in LDAP. In other cases, we recommend using SSL or TLS if deploying a service that stores and replicates sensible data in the database.

The choice of sync replication simplifies the following presentation. We preferred to leave SSL and TLS for the following parts in this book. Furthermore it is assumed that users do not make use of their userPassword in the principal LDAP service. Instead, there are situations were it is convenient to have another form of authentication available.

Slave Settings

On the slave machine, we have to install the slapd daemon and the LDAP client-side tools, the same way we previously did on the master, using the same settings especially the LDAP base setting. As we have seen before, Debian creates a stub tree with an administrator, hence we act as before removing the administrator by creating a new hard-wired entry in the slapd.conf file:

```
rootdn        "cn=replica,dc=example,dc=edu"
rootpw        ldappass
```

Our choice is to use a distinguished name that can be useful in the future, mimicking what we did on the master by using sysadmin to delete the unwanted entries in the database. In this case the replica user is used to synchronize the slave LDAP server with the master. The specific name is arbitrary.

After restarting the slave daemon, we can delete the administrator created during installation with the standard ldapdelete tool:

```
# ldapdelete -x -h localhost -D "cn=replica,dc=example,dc=edu" -w ldappass \
"cn=admin,dc=example,dc=edu"

# ldapsearch -x -h localhost -LLL
dn: dc=example,dc=edu
objectClass: top
objectClass: dcObject
objectClass: organization
o: Example Organization
dc: example
```

The rootpw item, containing the administrative password, can now be safely removed. In order to avoid any security issue about passwords, we set the field to an invalid hashed version of a password, a procedure we have already seen for user passwords:

```
rootdn        "cn=replica,dc=example,dc=edu"
rootpw        {CRYPT}*
```

Sync Settings

In the sync replication case, all other slave LDAP servers are mere clients, retrieving all the information from the master and modifying the local database. The settings about the replication process is stored in the slapd.conf file on the slave itself, in a stanza called syncrepl.

This part of the configuration file specifies a unique replication ID, the server where the slave should read the information from, and what and how often the process should be started. A minimal example of such a stanza is as follows, occurring at the very end of the configuration file:

```
syncrepl rid=123
        provider=ldap://ldap.example.edu:389
        type=refreshOnly
        interval=00:00:05:00
        searchbase="dc=example,dc=edu"
        filter="(objectClass=*)"
        scope=sub
        updatedn="cn=replica,dc=example,dc=edu"
        bindmethod=simple
```

Let us analyze the configuration in order to explain each part. The sync replication with `rid` 123 (Replica ID) reads the database from the `provider` every 5 minutes, as we can see from the `interval` field. The replica type is `refreshOnly`, so that no replication request should persist on the provider `slapd` server; the other possible option is `refreshAndPersist` which causes the synchronization search to be continuous. The contents that is to be replicated is given by the `filter`, the `searchbase` and `scope`: the slave queries the master for information based on a search inquiry, in our case we search for the entire LDAP tree. The last parameters define the distinguished name allowed to modify the replica: we use our `replica` administrator with a simple authentication meaning password based.

Restarting the slave LDAP server, almost instantly starts the replication process, as we can see by starting a query on the slave machine:

```
# ldapsearch -x -h localhost -LLL
dn: dc=example,dc=edu
objectClass: top
objectClass: dcObject
objectClass: organization
o: Example Organization
dc: example

dn: ou=users,dc=example,dc=edu
objectClass: organizationalUnit
ou: users

dn: ou=groups,dc=example,dc=edu
objectClass: organizationalUnit
ou: groups

dn: ou=aliases,dc=example,dc=edu
objectClass: organizationalUnit
ou: aliases
```

As the output shows clearly, the tree has been replicated by creating on the slave the three organizational units we have previously generated on the master machine.

The `replica` distinguished name is not allowed to make any further operation on the slave since we configured for this entity an invalid hashed password in the `slapd.conf`. The following examples show how any attempt to modify the slave by testing some passwords results in a failure:

```
# ldapdelete -x -h localhost "ou=aliases,dc=example,dc=edu"
Delete Result: Strong(er) authentication required (8)
Additional info: modifications require authentication

# ldapdelete -x -h localhost -D "cn=replica,dc=example,dc=edu" \
"ou=aliases,dc=example,dc=edu"
ldap_bind: Server is unwilling to perform (53)
        additional info: unauthenticated bind (DN with no password) disallowed

# ldapdelete -x -h localhost -D "cn=replica,dc=example,dc=edu" -w WrongPasword \
"ou=aliases,dc=example,dc=edu"
ldap_bind: Invalid credentials (49)

# ldapdelete -x -h localhost -D "cn=replica,dc=example,dc=edu" -w '*' \
"ou=aliases,dc=example,dc=edu"
ldap_bind: Invalid credentials (49)

# ldapdelete -x -h localhost -D "cn=replica,dc=example,dc=edu" -w '{CRYPT}*' \
"ou=aliases,dc=example,dc=edu"
ldap_bind: Invalid credentials (49)
```

4.4 Testing LDAP

In our network the LDAP servers contain non critical information that can be displayed publicly. As we already said, LDAP database can be employed to handle various types of details based on the description of such data. The LDAP schemas are a kind of type for the content in the tree, and in the following we are going to use LDAP as a means of UNIX information retrieval for users and groups.

4.4.1 Creating LDAP Entries

Commonly UNIX handles users and group information in the standard /etc/passwd and /etc/group files, and in the previous chapter we have already modified such files moving passwords from /etc/shadow to our KDCs.

For our testing purposes we are going to move all the remaining data regarding our **testuser** into LDAP. Let us first recall the properties of such a user, which has already the password moved into the Kerberos database:

```
# id testuser
uid=10000(testuser) gid=10000(testgroup) groups=10000(testgroup)

# cat /etc/passwd | grep testuser
testuser:x:10000:10000:Test User,001,555-123,1-123,none:/home/testuser:/bin/bash

# cat /etc/group | grep testgroup
testgroup:x:10000:
```

Group Information

The first entry to be moved into LDAP is the UNIX group `testgroup` with GID 10000, and then the entry in `/etc/group` has to be removed. We have already added sub-trees in our LDAP database, creating three objects with the standard `ldapadd` tool and an LDIF file. Our objective is to create now the replacement of the `testgroup` with the same information contained in the UNIX configuration file.

The distinguished name we are going to use in order to move the group into LDAP branches from the already created `ou=groups` entity, which contains all the groups in our network, and its common name matches the UNIX group name. The object class for the group, that provide all the necessary information, is the `posixGroup`, describing all the attributes of a POSIX group:

```
dn: cn=testgroup,ou=groups,dc=example,dc=edu
objectClass: top
objectClass: posixGroup
cn: testgroup
gidNumber: 10000
```

The GID is obviously identical with the `gidNumber` attribute, while the group name coincides with the common name entry `cn`. In order to create the needed item we have to possess a valid administrative credential, so after gaining the initial ticket for our `sysamdin`, we can add the above information described by that LDIF file:

```
# ldapadd -f group.ldif
SASL/GSSAPI authentication started
SASL username: sysadmin@EXAMPLE.EDU
SASL SSF: 56
SASL installing layers
adding new entry "cn=testgroup,ou=groups,dc=example,dc=edu"
```

The database should have been successfully updated, and we can easily check the result by querying the server:

```
# ldapsearch -LLL
SASL/GSSAPI authentication started
SASL username: sysadmin@EXAMPLE.EDU
SASL SSF: 56
SASL installing layers
dn: dc=example,dc=edu
objectClass: top
objectClass: dcObject
objectClass: organization
o: Example Organization
dc: example

dn: ou=users,dc=example,dc=edu
objectClass: organizationalUnit
ou: users

dn: ou=groups,dc=example,dc=edu
objectClass: organizationalUnit
```

```
ou: groups

dn: ou=aliases,dc=example,dc=edu
objectClass: organizationalUnit
ou: aliases

dn: cn=testgroup,ou=groups,dc=example,dc=edu
objectClass: top
objectClass: posixGroup
cn: testgroup
gidNumber: 10000
```

User Information

The creation of a `posixAccount` entry in the LDAP database allows us to represent all the user information. Our `testuser` has UID 10000 and belongs to the POSIX group `testgroup` with GID 10000.

In `/etc/passwd`, there is also a fifth field called GECOS, an acronym for *General Electric Comprehensive Operating Supervisor*. This field contains some generic information about users, such as the real name, room number, telephone number, and it varies among UNIX systems. One of the advantage for using LDAP is that this protocol standardizes the way such data is interpreted, allowing even a human-readable form as we see shortly. In the same file, we have also the home directory specification and the default shell for our user:

```
testuser:x:10000:10000:Test User,001,555-123,1-123,none:/home/testuser:/bin/bash
```

Symmetrically to the group information, we create an entry with object classes `posixAccount` and `shadowAccount`, providing all the needed specifications about UNIX details, such as GID, UID, home directory, and preferred shell. To include other useful details about users, we choose to add the `inetOrgPerson` object class, so that we can add certificates, department names, pictures and so on. The resulting LDIF file looks like the following:

```
dn: uid=testuser,ou=users,dc=example,dc=edu
objectClass: top
objectClass: posixAccount
objectClass: shadowAccount
objectClass: inetOrgPerson
cn: Test
sn: User
uid: testuser
uidNumber: 10000
gidNumber: 10000
homeDirectory: /home/testuser
loginShell: /bin/bash
gecos: Test User,001,555-123,1-123,none
```

The last step on the LDAP database is to add the above information as we did for the group `testgroup`:

```
# ldapadd -f user.ldif
SASL/GSSAPI authentication started
SASL username: sysadmin@EXAMPLE.EDU
SASL SSF: 56
SASL installing layers
adding new entry "uid=testuser,ou=users,dc=example,dc=edu"
```

At this point we are ready to remove the entries `testgroup` and `testuser` from the UNIX files. First we have to remove the user, since we cannot remove a non-empty group, and then we can safely remove the group, too, as follows:

```
# deluser testuser
Removing user 'testuser'...
done.

# delgroup testgroup
Removing group 'testgroup'...
done.
```

Note that if not explicitly requested, removing a user does not remove his home directory. We observe that the group and user information in this case are not resolved and remain just numerical because of the absence of the GID and UID information:

```
# ls -al /home/testuser/
total 20
drwxr-xr-x  2 10000 10000 4096 2006-06-22 11:39 ./
drwxrwsr-x  4 root  staff 4096 2006-06-22 11:34 ../
-rw-------  1 10000 10000   37 2006-06-22 11:57 .bash_history
-rw-r--r--  1 10000 10000  567 2006-06-22 11:34 .bash_profile
-rw-r--r--  1 10000 10000 1834 2006-06-22 11:34 .bashrc
```

4.4.2 Name Service Switch

By default, user information are retrieved through the common UNIX files as we have seen in the previous sections. In order to allow a centralized database of users and groups, Sun Microsystems developed a software that may access different sources of information called NSS, the *Name Service Switch*.

The NSS can be configured to retrieve information from the common UNIX files or from outer sources as NIS, or as in our case, from LDAP. This software has its main configuration file located in the `/etc/` directory, and called `nsswitch.conf`:

```
passwd:        compat
group:         compat
shadow:        compat

hosts:         files dns
networks:      files

protocols:     db files
services:      db files
```

```
ethers:          db files
rpc:             db files

netgroup:        nis
```

The syntax for this file is straightforward. It is a list of pairs indicating the key (the retrieved information) and the list of possible sources. In our example above, NSS recovers user passwords, group and shadow passwords from a *compatibility* source, that basically falls back into checking the common UNIX files /etc/passwd, /etc/group, and /etc/shadow.

By default NSS does not allow any LDAP connection, provided by an external library for NSS provided by the libnss-ldap package. We install the package and Debian configures it as usual. We have to provide the installer with all the obvious details about our network, such as our LDAP servers, the search base and the LDAP protocol version. Usually the default values for other queries are fine in Debian, but anyway we are going to configure NSS manually.

The first setting we modify is the nsswitch.conf file, adding the LDAP source to the list of possible system information services, leaving the compatibility mode as the first choice, thus allowing root or admin to login immediately even on LDAP failure:

```
passwd:          compat ldap
group:           compat ldap
shadow:          compat ldap
```

After the NSS configuration we have to modify the LDAP plugin settings, contained in the /etc/libnss-ldap.conf file:

```
# Your LDAP server.
host ldap.example.edu ldap2.example.edu ldap1.example.edu

# The distinguished name of the search base.
base dc=example,dc=edu

# The LDAP version to use (defaults to 3
# if supported by client library)
ldap_version 3

# Search timelimit
timelimit 30

# Bind/connect timelimit
bind_timelimit 30

# Idle timelimit; client will close connections
# (nss_ldap only) if the server has not been contacted
# for the number of seconds specified below.
idle_timelimit 60

# RFC2307bis naming contexts
nss_base_passwd ou=users,dc=example,dc=edu
nss_base_shadow ou=users,dc=example,dc=edu
nss_base_group  ou=groups,dc=example,dc=edu
```

As we can see, we added our LDAP hosts, with the `CNAME` alias for the master `ldap.example.edu`, and our search base with the `base` directive. The time limits introduced with the settings `timelimit`, `bind_timelimit`, and `idle_timelimit` prevents polluting the system with useless open sockets when querying the LDAP servers. The last three directives are the most important ones, directing the system information previously contained in the standard UNIX files to some sub-tree in the LDAP database.

For completeness we configure the LDAP client tools including SASL, too, and should be able to access the user data from LDAP:

```
# id testuser
uid=10000(testuser) gid=10000(testgroup) groups=10000(testgroup)

# groups testuser
testuser : testgroup
```

Having modified the NSS configuration, it should be possible to login with our `testuser`. At this point all the data regarding this user and its group are present only in the LDAP database, with its password securely stored in Kerberos. Upon login, PAM allows to obtain the tickets, and NSS automatically accesses the user information for this user:

```
Debian GNU/Linux 3.1 client tty6

client login: testuser
Password:
Last login: Thu Jun 22 12:02:45 2006 on tty6
Linux client 2.4.27-3-686 #1 Wed Feb 8 12:40:33 UTC 2006 i686 GNU/Linux

The programs included with the Debian GNU/Linux system are free software;
the exact distribution terms for each program are described in the
individual files in /usr/share/doc/*/copyright.

Debian GNU/Linux comes with ABSOLUTELY NO WARRANTY, to the extent
permitted by applicable law.

testuser@client:~$ klist
Ticket cache: FILE:/tmp/krb5cc_10000_gy3z06
Default principal: testuser@EXAMPLE.EDU

Valid starting     Expires            Service principal
06/22/06 12:03:22  06/22/06 22:03:22  host/client.example.edu@EXAMPLE.EDU
06/22/06 12:03:22  06/22/06 22:03:22  krbtgt/EXAMPLE.EDU@EXAMPLE.EDU


Kerberos 4 ticket cache: /tmp/tkt10000
klist: You have no tickets cached

testuser@client:~$ id
uid=10000(testuser) gid=10000(testgroup) groups=10000(testgroup)

testuser@client:~$ groups
testgroup

testuser@client:~$ ls -al
total 20
drwxr-xr-x  2 testuser testgroup 4096 2006-06-22 11:39 .
drwxrwsr-x  4 root     staff     4096 2006-06-22 11:34 ..
```

```
-rw-------  1 testuser testgroup  103 2006-06-22 12:03 .bash_history
-rw-r--r--  1 testuser testgroup  567 2006-06-22 11:34 .bash_profile
-rw-r--r--  1 testuser testgroup 1834 2006-06-22 11:34 .bashrc
```

Practice

Exercise 13. Check available schemas for LDAP in /etc/ldap/schema/: do those suffice for you or do you have to search for others? What are sensible ACL for your users, such that they can update some information about them?

Exercise 14. Test the replication based on the slurpd daemon. It is slightly more complicated to setup as the easier sync replication, requiring some configuration of the principal server, too.

Exercise 15. Consider to use LDAP as backend for DNS and Kerberos. Today this is principally possible. What are the advantages and what the disadvantages?

Exercise 16. Do you have a Windows-centered environment? The fundamental services so far as NTP, DNS, Kerberos, and LDAP are also available on Windows servers: the integration with the UNIX world and in particular with AFS is a real technical challenge if you prefer to have the principal administration delegated to Windows.

5

OpenAFS

The future is here. It's just not widely distributed yet.
William Gibson

5.1 The OpenAFS Distributed Filesystem

Data is probably the most expensive and valuable resource in a working environment: losing a hard drive is not as important as losing the data stored on it. Accessing documents reliably and securely is thus a main concern, especially when the data should be available through a network.

In 1983 the Carnegie Mellon University, in partnership with IBM, started the *Andrew Project* with the objective to provide the university with a distributed computing system that connected several affordable workstations with some administrative and more expensive servers. The Andrew project included centralized servers and tools, the *Vast Integrated Computing Environment* or VICE and the *Virtue Is Reached Through UNIX and Emacs* or VIRTUE, respectively, and consisted of four sub-projects:

AFS The Andrew File System, a highly scalable distributed file system based on TCP/IP networking;

ATK The Andrew Toolkit, providing tools to create documents containing various objects[1] (e.g. text and graphics);

AMS The Andrew Messaging System supplying an email and messaging tools, based on ATK;

AWM The Andrew Window Manager permitting to display remotely non overlapping windows, then replaced by X11 from the MIT.

The AFS was made commercially available in 1989 by the Transarc Corporation, a Carnegie Mellon University spin-off company, later acquired by IBM in 1998. In the year 2000 IBM decided to make the source code of AFS publicly available, announcing the OpenAFS open-source project.

OpenAFS is a distributed file system, based on the TCP/IP protocol (as its ancestor AFS) and designed on the base of a client-server architecture.

---

[1] ATK contained the *EZ Word* program, one of the first GUI-based editors made available on Linux.

Traditional networked file system as NFS or SMB basically share resources, meaning that a user attempting to access a file should know where the file physically resides. OpenAFS on the other hand is a distributed file system, completely transparent to the user, with the capability of being location and system independent: a file is natively accessible on a platform in the same way the platform usually displays resources. A UNIX system will access files as a directory in the file system, as well as a Windows client will obtain the same file as a shared location. OpenAFS is highly scalable, allowing the administration and maintenance of small to very large environments, providing replication and backup facilities, and ensures security via the Kerberos authentication and encrypted networked communication. As an example of the main characteristics of OpenAFS, we show in Table 5.1 the comparison between NFS and AFS, as provided by the Transarc documentation. In the following we will refer to AFS or OpenAFS as they were synonyms, since the old Transarc-IBM implementation is deprecated.

Table 5.1. The AFS-NFS comparison chart (from Transarc Corp.)

Property	AFS	NFS
File Access	Common name space	Different file names
File Location	Automatic	Mount-points
Performance	Client caching	No local disk caching
Andrew Benchmark	Average 210 sec. / client	Average 280 sec. / client
Scaling	Small to very large	Small to mid-size
	Excellent in wide-area	Best in local-area
Security	Kerberos	Unencrypted user ID
	ACLs	No ACLs
Availability	Data and AFS information	No replication
Backup	No downtime	Via UNIX tools
Reconfiguration	By volumes (groups of files)	Per-file movement
	No user impact or downtime	Mount-points need update
System Management	From any client	With connection to server

The core feature of OpenAFS—as well as AFS—is the concept of volumes. Groups of files and directories belong to a unit called *volume*, and reside on a partition of a physical machine. AFS offers the possibility to move volumes between *file servers*, machines running processes that handle volumes and provide access to files and directories for clients. In order to retrieve files from AFS file servers, clients contact a set of administrative servers. Such control machines run daemons that locate the volume a file belongs to, the machine where the volume physically resides, and check for user authorization on the requested resource. All the needed information about volumes and permissions are stored in databases, which is the reason such machines are called *database servers*. The set of all servers forming a single administrative unit is called an AFS *cell*.

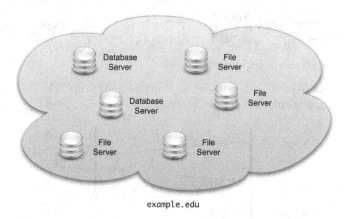

example.edu

Fig. 5.1. The OpenAFS cell `example.edu`

AFS is a distributed file system, and uses a particular technology called *Ubik* to maintain all the information among database servers consistent: this distributed database is implemented via remote procedure calls, and guarantees that data among all administrative databases are synchronized. The AFS servers are administered by a super-server called *Basic Overseer Server*, or BOS. The BOS server, running on every server, monitors all the AFS processes providing correctness of execution, and in case of failure it automatically restarts malfunctioning processes.

AFS servers work with different processes that are managed by BOS. Machines that act as pure file servers run the following servers:

File Server a process that actually handles files and directories residing on a given volume, giving access to them when a client has the proper authorization;

Salvager Server restores, if possible, any corrupted data stored in the volumes on the file server after a failure;

Volume Server administers all local volumes, creating, moving, replicating or deleting them from the file server.

On database servers, the BOS server starts and monitors the following processes, responsible of distributing and maintaining consistent information:

Backup Server administers all the backup operations on the database servers, managing the *backup database*;

Volume Location tracks all the information about volumes and their location on a file server, called the *Volume Location Database* or VLDB;

Protection Server manages all the entries in the *protection database*, containing information about user and group permissions.

The complete suite of servers is not limited to the above. There are some other processes that can be employed, but their use and description are out

cat /afs/example.edu/doc/README   Volume
                                           cell.doc

Fig. 5.2. Users request a file without any further knowledge. The AFS client retrieves the actual volume the data resides on

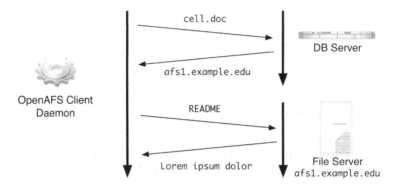

Fig. 5.3. The client daemon, using the information granted by a database server, retrieves data from the correct file server

of the scope of this book. Among these, we may mention the *authentication server* provided by the `kaserver` process: this process was in use before Open-AFS could interact with Kerberos V, and was based on an old Kerberos IV implementation, nowadays declared deprecated.

On the client side, there is complete transparency. The AFS file space is a common mount point in the file system, usually `/afs/`. Volumes are mounted in the AFS file space and appear to a client as any other mount point, that is, they are like any other directory. This makes it possible to move volumes from a file server to another without any reconfiguration, the path leading to a file remains the same, while the physical location of such a resource may change. Moving volumes brings no downtime, except for the initial and the final part of the operation, meaning that there is only a very low probability for a client to encounter any unusual behavior during this process.

A client requesting access to a location in the AFS file space, contacts the database servers providing its credentials, an AFS *token*[2]. If the user has sufficient privileges to access the location, then it retrieves the physical location of the resource, in other words, the file server machine and the partition. With the clearance and the machine name information, the client can fulfill the request: all the process is entirely transparent to a human user, who actually

---

[2] The equivalent of a Kerberos ticket: AFS was developed before Kerberos got standardized, so it has its own version of an authentication credential.

sees files and directories regardless of the location or actual implementation of such objects.

5.2 The First OpenAFS Server

In this section we are going to install and configure the first OpenAFS server. This machine will act as a database server, since without it a cell cannot operate; moreover, we plan to use this host as the first file server, too.

Being a file server means that we have to give the AFS processes the access to at least one dedicated partition on a disk. OpenAFS by default uses partitions names /vicepX, where X is one or two letters (e.g. /vicepa, /vicepb, /vicepiv). The name is a legacy to the already introduced VICE environment from the Andrew project. Our recommendation is to use a performing file system on the partitions, planned to be mounted as /vicepX. In our case we use XFS from the Silicon Graphics IRIX operating system. We will show in the course of this chapter the basic steps of creating an AFS cell file system.

We stress the fact that AFS relies on Kerberos as its authentication method: this means that our first server, called afs1.example.edu, needs to be synchronized with our NTP servers. Another obvious implication of using Kerberos, is that the machine should become a Kerberos client, as we have previously explained.

5.2.1 Preliminaries

Before proceeding with the installation of OpenAFS, we create the needed kernel module for the OpenAFS client. This operation is necessary in order to extend the normal Linux kernel and make it aware of the special treatment of the file space below /afs/. The availability of a client permits to test the system as the procedure advances. The first step is to check the currently installed kernel version:

```
# uname -a
Linux afs1 2.4.27-3-686 #1 Wed Feb 8 12:40:33 UTC 2006 i686 GNU/Linux
```

In order to create the proper kernel module, we need to install the kernel headers related to the installed kernel: a version mismatch puts the entire process in danger[3]. Let us proceed installing the kernel-headers package relative to our system:

```
# apt-get install kernel-headers-2.4.27-3-686
```

---

[3] The Linux kernel does not provide any guarantee on the API and its stability, as can be read in a document "Stable API Nonsense".

Debian provides the OpenAFS kernel module in its source code version, this means that after installing the `openafs-modules-source` package, we need to compile and create a suitable package for our Debian system:

```
# apt-get install openafs-modules-source
```

With the installation of the source code Debian also sets up the needed compilers and libraries, so that no further packages shall be installed in order to compile the kernel module. The installer does not attempt to uncompress the source code, located in `/usr/src/`, so let us proceed uncompressing the archive:

```
# ls -ls /usr/src/
total 35040
    4 drwxr-xr-x  5 root root     4096 2006-06-06 10:55 kernel-headers-2.4.27-3
    4 drwxr-xr-x  4 root root     4096 2006-06-06 10:55 kernel-headers-2.4.27-3-686
    4 drwxrwxr-x  3 root src      4096 2005-05-13 20:43 modules
 4496 -rw-r--r--  1 root root  4590818 2005-05-13 20:43 openafs.tar.gz

# tar zxf openafs.tar.gz

# ls modules/
openafs/
```

It is a good habit to create a symbolic link to the current kernel header directory with the name `linux`, since this directory is used as the default directory for many sources that might need to be recompiled:

```
# ln -s kernel-headers-2.4.27-3-686 linux
```

Now we are ready to start the kernel module configuration. Debian provides a standard tool that compiles kernel modules distributed in source code called `make-kpkg`. This tool compiles, links and creates a Debian package that can be installed via the Debian package tool `dpkg`:

```
# make-kpkg modules_image
```

The package should have been successfully created, as we shall see inspecting the `/usr/src/` directory on the AFS server machine. To install the package, use the `dpkg` tool providing the `-i` switch and the package name:

```
# ls /usr/src/
kernel-headers-2.4.27-3/
kernel-headers-2.4.27-3-686/
linux@
modules/
openafs-modules-2.4.27-3-686_1.3.81-3sarge1+2.4.27-10sarge2_i386.deb
openafs.tar.gz

# dpkg -i openafs-modules-2.4.27-3-686_1.3.81-3sarge1+2.4.27-10sarge2_i386.deb
```

The last step, before proceeding to install the OpenAFS servers, is to check the newly created module. To load a module, we could use the standard `modprobe` tool from the command line interface. Our choice is to use the Debian program `modconf`, which is an interface to the standard tools. The OpenAFS module can be found under the `fs` (file systems) category:

```
------------------------]] Select fs modules [[----------------------------
| The modules that are currently installed on your system have             |
| a "+" character to the right of their name. Modules that aren't           |
| installed have a "-" to the right of their name. In some modules,         |
| you can read a page about possible options of a module and then          |
| you can enable or disable it. To do so, use the up and down arrow        |
| keys to move the cursor to the line for the module, and then press ENTER. |
|                                                                           |
|        Exit         Finished. Return to previous menu.                    |
|                                                                           |
|        openafs.mp   - .mp                                                 |
|        openafs      - (No description available)          #               |
|                                                                           |
|                                                                           |
|           <Ok>                              <Cancel>                      |
|                                                                           |
----------------------------------------------------------------------------
```

As we can see, we have two new modules, one is `openafs.mp` which is designed for SMP machines, and the other one for single processor machines. After installing the module, we are warned that it "taints the kernel", meaning that the software, we have just loaded, has not been distributed under the GPL license. We can check, if the module has been loaded successfully, with the `lsmod` tool, and then we can remove it from the memory with `rmmod`:

```
# lsmod
Module               Size  Used by    Tainted: P
openafs            478720  0  (unused)
printer              7968  0  (unused)
usb-uhci            23344  0  (unused)
usbcore            62924  1  [printer usb-uhci]
i810_audio         24444  0  (unused)
ac97_codec         13300  0  [i810_audio]
soundcore           3940  2  [i810_audio]
ide-scsi           10032  0
scsi_mod           95140  1  [ide-scsi]
3c59x              27152  1
agpgart            46244  0  (unused)
ide-cd             31328  0
cdrom              29828  0  [ide-cd]
rtc                 6440  0  (autoclean)
ext3               81068  1  (autoclean)
jbd                42468  1  (autoclean) [ext3]
ide-detect           288  0  (autoclean) (unused)
piix                9096  1  (autoclean)
ide-disk           16864  2  (autoclean)
ide-core          108632  2  (autoclean) [ide-scsi ide-cd ide-detect piix ide-disk]
unix               14960  8  (autoclean)

# rmmod openafs
```

5.2.2 Installing OpenAFS

The first step in order to create our OpenAFS cell is to install the needed packages. We need to install the database server tools, as well as the OpenAFS-

Kerberos tools, since we rely on the already established Kerberos realm as a mean for authentication:

```
# apt-get install openafs-krb5 openafs-dbserver
```

Due to its dependencies, the package openafs-dbserver installs also all the needed programs to create an AFS file server. As usual Debian tries to configure the installed package. The first question is about the cell name: it is convenient to name our OpenAFS cell with the same name given to the DNS zone, so example.edu. Debian also asks about the database servers the machine should join, and in this case we have no running database server except the afs1.example.edu host. Debian asks also the amount of space to be used as cache, the default value of 50 megabytes is a possible choice, although you may want to use different sizes according to the free disk space on your system.

The AFS file space root can be created automatically using what is called a *dynamic root*, which is one of the questions posed by the Debian installer. Our choice is to discard this option and to decide on other mounted cells by ourselves.

Debian provides a useful script for creating a new AFS cell, symmetrically to the one we used for the Kerberos realm. This script, contrary to the Kerberos one that issued only one command, hides many steps that are essential to the understanding of the AFS infrastructure. We create all the needed volumes and entries in the databases by hand, explaining the role of each operation. At this point, we choose not to run the AFS client at boot time and finally stop the activated BOS server.

The last step for now is to create a partition that is used by AFS as global file space. These partitions as we already introduced, have a name in the form of /vicepX, so our first partition would be /vicepa, the second /vicepb and so on. Our choice is to use a partition formatted with the XFS file system, which works very well, especially for big disks:

```
# cat /etc/fstab
proc            /proc           proc    defaults        0       0
/dev/hda5       /               xfs     noatime         0       1
/dev/hda4       none            swap    sw              0       0
/dev/hdc        /media/cdrom0   iso9660 ro,user,noauto  0       0
/dev/fd0        /media/floppy0  auto    rw,user,noauto  0       0
/dev/hda6       /vicepa         xfs     noatime         0       1

# mkfs.xfs -f /dev/hda6
meta-data=/dev/hda6             isize=256    agcount=8, agsize=50202 blks
         =                      sectsz=512
data     =                      bsize=4096   blocks=401616, imaxpct=25
         =                      sunit=0      swidth=0 blks, unwritten=1
naming   =version 2             bsize=4096
log      =internal log          bsize=4096   blocks=2560, version=1
         =                      sectsz=512   sunit=0 blks
realtime =none                  extsz=65536  blocks=0, rtextents=0

# mkdir /vicepa
```

```
# mount /vicepa
```

The installation process creates two files located in the `/etc/openafs/` directory: `ThisCell` and `CellServDB`. The first configuration file contains the AFS cell name the machine belongs to, an this should be `example.edu`. The second file contains the list of all the known AFS cells with their database servers. The `CellServDB` has a predefined format, and at this point it should contain our cell name and the only database server we have:

```
# cat /etc/openafs/ThisCell
example.edu

# head -6 /etc/openafs/CellServDB
>example.edu            #Example Organization
192.168.127.154               #afs1.example.edu
>grand.central.org      #GCO Public CellServDB 27 Jan 2005
18.7.14.88                    #grand-opening.mit.edu
128.2.191.224                 #penn.central.org
130.237.48.87                 #andrew.e.kth.se
```

The `/etc/openafs/server/` directory should also contain a copy of these files, with entries only for our cell, but these files are configured afterwards.

5.2.3 Notes on the Cache

You may encounter problems using an AFS client on a system that uses a journaled file systems like XFS. The AFS cache is usually allowed to exist only on an `ext2` file system, although in the meantime also `ext3` is permitted. Since an in-memory cache is not recommended for production-level systems, our choice is to create a local on-file file system that gets mounted as any other file system through the `loop` device, just like an ISO CD-ROM image. The `/etc/openafs/cacheinfo` file contains the information about the location of the cache:

```
/afs:/var/cache/openafs:100000
```

The AFS cache is then located in `/var/cache/openafs/`, with an upper bound of 100 megabytes[4]. In the following procedure, we substitute the directory with an on-file file system.

Let us start by removing all the contents of `/var/cache/openafs/`, and then using the standard UNIX tool `dd`, we create a file from the `/dev/zero` device with the same size as the programmed AFS cache. Our choice is to make a file named `afscachefile` in the `/var/cache/` directory, and then to create an `ext2` file system in it with the standard `mkfs.ext2` program:

---

[4] OpenAFS expresses all sizes in kilobytes when not specified otherwise.

```
# dd if=/dev/zero bs=10240 count=10240 of=afscachefile
10240+0 records in
10240+0 records out
104857600 bytes transferred in 0.250042 seconds (419359837 bytes/sec)

# mkfs.ext2 afscachefile
mke2fs 1.37 (21-Mar-2005)
afscachefile is not a block special device.
Proceed anyway? (y,n) y
Filesystem label=
OS type: Linux
Block size=1024 (log=0)
Fragment size=1024 (log=0)
25688 inodes, 102400 blocks
5120 blocks (5.00%) reserved for the super user
First data block=1
13 block groups
8192 blocks per group, 8192 fragments per group
1976 inodes per group
Superblock backups stored on blocks:
        8193, 24577, 40961, 57345, 73729

Writing inode tables: done
Writing superblocks and filesystem accounting information: done

This filesystem will be automatically checked every 33 mounts or
180 days, whichever comes first.  Use tune2fs -c or -i to override.
```

The `mkfs.ext2` command complains about the given device file since it is not a *block device* (e.g. a hard disk): we can safely ignore the warning. After the creation, we can mount it in the directory where the old cache was located:

```
# mount -o loop afscachefile openafs/
```

The new file system behaves as any other present on this machine, we can create files in it and check that the created item still exists after we unmount and remount the on-file file system:

```
# cd openafs/

# echo "abcd" > hello

# ls -l
total 13
-rw-r--r--  1 root root     5 Jun 16 19:37 hello
drwx------  2 root root 12288 Jun 16 19:31 lost+found

# cd ..

# umount openafs/

# mount -o loop afscachefile openafs/

# ls openafs/
hello  lost+found/

# cat openafs/hello
abcd
```

Notice that the file system has a lost+found/ directory as other file systems might have. The last step in order to use this file system is to add it to the /etc/fstab such that it is mounted at boot time:

```
/var/cache/afscachefile  /var/cache/openafs ext2    defaults,loop   0   0
```

5.2.4 Kerberizing OpenAFS

The Andrew Project started before Kerberos became a standard, and its authentication server, the kaserver, was designed mimicking Kerberos IV. Our organization employes the new Kerberos V authentication protocol, which interacts with OpenAFS by translating Kerberos tickets into the AFS equivalent "tokens" with the help of a previously installed package.

The OpenAFS servers need, as any other Kerberized service, a principal in the Kerberos database, named afs/cellname. In our case we create the principal afs/example.edu:

```
kadmin:  add_principal -randkey afs/example.edu
WARNING: no policy specified for afs/example.edu@EXAMPLE.EDU; defaulting to no policy
Principal "afs/example.edu@EXAMPLE.EDU" created.
```

Next we import the keys belonging to our AFS principal in the server's own database. In order to do so, we must export the DES key in a keytab file, specifying the des-cbc-crc:afs3 encryption type, which at the time of writing is still the only supported type:

```
kadmin:  ktadd -k afs.keytab -e des-cbc-crc:afs3 afs/example.edu
Entry for principal afs/example.edu with kvno 3, encryption type \
DES cbc mode with CRC-32 added to keytab WRFILE:afs.keytab.
```

It is fundamental to observe the correct KVNO, since it is used to import the principal's secret key. We can check the validity of the exported key by issuing a klist command to view the contents of the keytab file:

```
# klist -ke afs.keytab
Keytab name: FILE:afs.keytab
KVNO Principal
---- --------------------------------------------------------------------
   3 afs/example.edu@EXAMPLE.EDU (DES cbc mode with CRC-32)
```

At this point we can import the secret key into the AFS security system through the asetkey command, provided by the Kerberos-OpenAFS tools. We have to feed the tool with the add subcommand, followed by the KVNO, the keytab file containing the key and the principal:

```
# asetkey add 3 afs.keytab afs/example.edu
```

The import process should end successfully, and we can then check the imported key issuing the `list` subcommand:

```
# asetkey list
kvno    3: key is: 0b6157dc3e575eea
All done.
```

At the end of this process, we have created in `/etc/openafs/server/` a file named `KeyFile` that contains the secret key for our AFS service principal:

```
# ls -ld /etc/openafs/server
drwxr-xr-x  2 root root 4096 2006-06-08 11:57 /etc/openafs/server/

# ls -ld /etc/openafs/server-local/
drwx------  2 root root 4096 2006-06-08 12:11 /etc/openafs/server-local/

# ls -l /etc/openafs/server
total 12
-rw-r--r--  1 root root  13 2006-06-06 12:14 CellServDB
-rw-------  1 root root 100 2006-06-06 12:14 KeyFile
-rw-r--r--  1 root root  12 2006-06-06 11:50 ThisCell
```

Note that the permission bits for all the critical files and directories should be set as shown above: in case of discrepancies the BOS server complains. It is safe on Debian to remove the `CellServDB` and `.ThisCell` files from the server configuration directory `/etc/openafs/server/` since these files are created during the first BOS server start.

5.2.5 Configuring the Database Server

Having initialized the secret key in our OpenAFS installation we can proceed starting the Basic Overseer Server, the BOS server. Even though everything is ready for an authenticated activation, our database server is going to run in the first instance as an *unauthenticated* daemon, since we have no administrative user: this procedure is similar to the use of `kadmin.local` in the KDC creation.

As we have already introduced, BOS is the main daemon, responsible of starting, stopping, and managing all the processes in an AFS cell. Let us start the daemon by issuing the `bosserver` command with the `-noauth` switch, and then check for its state in memory:

```
# /usr/sbin/bosserver -noauth

# ps auxg | grep bos
root      1716  0.3  0.5  3872 2804 ?        S    11:39   0:00 /usr/sbin/bosserver -noauth
```

The first operation we have to perform is assigning a cell name, by issuing a `setcellname` to the `bos` command, which interacts with the BOS server:

```
# bos setcellname -server afs1.example.edu -name example.edu -noauth
```

Every database server knows all its peers, and as we said in the introduction, all the information is distributed via the Ubik technology so that a cell may function with only one of the database servers being up and running. Debian adds the local host name to the list of database servers, viewable by issuing the `listhosts` command:

```
# bos listhosts -server afs1.example.edu -noauth
Cell name is example.edu
    Host 1 is afs1
```

OpenAFS requires the fully qualified domain name in the server list, so we need to add the correct host name and then remove the short one, using the `addhost` and `removehost` subcommands of the BOS interface tool:

```
# bos addhost -server afs1.example.edu -host af1.example.edu -noauth

# bos listhosts -server dns.example.edu -noauth
Cell name is example.edu
    Host 1 is afs1
    Host 2 is asf1.example.edu

# bos removehost -server afs1.example.edu -host afs1 -noauth

# bos listhosts -server afs1.example.edu -noauth
Cell name is example.edu
    Host 1 is afs1.example.edu
```

From now on, in all the AFS commands we will omit the switches (e.g. `-server` and `-cell`) since they are not mandatory, as long as we specify the parameters in the same order in which they appear in the command syntax. Every program in the OpenAFS suite presents a `help` subcommand which gives hints about all the available commands, and eventually displays their parameters and explanation:

```
# bos help
bos: Commands are:
addhost        add host to cell dbase
addkey         add keys to key dbase (kvno 999 is bcrypt)
adduser        add users to super-user list
apropos        search by help text
blockscanner   block scanner daemon from making migration requests
create         create a new server instance
delete         delete a server instance
exec           execute shell command on server
getdate        get dates for programs
getlog         examine log file
getrestart     get restart times
help           get help on commands
install        install program
listhosts      get cell host list
listkeys       list keys
listusers      list super-users
prune          prune server files
removehost     remove host from cell dbase
```

```
removekey       remove keys from key dbase
removeuser      remove users from super-user list
restart         restart processes
salvage         salvage partition or volumes
setauth         set authentication required flag
setcellname     set cell name
setrestart      set restart times
shutdown        shutdown all processes
start           start running a server
startup         start all processes
status          show server instance status
stop            halt a server instance
unblockscanner  allow scanner daemon to make migration requests again
uninstall       uninstall program

# bos help addhost
bos addhost: add host to cell dbase
Usage: bos addhost -server <machine name> -host <host name>+ [-clone] \
[-cell <cell name>] [-noauth] [-localauth] [-help]
Where: -clone      vote doesn't count
       -noauth     don't authenticate
       -localauth  create tickets from KeyFile
```

In the **addhost** procedure we have performed before, the **-server** and **-host** switches could have been omitted, provided that the command line specifies the parameters in the right order.

The BOS server is ready now to be configured in order to handle the needed database servers. Each server is controlled through a *server instance*, that is the name of the AFS process to manage (e.g. a backup server, a file server, a volume location server):

```
# bos help create
bos create: create a new server instance
Usage: bos create -server <machine name> -instance <server process name> \
-type <server type> -cmd <command lines>+ [-notifier <Notifier program>] \
[-cell <cell name>] [-noauth] [-localauth] [-help]
Where: -noauth     don't authenticate
       -localauth  create tickets from KeyFile
```

The instance specification needs also a type, that define the process class handled by the BOS server. These values range in a predefined set of types, such as a **simple** type (any process except those used in a file server), a **cron** (used to schedule operations) or a **fs** type used only when BOS should manage a file server. As a side note, all the processes with the exception of the **salvager** should not be run directly on the command line, since BOS has been created in order to start and stop them properly.

The first instance we create in the BOS process database is the backup server, handled by the **buserver** command. The command line has to specify the host where the server should run, in our case then **afs1**, the only database server we have. We need also to specify the instance, which is equal to the command name that BOS runs, and the complete path of the executable:

```
# bos create afs1 buserver simple /usr/lib/openafs/buserver -noauth
```

The instance type we have specified above is `simple`: we have already specified that `simple` is suitable for all processes except for scheduled commands and file server daemons. The switch `-noauth` is necessary until the AFS infrastructure is provided with a Kerberized administrator.

The second instance is the protection database server, run by the `ptserver` process. This process is responsible of handling users and groups, providing authorization over AFS objects, and is started by the `simple` typed instance specified as follows:

```
# bos create afs1 ptserver simple /usr/lib/openafs/ptserver -noauth
```

The last database server we run on our machine is the volume location process, which tracks all the information about the physical location of objects in all file servers. The `vlserver` instance is created symmetrically to all the previous ones:

```
# bos create afs1 vlserver simple /usr/lib/openafs/vlserver -noauth
```

The BOS server knows at any time the state of all the processes in its database, and may provide useful information such as the command line, the last startup time, and the status of the daemon:

```
# bos status afs1 -long -noauth
Instance buserver, (type is simple) currently running normally.
    Process last started at Thu Jun  8 11:52:34 2006 (1 proc starts)
    Command 1 is '/usr/lib/openafs/buserver'

Instance ptserver, (type is simple) currently running normally.
    Process last started at Thu Jun  8 11:53:01 2006 (1 proc starts)
    Command 1 is '/usr/lib/openafs/ptserver'

Instance vlserver, (type is simple) currently running normally.
    Process last started at Thu Jun  8 11:53:34 2006 (1 proc starts)
    Command 1 is '/usr/lib/openafs/vlserver'
```

Administrative Users

In order to administer the AFS cell we need some superusers. Remember that the `sysadmin` was planned to administer the main servers in the network, from Kerberos to AFS, so all we need now is to add a new administrative user to the BOS super-users database:

```
# bos adduser afs1 sysadmin -noauth

# bos listuser afs1 -noauth
SUsers are: sysadmin
```

Having created a user that can administer BOS, we need to populate the protection database with the needed items. This database, handled by the `ptserver` instance, contains all the users and groups known to AFS, and by default the set of known users is constituted by a single item. In order to query the protection server, we use the `pts` interface program:

```
# pts listentries -users -noauth
Name                        ID  Owner Creator
anonymous                32766  -204    -204
```

We may also want to view all the known groups in the protection database. Contrary to the list of users, constituted just by **anonymous**, the list of default groups is longer:

```
# pts listentries -groups -noauth
Name                        ID  Owner Creator
system:administrators     -204   -204    -204
system:backup             -205   -204    -204
system:anyuser            -101   -204    -204
system:authuser           -102   -204    -204
system:ptsviewers         -203   -204    -204
```

The default groups are self-explaining: `system:administrators` contain the AFS administrators, `system:anyuser` stands for any user (authenticated or not) and `system:authuser` is a placeholder for all authenticated users. The `system:ptsviewers` contains all the users entitled to query the protection database, but they are not allowed to modify any of its items. The group `system:backup` allows the backup process to read volumes, as we shall see in the proper section.

Now the `sysadmin` user has to be created in the protection database, and added to the list of administrative users. Using the `pts` tool we first create the entry in the database with an AFS ID of our choice, and then add the user to the proper group:

```
# pts createuser sysadmin -id 1 -noauth
User sysadmin has id 1

# pts adduser sysadmin system:administrators -noauth
```

The process should end successfully, and the results may be viewed by querying the protection database about the members of the administrative `system:administrators` group, and the groups the `sysadmin` user belongs to:

```
# pts membership system:administrators -noauth
Members of system:administrators (id: -204) are:
  sysadmin

# pts membership sysadmin -noauth
Groups sysadmin (id: 1) is a member of:
  system:administrators
```

We are now prepared to shutdown the BOS server, running until now unauthenticated. Having created an administrative user, from now on we use either that user or the local authentication that makes use of the secret key we previously stored in the KeyFile, imported from the Kerberos database. Let us proceed stopping the service, and immediately restarting it:

```
# bos shutdown afs1 -noauth

# pkill bosserver

# /etc/init.d/openafs-fileserver start
Starting AFS Server: bosserver.
```

We have now the rights to use authenticated commands through the -localauth switch. We can also test the system in order to prove that a non-authenticated command as we used up to this moment is rejected:

```
# bos status afs1 -long -localauth
Instance buserver, (type is simple) currently running normally.
    Process last started at Thu Jun  8 12:11:32 2006 (1 proc starts)
    Command 1 is '/usr/lib/openafs/buserver'

Instance ptserver, (type is simple) currently running normally.
    Process last started at Thu Jun  8 12:11:32 2006 (1 proc starts)
    Command 1 is '/usr/lib/openafs/ptserver'

Instance vlserver, (type is simple) currently running normally.
    Process last started at Thu Jun  8 12:11:32 2006 (1 proc starts)
    Command 1 is '/usr/lib/openafs/vlserver'

# bos stop afs1 vlserver -noauth
bos: failed to change stop instance 'vlserver' (you are not authorized for this operation)
```

At the end of the configuration process, we start the OpenAFS client that allows us to use the sysadmin user, previously created and potentially from any AFS client machine.

5.2.6 Configuring the File Server

The first database server also acts like a file server, as we previewed before. In the future this can be changed but it simplifies the procedure for the moment. We have created a partition to be used by the file serving processes, the /vicepa partition, formatted with the XFS file system.

As any other AFS process, the file server daemons are manged by the BOS server, started with the instance fs and type fs. As we have previously explained, a file server needs three processes to be run on the machine: the file server itself, the volume server and the salvager. Let us create the needed instance providing the bos command the full path of all the daemons:

```
# bos create afs1 fs fs -cmd /usr/lib/openafs/fileserver \
-cmd /usr/lib/openafs/volserver -cmd /usr/lib/openafs/salvager -localauth
```

The BOS server now handles both database processes and file serving daemons, as we can see by querying its status with the bos command:

```
# bos status afs1 -long -localauth
Instance buserver, (type is simple) currently running normally.
    Process last started at Thu Jun  8 12:19:16 2006 (1 proc starts)
    Command 1 is '/usr/lib/openafs/buserver'

Instance ptserver, (type is simple) currently running normally.
    Process last started at Thu Jun  8 12:19:16 2006 (1 proc starts)
    Command 1 is '/usr/lib/openafs/ptserver'

Instance vlserver, (type is simple) currently running normally.
    Process last started at Thu Jun  8 12:19:16 2006 (1 proc starts)
    Command 1 is '/usr/lib/openafs/vlserver'

Instance fs, (type is fs) currently running normally.
    Auxiliary status is: file server running.
    Process last started at Thu Jun  8 12:22:42 2006 (2 proc starts)
    Command 1 is '/usr/lib/openafs/fileserver'
    Command 2 is '/usr/lib/openafs/volserver'
    Command 3 is '/usr/lib/openafs/salvager'
```

5.2.7 Volume Creation

We have previously explained that volumes are at the core of the AFS file system. They are the logical equivalent of local partitions in the network: a space where files and directories are stored with the appearance of a directory.

The AFS file space needs at least two volumes in order to manage a cell: the AFS root volume and the cell root volume. The first contains all the other volumes, and may be used to mount external AFS cells as we will see in the proceeding. The cell root volume contains all the files and volumes belonging to our AFS cell, and like any other volume, it is mounted and appears as a normal directory.

In order to create volumes we need to provide the vos command all the information about the physical location of such a space. The first volume is root.afs, automatically mounted as the root of all our AFS space in /afs/. The needed data include the host, the partition, the volume name and an eventual disk quota[5]:

```
# vos create afs1 vicepa root.afs -localauth
Volume 536870912 created on partition /vicepa of afs1
```

A volume, as we see from the vos output, has an ID, a unique number in the cell, and is created on a particular partition on a specified host, provided that the host runs the file server processes. Without any further option this command defines a default quota of 5000 KB.

Using Kerberized AFS

Now we are ready to start the OpenAFS client in order to use a fully Kerberized system. Until this moment our AFS file space is constituted by the root

---

[5] The upper bound of disk space to be used, but not immediately allocated.

volume, with no cell volume: starting the client normally does obviously result in a failure. Debian provides a `force-start` command to the OpenAFS client script that allows us to start the daemon regardless of the cell root volume:

```
# /etc/init.d/openafs-client force-start
Warning: loading /lib/modules/2.4.27-3-686/fs/openafs.o will taint the kernel: no license
  See http://www.tux.org/lkml/#export-tainted for information about tainted modules
Module openafs loaded, with warnings
Starting AFS services: afsd: All AFS daemons started.
 afsd.
```

As usual the Linux kernel tools complain about the non-GPL license of the OpenAFS module, and we can safely ignore the legal warning. Having the client up and running, we can now use the `sysadmin` user in order to create our AFS cell. We may recall that AFS was created before the Kerberos standardization, so it has its own version of a Kerberos ticket, called token. The Kerberos-OpenAFS interaction package provides the `aklog` tool that converts a Kerberos ticket into an AFS token, as we can see by converting the initial ticket for `sysadmin` into an AFS token:

```
# kinit sysadmin
Password for sysadmin@EXAMPLE.EDU:

# aklog
```

As usual no output gets printed on the console. The AFS equivalent of the `klist` command is `tokens`, which displays all the AFS tokens provided to the current user:

```
# tokens

Tokens held by the Cache Manager:

User's (AFS ID 1) tokens for afs@example.edu [Expires Jun  8 22:44]
   --End of list--
```

As a sidenote we mention that older cells might still use the old `kaserver` for authentication having `kas` as the client side command. authenticated in several cells at the same time. In that case one needs the previous `klog` command for authentication.

We can test the access to the AFS file space in `/afs/`, possessing the administrative AFS token:

```
# ls -al /afs
total 6
drwxrwxrwx   2 root root 2048 2006-06-08 12:42 .
drwxr-xr-x  23 root root 4096 2006-06-08 10:36 ..
```

The equivalent of `kdestroy` to AFS tokens is the `unlog` command, which discards all the AFS tokens. Discarding the token for `sysadmin` disallows us to access the AFS file space:

```
# unlog

# ls /afs/
ls: /afs/: Permission denied
```

Creating the Cell Root

The AFS file space is constituted of volumes mounted as directories and accessible based on a set of access control lists. OpenAFS, like its predecessor AFS, permits to specify ACLs with a directory-based granularity: since volumes are mounted as directories, this property holds also for volumes. The set of ACLs are described in Table 5.2.

Table 5.2. The OpenAFS access control list attributes

Permission	Meaning
l	List contents (lookup)
i	Create new files or directories (insert)
d	Delete files or directories
a	Change ACL attributes of directories (administer)
r	Read contents of files
w	Modify contents of files (write)
k	Lock files for reading
read	Equivalent to rl
write	Equivalent to rlidwk (no administrative rights)
all	Equivalent to rlidwka
none	Remove all ACL permissions

The most important access control property is the list bit l: without this bit set it is impossible to access any directory or list its attributes, any other permission is subsidiary to the list attribute.

The AFS tool that allows us to view and change the properties of directories and volumes in the AFS file space is fs, which directly interacts with the file server. To list all the associated access control lists, we feed the program the listacl command, followed by the directory under analysis:

```
# fs listacl /afs
Access list for /afs is
Normal rights:
  system:administrators rlidwka
```

We got the token for the user **sysadmin** before this operation. By default, as we can see, the AFS file space is accessible only by system administrators. This choice is of no use since in a real environment we should give access to this space to users, granting their writing and reading privileges with care. It is recommended to allow any user to read from the AFS root, using the fs tool and setting the proper ACL to /afs/ by issuing the setacl command[6]:

```
# fs setacl /afs system:anyuser rl

# fs listacl /afs
Access list for /afs is
Normal rights:
  system:administrators rlidwka
  system:anyuser rl
```

A rather restrictive setting is to allow read just to the system:authuser group permitting only locally authenticated users. Having created the AFS root volume, we next need to make the cell root volume called root.cell:

```
# vos create afs1 vicepa root.cell
Volume 536870918 created on partition /vicepa of afs1
```

The same vos tool allows us to analyze all the volumes present on a particular host, in our case just the afs1 machine, using the listvol command:

```
# vos listvol afs1
Total number of volumes on server afs1 partition /vicepa: 2
root.afs                    536870915 RW          2 K On-line
root.cell                   536870918 RW          2 K On-line

Total volumes onLine 2 ; Total volumes offLine 0 ; Total busy 0
```

We have previewed some properties associated to volumes, and one of this attribute is the disk quota. By default the disk quota assigned to a volume is 5 megabytes, as we can see from the output of the listquota command of the fs tool:

```
# fs listquota /afs
Volume Name                 Quota     Used %Used   Partition
root.afs                    5000        2    0%          0%
```

The AFS root and the cell root are supposed to be containers for other volumes, and thus such a small disk quota is understandably sufficient. The last step in starting our cell is to mount the root volume under the AFS file space. Usually the cell root is mounted under a meaningful name, which generally coincides with the cell name, in our case, with example.edu. The command to be fed to fs in order to mount a volume is mkmount, specifying the mount name—which appears as a directory—and the volume:

```
# fs mkmount /afs/example.edu root.cell
```

---

[6] Although not recommended in practical uses, permissions may be also specified in their negative form with the -negative switch, describing explicitly an access denial.

The mounted volume needs a proper ACL as we have seen for the AFS root volume:

```
# fs listacl /afs/example.edu/
Access list for /afs/example.edu/ is
Normal rights:
  system:administrators rlidwka

# fs setacl /afs/example.edu system:anyuser read

# fs listacl /afs/example.edu
Access list for /afs/example.edu is
Normal rights:
  system:administrators rlidwka
  system:anyuser rl
```

In order to view the volume associated with a mount point, the `lsmount` command can be fed to `fs`, along with the directory we intend to analyze:

```
# fs lsmount /afs/example.edu
'/afs/example.edu' is a mount point for volume '#root.cell'
```

A side-note to volumes and mount points: contrary to a normal UNIX mount operation, in the AFS file space a mount point directory should not exist beforehand. An AFS cell is then usually seen as a directory named as the cell itself, in our case /afs/example.edu/; in the following of this chapter we will explain how to mount also foreign AFS cells.

In order to enable the client permanently on our system, we have to edit the client configuration file /etc/openafs/afs.conf.client changing the AFS_CLIENT value to `true`:

```
AFS_CLIENT=true
AFS_AFSDB=true
AFS_CRYPT=true
AFS_DYNROOT=false
AFS_FAKESTAT=true
```

We notice in the configuration file that by default Debian allows an encrypted AFS communication, which may be confirmed by the `getcrypt` command of `fs`:

```
# fs getcrypt
Security level is currently crypt (data security).
```

This encryption means that file data is encrypted on transmission between file server and client cache.

5.2.8 Structuring the Cell

The AFS file space is similar to any other part of the file system, except for the fact that files and directories are physically spread among different file servers—a fact that users ignore since they experience just a set of directories.

Like any file system, we need to give the cell a structure that suites the need of our organization. A typical company provides users with a personal space, and may distribute software for various platforms. In the following we are going to create an organization that allows us to supply such services. The organization of an AFS cell is an important task and should not be underestimated.

Commonly volumes in a cell are given a meaningful name. We have already seen that the AFS root and the cell root volumes are labeled root.X: our choice for the container volumes for users and software is to create volumes named cell.users and cell.software. The name given to volumes, in the current OpenAFS implementation provided by Debian, cannot exceed 22 characters.

User Space

The cell.users volume we are about to create shall act as another container volume. Inside this space we mount our users' home directories, provided by user-specific volumes as we shall see later on. Creating volumes on a user basis gives the administrator the possibility to move home directories from a file server to another without changing the mount point, allowing load and space balancing between all server machines in the AFS space.

Let us start creating the container volume on the /vicepa partition of afs1, the only server in our AFS cell:

```
# vos create afs1 a cell.users
Volume 536870921 created on partition /vicepa of afs1
```

The above command shows another shortcut provided by the OpenAFS tools, other than avoiding the switches: partition names are by default in the format /vicepX, so all is needed by the fs tool is the X part, in our case, we specified just a instead of vicepa. After creating the volume, we mount it with a meaningful name. We create a mount point called users:

```
# cd /afs/example.edu

# fs mkmount users cell.users
```

A volume does not directly inherit the ACL property from its parent, as we already showed for the root.cell volume which did not assume the ACL applied to root.afs. We need then to modify the properties of the newly mounted volume with the fs tool:

```
# fs listacl users
Access list for users is
Normal rights:
  system:administrators rlidwka

# fs setacl users system:anyuser read
```

```
# fs listacl users
Access list for users is
Normal rights:
  system:administrators rlidwka
  system:anyuser rl
```

Giving access to anyone for the users space is of no harm since user volumes are mounted with a more strict policy, as we will see. Since we are acting on a UNIX system we may want to check the standard permission bits for the new volume:

```
# ls -l /afs/example.edu/
total 2
drwxrwxrwx  2 root root 2048 2006-06-15 11:07 users/
```

Although it seems, that this is a completely open space, we are located below /afs/ and consequently the AFS ACLs determine the real permissions.

Software Space

The AFS file space provides a commodity to distribute software among various platforms, with a transparent per-platform facility we are going to introduce. Let us first create the container volume cell.software, and mount it in our AFS file space:

```
# vos create afs1 a cell.software
Volume 536870924 created on partition /vicepa of afs1

# fs mkmount software cell.software

# ls -l
total 4
drwxrwxrwx  2 root root 2048 2006-06-15 11:16 software/
drwxrwxrwx  2 root root 2048 2006-06-15 11:07 users/
```

In a real situation distributing software may rise legal problems due to licenses and copyrights. Let us suppose we want to give access to free and also commercial software our organization is legally entitled to use, limiting the access to all individuals belonging to our company: as we already previewed, AFS has a special group called system:authuser that contains all the authenticated users. Such a group is a perfect candidate for setting the accessibility to our software distribution center:

```
# fs setacl software system:anyuser l

# fs setacl software system:authuser read

# fs listacl software
Access list for software is
Normal rights:
  system:administrators rlidwka
  system:authuser rl
  system:anyuser l
```

With these settings, authenticated users are allowed to read and list all the distributed software, while non authenticated visitors are allowed just to list the contents. System administrators are granted any operation on the volume.

Recalling the fact that the software volume is a container, we show how to distribute transparently software for various platforms. Let us suppose we want to give access to the Debian Linux CD-ROM ISO images: then we create a volume with a significant name with a sufficient disk quota to allow the distribution of the ISO images (in this example we use two different platforms):

```
# vos create afs1 a software.debian -maxquota 200000
Volume 536870927 created on partition /vicepa of afs1

# fs mkmount debian software.debian

# fs listquota debian
Volume Name                    Quota    Used %Used    Partition
software.debian                200000      2   0%           0%
```

We have given the volume the name **software.debian** with a disk quota of 200 megabytes, and mounted it as **/afs/example.edu/software/debian/**: it is possible to change the disk quota later with the **fs** command **setquota**. As previously explained, volumes do not inherit the properties belonging to the parent, so we have to change the ACL for the new volume:

```
# fs listacl debian
Access list for debian is
Normal rights:
  system:administrators rlidwka

# fs setacl debian system:anyuser l

# fs setacl debian system:authuser rlk

# fs listacl debian
Access list for debian is
Normal rights:
  system:administrators rlidwka
  system:authuser rlk
  system:anyuser l
```

Note as we added the lock k property to authorized users, since some software run directly from the AFS file space may require the ability to lock files for reading.

The AFS file space provides a particular symbolic link name that a client translates into the current system name: this link is called @sys, and Table 5.3 we show the most recurring system names[7]. Usually such names are in the form **hardware_OS**, where **hardware** describes the architecture (e.g. **i386** for Intel 386 and compatibles, **ppc** for IBM PowerPC), and **OS** is the operating system and its version.

In order to get the system name of the current client we have to query the system using the **fs** command **sysname**:

---

[7] A complete list of system names may be found in the OpenAFS documentation.

Table 5.3. The OpenAFS @sys names (excerpt)

@sys	Architecture
alpha_dux40	Digital UNIX 4 on an Alpha
alpha_dux50	Digital UNIX 5 on an Alpha
i386_linux24	Linux Kernel 2.4 on Intel and compatible
i386_linux26	Linux Kernel 2.6 on Intel and compatible
i386_nt40	Microsoft Windows NT and later on Intel and compatible
ppc_darwin70	Apple MacOS X 10.3 on a PowerPC Macintosh
ppc_darwin80	Apple MacOS X 10.4 on a PowerPC Macintosh
ppc_darwin90	Apple MacOS X 10.5 on a PowerPC Macintosh
rs_aix52	IBM AIX 5.2 on a pSeries
rs_aix53	IBM AIX 5.3 on a pSeries
sgi_65	SGI Irix 6.5 on a MPIS
x86_darwin80	Apple MacOS X 10.4 on an Intel Macintosh
x86_darwin90	Apple MacOS X 10.5 on an Intel Macintosh

```
# fs sysname
Current sysname is 'i386_linux24'
```

In this case we are using a Linux Kernel version 2.4 on an Intel 386 CPU or compatible processors (notably the 486, the Pentium series, AMD K6 and K7 processors). Our purely didactic objective is to store the Debian ISO images so that a user may easily find the source of the currently running system. Let us start by creating a directory named **platform** that contains a list of @sys subdirectories:

```
# mkdir platforms

# cd platforms

# mkdir i386_linux26
# mkdir i386_linux24
# mkdir ppc_darwin_70
# mkdir ppc_darwin_80
# mkdir i386_nt40
```

Note that a directory, unlike volumes, do actually inherit the ACLs of the parent directory:

```
# fs la /afs/example.edu/software/debian
Access list for /afs/example.edu/software/debian is
Normal rights:
  system:administrators rlidwka
  system:authuser rlk
  system:anyuser l

# fs la /afs/example.edu/software/debian/platforms
Access list for /afs/example.edu/software/debian/platforms is
Normal rights:
  system:administrators rlidwka
  system:authuser rlk
  system:anyuser l
```

We can now create a symbolic link named ISO pointing to the special @sys name like the following example:

```
# ln -s platforms/@sys ISO

# ls -l
total 3
lrwxr-xr-x  1 daemon root    14 2006-06-15 11:40 ISO -> platforms/@sys/
drwxr-xr-x  7 daemon root  2048 2006-06-15 11:38 platforms/
```

Thus a client accessing the ISO subdirectory is transparently redirected to that subdirectory of **platforms** corresponding the the operating system and architecture:

```
# ls -l ISO/
total 111225
-rw-r--r--  1 daemon root 113893376 2006-06-15 11:50 debian-31r2-i386-netinst.iso
-rw-r--r--  1 daemon root        43 2006-06-15 11:51 README

# cat ISO/README
This is platform i368 for Linux Kernel 2.4
```

The translation from a @sys link into a name is done on the client-side. Let us suppose a client accesses to the AFS file space using Microsoft Windows, with a user entering a directory that is actually a symbolic link to @sys: the client recognizes the link, and translates it to the proper string, in this case to i386_nt40.

As a live example of this powerful facility we show a per-platform installation of the Condor High Throughput Computing software developed by the University of Wisconsin-Madison. The software is organized in the AFS cell as follows:

```
# ls -l
total 56
lrwxr-xr-x  1 daemon  root       28 Feb 25 2005  THIS_PC@ -> platforms/@sys/THIS_PC
-rw-r--r--  1 daemon  root     3138 Feb 28 2005  README
lrwxr-xr-x  1 daemon  root       18 Feb 23 2005  bin@ -> platforms/@sys/bin/
drwxr-xr-x  3 daemon  root     2048 Nov 22 2005  etc/
drwxr-xr-x  4 daemon  root     2048 Jan 27 2005  examples/
drwxr-xr-x 11 daemon  root     2048 Nov 22 2005  hosts/
drwxr-xr-x  2 daemon  root     2048 Jan 27 2005  include/
lrwxr-xr-x  1 daemon  root       18 Feb 23 2005  lib@ -> platforms/@sys/lib/
drwxr-xr-x  3 daemon  root     2048 Jan 27 2005  man/
drwxr-xr-x  2 daemon  root     8192 Feb 11 2005  manual/
drwxr-xr-x  7 daemon  root     2048 Feb 25 2005  platforms/
lrwxr-xr-x  1 daemon  root       19 Feb 23 2005  sbin@ -> platforms/@sys/sbin/

# ls platforms/
i386_linux24/   i386_linux26/   i386_nt40/     ppc_darwin_70/  rs_aix52/
```

The core directories (**bin**, **sbin**, and **sbin**) point at the homonymous subdirectory inside **platform/@sys**, as well as THIS_PC points to a file. Inside each subdirectory present in **platforms** we have installed the necessary files:

```
# ls platforms/i386_linux24
THIS_PC   bin/           lib/              sbin/

# ls platforms/i386_linux26
THIS_PC   bin/           lib/              sbin/

# ls platforms/i386_nt40/
CondorJavaInfo.class*     condor_hold.exe*        condor_shadow.dbg*
CondorJavaWrapper.class*  condor_kbdd_dll.dll*    condor_shadow.exe*
Msvcrt.dll*               condor_mail.exe*        condor_startd.dbg*
THIS_PC                   condor_master.dbg*      condor_startd.exe*
bin@                      condor_master.exe*      condor_starter.dbg*
condor.exe*               condor_negotiator.dbg*  condor_starter.exe*
condor_advertise.exe*     condor_negotiator.exe*  condor_stats.exe*
condor_birdwatcher.exe*   condor_off.exe*         condor_status.exe*
condor_cod.exe*           condor_on.exe*          condor_store_cred.exe*
condor_cod_request.exe*   condor_preen.exe*       condor_submit.exe*
condor_collector.dbg*     condor_prio.exe*        condor_submit_dag.exe*
condor_collector.exe*     condor_q.exe*           condor_userlog.exe*
condor_config_val.exe*    condor_qedit.exe*       condor_userprio.exe*
condor_dagman.exe*        condor_reconfig.exe*    condor_vacate.exe*
condor_eventd.dbg*        condor_release.exe*     condor_version.exe*
condor_eventd.exe*        condor_reschedule.exe*  condor_wait.exe*
condor_fetchlog.exe*      condor_restart.exe*     lib@
condor_findhost.exe*      condor_rm.exe*          msvcirt.dll*
condor_gridmanager.exe*   condor_schedd.dbg*      pdh.dll*
condor_history.exe*       condor_schedd.exe*      sbin@

# ls platforms/ppc_darwin_70/
THIS_PC   bin/           lib/              sbin/

# ls platforms/rs_aix52/
THIS_PC   bin/           lib/              sbin/
```

Different clients accessing files and directories in the Condor distribution experience different behaviors, as we can see from the following example showing the content of THIS_PC from different platforms:

```
# uname -a
AIX aixserver 2 5 0053447A4C00

# cat THIS_PC
This platform is:
IBM pSeries Processor, IBM AIX 5.2
```

```
# uname -a
Linux dns 2.4.27-3-686 #1 Tue Dec 5 21:03:54 UTC 2006 i686 GNU/Linux

# cat THIS_PC
This platform is:
i386 Processor, Linux Kernel 2.4.x
```

Foreign AFS Cells

It is possible to mount foreign AFS cells in our file space so that we may gain access to some resources that are not available via web or too expensive to send via email. We choose to mount the grand.central.org cell, a community resource for AFS users. We may recall that the main volume for a cell is called root.cell, since the root.afs volume is the AFS file space container.

With the usual **fs** tool, specifying the cell, the volume and the mount point name, we can access the **grand.central.org** AFS cell:

```
# fs mkmount grand.central.org root.cell -cell grand.central.org

# ls -l
total 4
drwxrwxrwx  2 root root 2048 2006-06-15 11:16 example.edu/
drwxrwxrwx  2 root root 2048 2006-05-07 01:21 grand.central.org/
```

The **fs** command **whichcell** shows the AFS cell a given file or directory belongs to, and since the mounted cell gives access to unauthenticated users (at least in the root of the cell), we can show its contents:

```
# fs whichcell grand.central.org
File grand.central.org lives in cell 'grand.central.org'

# ls -l grand.central.org
total 18
drwxrwxrwx  3 root root 2048 2004-06-17 23:27 archive/
drwxrwxrwx  2 root root 2048 2006-05-07 00:33 cvs/
drwxrwxrwx  3 root root 2048 2003-03-21 18:08 doc/
drwxrwxrwx  7 root root 2048 2006-05-07 05:58 local/
drwxrwxrwx  2 root root 2048 2005-06-17 08:00 project/
drwxrwxrwx  4 root root 2048 2006-05-07 01:29 service/
drwxrwxrwx  2 root root 2048 2006-05-30 00:24 software/
drwxrwxrwx  2 root root 2048 2003-11-20 23:34 user/
drwxrwxrwx  4 root root 2048 2006-05-07 02:43 www/
```

A user does not notice that the directory /afs/grand.central.org/ is actually a volume that is geographically distant from the terminal in use: a complete transparency, that is one of the major features of the AFS file system. Note that it is a good option to mount any external cell right now, since in the following sections we will add features that prohibit any direct modification to our main AFS file space volume[8].

5.3 Additional Servers

For redundancy reasons it is a good practice to have more than one database server in an AFS cell, so that even software upgrades on hosts may be performed without any downtime as long as one database server is up and running. The actual implementation of the Ubik makes 3 or 5 database servers the best choice for the moment and the first server should have the lowest IP address.

The new database host, called **afs2**, is a pure database server, since we do not ask BOS to manage any file server instance: no /vicepX partition are needed. Additionally, we install a pure file serving machine called **fs01** which runs only the file server instance and no database services.

---

[8] Actually mounting foreign cells is not exactly prohibited, but the procedure becomes more complicated: in the following we also show how to overcome such difficulties.

5.3.1 Secondary Database Servers

The new afs2 host acts as a database server for our AFS cell: all is needed is to perform an installation similar to the one we have already performed to start the AFS cell. Remember that all AFS machines are Kerberos clients and that time synchronization is of primary importance to avoid malfunctioning due to a high clock skew. We briefly show the installation process for didactic purposes, using a different kernel version.

The new machine is to run a 2.6 kernel series, as we can see from the uname output, and the first step is to install the kernel headers matching the current version:

```
# uname -a
Linux afs2 2.6.8-3-686 #1 Thu Feb 9 07:39:48 UTC 2006 i686 GNU/Linux

# apt-get install kernel-headers-2.6.8-3-686
```

As we did for the first server, we have to install the OpenAFS kernel module source, unpack it and finally produce the Debian package with the make-kpkg tool:

```
# make-kpkg clean

# make-kpkg configure

# make-kpkg modules_image
```

Note that the compilation process on a Linux kernel series 2.4 and 2.6 show different outputs. It is a good practice to install the kernel module and test it with modconf or modprobe before proceeding with the installation of the OpenAFS database server package openafs-dbserver, and the Kerberos-OpenAFS interaction package openafs-krb5.

Kerberized AFS Server

The installation of the openafs-dbserver package configures the services: the same rules for the first server apply also to the secondary machine, with the exception of the database server list which includes the new afs2 host. As usual, we need to stop the OpenAFS daemon before proceeding.

After removing the CellServDB and ThisCell files from the OpenAFS server configuration directory, we need to transfer the keytab file we have created on the primary machine with a secure method (e.g. SSH, USB pendrive). Note that exporting the principals key to a new keytab file on the secondary database server results in a KVNO mismatch, potentially harming the following steps. As we already did on the afs1 machine, we need to add the secret key with the asetkey tool:

```
# klist -ke afs.keytab
Keytab name: FILE:afs.keytab
KVNO Principal
---- -----------------------------------------------------------------------
   3 afs/example.edu@EXAMPLE.EDU (DES cbc mode with CRC-32)

# asetkey add 3 afs.keytab afs/example.edu

# asetkey list
kvno    3: key is: 0b6157dc3e575eea
All done.
```

Having successfully created the KeyFile containing the afs/example.edu service principal key, we can safely start both the OpenAFS server and client:

```
# /etc/init.d/openafs-fileserver start
Starting AFS Server: bosserver.

# /etc/init.d/openafs-client start
Starting AFS services: afsd: All AFS daemons started.
 afsd.
```

Our current AFS cell permits free access to the cell root to any unauthenticated user:

```
# klist
klist: No credentials cache found (ticket cache FILE:/tmp/krb5cc_0)


Kerberos 4 ticket cache: /tmp/tkt0
klist: You have no tickets cached

# tokens

Tokens held by the Cache Manager:

   --End of list--

# ls /afs
example.edu/  grand.central.org/
```

Anyway, when accessing the software distribution directory we have previously created, a non authenticated user experiences a permission denial:

```
# cat ISO/README
cat: ISO/README: Permission denied
```

Configuring the Database Server

Now we are ready to configure a new pure database server in our cell, but before proceeding we need to set the cell name and add the sysadmin user to the administrative entries in the BOS database with a local authentication (i.e. using the KeyFile as an authentication means):

```
# bos setcellname
afs2.example.edu example.edu -localauth

# bos adduser afs2.example.edu sysadmin -localauth
```

The last step, before fully employing the Kerberos principal to administer the cell, is to add the current FQDN of afs2 to the list of known database servers:

```
# bos listhosts afs2.example.edu
Cell name is example.edu
    Host 1 is afs2

# bos addhost afs2 afs1.example.edu -localauth
# bos addhost afs2 afs2.example.edu -localauth

# bos removehost afs2.example.edu afs2 -localauth

# bos listhosts afs2 -localauth
Cell name is example.edu
    Host 1 is afs1.example.edu
    Host 2 is afs2.example.edu
```

As we have seen previously, we removed the entry for the machine that was added by BOS itself. It is possible now to run all the commands with the sysadmin user, obtaining the initial ticket and then translating it to an AFS token:

```
# kinit sysadmin
Password for sysadmin@EXAMPLE.EDU:

# aklog
```

The known hosts for afs2 has been already set, so we need to add the new database server to the list on afs1. This operation can be done using the bos command on the secondary database machine, provided that we have a valid token as an administrative user:

```
# bos listhosts afs1.example.edu
Cell name is example.edu
    Host 1 is afs1.example.edu

# bos addhost afs1.example.edu afs2.example.edu

# bos listhosts afs1.example.edu
Cell name is example.edu
    Host 1 is afs1.example.edu
    Host 2 is afs2.example.edu
```

As the database list of both servers are synchronized, we can restart the server and client-side services, and then add the necessary backup, protection and volume location instances to the BOS server running on afs2:

```
# bos create afs2 buserver simple /usr/lib/openafs/buserver

# bos create afs2 ptserver simple /usr/lib/openafs/ptserver

# bos create afs2 vlserver simple /usr/lib/openafs/vlserver

# bos status afs2 -long
Instance buserver, (type is simple) currently running normally.
    Process last started at Thu Jun 15 12:50:22 2006 (1 proc starts)
    Command 1 is '/usr/lib/openafs/buserver'

Instance ptserver, (type is simple) currently running normally.
    Process last started at Thu Jun 15 12:52:48 2006 (1 proc starts)
    Command 1 is '/usr/lib/openafs/ptserver'

Instance vlserver, (type is simple) currently running normally.
    Process last started at Thu Jun 15 12:52:55 2006 (1 proc starts)
    Command 1 is '/usr/lib/openafs/vlserver'
```

The database entries on `afs2` are automatically synchronized with the items present on the first machine, and no further human intervention is needed to keep the AFS databases synchronized. We may notice that we could proceed creating a file server instance on the secondary machine—supplying a valid `/vicepX` partition—in case we wanted `afs2` to be also a file server. Clients can benefit from more database server hosts from the moment that these are configured in their `CellServDB` files.

5.3.2 Secondary File Servers

Large installations may need a great quantity of disk space, and this fact is reflected for AFS by the number of file servers in a cell. Adding numerous file servers allows the administrators to distribute resources—volumes in the AFS terminology—across the network, and thanks to the volume location process, the distribution is not limited to a local connection[9].

In the following we are going to create a pure file server called `fs01`, following the same steps we have seen before. Pure file servers are meant to add disk space to an AFS cell, so they are usually machines with a large amount of hard drive space, and possibly various `/vicepX` partitions. We assume that the `fs01` machine has already been configured to be a Kerberos client, with mounted `/vicepX` partitions.

Configuring the File Server

Instead of installing the `openafs-dbserver` which installs the database and the file server tools, we install the `openafs-fileserver` package along with the usual Kerberos-OpenAFS tools. As usual Debian configures the package and finally asks whether or not to start the OpenAFS client. It is safe to start the client at this point since all the database servers are up and running, while

---

[9] An AFS cell does not require a LAN locality, servers may be on different networks and continents, as long as the database servers are accessible.

the BOS server is automatically started by the Debian installer without any inquiry.

Let us proceed then stopping the BOS server and using the `asetkey` tool to import the secret key from the keytab file which we transfer on the file server with a safe medium. After removing the server configuration files, we can start BOS and configure it by setting the cell name and the database servers with the local authentication:

```
# bos setcellname
fs01.example.edu example.edu -localauth

# bos addhost fs01 afs1.example.edu -localauth

# bos addhost fs01 afs2.example.edu -localauth

# bos removehost fs01 fs01 -localauth
```

After this preliminary configuration we can add the `sysadmin` user to the privileged users list and then restart the file server in order to make changes take effect:

```
# bos adduser fs01.example.edu sysadmin -localauth

# bos listusers fs01 -localauth
SUsers are: sysadmin

# /etc/init.d/openafs-fileserver start
Starting AFS Server: bosserver.
```

We are now ready to fully employ the Kerberized server by getting the initial ticket for `sysadmin` and converting it to the corresponding AFS token. The BOS server on the new machine does not handle any instance, as we can see from its status:

```
# bos status fs01 -long
```

The new file server needs to be completed by adding the new `fs` instance with type `fs` to the BOS instance list:

```
# bos create fs01 fs fs -cmd /usr/lib/openafs/fileserver \
-cmd /usr/lib/openafs/volserver -cmd /usr/lib/openafs/salvager

# bos status fs01 -long
Instance fs, (type is fs) currently running normally.
    Auxiliary status is: file server running.
    Process last started at Thu Jun 15 15:26:04 2006 (2 proc starts)
    Command 1 is '/usr/lib/openafs/fileserver'
    Command 2 is '/usr/lib/openafs/volserver'
    Command 3 is '/usr/lib/openafs/salvager'
```

5.3.3 Volume Management

The ability to move volumes among AFS file servers is one of the major features of this architecture. This characteristic has a great impact on large installations where file servers may be sensibly placed and administered in order to create a load balancing and concentrate disk space where it is needed.

OpenAFS can easily move volumes without creating downtime during this process: a lock is retained on the first and very last instants of the operation. Let us move one of the volumes previously created on `afs1` to the new file server `fs01`. The list of volumes present on `afs1` is as follows:

```
# vos listvol afs1
Total number of volumes on server afs1 partition /vicepa: 5
cell.software               536870924 RW          3 K On-line
cell.users                  536870921 RW          2 K On-line
root.afs                    536870915 RW          4 K On-line
root.cell                   536870918 RW          4 K On-line
software.debian             536870927 RW     111241 K On-line

Total volumes onLine 5 ; Total volumes offLine 0 ; Total busy 0
```

The `vos` tool can move volumes among file servers with the `move` command, feeding it with the volume ID or its name, the originating server and partition, and the destination server and partition, as we can see in the following example that moves the `software.debian` volume:

```
# vos move -id software.debian -fromserver afs1 -frompartition vicepa \
-toserver fs01 -topartition vicepa
Volume 536870927 moved from afs1 /vicepa to fs01 /vicepa
```

The same rule of shortcutting commands is applied also to `vos` services, removing the switch `-id`, and avoid the prefix `vicep` from partition names (e.g. `a` would be assumed to be `vicepa`).

The moving process is displayed on both target and origin file servers, showing a busy volume on both sides:

```
# vos listvol afs1
Total number of volumes on server afs1 partition /vicepa: 6
cell.software               536870924 RW          3 K On-line
cell.users                  536870921 RW          2 K On-line
root.afs                    536870915 RW          4 K On-line
root.cell                   536870918 RW          4 K On-line
software.debian             536870927 RW     111241 K On-line
**** Volume 536870930 is busy ****

Total volumes onLine 5 ; Total volumes offLine 0 ; Total busy 1

# vos listvol fs01
Total number of volumes on server fs01 partition /vicepa: 1
**** Volume 536870927 is busy ****

Total volumes onLine 0 ; Total volumes offLine 0 ; Total busy 1
```

We can notice that the volume ID of the busy volume on the source file server differs from the ID of the volume we are actually moving, while on the target side the same ID appears correctly: a volume *clone* is created so that users can continue to read ad write while the operation is in progress. The volumes at the end of the process retain the original ID and the clone is finally removed:

```
# vos listvol afs1
Total number of volumes on server afs1 partition /vicepa: 4
cell.software                536870924 RW           3 K On-line
cell.users                   536870921 RW           2 K On-line
root.afs                     536870915 RW           4 K On-line
root.cell                    536870918 RW           4 K On-line

Total volumes onLine 4 ; Total volumes offLine 0 ; Total busy 0

# vos listvol fs01
Total number of volumes on server fs01 partition /vicepa: 1
software.debian              536870927 RW       111241 K On-line

Total volumes onLine 1 ; Total volumes offLine 0 ; Total busy 0
```

5.4 Replication and Backup

OpenAFS provides the ability to replicate volumes on file servers, although replicas are limited to just one read and write enabled volume, with several read-only replicas. Replicating volumes, and automatically synchronizing the read-only replicas can be a straightforward backup facility.

Replication is one of the many possible implementation for backups, one of the most important tasks to ensure a fairly low probability of data loss. In the following sections we will first illustrate the replication process, and next we will provide a view over some backup procedures that employ current AFS capabilities.

5.4.1 Replicas

Replicating volumes inside a cell provides an easy way of creating backups of critical data. Clients accessing the AFS file space choose to read data from read-only volumes as long as it is possible, avoiding possible connection failures. The first volume to be replicated is the main cell volume `root.cell`. Before proceeding in replica creation, we create a new mount point for our cell volume forcing it to be write-enabled adding the `-rw` switch:

```
# fs mkmount /afs/.example.edu root.cell -rw
```

The choice of the mount point name is not arbitrary: on UNIX systems files whose name begin with a dot are considered hidden:

```
# ls -a /afs
./  ../  .example.edu/  example.edu/  grand.central.org/
```

Volume names also differ when querying the file server about the two different mount points:

```
# fs lsmount /afs/example.edu
'/afs/example.edu' is a mount point for volume '#root.cell'

# fs lsmount /afs/.example.edu
'/afs/.example.edu' is a mount point for volume '%root.cell'
```

Here # indicate a regular mount point and % indicate a read/write mount point followed by the name of the volume.

Creating Replicas

The replicas of a volume are called in the correct AFS terminology *replication sites*, and we are allowed to have up to 11 RO replicas for one RW volume which might have a backup volume introduced later. The **vos** program is used to create replication sites with the **addsite** command, specifying the file server and the partition where the replica should be created, along with the volume ID of the chosen volume. Let us create a replica for the **root.afs** volume on both our file servers, **afs1** and **fs01**:

```
# vos addsite -server afs1 -partition a -id root.afs
Added replication site afs1 /vicepa for volume root.afs

# vos addsite -server fs01 -partition a -id root.afs
Added replication site fs01 /vicepa for volume root.afs
```

The same procedure can be applied to the cell root volume, **root.cell**, on both file servers:

```
# vos addsite -server afs1 -partition a -id root.cell
Added replication site afs1 /vicepa for volume root.cell

# vos addsite -server fs01 -partition a -id root.cell
Added replication site fs01 /vicepa for volume root.cell
```

Thus we have created two replication sites for each root volume, but no change has been made to the read-write volume:

```
# vos volinfo root.afs
root.afs                      536870915 RW          4 K  On-line
    afs1.example.edu /vicepa
    RWrite  536870915 ROnly         0 Backup        0
    MaxQuota     5000 K
    Creation    Thu Jun  8 12:42:45 2006
    Copy        Thu Jun  8 12:42:45 2006
    Backup      Never
    Last Update Thu Jun 15 11:59:46 2006
    50 accesses in the past day (i.e., vnode references)

    RWrite: 536870915
    number of sites -> 3
       server afs1.example.edu partition /vicepa RW Site
       server afs1.example.edu partition /vicepa RO Site  -- Not released
       server fs01.example.edu partition /vicepa RO Site  -- Not released

# vos volinfo root.cell
```

```
root.cell                       536870918 RW              4 K  On-line
    afs1.example.edu /vicepa
    RWrite  536870918 ROnly           0 Backup           0
    MaxQuota        5000 K
    Creation    Thu Jun  8 13:00:59 2006
    Copy        Thu Jun  8 13:00:59 2006
    Backup      Never
    Last Update Thu Jun 15 11:16:49 2006
    21 accesses in the past day (i.e., vnode references)

    RWrite: 536870918
    number of sites -> 3
        server afs1.example.edu partition /vicepa RW Site
        server afs1.example.edu partition /vicepa RO Site   -- Not released
        server fs01.example.edu partition /vicepa RO Site   -- Not released
```

In order to allow changes take effect we need to *release* the root.cell and
root.afs volumes, an operation performed by the vos tool with the release
command followed by the volume ID:

```
# vos release root.afs
Released volume root.afs successfully

# vos release root.cell
Released volume root.cell successfully
```

Working with Replicas

Once that replication sites have been created, the read-only volume cannot
be modified easily and all the changes take effect only upon a volume release,
in other words, all the changes must be made to the read-write volume and
successively released.

In this case, the example.edu mount point has become a read-only location, and no changes are ever made available to users until the volume
associated to .example.edu gets released. We can test that effectively the
/afs/example.edu/ location is non-modifiable even by the system administrator sysadmin:

```
# tokens

Tokens held by the Cache Manager:

User's (AFS ID 1) tokens for afs@example.edu [Expires Jun 16 02:29]
   --End of list--

# cd /afs/example.edu/

# touch aaa
touch: cannot touch 'aaa': Read-only file system
```

The property does not affect volumes with no replication sites. For instance, the cell.users volume we have previously created is write-enabled:

```
# cd /afs/example.edu/users

# mkdir aaa

# ls -l
total 2
drwxr-xr-x  2 daemon root 2048 2006-06-15 16:35 aaa/

# rmdir aaa
```

A read-only volume as replication site is modified only upon a volume release command, as we have previously explained. Let us show how this behavior affects users and administrators by creating a new volume for network services called `cell.services`:

```
# vos create afs1 a cell.services
Volume 536870931 created on partition /vicepa of afs1
```

The new volume should now be mounted in a proper location, we decide to have a directory named `/afs/example.edu/services/` that contains service data, for instance web pages. Trying to mount the volume directly as `/afs/example.edu/services/` results in a failure, since the location is a read-only site with replicas. Mounting the volume in the write-enabled location `.example.edu` results in success:

```
# fs mkmount example.edu/services cell.services
fs: You can not change a backup or readonly volume

# fs mkmount .example.edu/services cell.services
```

The volume we have modified is the write-enabled version of `root.cell` which is commonly accessed by users. In fact, when inspecting both locations we notice that the read-only volume still has no knowledge about the newly mounted service volume:

```
# ls example.edu/
software/  users/

# ls .example.edu/
services/  software/  users/
```

After releasing the `root.cell` volume we can notice that the two sites have been synchronized, and changes are made visible to clients:

```
# vos release root.cell
Released volume root.cell successfully

# ls example.edu/
services/  software/  users/

# ls .example.edu/
services/  software/  users/
```

Modifying the AFS File Space

In the past we have advised to mount all the foreign cells before proceeding. As we introduced the replication sites for the `root.afs` volume, which contains the AFS file space, no modifications are allowed anymore: currently there is no read-write volume mounted for the `/afs/` space. It is possible to mount other cells even when a replication site for the root volume has been created, although the procedure is a bit tricky.

Suppose we want to mount the AFS cell of the School of Computer Science from the Carnegie Mellon University, whose cell name is `cs.cmu.edu`:

```
# cd /afs

# fs mkmount cs.cmu.edu root.cell -cell cs.cmu.edu
fs: You can not change a backup or readonly volume
```

In order to mount the foreign cell we need a read-write mount point. The operation is simple: mount the AFS root volume in a temporary mount point as a write-enabled location which contains then a modifiable version of our AFS file space. Let us proceed then mounting the AFS file space into that auxiliary location under the write-enabled location `.example.edu`, using the forcing switch `-rw`:

```
# cd .example.edu/

# fs mkmount temp root.afs -rw
```

We see now that the `temp` directory contains the AFS file space as in `/afs/`, with the exception that in this location we are cleared to modify the mounted volume:

```
# cd temp

# ls
example.edu/  grand.central.org/

# fs mkmount cs.cmu.edu root.cell -cell cs.cmu.edu
```

The `fs` command should end successfully mounting the external AFS cell:

```
# ls /afs/.example.edu/temp/
cs.cmu.edu/  example.edu/  grand.central.org/

# ls /afs/.example.edu/temp/cs.cmu.edu/
academic/      hp700_ux100/   misc/          rt_mach/      sun4_413/     system/
alpha_dux40/   hp700_ux90/    mmax_mach/     service/      sun4_53/      unix@
alpha_osf1/    i386_fc3/      next_mach@     sgi_53/       sun4_54/      user/
alpha_osf20/   i386_linux1/   org/           sgi_62/       sun4_55/      usr@
alpha_osf32/   i386_mach/     os/            sun3_40/      sun4c_40@     vax_22/
amd64_fc3/     ibmrt_mach@    pmax_mach/     sun3_41/      sun4c_41/     vax_mach/
archive/       links_mach/    pmax_ul43a/    sun3_mach/    sun4c_411/    Web/
common/        local@         project/       sun4_40/      sun4m_412@
data/          luna88k_mach/  publications/  sun4_40c/     sun4_mach/
```

```
help/        mach/        root@        sun4_41/    sun4x_57/
host/        mac_sys7/    rs_aix32/    sun4_411/   sunos/
```

At this point we can safely remove the temporary mount point:

```
# fs rmmount temp
```

The current version of our AFS cell is not affected by any change: in fact, since we added a replication site, the /afs/ location is read-only and becomes synchronized with the read-write volume only upon release:

```
# ls /afs
example.edu/  grand.central.org/

# vos release root.afs
Released volume root.afs successfully
```

After releasing the root.afs volume our AFS file space reflects the changes previously made to the temporary mount point, correctly showing cs.cmu.edu mounted in the cell root:

```
# ls /afs
cs.cmu.edu/   example.edu/  grand.central.org/
```

5.4.2 Backup

A good network architecture should involve fault-tolerance techniques, along with a careful disaster recovery facility. Backups must be carefully planned in order to lower as much as possible the probability of data loss in case of hardware failures. We have already said that an AFS database server runs an instance called buserver, which is specifically designed to keep track of total and incremental backups. In the following we will describe the principal backup commands used in an AFS file space. We stress the fact that such commands require privileged access to the AFS volumes, so we will assume that all the described operations are run by the sysadmin user possessing a valid AFS token.

Volume Dump

The easiest method of backing up data from the AFS file space is to dump the contents of a volume on a file. The vos tool, instructed with the dump command, can perform a complete binary dump of a volume:

```
# vos help dump
vos dump: dump a volume
Usage: vos dump -id <volume name or ID> [-time <dump from time>] [-file <dump file>] \
[-server <server>] [-partition <partition>] [-clone] [-cell <cell name>] [-noauth] \
[-localauth] [-verbose] [-encrypt] [-help]
```

```
Where:  -clone     dump a clone of the volume
        -noauth    don't authenticate
        -localauth use server tickets
        -verbose   verbose
        -encrypt   encrypt commands
```

Let us dump the `software.debian` volume on a file in the local file system. The dump operation exclusively locks a volume, denying any modification to the contents while the process is running: for this reason a careful schedule plan should be made in advance. The dump may require several minutes to operate when employed as a full dump as in the following example:

```
# vos dump -id software.debian -file /tmp/software-debian.dump
Dumped volume software.debian in file /tmp/software-debian.dump
```

Note that server and partition can be omitted in the command line, since volumes are univocally located by the volume location server. The `vos dump` operation allows also a `-clone` switch that avoids the exclusive volume lock:

```
# vos dump -id software.debian -file /tmp/software-debian.clone-dump -clone
Dumped volume software.debian in file /tmp/software-debian.clone-dump
```

Although necessary, complete dumps are not always the best choice for backing up data. The AFS tools allow also incremental dumps of a volume, provided a time specification through the `-time` switch of the `dump` command. The date specification is given in the format `mm/dd/yyyy hh:MM`, where the date is mandatory and time is optional (a date equal to 0 indicates a full dump).

In case of failure a volume can be restored from a dump with the `restore` command issued to the `vos` program:

```
# vos help restore
vos restore: restore a volume
Usage: vos restore -server <machine name> -partition <partition name> \
-name <name of volume to be restored> [-file <dump file>] [-id <volume ID>] \
[-overwrite <abort | full | incremental>] [-offline] [-readonly] \
[-creation <dump | keep | new>] [-lastupdate <dump | keep | new>] \
[-cell <cell name>] [-noauth] [-localauth] [-verbose] [-encrypt] [-help]
Where:  -offline   leave restored volume offline
        -readonly  make restored volume read-only
        -noauth    don't authenticate
        -localauth use server tickets
        -verbose   verbose
        -encrypt   encrypt commands
```

In order to restore a volume, we must specify the file server and partition where the dump should be restored, as well as the target volume ID. In the following example we restore from a dump file the volume `software.debian` on the partition `/vicepa` of `afs1`:

```
# vos restore afs1 a software.debian -file /tmp/software-debian.dump
Restoring volume software.debian Id 536870935 on server afs1.example.edu \
partition /vicepa .. done
Restored volume software.debian on afs1 /vicepa
```

Note that a restore actually restores both data and permissions as they were before dumping the contents of a volume. Symmetrically to an incremental dump, restoring a volume may be an incremental process, specified with the -overwrite option which allows different behaviors in case we are overwriting an existing volume: an abortion (-overwrite a) of the process, a full restore (-overwrite f) or an incremental one (-overwrite i). Although appealing, we would recommend to avoid the use of dump files for backups, since AFS provides a more sophisticated method.

Backup Volumes

The AFS services provide a specific backup solution similar to the replication sites we have previously introduced: a particular volume type called *backup volume*. This particular kind of volumes are employed for full backups, which can be scheduled by the BOS server.

Backup volumes are created as usual via the vos program with the backup command, feeding it with the volume ID or name, as we can see from the command help output:

```
# vos help backup
vos backup: make backup of a volume
Usage: vos backup -id <volume name or ID> [-cell <cell name>] [-noauth] [-localauth] \
[-verbose] [-encrypt] [-help]
Where: -noauth     don't authenticate
       -localauth  use server tickets
       -verbose    verbose
       -encrypt    encrypt commands
```

The command creates a new volume with the .backup suffix. This particular type of volumes, contrary to a replication site, are bound to be created on the same file server where the original volume is stored, as we can see by listing the available volumes after creating the backup for both the AFS and the cell root volumes:

```
# vos backup root.afs
Created backup volume for root.afs

# vos backup root.cell
Created backup volume for root.cell

# vos listvol afs1
Total number of volumes on server afs1 partition /vicepa: 10
cell.services            536870931 RW       2 K On-line
cell.software            536870924 RW       3 K On-line
cell.users               536870921 RW       2 K On-line
root.afs                 536870915 RW       6 K On-line
root.afs.backup          536870917 BK       6 K On-line
root.afs.readonly        536870916 RO       6 K On-line
```

```
root.cell                          536870918 RW        5 K On-line
root.cell.backup                   536870920 BK        5 K On-line
root.cell.readonly                 536870919 RO        5 K On-line
software.debian                    536870935 RW   111241 K On-line

Total volumes onLine 10 ; Total volumes offLine 0 ; Total busy 0
```

It is possible to create backup volumes specifying a common prefix for the volume ID, using the **backupsys** command of **vos**. The command allows us also to apply negative prefixes and show the proceeding of a backup operation without actually performing it:

```
# vos help backupsys
vos backupsys: en masse backups
Usage: vos backupsys [-prefix <common prefix on volume(s)>+] [-server <machine name>] \
[-partition <partition name>] [-exclude] [-xprefix <negative prefix on volume(s)>+] \
[-dryrun] [-cell <cell name>] [-noauth] [-localauth] [-verbose] [-encrypt] [-help]
Where: -exclude    exclude common prefix volumes
       -dryrun     no action
       -noauth     don't authenticate
       -localauth  use server tickets
       -verbose    verbose
       -encrypt    encrypt commands
```

As an example we could create backups for all the volumes whose names begin with **cell**, by using the **-prefix** switch followed by the prefixed string:

```
# vos backupsys -prefix cell
done
Total volumes backed up: 3; failed to backup: 0

# vos listvol afs1
Total number of volumes on server afs1 partition /vicepa: 13
cell.services                      536870931 RW        2 K On-line
cell.services.backup               536870933 BK        2 K On-line
cell.software                      536870924 RW        3 K On-line
cell.software.backup               536870926 BK        3 K On-line
cell.users                         536870921 RW        2 K On-line
cell.users.backup                  536870923 BK        2 K On-line
root.afs                           536870915 RW        6 K On-line
root.afs.backup                    536870917 BK        6 K On-line
root.afs.readonly                  536870916 RO        6 K On-line
root.cell                          536870918 RW        5 K On-line
root.cell.backup                   536870920 BK        5 K On-line
root.cell.readonly                 536870919 RO        5 K On-line
software.debian                    536870935 RW   111241 K On-line

Total volumes onLine 13 ; Total volumes offLine 0 ; Total busy 0
```

The **-dryrun** switch is useful in case we want to inspect the volumes that would be affected by the process without actually running a backup operation:

```
# vos backupsys -prefix cell -dryrun
    cell.users
    cell.software
    cell.services
done
Total volumes backed up: 0; failed to backup: 0
```

Backing up volumes is a critical operation and should be done regularly and automatically. The BOS server provides a special instance type for scheduled jobs called **cron**, as the common UNIX daemon. As usual BOS runs and monitors all the processes it is demanded to handle, allowing an AFS server to securely handle a crucial task as backups. Usually these are scheduled at night in order to avoid interferences with business time. The name given to the **cron** instance is customary, although as any other choice in a working environment, should be chosen with certain criteria.

As an example, we create an instance called **backuproot** on the **afs1** database server, with type **cron**, that creates backup volumes at 1am, targeting the **root** volumes (i.e. **root.afs** and **root.cell**):

```
# bos create -server afs1 -instance backuproot -type cron -cmd "/usr/bin/vos backupsys \
-prefix root -localauth" "01:00"
```

Note that a local authentication via the **KeyFile** is needed by the issued **vos** command: a backup accesses privileged information in the AFS file space an thus it must be run with administrative privileges. The **cron** instance is shown correctly when querying the BOS status, displaying also the next scheduled run:

```
# bos status -long afs1
Instance buserver, (type is simple) currently running normally.
    Process last started at Tue Jun 20 10:01:56 2006 (1 proc starts)
    Command 1 is '/usr/lib/openafs/buserver'

Instance ptserver, (type is simple) currently running normally.
    Process last started at Tue Jun 20 10:01:56 2006 (1 proc starts)
    Command 1 is '/usr/lib/openafs/ptserver'

Instance vlserver, (type is simple) currently running normally.
    Process last started at Tue Jun 20 10:01:56 2006 (1 proc starts)
    Command 1 is '/usr/lib/openafs/vlserver'

Instance fs, (type is fs) currently running normally.
    Auxiliary status is: file server running.
    Process last started at Tue Jun 20 10:01:56 2006 (2 proc starts)
    Command 1 is '/usr/lib/openafs/fileserver'
    Command 2 is '/usr/lib/openafs/volserver'
    Command 3 is '/usr/lib/openafs/salvager'

Instance backuproot, (type is cron) currently running normally.
    Auxiliary status is: run next at Wed Jun 21 01:00:00 2006.
    Command 1 is '/usr/bin/vos backupsys -prefix root -localauth'
    Command 2 is '01:00'
```

It is possible to schedule several **cron**-driven operations, for instance creating backups for all the volumes whose names start with **cell** at 3am:

```
# bos create -server afs1 -instance backupcell -type cron -cmd "/usr/bin/vos backupsys \
-prefix cell -localauth" "03:00"

# bos status -long afs1
Instance buserver, (type is simple) currently running normally.
    Process last started at Tue Jun 20 10:01:56 2006 (1 proc starts)
```

```
      Command 1 is '/usr/lib/openafs/buserver'

Instance ptserver, (type is simple) currently running normally.
      Process last started at Tue Jun 20 10:01:56 2006 (1 proc starts)
      Command 1 is '/usr/lib/openafs/ptserver'

Instance vlserver, (type is simple) currently running normally.
      Process last started at Tue Jun 20 10:01:56 2006 (1 proc starts)
      Command 1 is '/usr/lib/openafs/vlserver'

Instance fs, (type is fs) currently running normally.
      Auxiliary status is: file server running.
      Process last started at Tue Jun 20 10:01:56 2006 (2 proc starts)
      Command 1 is '/usr/lib/openafs/fileserver'
      Command 2 is '/usr/lib/openafs/volserver'
      Command 3 is '/usr/lib/openafs/salvager'

Instance backuproot, (type is cron) currently running normally.
      Auxiliary status is: run next at Wed Jun 21 01:00:00 2006.
      Command 1 is '/usr/bin/vos backupsys -prefix root -localauth'
      Command 2 is '01:00'

Instance backupcell, (type is cron) currently running normally.
      Auxiliary status is: run next at Wed Jun 21 03:00:00 2006.
      Command 1 is '/usr/bin/vos backupsys -prefix cell -localauth'
      Command 2 is '03:00'
```

Backup batch jobs are usually executed when the AFS file space is less unused, since such operations lock the volumes for a very short time.

The Backup Tape Coordinator

The backup volumes are created in order to support a powerful backup manager. Similarly to a dump, our objective is to save this particular type of volumes in case of data loss. The privileged legacy medium, but still in use in many companies, are magnetic tapes.

In our environment, in order to show how to implement a backup system, we choose to save the backup volumes on the secondary database server afs2, but it would be sufficient to be a normal client of the cell. Let us first create the location where the backup system reads its configuration settings. By default this location is named **backup** under the **/var/lib/openafs/** directory:

```
# ls -l /var/lib/openafs/
total 12
drwxr-xr-x  2 root root 4096 2006-06-20 12:05 backup/
drwx------  2 root root 4096 2005-05-14 21:49 cores/
drwx------  2 root root 4096 2006-06-15 12:52 db/
```

At this point we have to decide the backup medium. Usually the process would start a tape device by opening the special file under **/dev/**, dumping the contents to the magnetic tape. This process is entirely driven by the **butc** tool, the *backup tape coordinator*. The program allows us also to use different device files, including a mounted partition, which is our preferred medium to show the backup process. The **butc** configuration highly relies on the device file name we intend to use, and we choose to use a device called **/dev/backup** which is a symbolic link to a file that the tool creates upon completing the operation. The /butc/ directory is a local mount point with enough free disk space:

```
# ls -l /dev/backup
lrwxrwxrwx  1 root root 18 2006-06-20 12:17 /dev/backup -> /butc/afsbackup
```

In the /var/lib/openafs/backup/ subdirectory we have to create the configuration file for the backup tape coordinator named tapeconfig. This configuration file specifies the size of the backup, a number followed by K, M, G, or T—or their respective lowercase versions—indicating kilobytes, megabytes, gigabytes or terabytes, respectively. The second parameter is the *End-Of-File* marker which specifies the separating sign between different volumes, and it is established by the manufacturer: if using a file as a backup medium then the value should be set to 0, although disregarded by butc in this case[10]. Following the mark, we need to specify the device and the port offset associated with the backup tape, which is a unique integer number among tape coordinators in the cell. In our example, we choose to use /dev/backup with 100 gigabytes of size:

```
100G 0 /dev/backup 0
```

The device name specified in tapeconfig decides the device configuration file. Each backup medium must be properly configured in the same directory as tapeconfig with a file whose name is in the format CFG_device, in our case then CFG_backup. This file contains a list of options for the device operation, as whether or not it is a file, or if the process should ask for human intervention:

```
AUTOQUERY NO
FILE YES
NAME_CHECK NO
```

The AUTOQUERY parameter specifies whether the system should prompt a human user about inserting the first tape, and the NAME_CHECK specifies if the tape name should be checked before processing the backup. The FILE parameter is obviously describing whether the backup is done on a file or on a real device. Both the tape coordinator and device are set up and we can safely start the butc tool on the afs2 server:

```
# butc -localauth
Auto query is disabled
Will dump to a file
Dump tape name check is disabled
Starting Tape Coordinator: Port offset 0    Debug level 0
Token expires: NEVER
```

The command is idle until we send a backup start command.

---

[10] The EOF specification follows the same rule as the backup size, with the default size set to bytes.

Backup Sets

The backup tape coordinator along with the backup program can be employed to run scheduled operations, configuring these with the `backup` AFS tool. Contrary to all other programs we have used until this point, the `backup` can be either run from the command line as `fs` and `vos`, or it can be used interactively like the `kadmin` tool:

```
# backup
backup> help
Commands are:
adddump         add dump schedule
addhost         add host to config
addvolentry     add a new volume entry
addvolset       create a new volume set
apropos         search by help text
dbverify        check ubik database integrity
deldump         delete dump schedule
deletedump      delete dumps from the database
delhost         delete host to config
delvolentry     delete a volume set sub-entry
delvolset       delete a volume set
diskrestore     restore partition
dump            start dump
dumpinfo        provide information about a dump in the database
help            get help on commands
interactive     enter interactive mode
jobs            list running jobs
kill            kill running job
labeltape       label a tape
listdumps       list dump schedules
listhosts       list config hosts
listvolsets     list volume sets
quit            leave the program
readlabel       read the label on tape
restoredb       restore backup database
savedb          save backup database
scantape        dump information recovery from tape
setexp          set/clear dump expiration dates
status          get tape coordinator status
volinfo         query the backup database
volrestore      restore volume
volsetrestore   restore a set of volumes
backup>
```

The backup server is not aware of the backup host running `butc`, so we first need to add the `afs2` machine to the backup tape hosts with the `addhost` command followed by the tape port offset. The status of the `butc` process running on `afs2` should be idle, viewable via `status`:

```
backup> addhost afs2.example.edu 0
Adding host afs2.example.edu offset 0 to tape list...done

backup> status
Tape coordinator is idle
```

The backup system may handle several backup configurations, called *volume sets*, each of them with a meaningful name (e.g. users, homes, web). In our example we specify a unique volume set for all the backup volumes called

backups. Adding a volume set is possible through the **addvolset** command of **backup**:

```
backup> addvolset -name backups
```

Now the volume set must be configured assigning all the volume IDs, partitions and hosts that should be added to the backup operation when processing the **backups** volume set. All the parameters may be expressed with regular expressions fed to the **addvolentry** command. The example shows how to add all the volumes, on every server, regardless of the partition, whose names end with .**backup**:

```
backup> addvolentry -name backups -server .* -partition .* -volumes .*\.backup
```

Note that since the dot is a special character in regular expressions, we had to protect it with a backslash. The list of volume sets can be viewed with the **listvolset** command:

```
backup> listvolsets
Volume set backups:
    Entry  1: server .*, partition .*, volumes: .*\.backup
```

The backup dumping system is similar to a directory specification. A dump name beginning with a slash, for instance /**full**, indicate a full backup dump. Subsequent "sub-dumps" can be specified adding the name as if it were a subdirectory, as in /**full/w1**. The last specification indicates an incremental backup named **w1**, done with respect to the full back /**full**: a backup named /**full/w1/w2** stands for an incremental backup with respect to **w1**, which is actually an incremental backup with respect to the parent /**full**.

This specification makes it possible to design a complete backup hierarchy, where each dump is added through the **adddump** command, and the name specifies whether it is a full or an incremental backup. The following commands add five backup dumps, the first being full, while all the others are incremental backups with respect to the first:

```
backup> adddump -dump /full
backup: Created new dump schedule /full

backup> adddump -dump /full/w1
backup: Created new dump schedule /full/w1

backup> adddump -dump /full/w2
backup: Created new dump schedule /full/w2

backup> adddump -dump /full/w3
backup: Created new dump schedule /full/w3

backup> adddump -dump /full/w4
backup: Created new dump schedule /full/w4
```

The names given to dumps are completely customary, although meaningful names may help. In this example, we are implying to make weekly backups incrementally from the first full dump. It is also possible to create incremental backups that rely on the preceding one. Since we have already created the w1 dump, we have to add the following three weekly operations:

```
backup> adddump -dump /full/w1/w2
backup: Created new dump schedule /full/w1/w2

backup> adddump -dump /full/w1/w2/w3
backup: Created new dump schedule /full/w1/w2/w3

backup> adddump -dump /full/w1/w2/w3/w4
backup: Created new dump schedule /full/w1/w2/w3/w4
```

The listdumps command shows the complete hierarchy we have previously specified:

```
backup> listdumps
/full
    /w1
        /w2
            /w3
                /w4
    /w2
    /w3
    /w4
```

Dumping Backups

After specifying the backup hierarchy we are ready to create the backup dumps using the dump command, followed by the volume set and the backup level, which is obviously /full since it is the first backup process we ever started:

```
backup> dump backups /full
Starting dump of volume set 'backups' (dump level '/full')
Total number of volumes : 5
Preparing to dump the following volumes:
        cell.services.backup (536870933)
        cell.software.backup (536870926)
        cell.users.backup (536870923)
        root.cell.backup (536870920)
        root.afs.backup (536870917)
backup> Starting dump
backup: Task 1: Dump (backups.full)
Job 1: Dump (backups.full) finished. 5 volumes dumped
```

On the afs2 host we can notice that the backup device, in this case the /butc/afsbackup file as declared in the configuration, has been used success- fully:

```
# ls -l /butc/afsbackup
-rwxr-xr-x  1 root root 360448 2006-06-20 13:02 afsbackup*
```

As expected, the backup tape coordinator `butc`, once idle, now shows that the dump process has been successfully performed:

```
# butc -localauth
Auto query is disabled
Will dump to a file
Dump tape name check is disabled
Starting Tape Coordinator: Port offset 0    Debug level 0
Token expires: NEVER


Dump backups.full (DumpID 1150801336)
Updating database
Updating database - done
backups.full (DumpId 1150801336): Finished. 5 volumes dumped
```

It is then straightforward to implement incremental backups, since all is needed is the hierarchy specification fed to the `backup dump` command (e.g. `/full/w1/w2`).

The `butc` program we have run interactively is configured to use the device `/dev/backup`. If this file were a real tape device we could avoid the following consideration: every time a backup is performed, `butc` opens the device and writes onto it. This detail is of primary importance when using on-file dumps, since the `/butc/afsbackup` file gets overwritten each time a dump is performed. It is then essential to rename the backup dump file at each run:

```
# ls -l /butc/full*
-rwxr-xr-x  1 root root 360448 2006-06-20 13:02 full-2006-06-20*
```

Actually it is not strictly necessary to restart `butc` every time, but the file should be renamed according to some scheme. As another backup operation we can save the backup database contents to the `/dev/backup` device with the `savedb` command:

```
> savedb
backup> Job 1: SaveDb finished
```

Note that all the commands in `backup` are started as background jobs, and in the last example the `butc` output shows that the database has been correctly dumped:

```
# butc -localauth
Auto query is disabled
Will dump to a file
Dump tape name check is disabled
Starting Tape Coordinator: Port offset 0    Debug level 0
Token expires: NEVER



SaveDb
SaveDb: Finished
```

Again, the `afsbackup` file has been created and should be promptly renamed in order to avoid data loss. The backup process takes place each time a backup volume has been created, and `backup` refuses to run if no modifications have been made since the last backup volume creation:

```
# butc -localauth
Auto query is disabled
Will dump to a file
Dump tape name check is disabled
Starting Tape Coordinator: Port offset 0    Debug level 0
Token expires: NEVER


Dump backups.w1 (DumpID 1150806686)
Volume cell.services.backup (536870933) not dumped - has not been re-cloned since last dump
Volume cell.software.backup (536870926) not dumped - has not been re-cloned since last dump
Volume cell.users.backup (536870923) not dumped - has not been re-cloned since last dump
Volume root.cell.backup (536870920) not dumped - has not been re-cloned since last dump
Volume root.afs.backup (536870917) not dumped - has not been re-cloned since last dump
Volume cell.services.backup (536870933) not dumped - has not been re-cloned since last dump

Dump of volume cell.services.backup (536870933) failed

Please select action to be taken for this volume
r - retry, try dumping this volume again
o - omit,  this volume from this dump
a - abort, the entire dump
```

The process of creating backup volumes, starting `butc` and then issuing a `backup dump` has been shown interactively for didactic purposes. In real environments a careful and fully-automated backup plan is vital and should be carefully scheduled.

Restoring Backups

Volume restoration is symmetrical to volume creation, performed by `backup` with the `volrestore` command. In order to illustrate this feature, we perform an incremental backup with respect to the full backup we have previously created, and then restore one of the volumes. Let us first show the `backup` output along with `butc`:

```
backup> dump backups /full/w1
Starting dump of volume set 'backups' (dump level '/full/w1')
Found parent: dump backups.full (DumpID 1150801336)
Total number of volumes : 6
Preparing to dump the following volumes:
        cell.services.backup (536870933)
        software.debian.backup (536870936)
        cell.software.backup (536870926)
        cell.users.backup (536870923)
        root.cell.backup (536870920)
        root.afs.backup (536870917)
backup> Starting dump
backup: Task 1: Dump (backups.w1)
Job 1: Dump (backups.w1) finished. 6 volumes dumped

# butc
```

```
Auto query is disabled
Will dump to a file
Dump tape name check is disabled
Starting Tape Coordinator: Port offset 0    Debug level 0
Token expires: Tue Jun 20 22:35:00 2006


Dump backups.w1 (DumpID 1150807202)
Updating database
Updating database - done
backups.w1 (DumpId 1150807202): Finished. 1 volumes dumped, 5 unchanged
```

The `volrestore` command replaces a given volume with the backup stored during the last backup operation, restoring the volume on a particular partition of a given file server:

```
backup> volrestore -server afs1 -partition a -volume software.debian
backup> Starting restore

Incremental restore being processed on port 0
Job 1: Incremental Restore finished
```

Restoring the same volume twice, even on a different file server results in a failure as the output of `butc` testifies:

```
backup> volrestore -server fs01 -partition a -volume software.debian
backup> Starting restore

Incremental restore being processed on port 0
Job 1: Incremental Restore finished

# butc -localauth
Auto query is disabled
Will dump to a file
Dump tape name check is disabled
Starting Tape Coordinator: Port offset 0    Debug level 0
Token expires: NEVER


Restore
Restoring volume software.debian Id 536870935 on server fs01.example.edu partition \
/vicepa .. done

Failed to get info about server's -1851667263 address(es) from vlserver (err=0)
   Restore: Finished
```

Analyzing the situation on both file servers, we find an inconsistency between the volumes and the situation as reported by `afs1`, having on this host an orphan backup volume `software.debian.backup`:

```
# vos listvol afs1
Total number of volumes on server afs1 partition /vicepa: 13
cell.services                   536870931 RW         2 K On-line
cell.services.backup            536870933 BK         2 K On-line
cell.software                   536870924 RW         3 K On-line
cell.software.backup            536870926 BK         3 K On-line
cell.users                      536870921 RW         2 K On-line
```

```
cell.users.backup              536870923 BK         2 K On-line
root.afs                       536870915 RW         6 K On-line
root.afs.backup                536870917 BK         6 K On-line
root.afs.readonly              536870916 RO         6 K On-line
root.cell                      536870918 RW         5 K On-line
root.cell.backup               536870920 BK         5 K On-line
root.cell.readonly             536870919 RO         5 K On-line
software.debian.backup         536870936 BK    111241 K On-line

Total volumes onLine 13 ; Total volumes offLine 0 ; Total busy 0


# vos listvol fs01
Total number of volumes on server fs01 partition /vicepa: 4
root.afs.readonly              536870916 RO         6 K On-line
root.cell.readonly             536870919 RO         5 K On-line
software.debian                536870935 RW    111241 K On-line
software.debian.backup         536870936 BK    111241 K On-line

Total volumes onLine 4 ; Total volumes offLine 0 ; Total busy 0
```

The server partition has not been synchronized with the volume location database (VLDB). By issuing a `syncserv` command to `vos` we can force `afs1` to synchronize its status with the VLDB, and thus correcting the inconsistencies:

```
# vos syncserv afs1 a
Server afs1 partition /vicepa synchronized with VLDB

# vos listvol afs1
Total number of volumes on server afs1 partition /vicepa: 12
cell.services                  536870931 RW         2 K On-line
cell.services.backup           536870933 BK         2 K On-line
cell.software                  536870924 RW         3 K On-line
cell.software.backup           536870926 BK         3 K On-line
cell.users                     536870921 RW         2 K On-line
cell.users.backup              536870923 BK         2 K On-line
root.afs                       536870915 RW         6 K On-line
root.afs.backup                536870917 BK         6 K On-line
root.afs.readonly              536870916 RO         6 K On-line
root.cell                      536870918 RW         5 K On-line
root.cell.backup               536870920 BK         5 K On-line
root.cell.readonly             536870919 RO         5 K On-line

Total volumes onLine 12 ; Total volumes offLine 0 ; Total busy 0

# vos listvol fs01
Total number of volumes on server fs01 partition /vicepa: 4
root.afs.readonly              536870916 RO         6 K On-line
root.cell.readonly             536870919 RO         5 K On-line
software.debian                536870935 RW    111241 K On-line
software.debian.backup         536870936 BK    111241 K On-line

Total volumes onLine 4 ; Total volumes offLine 0 ; Total busy 0
```

Copy and Rename as Backup

The volume copy facility is a newly added feature present on OpenAFS and not on legacy systems still running the Transarc or IBM AFS implementation. The `vos` tool can be used with the `copy` command to create copies of a given volume on different file servers, and the `rename` command may be employed to restore it in case of data loss. For the example let us start by listing all the volumes known to the VLDB on all servers by issuing the `listvldb` command to `vos`:

```
# vos listvldb
VLDB entries for all servers

cell.services
    RWrite: 536870931    Backup: 536870933
    number of sites -> 1
       server afs1.example.edu partition /vicepa RW Site

cell.software
    RWrite: 536870924    Backup: 536870926
    number of sites -> 1
       server afs1.example.edu partition /vicepa RW Site

cell.users
    RWrite: 536870921    Backup: 536870923
    number of sites -> 1
       server afs1.example.edu partition /vicepa RW Site

root.afs
    RWrite: 536870915    ROnly: 536870916    Backup: 536870917
    number of sites -> 3
       server afs1.example.edu partition /vicepa RW Site
       server afs1.example.edu partition /vicepa RO Site
       server fs01.example.edu partition /vicepa RO Site

root.cell
    RWrite: 536870918    ROnly: 536870919    Backup: 536870920
    number of sites -> 3
       server afs1.example.edu partition /vicepa RW Site
       server afs1.example.edu partition /vicepa RO Site
       server fs01.example.edu partition /vicepa RO Site

software.debian
    RWrite: 536870935
    number of sites -> 1
       server fs01.example.edu partition /vicepa RW Site

Total entries: 6
```

The `software.debian` volume is copied from the `fs01` file server to `afs1` with `vos copy`. This command has a syntax similar to `move`, with the specification of the origin host and partition and the destination ones. The switch `-offline` is used in this case to render the copy inaccessible to clients:

```
# vos copy -id software.debian -fromserver fs01 -frompartition a \
-toname software.debian.copy -toserver afs1 -topartition a -offline
Volume 536870935 copied from fs01 /vicepa to software.debian.copy on afs1 /vicepa
```

The volumes on both file servers reflect the new situation, showing the new offline `software.debian.copy` volume:

```
# vos listvol afs1
Total number of volumes on server afs1 partition /vicepa: 13
cell.services              536870931 RW        2 K On-line
cell.services.backup       536870933 BK        2 K On-line
cell.software              536870924 RW        3 K On-line
```

```
cell.software.backup            536870926 BK          3 K On-line
cell.users                      536870921 RW          2 K On-line
cell.users.backup               536870923 BK          2 K On-line
root.afs                        536870915 RW          6 K On-line
root.afs.backup                 536870917 BK          6 K On-line
root.afs.readonly               536870916 RO          6 K On-line
root.cell                       536870918 RW          5 K On-line
root.cell.backup                536870920 BK          5 K On-line
root.cell.readonly              536870919 RO          5 K On-line
software.debian.copy            536870940 RW     111241 K Off-line

Total volumes onLine 12 ; Total volumes offLine 1 ; Total busy 0

# vos listvol fs01
Total number of volumes on server fs01 partition /vicepa: 3
root.afs.readonly               536870916 RO          6 K On-line
root.cell.readonly              536870919 RO          5 K On-line
software.debian                 536870935 RW     111241 K On-line

Total volumes onLine 3 ; Total volumes offLine 0 ; Total busy 0
```

Since the copied volume is offline, we can simulate a file server crash by
suddenly removing the network cable, a fact that results in an access error
when a client tries to read data from fs01 which stored the mounted online
volume:

```
# ping fs01
PING fs01.example.edu (192.168.127.145) 56(84) bytes of data.
From afs1.example.edu (192.168.127.154) icmp_seq=1 Destination Host Unreachable
From afs1.example.edu (192.168.127.154) icmp_seq=2 Destination Host Unreachable
From afs1.example.edu (192.168.127.154) icmp_seq=3 Destination Host Unreachable

--- fs01.example.edu ping statistics ---
5 packets transmitted, 0 received, +3 errors, 100% packet loss, time 4026ms, pipe 3

# ls /afs/example.edu/software/debian
ls: debian: Connection timed out
```

Note that a file server error affects only the volumes physically stored on
that particular host, while other parts of the AFS cell are not influenced by
the connection loss. Although the cell is up and running the VLDB still retains
an invalid information about the software.debian volume, locating it on the
failed server:

```
# vos listvldb -server fs01
VLDB entries for server fs01

root.afs
    RWrite: 536870915    ROnly: 536870916    Backup: 536870917
    number of sites -> 3
        server afs1.example.edu partition /vicepa RW Site
        server afs1.example.edu partition /vicepa RO Site
        server fs01.example.edu partition /vicepa RO Site

root.cell
    RWrite: 536870918    ROnly: 536870919    Backup: 536870920
    number of sites -> 3
        server afs1.example.edu partition /vicepa RW Site
        server afs1.example.edu partition /vicepa RO Site
        server fs01.example.edu partition /vicepa RO Site
```

```
software.debian
   RWrite: 536870935
   number of sites -> 1
      server fs01.example.edu partition /vicepa RW Site

Total entries: 3
```

To avoid any further errors and connection problems, first we remove all the references to `fs01` with the `remove` command of the `vos` tool, which removes all the information about a particular volume, partition or host in the VLDB:

```
# vos delentry -server fs01 -partition a
Deleting VLDB entries for server fs01 partition /vicepa
----------------------
Total VLDB entries deleted: 3; failed to delete: 0
```

The VLDB should be synchronized with the state of a currently working server in this case `afs1`. The synchronization process is done via `vos syncvldb`, a command symmetric to `syncserv`, correcting the invalid references to `fs01`:

```
# vos syncvldb -server afs1
VLDB synchronized with state of server afs1

# vos listvldb
VLDB entries for all servers

cell.services
   RWrite: 536870931    Backup: 536870933
   number of sites -> 1
      server afs1.example.edu partition /vicepa RW Site

cell.software
   RWrite: 536870924    Backup: 536870926
   number of sites -> 1
      server afs1.example.edu partition /vicepa RW Site

cell.users
   RWrite: 536870921    Backup: 536870923
   number of sites -> 1
      server afs1.example.edu partition /vicepa RW Site

root.afs
   RWrite: 536870915    ROnly: 536870916    Backup: 536870917
   number of sites -> 2
      server afs1.example.edu partition /vicepa RW Site
      server afs1.example.edu partition /vicepa RO Site

root.cell
   RWrite: 536870918    ROnly: 536870919    Backup: 536870920
   number of sites -> 2
      server afs1.example.edu partition /vicepa RW Site
      server afs1.example.edu partition /vicepa RO Site

software.debian.copy
   RWrite: 536870940
   number of sites -> 1
      server afs1.example.edu partition /vicepa RW Site
```

```
Total entries: 6
```

In order to restore the failed volume, all we need is to bring online the copy, and rename it to `software.debian` with the `rename` command fed to the `vos` tool:

```
# vos online afs1 a software.debian.copy

# vos listvol afs1
Total number of volumes on server afs1 partition /vicepa: 13
cell.services               536870931 RW        2 K On-line
cell.services.backup        536870933 BK        2 K On-line
cell.software               536870924 RW        3 K On-line
cell.software.backup        536870926 BK        3 K On-line
cell.users                  536870921 RW        2 K On-line
cell.users.backup           536870923 BK        2 K On-line
root.afs                    536870915 RW        6 K On-line
root.afs.backup             536870917 BK        6 K On-line
root.afs.readonly           536870916 RO        6 K On-line
root.cell                   536870918 RW        5 K On-line
root.cell.backup            536870920 BK        5 K On-line
root.cell.readonly          536870919 RO        5 K On-line
software.debian.copy        536870940 RW   111241 K On-line

Total volumes onLine 13 ; Total volumes offLine 0 ; Total busy 0

# vos rename software.debian.copy software.debian
Renamed volume software.debian.copy to software.debian
```

After the volume is restored to the original name, the mount point associated with it is repaired and all its contents are again accessible to clients:

```
# cd debian/

# ls
ISO@  platforms/

# ls platforms/
i386_linux24/  i386_linux26/  i386_nt40/  ppc_darwin_70/  ppc_darwin_80/
```

Note that clients may require time to synchronize their caches to the new volume configuration. When the file server is capable again of communicating with the database servers, its internal volume database retains knowledge of `software.debian`, which has been actually replaced. A `vos remove` command is not applicable in this situation since the VLDB correctly locates the volume on `afs1`. The AFS `vos` tool provides a command named `zap` that removes a volume from a file server regardless of any information on the VLDB. In order to restore a valid situation on the file server we need to `zap` the volume on `fs01` using its numerical ID, thus avoiding any volume name conflicts:

```
# vos zap fs01 a -id 536870935
Volume 536870935 deleted
```

Read-Only Volumes as Backups

Another new feature added to OpenAFS, and again not back-compatible with Transarc or IBM versions of the AFS file system, is the ability to convert read-only volumes to write-enabled ones. Again for didactic and testing purposes we focus on the `software.debian` volume, which is correctly mounted as the following output shows:

```
# cd /afs/example.edu/software/

# fs lsmount debian
'debian' is a mount point for volume '#software.debian'
```

We are now going to explicitly mount the volume in a write-enabled state and create replication sites, and release the read-write volume so that all changes are synchronized with its replicas. Let us first create a write-enabled mount point:

```
# fs rmmount debian

# fs mkmount debian software.debian -rw

# fs lsmount debian
'debian' is a mount point for volume '%software.debian'
```

Next a replication site is created on the `afs1` host, and then synchronized with the write-enabled volume:

```
# vos addsite afs1 a software.debian
Added replication site afs1 /vicepa for volume software.debian

# vos release software.debian
Released volume software.debian successfully

# vos listvol afs1
Total number of volumes on server afs1 partition /vicepa: 13
cell.services               536870931 RW          2 K On-line
cell.services.backup        536870933 BK          2 K On-line
cell.software               536870924 RW          3 K On-line
cell.software.backup        536870926 BK          3 K On-line
cell.users                  536870921 RW          2 K On-line
cell.users.backup           536870923 BK          2 K On-line
root.afs                    536870915 RW          6 K On-line
root.afs.backup             536870917 BK          6 K On-line
root.afs.readonly           536870916 RO          6 K On-line
root.cell                   536870918 RW          5 K On-line
root.cell.backup            536870920 BK          5 K On-line
root.cell.readonly          536870919 RO          5 K On-line
software.debian.readonly    536870942 RO     111241 K On-line

Total volumes onLine 13 ; Total volumes offLine 0 ; Total busy 0

# vos listvol fs01
Total number of volumes on server fs01 partition /vicepa: 1
software.debian             536870940 RW     111241 K On-line

Total volumes onLine 1 ; Total volumes offLine 0 ; Total busy 0
```

We notice the presence of a `software.debian.readonly` volume on `afs1`. As we have previously shown, we simulate a file server loss by detaching the network cable of `fs01` which contains the `software.debian` volume. The `/afs/example.edu/software/debian` mount point is no longer available:

```
# touch /afs/example.edu/software/debian/ddd
touch: cannot touch '/afs/example.edu/software/debian/ddd': Connection timed out
```

The `vos` tool can be used with the `convertROtoRW` command that actually converts a replica to a fully operable write-enabled volume, asking for confirmation first:

```
# vos convertROtoRW afs1 a software.debian.readonly
VLDB indicates that a RW volume exists already on fs01.example.edu in partition /vicepa.
Overwrite this VLDB entry? [y|n] (n)
y
```

At this point, the new volume may require a `salvage` command in case some data has been modified creating inconsistencies between the read-only and the write-enabled volumes. The command can be easily issued by the `bos` tool, and the results can be seen in the following output:

```
# bos salvage afs1 a software.debian
Starting salvage.
bos: salvage completed

# vos listvol afs1
Total number of volumes on server afs1 partition /vicepa: 13
cell.services                536870931 RW        2 K On-line
cell.services.backup         536870933 BK        2 K On-line
cell.software                536870924 RW        3 K On-line
cell.software.backup         536870926 BK        3 K On-line
cell.users                   536870921 RW        2 K On-line
cell.users.backup            536870923 BK        2 K On-line
root.afs                     536870915 RW        6 K On-line
root.afs.backup              536870917 BK        6 K On-line
root.afs.readonly            536870916 RO        6 K On-line
root.cell                    536870918 RW        5 K On-line
root.cell.backup             536870920 BK        5 K On-line
root.cell.readonly           536870919 RO        5 K On-line
software.debian              536870940 RW   111241 K On-line

Total volumes onLine 13 ; Total volumes offLine 0 ; Total busy 0
```

Again, clients may require some time to cope with the new configuration. When the file server is brought online it needs a small adjustment removing the `software.debian` volume:

```
# vos remove -server fs01 -partition vicepa -id software.debian
WARNING: Volume 536870940 does not exist in VLDB on server and partition
Volume 536870940 on partition /vicepa server fs01.example.edu deleted
```

5.5 Testing OpenAFS

In the previous chapters we moved the password of the `testuser` entry into the Kerberos database, and all the information (e.g. shell, home directory, real name) in the LDAP tree. OpenAFS gets now employed to remove the `testuser` home directory, creating a volume and placing it in the AFS file space.

5.5.1 Users and Groups

The `testuser` has access to a private location in the AFS file space, which contains its home directory. In order to allow specified users and groups, including `testuser`, to access AFS volumes, we need to create the proper entries in the protection database. The `testuser` item is created via `pts createuser` matching the name with the user name in the LDAP tree:

```
# pts createuser testuser -id 10000
User testuser has id 10000
```

Note as we chose the protection database user ID duplicating the UNIX UID, but this is a completely customary choice. Next we need to create the proper group and assign `testuser` to the `testgroup`, whose ID is again matched with the UNIX GID:

```
# pts creategroup testgroup -id -10000
group testgroup has id -10000

# pts adduser testuser testgroup

# pts membership testuser
Groups testuser (id: 10000) is a member of:
  testgroup

# pts membership testgroup
Members of testgroup (id: -10000) are:
  testuser
```

5.5.2 User Volumes

The private home space becomes an AFS volume mounted in the previously created container volume `cell.users`, with a proper disk quota depending on the needs of the user. In this example we grant 1 gigabyte of disk quota on the `fs01` file server. The user volumes are named with a particular format that would help an automated backup operation, our choice is `user.username`, in this case it would be `user.testuser`:

```
# vos create fs01 a user.testuser -maxquota 1000000
Volume 536870946 created on partition /vicepa of fs01

# cd /afs/example.edu/users
```

```
# fs mkmount testuser user.testuser

# ls -l
total 2
drwxrwxrwx  2 root root 2048 2006-06-22 12:17 testuser/
```

Note that we were allowed to mount the volume directly in the AFS space belonging to `cell.users`, since this container volume has no read-only counterpart. In case it had one, we should have mounted the `user.testuser` volume in the read-write enabled one and then release the container.

Home Structure

The volume `user.testuser` as we know inherits the standard ACLs for the system administrators. Obviously we shall grant all the privileges to the volume owner, `testuser`, who is entitled to use the disk space at its will:

```
# fs setacl -dir testuser -acl testuser all

# fs listacl testuser
Access list for testuser is
Normal rights:
  system:administrators rlidwka
  testuser rlidwka
```

Note that usually any user is be allowed to list the contents, a property that is useful for some services you may want to implement in the AFS file space:

```
# fs setacl -dir testuser -acl system:anyuser l

# fs listacl testuser
Access list for testuser is
Normal rights:
  system:administrators rlidwka
  system:anyuser l
  testuser rlidwka
```

A user space usually comprehends some directories that are used by services and other users. A common practice is to provide users with three directories: a private one, a completely public space (which is going to be used by a future web service for personal home pages), and another one accessible by cell users as for the `software.debian` volume. It is better to change the ownership of the home directory to the proper values, since OpenAFS relies on a UNIX architecture and just the access control lists might not be sufficient privileges:

```
# fs listacl local/
Access list for local/ is
Normal rights:
  system:administrators rlidwka
  system:authuser rl
  testuser rlidwka
```

```
# fs listacl private/
Access list for private/ is
Normal rights:
  system:administrators rlidwka
  testuser rlidwka

# fs listacl public/
Access list for public/ is
Normal rights:
  system:administrators rlidwka
  system:anyuser rl
  testuser rlidwka

# chown -R testuser:testgroup testuser/
```

5.5.3 Backup Volumes

A usual practice is to provide users backup volumes in order to lessen the probability of data loss. The preferred method of providing a backup facility is through the employment of backup volumes, since it allows system administrators to schedule massive dumps for all the user volumes, or part of it. Let us create the backup volume for the new **testuser**:

```
# vos backup user.testuser
Created backup volume for user.testuser

# vos listvol fs01
Total number of volumes on server fs01 partition /vicepa: 2
user.testuser                  536870946 RW          8 K On-line
user.testuser.backup           536870948 BK          8 K On-line

Total volumes onLine 2 ; Total volumes offLine 0 ; Total busy 0
```

The BOS server should now be instructed to handle a **cron** type instance that we call **backupuser**, which starts a backup dump for all the volumes whose names begin with **user** at 5am:

```
# bos create afs1 backupuser cron -cmd "/usr/bin/vos backupsys -prefix user -localauth" \
"05:00"

# bos status -long afs1
Instance buserver, (type is simple) currently running normally.
    Process last started at Thu Jun 22 11:12:10 2006 (1 proc starts)
    Command 1 is '/usr/lib/openafs/buserver'

Instance ptserver, (type is simple) currently running normally.
    Process last started at Thu Jun 22 11:12:10 2006 (1 proc starts)
    Command 1 is '/usr/lib/openafs/ptserver'

Instance vlserver, (type is simple) currently running normally.
    Process last started at Thu Jun 22 11:12:10 2006 (1 proc starts)
    Command 1 is '/usr/lib/openafs/vlserver'

Instance fs, (type is fs) currently running normally.
    Auxiliary status is: file server running.
    Process last started at Thu Jun 22 11:12:10 2006 (2 proc starts)
    Command 1 is '/usr/lib/openafs/fileserver'
```

```
    Command 2 is '/usr/lib/openafs/volserver'
    Command 3 is '/usr/lib/openafs/salvager'

Instance backuproot, (type is cron) currently running normally.
    Auxiliary status is: run next at Fri Jun 23 01:00:00 2006.
    Command 1 is '/usr/bin/vos backupsys -prefix root -localauth'
    Command 2 is '01:00'

Instance backupcell, (type is cron) currently running normally.
    Auxiliary status is: run next at Fri Jun 23 03:00:00 2006.
    Command 1 is '/usr/bin/vos backupsys -prefix cell -localauth'
    Command 2 is '03:00'

Instance backupuser, (type is cron) currently running normally.
    Auxiliary status is: run next at Fri Jun 23 05:00:00 2006.
    Command 1 is '/usr/bin/vos backupsys -prefix user -localauth'
    Command 2 is '05:00'
```

Mounting Backup Volumes

It is a useful policy to make backup volumes available to users. Each time a
backupsys operation is performed, all the .backup volumes are updated. By
making these volumes available to users we allow them to have an easy access
to an old version of their own home directory:

```
# cd testuser/

# fs mkmount .backup user.testuser.backup
```

The new mount point gives users the ability to retrieve deleted files, up to
the last executed backup operation:

```
# ls -al
total 12
drwxrwxrwx  5 testuser testgroup 2048 2006-06-22 12:46 ./
drwxrwxrwx  2 root     root      2048 2006-06-22 12:17 ../
drwxrwxrwx  5 testuser testgroup 2048 2006-06-22 12:32 .backup/
drwxr-xr-x  2 testuser testgroup 2048 2006-06-22 12:27 local/
drwxr-xr-x  2 testuser testgroup 2048 2006-06-22 12:27 private/
drwxr-xr-x  2 testuser testgroup 2048 2006-06-22 12:27 public/

# ls -al .backup/
total 10
drwxrwxrwx  5 testuser testgroup 2048 2006-06-22 12:32 ./
drwxrwxrwx  5 testuser testgroup 2048 2006-06-22 12:46 ../
drwxr-xr-x  2 testuser testgroup 2048 2006-06-22 12:27 local/
drwxr-xr-x  2 testuser testgroup 2048 2006-06-22 12:27 private/
drwxr-xr-x  2 testuser testgroup 2048 2006-06-22 12:27 public/
```

5.5.4 LDAP Information

Users in our organization rely on AFS for their home directories. The LDAP
database should now be updated by removing the reference to the local
/home/testuser/ directory. Then the testuser entry should be modified
by changing its homeDirectory attribute with the following LDIF file, and
by issuing an ldapmodify command:

```
# cat diff.ldif
dn: uid=testuser,ou=users,dc=example,dc=edu
homeDirectory: /afs/example.edu/users/testuser

# ldapmodify -f diff.ldif
SASL/GSSAPI authentication started
SASL username: sysadmin@EXAMPLE.EDU
SASL SSF: 56
SASL installing layers
modifying entry "uid=testuser,ou=users,dc=example,dc=edu"
```

Note that we have been authenticated successfully as **sysadmin** via SASL using the GSSAPI library for MIT Kerberos V. The command exited successfully, and the updated attribute can be searched as usual:

```
# ldapsearch -LLL "uid=testuser" homeDirectory
SASL/GSSAPI authentication started
SASL username: sysadmin@EXAMPLE.EDU
SASL SSF: 56
SASL installing layers
dn: uid=testuser,ou=users,dc=example,dc=edu
homeDirectory: /afs/example.edu/users/testuser
```

5.5.5 PAM and OpenAFS

The incremental tests of our infrastructure led to move all the information to a distributed system of databases, as we have done in the preceding chapters. User information was moved from the legacy UNIX files to LDAP and passwords to the Kerberos database. In order to relocate passwords and let users login in the system, we introduced PAM and the Kerberos authentication module.

Our **testuser** is allowed to login, but **testuser** is not allowed to access the home directory on AFS: there are Kerberos tickets, but no AFS tokens. Users may be forced to use the **aklog** tool upon login in textual mode, but in a fully-fledged system the process should be automated. The PAM authentication modules provide a way of achieving the goal of obtaining an AFS token upon login, installing the **libpam-openafs-session** package. This package provides a session module that basically runs **aklog** upon login, and should be made available in the **common-session** PAM configuration file:

```
# cat common-session
session required        pam_unix.so
session optional        pam_openafs_session.so
```

The above modification is sufficient to allow **testuser**, as any other user in our organization, to login via a Kerberos password, and obtaining from the initial ticket a valid AFS token that allows a full access to the home directory. The output of a typical login session is as follows:

```
Debian GNU/Linux 3.1 client tty6

client login: testuser
Password:
Last login: Thu Jun 22 13:05:11 2006 on tty6
Linux client 2.4.27-3-686 #1 Wed Feb 8 12:40:33 UTC 2006 i686 GNU/Linux

The programs included with the Debian GNU/Linux system are free software;
the exact distribution terms for each program are described in the
individual files in /usr/share/doc/*/copyright.

Debian GNU/Linux comes with ABSOLUTELY NO WARRANTY, to the extent
permitted by applicable law.

testuser@client:~$ tokens

Tokens held by the Cache Manager:

User's (AFS ID 10000) tokens for afs@example.edu [Expires Jun 22 23:05]
   --End of list--

testuser@client:~$ klist
Ticket cache: FILE:/tmp/krb5cc_10000_MLnruP
Default principal: testuser@EXAMPLE.EDU

Valid starting      Expires            Service principal
06/22/06 13:05:28   06/22/06 23:05:28  host/client.example.edu@EXAMPLE.EDU
06/22/06 13:05:28   06/22/06 23:05:28  krbtgt/EXAMPLE.EDU@EXAMPLE.EDU
06/22/06 13:05:28   06/22/06 23:05:28  afs/example.edu@EXAMPLE.EDU


Kerberos 4 ticket cache: /tmp/tkt10000
klist: You have no tickets cached
```

Note as the pam_openafs_session.so provides the user with a token for
the AFS service.

Practice

Exercise 17. Plan an AFS cell for your needs. Will you make it available
world-wide, how are your default permissions, and which platforms do you
want to support? It is recommended to change the secret of the afs/CELLNAME
principal regularly and to update all database and file servers accordingly.

Exercise 18. What can be a good backup strategy for you, are tapes or
disks sufficient? Which is the method of your choice taking new OpenAFS
commands into account? Where do you mount backup or some other previous
state volumes?

Exercise 19. PTS groups do not have to be reflected in LDAP, nevertheless
some LDAP groups might be convenient to restrict access via PAM. What
about project organization? Those need project space and maybe two PTS
groups, an administrative one managing another member group.

Exercise 20. Sun Microsystems released a version of its operating system as
open source called OpenSolaris. The Nexenta operating system has the goal

to combine the OpenSoaris kernel with the package mechanism known from Debian and Ubuntu. Try a Nexenta host as a file server machine compiled with the `namei` option, having the `/vicepX` partitions on the new ZFS file system.

6

Samba

Opening Windows to a wider world.
The Samba Team

6.1 Samba and Server Message Block

Back in time when networking was expensive, and equipment was owned by few institutions, IBM commissioned the Sytek Inc. to develop a solution for small networks. The resulting protocol, released with the PC-Network platform in 1983, was called NetBIOS, the *Network Basic Input Output System*, and soon became the de-facto standard working over IPX/SPX used by Novell for their Netware OS, as well as over the TCP protocol. The NetBIOS protocol provided name and service resolution in IP addresses, although these names are not to be confused with the host names. This resolution of names, limited to 16 bytes, allows clients to communicate between each other establishing a *session*.

On the top of NetBIOS, IBM developed the SMB protocol, the acronym of *Server Message Block*, mainly used in the DOS operating system, and later renamed by Microsoft in 1986 as CIFS, or *Common Internet File System*, adding features like symbolic links and the ability of working without NetBIOS: besides the efforts to avoid NetBIOS, its support is still critical in Windows-based networks. This protocol involves frequent broadcasts of a client's presence on the network, a fact usually avoidable employing a WINS server, *Windows Internet Naming Service.*

Originally Microsoft implemented a client to client infrastructure based on SMB called *Workgroup*, where each host could be considered independent, allowing other computers to access resources that the host voluntarily shared. Later the concept of *Domain* was introduced, a logical group of connected computers, sharing a common centralized security database.

A domain is administered by a set of *controllers*, a *Primary Domain Controller*, or PDC, and possibly several *Backup Domain Controllers*. These servers contain the administrative information about computers, users, and groups, and may be compared with the previous servers we have implemented, with LDAP and Kerberos. In fact, the new version of Windows Domains released by Microsoft with Windows 2000, called *Active Directory*, or AD, re-

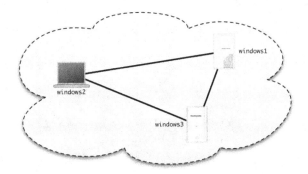

Fig. 6.1. A Windows Workgroup as a loose group of peers

moves the primary and backup domain controller distinction, and actually uses LDAP for information retrieval and Kerberos V for authentication. The Samba software is the open-source implementation of a Windows Domain controller, and can act both as a PDC and BDC. Although Samba can fully cooperate with a real Active Directory domain, it cannot perform as a primary server in this case. The future version Samba 4 should implement all the requirements (LDAP and Kerberos) to emulate a complete AD domain.

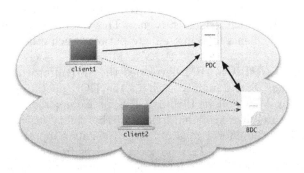

Fig. 6.2. A Windows Domain administered by a PDC and an eventual BDC

The path we will follow in this chapter differs slightly from the previous ones. We first install Samba emulating the old Windows Workgroup for sharing a directory, then we implement a local PDC. Once accustomed with the terminology used in Windows networks, we create an LDAP based Samba PDC and BDC. Since Windows networking information may get quite complicated, we avoid to use our previously installed LDAP servers: we create a brand new LDAP master for out PDC and a slave when implementing the BDC.

6.2 Understanding Samba

In the following sections we are going to install and configure Samba by first creating a simple share within a legacy Windows Workgroup, and then we focus on creating a Primary Domain Controller, where all the security information gets stored on the equivalent of UNIX files like /etc/passwd, /etc/group, and /etc/shadow.

Our Samba domain name will be WIN.EXAMPLE.EDU, and the workgroup name, coincides with it: this choice was made in order to avoid interferences with the DNS name or the LDAP root. The host running Samba is called smb1.example.edu, and should be properly available through the DNS service.

6.2.1 A Windows Workgroup

The Samba server is provided by Debian with the samba package, installable via the standard apt-get tool:

```
# apt-get install samba
```

As usual Debian configures the Samba server. The workgroup name is WIN.EXAMPLE.EDU as said before, and in our installation we do not make use of any WINS servers. The Samba server we are installing runs as a daemon and not on demand as we did for the kpropd process. The installer asks if we would like to populate the Samba security database with the UNIX users present on our system: our choice is to avoid this automated process since we create our users by hand for didactic purposes. Finally Debian starts the Samba daemon, and we need to stop it before proceeding with the configuration.

Simple File Sharing

As previously introduced, Windows Workgroups actually share resources but do not share any other security information. Our choice is to provide a simple read-only shared directory located on the Samba server in /home/shared/. This directory contains a simple text file which is accessible to any guest user, meaning that on the server side, the location should retain the following permission bits:

```
# ls -ld shared
drwxr-xr-x  2 root staff 4096 2006-06-22 17:05 shared/
```

In this location we then create a file in order to test the access from a Windows client. The Samba configuration file is located in /etc/samba/ and is named smb.conf. The file has been created by the Debian installer so it is safe to remove or rename it since we are going to modify it completely. The syntax is similar to the the legacy Windows configuration files WIN.INI and

SYSTEM.INI, with stanzas in the form [SECTION], with semicolon and pound
(; and #, the legacy sign and the usual UNIX character) indicating comments.

The mandatory section for both workgroup and domain is called [global]
and contains all the primary information about the Samba server. Our configuration sets the current workgroup name to WIN.EXAMPLE.EDU, the host
NetBIOS name to SMB1, and the Samba security level to share. The resulting
configuration file looks like the following:

```
[global]
workgroup = WIN.EXAMPLE.EDU
netbios name = SMB1
server string = Samba Sharing Server
security = share

[share]
path = /home/shared
comment = Our Samba Share
read only = yes
guest ok = yes
```

We have already introduced the meaning of the workgroup name (or Domain name) comparing it to the Kerberos realm, and the NetBIOS name to
a DNS host name, while the directive server string is a comment that will
appear on clients.

The security field, which identifies how the Samba server behaves on the
network, accepts the following settings:

ads Samba joins an existing Windows Active Directory Domain;
domain Samba joins an existing Windows Domain;
server Legacy security mode, currently deprecated;
share Samba joins a Windows Workgroup with host sharing resources;
user Samba acts as a Domain Controller of a Windows Domain.

Since our primary objective is to share a directory, we choose the share security level, actually instructing Samba to act as a normal Windows machine.
The shared resources are described by the following stanzas in the configuration file. In our example, we have prepared a shared resource named share, as
indicated by the stanza [share]. It is mandatory in our file sharing example
to set the path of the resource, and we allow guests to access directories and
read files, as the guest ok setting imply. We can test the configuration file
with the testparm tool:

```
# testparm
Load smb config files from /etc/samba/smb.conf
Processing section "[share]"
Loaded services file OK.
Server role: ROLE_STANDALONE
Press enter to see a dump of your service definitions

# Global parameters
[global]
        workgroup = WIN.EXAMPLE.EDU
        netbios name = SMB1
```

```
        server string = Samba Sharing Server
        security = SHARE

[share]
        comment = Our Samba Share
        path = /home/share
        guest ok = Yes
```

The program loads the `smb.conf` file and analyzes it for syntactical errors. Moreover, it determines the role of our Samba server in the network, in this case a simple stand-alone host. It is safe to start the server which runs both the NetBIOS and SMB daemons:

```
# /etc/init.d/samba start
Starting Samba daemons: nmbd smbd.
```

In order to try the new service, we install the `smbclient` package, allowing us to query the Samba server directly. The `smbclient` tool can be used to contact the server and query all the running services on the machine with the -L switch:

```
# smbclient -L localhost
Password:
Domain=[WIN.EXAMPLE.EDU] OS=[Unix] Server=[Samba 3.0.14a-Debian]

        Sharename       Type        Comment
        ---------       ----        -------
        share           Disk        Our Samba Share
        IPC$            IPC         IPC Service (Samba Sharing Server)
        ADMIN$          IPC         IPC Service (Samba Sharing Server)
Domain=[WIN.EXAMPLE.EDU] OS=[Unix] Server=[Samba 3.0.14a-Debian]

        Server                  Comment
        ---------               -------
        SMB1                    Samba Sharing Server

        Workgroup               Master
        ---------               -------
        WIN.EXAMPLE.EDU
```

The password is not specified by the system, so leaving it blank (i.e. hitting return without entering any string) should work properly. As we can see from the output, we are running a Debian-based Samba server with NetBIOS name SMB1 and a custom shared resource, whose type is Disk, named share. The shared directory and its contents appears on a Windows client after joining the WIN.EXAMPLE.EDU workgroup and viewing all the workgroup computers under *My Network Places*. Samba creates the /etc/samba/smbpasswd file which contains all Samba passwords for Windows users, the analogous of /etc/shadow. Our file sharing server has a guest account enabled, which is identified on the Samba side by a nobody user, with an invalid password:

```
# cat /etc/samba/smbpasswd
nobody:65534:XXXXXXXXXXXXXXXXXXXXXXXXXXXXXXXX:XXXXXXXXXXXXXXXXXXXXXXXXXXXXXXXX:\
[DU         ]:LCT-00000000:
```

6.2.2 A Simple Windows Domain

A Domain, as we previewed, is a group of computers sharing security information about machines, groups, and users. Samba may act as a Primary Domain Controller, as we will see in the following of this section, and the Samba server may be compared to both LDAP and Kerberos services we have previously configured. Windows clients then login using the Domain security accounts, and have their profile—the equivalent of the home directory in UNIX, containing personal files and settings—created on the server (actually profiles are cached by default on the client).

In the following we are going to create a Domain called WIN.EXAMPLE.EDU, assuming we have installed a brand new Samba server as previously seen. In case we have the intention of removing completely the previous installation, we may issue the following command:

```
# apt-get remove --purge samba samba-common
```

The --purge indicates the Debian tool to completely remove the package including all configuration files. So let us reinstall the samba package and configure it as required by Debian, and finally stop the service.

The domain name is described in the smb.conf file in the workgroup field, and the NetBIOS name we are going to use for the PDC is SMBPDC: in the following sections we are going to create a Backup Domain Controller for redundancy reasons. The security level for the Samba server is user since our machine behaves as a PDC on the network, and we allow users to login in the domain with the domain logons setting. A primary domain controller is the domain master server on the network, and there should be only one: Samba allows also an auto setting for an automatic master election. All these settings concur with the [global] stanza:

```
[global]
workgroup = WIN.EXAMPLE.EDU
netbios name = SMBPDC
server string = Samba Domain Master
security = user
add machine script = /usr/sbin/useradd -s /bin/false -d /tmp '%u'
domain logons = yes
domain master = yes
enable privileges = yes

[netlogon]
path = /home/%U
comment = Samba Domain Login Service
valid users = %S
read only = no

[profiles]
path = /home/%U
comment = User Profile Service
valid users = %S
guest ok = no
read only = no
writable = yes
```

```
browsable = no

[homes]
path = /home/%U
comment = User Home Directory
valid users = %S
guest ok = no
read only = no
writable = yes
browsable = no
```

Let us inspect the configuration file analyzing its contents. The last setting in the [global] stanza allows us to set privileges to groups and users, forcing Samba to honor the granted rights: this setting is the analogous of adding an AFS user to the system:administrators group when dealing with domain administrators, as we shall see shortly. The directive add machine script tells Samba how to add a host joining the domain: Samba relies on UNIX users and needs accounts for hosts in /etc/passwd. The script used by our configuration adds a new user with no login capability—the shell is the /bin/false program—and with a username equal to the client machine name. Without adding the UNIX entity Samba will deny domain logins.

The special stanza [netlogon] is the mandatory share when enabling users to perform domain logins. Users may be issued a special login script—the analogous of a .profile or .bashrc in the UNIX world—and such a script must be a relative path to the netlogon service, which in this case is translated into a subdirectory of /home/. The special variables %U and %S indicate the session user name and the requested service, respectively. The most used variables are shown in Table 6.1, but for a more comprehensive list of variables consult the manual page of smb.conf shipped with your Samba distribution. An eventual user login script is then referred to a relative path

Table 6.1. Variable substitution in the Samba configuration file (excerpt)

Variable	Substitution
%D	Domain or workgroup name for the current user
%h	Internet host name of the Samba server
%L	NetBIOS Samba server name
%m	NetBIOS client name
%M	Internet host name of the client
%S	Current requested service name
%U	Session username as indicated by the client

inside the directory /home/%U, for instance our testuser has a login script file inside /home/testuser/. Domain logins are restricted by the valid users directive to valid service names, and such a share is write-enabled.

The Windows-counterparts of home directories are the *user profiles*, configured in the [profiles] stanza. The current setting locate user profiles in their home directory, since the path field is replaced by variable substitution.

It is fairly understandable to set profiles as write-enabled and disallow guest users for security reasons. A Windows user profile contains its registry information, application settings, and special folders as My Documents, Desktop, and Start Menu.

Last, the [homes] section indicates the current user home directory. The home directory is mounted as a new shared hard drive letter (e.g. Z:), and the same write policy has been applied to this share. We can use the testparm tool to check the settings:

```
# testparm
Load smb config files from /etc/samba/smb.conf
Processing section "[netlogon]"
Processing section "[profiles]"
Processing section "[homes]"
Loaded services file OK.
Server role: ROLE_DOMAIN_PDC
Press enter to see a dump of your service definitions

# Global parameters
[global]
        workgroup = WIN.EXAMPLE.EDU
        netbios name = SMBPDC
        server string = Samba Domain Master
        enable privileges = Yes
        add machine script = /usr/sbin/useradd -s /bin/false -d /tmp '%u'
        domain logons = Yes
        domain master = Yes

[netlogon]
        comment = Samba Domain Login Service
        path = /home/%U
        valid users = %S
        read only = No

[profiles]
        comment = User Profile Service
        path = /home/%U
        valid users = %S
        read only = No
        browseable = No

[homes]
        comment = User Home Directory
        path = /home/%U
        valid users = %S
        read only = No
```

The output correctly shows that the host will be a PDC on the network for our WIN.EXAMPLE.EDU domain, and its NetBIOS name will be SMBPDC. Now the Samba server can be started.

User Mapping

Unfortunately Samba needs the root user to be in its security database, a fact that we will avoid later with the help of the admin group which has been created together with the admin user. The first operation is to provide the Samba server with the root password, adding this new user to the security list. This is achieved with the `smbpasswd` tool, which changes Samba user passwords providing the `-a` switch to add new entries:

```
# smbpasswd -a root
New SMB password:
Retype new SMB password:
Added user root.
```

The Samba server may be configured and queried via the `net` tool. This program is fed with commands intended to interact with a Windows domain using `rpc`, an AD domain using `ads`, and a legacy support using `rap` (e.g. the OS/2 system and earlier Samba versions). Our objective is to grant the `admin` user all administrative rights so that we can remove `root`. To query the list of Samba rights, we issue the following command with the help of the only administrative user, `root`:

```
# net rpc rights list -U root
Password:
    SeMachineAccountPrivilege  Add machines to domain
     SePrintOperatorPrivilege  Manage printers
          SeAddUsersPrivilege  Add users and groups to the domain
    SeRemoteShutdownPrivilege  Force shutdown from a remote system
       SeDiskOperatorPrivilege  Manage disk shares
```

Currently we have no privileges assigned to any account, as we can see in the following output:

```
# net rpc rights list accounts -U root
Password:
BUILTIN\Print Operators
No privileges assigned

BUILTIN\Account Operators
No privileges assigned

BUILTIN\Backup Operators
No privileges assigned

BUILTIN\Server Operators
No privileges assigned

WIN.EXAMPLE.EDU\root
No privileges assigned

BUILTIN\Administrators
No privileges assigned

Everyone
No privileges assigned
```

Windows domains have predefined user and groups, similar to the AFS predefined ones: one of these groups is for instance the `Domain Admins`, the equivalent of our `system:administrators` in the AFS space. Any user belonging to this group of our domain gets granted all the rights, with the following `net` command:

```
# net rpc rights grant "WIN.EXAMPLE.EDU\Domain Admins" SeMachineAccountPrivilege \
SePrintOperatorPrivilege SeAddUsersPrivilege SeRemoteShutdownPrivilege \
SeDiskOperatorPrivilege -U root
Password:
Successfully granted rights.

# net rpc rights list accounts -U root
Password:
BUILTIN\Print Operators
No privileges assigned

BUILTIN\Account Operators
No privileges assigned

BUILTIN\Backup Operators
No privileges assigned

BUILTIN\Server Operators
No privileges assigned

WIN.EXAMPLE.EDU\root
No privileges assigned

WIN.EXAMPLE.EDU\Domain Admins
SeMachineAccountPrivilege
SePrintOperatorPrivilege
SeAddUsersPrivilege
SeRemoteShutdownPrivilege
SeDiskOperatorPrivilege

BUILTIN\Administrators
No privileges assigned

Everyone
No privileges assigned
```

The operation ended successfully as we see in the output shown above. What we need now, is to map the UNIX group called admin to Domain Admins, so that any UNIX user in the group could administer the Windows domain. The mapping operation is done with the groupmap command of the net tool:

```
# net groupmap modify ntgroup="Domain Admins" unixgroup="admin"
Updated mapping entry for Domain Admins

# net groupmap list
System Operators (S-1-5-32-549) -> -1
Domain Admins (S-1-5-21-3266971356-1389114676-386038377-512) -> admin
Replicators (S-1-5-32-552) -> -1
Guests (S-1-5-32-546) -> -1
Domain Guests (S-1-5-21-3266971356-1389114676-386038377-514) -> -1
Domain Users (S-1-5-21-3266971356-1389114676-386038377-513) -> -1
Domain Admins (S-1-5-21-3314377433-826363095-127981249-512) -> -1
Power Users (S-1-5-32-547) -> -1
Print Operators (S-1-5-32-550) -> -1
Administrators (S-1-5-32-544) -> -1
Domain Users (S-1-5-21-3314377433-826363095-127981249-513) -> -1
Account Operators (S-1-5-32-548) -> -1
Backup Operators (S-1-5-32-551) -> -1
Domain Guests (S-1-5-21-3314377433-826363095-127981249-514) -> -1
Users (S-1-5-32-545) -> -1
```

The meaning of the strings between parentheses will be explained later in this chapter. Additionally to the `admin` group we had an homonymous user belonging to this group. We finish the user configuration by adding the `admin` user to the Samba security list, and then safely remove the `root` user:

```
# smbpasswd -a admin
New SMB password:
Retype new SMB password:
Added user admin.

# smbpasswd -x root
Deleted user root.
```

We stress the fact that the `admin` UNIX user belongs to the `admin` group previously mapped to the `Domain Admins`: this allows `admin` to administer the domain avoiding the use of `root`.

Domain Join

Microsoft Windows XP can join our domain provided that the version of XP is not the "Home Edition", and that the Administrator modifies a value in the Windows registry. The field that needs to be modified is called `RequireSignOrSeal` in the net logon subsection:

```
[HKEY_LOCAL_MACHINE\SYSTEM\CurrentControlSet\Services\Netlogon\Parameters]
requiresignorseal=dword:00000000
```

Setting the parameter to 0, instead of the default value 1, enables Windows XP Professional to join other types of domains besides Active Directory. Joining a domain is a procedure that a Windows system administrator can

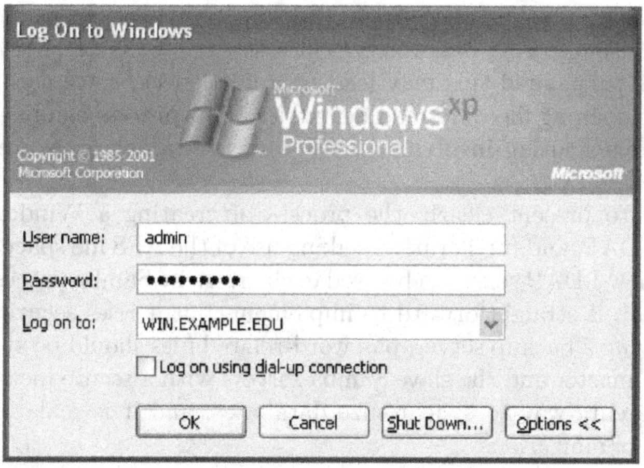

Fig. 6.3. The Windows XP login dialog box

perform through the control panel, specifying the domain name, in our case WIN.EXAMPLE.EDU. The system prompts for an administrative login: a system may join a domain if a domain administrator allows this operation. Our domain administrator is the admin user, and after successfully logging into the domain and rebooting the system, we are prompted with the login dialog box as in Fig. 6.3.

The only known domain user is admin, the domain administrator itself. Logging into the system creates the proper profile both on the client and on the server. On the server side we observe that the profile has been successfully created according to the [profiles] section of smb.conf, in the user's home directory, with the default directory name profile:

```
# cd /home/admin/

# ls
profile/

# ls profile/
Application Data/  Favorites/     NTUSER.DAT*      PrintHood/  Start Menu/
Cookies/           My Documents/  NTUSER.DAT.LOG*  Recent/     Templates/
Desktop/           NetHood/       ntuser.ini       SendTo/
```

The [homes] share allows users to browse in their home directory on the Samba server, which is mounted on the client as a shared network drive. As a machine joins the domain, the add machine script command is executed, and a new UNIX user for the machine is created.

6.3 The Samba Domain

Our objective is to create a reliable Windows Domain, providing users a Primary Domain Controller as well as a Backup controller. In a real situation with several users storing passwords in files as /etc/passwd, /etc/shadow or /etc/samba/smbpasswd this may lead to a bottleneck, since each login process involves opening files and reading entries. This process can be speeded up with a scalable solution involving LDAP servers for lookup, as we have seen already.

In order to present clearly the process of creating a Windows domain employing LDAP, and furthermore making use of the AFS file space, we choose to install a new LDAP server to be used exclusively by Samba processes. A file-based solution is straightforward to implement, but it rises security concerns when deploying a backup server: password-related files should be synchronized between the master and the slave Samba servers with a secure method. LDAP provides a secure way to synchronize databases, and it is scalable from few users to big organizations.

6.3.1 LDAP Configuration

An LDAP-based architecture is a scalable solution for information retrieval, allowing administrators to create a network of servers mirroring the database for reliability reasons. Samba can make use of LDAP to store user information and critical data such as passwords, and it is the recommended architectural choice for production systems.

This section outlines the installation process of an LDAP server suitable for Samba, revealing the important differences with the operations introduced in the LDAP chapter. For a deeper discussion about configuration issues refer to the appropriate chapter.

The LDAP server we are about to install serves as a back-end for the Samba server, anyway Debian configures the `slapd` package asking for the DNS domain name. Debian uses this field to build the LDAP root's distinguished name: answering `win.example.edu` then causes the system to generate the root as `dc=win,dc=example,dc=edu`.

So now we have to create an LDAP server as we did before, installing the `slapd` package and configuring it: take as a reference the previous chapter with the following differences. Debian asks for the DNS domain to use, used to generate the root of the database. Therefore we use `win.example.edu` such that we have the root as said before. Stop LDAP after the installation. We apply the same procedure for the removal of the administrative entry by adding a hard coded administrator called `ldapadmin` in the `slapd.conf` configuration file:

```
rootdn   "cn=ldapadmin,dc=win,dc=example,dc=edu"
rootpw   ldapadmin
```

Note that the administrative password does not have to be in clear text, even though the file has restrictive permissions: `rootpw` line can contain encoded passwords as {CRYPT}password, {MD5}password, or {SHA}password, and can be generated with the help of the `slappasswd` command.

It is useful to install and configure the client-side tools so that after restarting the LDAP server, we can safely remove the entry `admin`—created by the Debian installer—using the `ldapadmin` distinguished name:

```
# ldapdelete -x -D "cn=ldapadmin,dc=win,dc=example,dc=edu" -w ldapadmin \
"cn=admin,dc=win,dc=example,dc=edu"
```

Samba Schema

In order to have `slapd` handle coherently all the attributes needed by Samba, we need to add the appropriate schema to the server configuration. The package shipping the configuration files is called `samba-doc`, and in `/usr/share/doc/samba-doc/examples/LDAP/` we find a compressed version of the schema file. Hence all we need is to decompress the archive in the proper location, that is `/etc/ldap/schema/`:

```
# cd /etc/ldap/schema/

# cp /usr/share/doc/samba-doc/examples/LDAP/samba.schema.gz

# gunzip samba.schema.gz
```

From now on there is a `samba.schema` file in the default schema location, and we can add it to the known LDAP schemas in `slapd.conf`:

```
include        /etc/ldap/schema/samba.schema
```

The last step before proceeding to install Samba is to allow users to modify their passwords. This operation cannot be accomplished by just allowing changes to the `userPassword` attribute, since Samba stores the Domain password and the legacy LanManager[1] one. The access control for these fields needs to be like the following:

```
access to attrs=userPassword,sambaNTPassword,sambaLMPassword
        by anonymous auth
        by self write
        by * none
```

The `slapd.conf` contains now the administrative password, and it should be readable by `root` only. After restarting `slapd` we may proceed installing Samba. It is assumed that this is going to be a fresh Samaba installation.

6.3.2 Installing Samba

It is a good option to install the `samba` server package along with the client tool `smbclient`. Additionally, we need to install the Samba-LDAP interaction tools, provided by Debian with the package named `smbldap-tools`. As usual the installer configures the services and starts the daemons, so we need to stop the Samba service before proceeding:

```
# apt-get install samba smbclient smbldap-tools

# /etc/init.d/samba stop
Stopping Samba daemons: nmbd smbd.
```

The [global] section of `smb.conf` undergoes a major change: the most important one is about the password back-end used by the service. Samba stores all the needed information in the LDAP tree, so we need to instruct the daemon about the server it is supposed to use through the `passdb backend` directive. This option is in the form `method:URI`, where the method can be for instance `tdbsam` or `smbpasswd` for a file-based solution, or `ldapsam` for an

---

[1] This is the old authentication method NTLMv1 derived from the first SMB implementation by IBM, called LanManager, using DES.

LDAP server; the URI specification is optional, and in our case it just specifies the local host 127.0.0.1.

Additionally we need to configure the LDAP suffix, the sub-trees devoted to the storage of Samba information, and the administrator distinguished name: this is needed since the service shall deeply interact with the LDAP daemon at an administrative level (e.g. in case a user changes its password). The Samba configuration file can look like the following:

```
[global]
workgroup = WIN.EXAMPLE.EDU
netbios name = SMBPDC
server string = Samba Domain Master
security = user
ldap passwd sync = yes
passdb backend = ldapsam:ldap://127.0.0.1/
ldap admin dn = cn=ldapadmin,dc=win,dc=example,dc=edu
ldap suffix = dc=win,dc=example,dc=edu
ldap group suffix = ou=Groups
ldap user suffix = ou=Users
ldap machine suffix = ou=Machines
add machine script = /usr/sbin/smbldap-useradd -w '%u'
domain logons = yes
domain master = yes
enable privileges = yes

[netlogon]
path = /home/%U
comment = Samba Domain Login Service
valid users = %S
read only = no
browsable = no

[profiles]
path = /home/%U
comment = User Profile Service
valid users = %U
guest ok = no
read only = no
writable = yes
browsable = no

[homes]
path = /home/%U
comment = User Home Directory
valid users = %U
guest ok = no
read only = no
writable = yes
browsable = no
```

We notice that the automatic machine adding script was modified in order to use the Samba-LDAP interaction tools. The LDAP administrator password shall now be added to the known passwords, observing how the LDAP configuration is already in use by the Samba tools:

```
# smbpasswd -w ldapadmin
Setting stored password for "cn=ldapadmin,dc=win,dc=example,dc=edu" in secrets.tdb
```

Domain Configuration

Windows domains are associated with a distinct identification string called *Security Identifier*, or SID, which is generated by the domain controller and uniquely determines the entries in the domain. The SID along with some ID determine an entry in the domain (e.g. a group or a user): UNIX users will be mapped to a Windows ID based on the domain SID.

There are known IDs in a domain symmetrically to UNIX UIDs, for instance an identifier SID-512 is the default domain administrators group, and SID-513 is the domain users group. Based on this mapping, we are able to use UNIX accounts on Windows clients through our Samba domain controller.

In order to retrieve the SID of our domain we need to use the **net** program with the **getlocalsid** command:

```
# net getlocalsid
SID for domain SMBPDC is: S-1-5-21-785093230-3453868100-3778353011
```

The SID S-1-5-21-785093230-3453868100-3778353011-512 then identifies our domain administrators group. Once read the SID, we may proceed configuring the LDAP interaction tools in /etc/smbldap-tools/. In this location we need to create the smbldap_bind.conf and smbldap.conf files, shipped by Debian with the tools themselves:

```
# cd /etc/smbldap-tools/

# cp /usr/share/doc/smbldap-tools/examples/smbldap_bind.conf .

# cp /usr/share/doc/smbldap-tools/examples/smbldap.conf.gz .

# gunzip smbldap.conf.gz

# ls -l
total 12
-rw-------  1 root root  428 2006-07-06 12:22 smbldap_bind.conf
-rw-r--r--  1 root root 6504 2006-07-06 12:22 smbldap.conf
```

The permission bits are critical since the smbldap_bind.conf file contains the necessary LDAP binding information, in other words, the administrative user and password used by Samba to store and modify the LDAP database:

```
slaveDN="cn=ldapadmin,dc=win,dc=example,dc=edu"
slavePw="ldapadmin"
masterDN="cn=ldapadmin,dc=win,dc=example,dc=edu"
masterPw="ldapadmin"
```

Note that we have only one LDAP server for our domain, so slave and master point to the same host, that is localhost. The other configuration file called smbldap.conf directs the tools to create correct LDAP entries suitable for Samba. This configuration file matches the entries in smb.conf, requiring for instance that users are stored in the Users organization unit; moreover, it

specifies the default UNIX properties and the encryption algorithm used by
Samba to store the password in the LDAP database:

```
SID="S-1-5-21-785093230-3453868100-3778353011"

slaveLDAP="127.0.0.1"
slavePort="389"

masterLDAP="127.0.0.1"
masterPort="389"

ldapTLS="0"
verify="require"
cafile="/etc/smbldap-tools/ca.pem"
clientcert="/etc/smbldap-tools/smbldap-tools.pem"
clientkey="/etc/smbldap-tools/smbldap-tools.key"

suffix="dc=win,dc=example,dc=edu"
usersdn="ou=Users,${suffix}"
computersdn="ou=Machines,${suffix}"
groupsdn="ou=Groups,${suffix}"
idmapdn="ou=Idmap,${suffix}"

sambaUnixIdPooldn="sambaDomainName=WIN.EXAMPLE.EDU,${suffix}"
scope="sub"
hash_encrypt="SSHA"
crypt_salt_format="%s"

userLoginShell="/bin/bash"
userHome="/home/%U"
userGecos="Samba User"
defaultUserGid="513"
defaultComputerGid="515"
skeletonDir="/etc/skel"
defaultMaxPasswordAge="99"

userSmbHome="\\%L\homes"
userProfile="\\%L\profiles\profile"
userHomeDrive="Z:"

userScript="%U.cmd"
mailDomain="example.edu"

with_smbpasswd="0"
smbpasswd="/usr/bin/smbpasswd"
with_slappasswd="0"
slappasswd="/usr/sbin/slappasswd"
```

The userSmbHome and userProfile are the Windows user home directory and profile, respectively, described by a Windows UNC following the
Universal Naming Convention. In UNIX systems the separator is the slash
character / while on Windows the backslash \ is used. The convention defines
then resources as \\server\name: the server name %L will be substituted with
SMBPDC, while homes and profiles will point to the path indicated by the
smb.conf shares [homes] and [profiles]: the user profile will be then located under the profile folder inside the user's home directory. We are now
ready to populate the LDAP tree with all the needed organizational units
using the smbldap-populate tool:

```
# smbldap-populate
Using workgroup name from sambaUnixIdPooldn (smbldap.conf): sambaDomainName=WIN.EXAMPLE.EDU
Using builtin directory structure
entry dc=win,dc=example,dc=edu already exist.
adding new entry: ou=Users,dc=win,dc=example,dc=edu
adding new entry: ou=Groups,dc=win,dc=example,dc=edu
adding new entry: ou=Machines,dc=win,dc=example,dc=edu
adding new entry: ou=Idmap,dc=win,dc=example,dc=edu
adding new entry: sambaDomainName=WIN.EXAMPLE.EDU,dc=win,dc=example,dc=edu
adding new entry: uid=Administrator,ou=Users,dc=win,dc=example,dc=edu
adding new entry: uid=nobody,ou=Users,dc=win,dc=example,dc=edu
adding new entry: cn=Domain Admins,ou=Groups,dc=win,dc=example,dc=edu
adding new entry: cn=Domain Users,ou=Groups,dc=win,dc=example,dc=edu
adding new entry: cn=Domain Guests,ou=Groups,dc=win,dc=example,dc=edu
adding new entry: cn=Domain Computers,ou=Groups,dc=win,dc=example,dc=edu
adding new entry: cn=Administrators,ou=Groups,dc=win,dc=example,dc=edu
adding new entry: cn=Print Operators,ou=Groups,dc=win,dc=example,dc=edu
adding new entry: cn=Backup Operators,ou=Groups,dc=win,dc=example,dc=edu
adding new entry: cn=Replicators,ou=Groups,dc=win,dc=example,dc=edu
```

The LDAP interaction tools, as we can see from the above output, read the configuration file and use the `sambaUnixIdPooldn` option to identify the domain name, pointing to the `sambaDomainName` distinguished name. The entry contains also the needed data to map UNIX UIDs and GIDs to Windows users and groups.

The default domain administrator is called `Administrator`, whose password should be immediately set with the `smbldap-passwd` program:

```
# smbldap-passwd Administrator
Changing password for Administrator
New password :
Retype new password :
```

We can now query the LDAP server to retrieve all the domain administrators, so all the entries belonging to the `Domain Admins` group with identifier `SID-512`. Apart from querying the service directly, we can use the Samba-LDAP `smbldap-groupshow` tool:

```
# smbldap-groupshow "Domain Admins"
dn: cn=Domain Admins,ou=Groups,dc=win,dc=example,dc=edu
objectClass: posixGroup,sambaGroupMapping
gidNumber: 512
cn: Domain Admins
memberUid: Administrator
description: Netbios Domain Administrators
sambaSID: S-1-5-21-785093230-3453868100-3778353011-512
sambaGroupType: 2
displayName: Domain Admins
```

It is interesting noticing that the entry is mapped to a UNIX group with the same name and GID 512. Samba needs then to retrieve the UNIX information from the LDAP database in order to function properly: we need to install and configure the name service switch to use LDAP, as we have seen in the chapter regarding the LDAP service. It is critical to match user, group, and machine passwords to the appropriate LDAP entries as we can see from the following `libnss-ldap.conf` configuration file:

```
host 127.0.0.1
base dc=win,dc=example,dc=edu
ldap_version 3

nss_base_passwd ou=Users,dc=win,dc=example,dc=edu
nss_base_passwd ou=Machines,dc=win,dc=example,dc=edu

nss_base_shadow ou=Users,dc=win,dc=example,dc=edu
nss_base_shadow ou=Machines,dc=win,dc=example,dc=edu

nss_base_group  ou=Groups,dc=win,dc=example,dc=edu
```

In fact, we already observed that users as well as client machines have entries in a domain, and also a specific password. The changes take effect immediately, and we can test our configuration by querying the UNIX groups the `Administrator` user belongs to:

```
# groups Administrator
Administrator : Domain Admins
```

At this point, we can start the Samba service and progress to configure the administrative privileges. As we have previewed in the previous section, the domain administrator should be granted all privileges, or better, all domain administrators should be able to perform managerial actions. We can then issue a `net rights grant` command specifying the domain administrators as in the following command:

```
# net rpc rights grant "WIN.EXAMPLE.EDU\Domain Admins" SeMachineAccountPrivilege \
SePrintOperatorPrivilege SeAddUsersPrivilege SeRemoteShutdownPrivilege \
SeDiskOperatorPrivilege -U Administrator
Password:
Successfully granted rights.

# net rpc rights list "WIN.EXAMPLE.EDU\Domain Admins" -U Administrator
Password:
SeMachineAccountPrivilege
SePrintOperatorPrivilege
SeAddUsersPrivilege
SeRemoteShutdownPrivilege
SeDiskOperatorPrivilege
```

6.3.3 Samba Users

As we introduced earlier, the `sambaDomainName` item in the LDAP database identifies the domain, and thus contains apart from the name itself, also the domain SID:

```
# ldapsearch -x -LLL "sambaDomainName=WIN.EXAMPLE.EDU"
dn: sambaDomainName=WIN.EXAMPLE.EDU,dc=win,dc=example,dc=edu
sambaAlgorithmicRidBase: 1000
gidNumber: 1000
objectClass: sambaDomain
objectClass: sambaUnixIdPool
sambaSID: S-1-5-21-785093230-3453868100-3778353011
sambaDomainName: WIN.EXAMPLE.EDU
uidNumber: 1001
```

The `sambaAlgorithmicRidBase` attribute specifies the base to calculate the mapping between Windows IDs and UNIX GIDs or UIDs. Our choice is to select our UIDs, since our prospective users will be AFS users and have their own UID and GID. We can now add the `testuser` entry to the domain users through the `smbldap-useradd` tool, specifying the add switch `-a` (creating both UNIX and Samba entries), its UID 10000 and of course the user name. The `-c` option specifies the GECOS field, and will appear on the top of the Start menu in a Windows client. Watch the `-m` option that directs the tool to create the user's home directory, if none exists. We shall remember that until this point, our Samba server does not interact with the pre-existing OpenAFS, LDAP or Kerberos services, and thus `testuser` is just a local user. We will modify this behavior shortly by making the PDC an OpenAFS client and enable it to read and write from our AFS file space.

Let us proceed creating the `testuser` entry, changing its password and analyzing the item created by the tools in the LDAP database:

```
# smbldap-useradd -a -m -c "Samba Testuser" -u 10000 testuser

# smbldap-passwd testuser
Changing password for testuser
New password :
Retype new password :

# ldapsearch -x -LLL "uid=testuser"
dn: uid=testuser,ou=Users,dc=win,dc=example,dc=edu
objectClass: top
objectClass: inetOrgPerson
objectClass: posixAccount
objectClass: shadowAccount
objectClass: sambaSamAccount
cn: Samba Testuser
sn: testuser
uid: testuser
uidNumber: 10000
gidNumber: 513
homeDirectory: /home/testuser
loginShell: /bin/bash
gecos: Samba Testuser
description: Samba Testuser
sambaLogonTime: 0
sambaLogoffTime: 2147483647
sambaKickoffTime: 2147483647
sambaPwdCanChange: 0
displayName: Samba Testuser
sambaSID: S-1-5-21-785093230-3453868100-3778353011-21000
sambaPrimaryGroupSID: S-1-5-21-785093230-3453868100-3778353011-513
sambaLogonScript: testuser.cmd
sambaProfilePath: \\SMBPDC\profiles\profile
sambaHomePath: \\SMBPDC\homes
sambaHomeDrive: Z:
sambaAcctFlags: [U]
sambaPwdLastSet: 1152269496
sambaPwdMustChange: 1160823096
```

Let us analyze the attributes above. Any user created by Samba tools belongs to `Domain Users` primary group with GID 513, as we can see from both the UNIX `gidNumber` and the Windows `sambaPrimaryGroupSID`. Users upon a successful login will have their [homes] shared resource mounted as the Z: drive, with their profiles stored under the profile directory located in the [profiles] share: this UNC gets then translated to the UNIX path /home/testuser/profile. The sambaAcctFlags contains the account flags identifying the Windows properties, in this case U specifies a normal user account. The available flags are described in Table 6.2. Like Kerberos passwords,

Table 6.2. Samba account flags

Flag	Description
D	Disabled account
H	Account requires a home directory
I	Inter-domain account trust
L	The account has been locked
M	A Microsoft Network Service (MSN) account
N	No password is required
S	Server trust account
T	A temporarily duplicated account
U	Normal user account
W	Workstation trust account
X	Password does not expire

Samba may have policies and expiration dates: it is important to match these properties between the domain and the realm, since users may be confused by different time-schedules for passwords.

As a side-note, a direct UID choice, when creating a user, will not modify the sambaDomainName entry, which contains the next-available UID if we let Samba choose UIDs and Windows IDs:

```
# ldapsearch -x -LLL "sambaDomainName=WIN.EXAMPLE.EDU"
dn: sambaDomainName=WIN.EXAMPLE.EDU,dc=win,dc=example,dc=edu
sambaAlgorithmicRidBase: 1000
gidNumber: 1000
objectClass: sambaDomain
objectClass: sambaUnixIdPool
sambaSID: S-1-5-21-785093230-3453868100-3778353011
sambaDomainName: WIN.EXAMPLE.EDU
uidNumber: 1001
```

We are ready to test the WIN.EXAMPLE.EDU domain based on LDAP by letting a Windows client join. Note that Windows XP Professional needs a small modification in the registry as we have seen in the previous section. After joining the domain using the domain Administrator user, we can login as testuser as we can see in Fig. 6.4.

6.3.4 Samba and OpenAFS

Samba is neither a Kerberized service nor AFS-aware. In the following we are going to introduce a workaround for this issue, allowing the domain controller

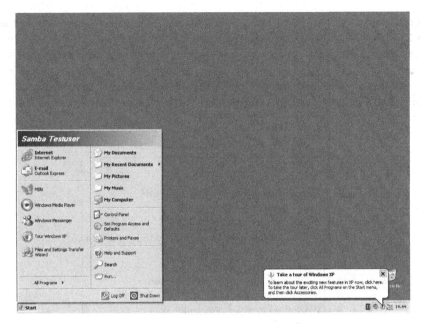

Fig. 6.4. The Windows XP desktop upon login

a dedicated access to the AFS file space, and thus enabling users to access their personal files transparently.

To achieve this we have to transform the machine running Samba into a fully-functioning Kerberos and OpenAFS client as we have seen in previous chapters. Note that we are not going to use the previous LDAP service since we chose to create a new one for the domain controller for didactic reasons. Creating a Samba LDAP database enables also UNIX users, as we have seen from the attributes needed by the domain controller. It is a simple task to create a single LDAP tree suitable for both Windows and UNIX clients but with security concerns.

Kerberos Serivce

Samba is not Kerberos-aware, as we have already introduced, but this fact does not necessarily mean that we cannot use OpenAFS. We have explained before that a keytab file contains the secret keys for a principal, and thus it is completely equivalent to a password: through a keytab access we can obtain a Kerberos ticket.

We have then to create a principal for our Samba service and to export its secret keys to a keytab file, so let us start creating the principal `windows` with a random password and export its keys to a keytab file:

```
kadmin:  add_principal -randkey windows
WARNING: no policy specified for windows@EXAMPLE.EDU; defaulting to no policy
Principal "windows@EXAMPLE.EDU" created.

kadmin:  ktadd -k /etc/samba/windows.keytab windows
Entry for principal windows with kvno 3, encryption type \
Triple DES cbc mode with HMAC/sha1 added to keytab WRFILE:/etc/samba/windows.keytab.
Entry for principal windows with kvno 3, encryption type \
DES cbc mode with CRC-32 added to keytab WRFILE:/etc/samba/windows.keytab.
```

The keytab file is accessible only by `root` for security reasons, and will contain one or more secret keys, viewable with the `klist` tool:

```
# cd /etc/samba/

# ls -l
total 16
-rw-r--r--  1 root root   8 2005-07-13 01:10 gdbcommands
-rw-r--r--  1 root root 912 2006-07-07 15:39 smb.conf
-rw-------  1 root root 116 2006-07-07 15:54 windows.keytab

# klist -ke windows.keytab
Keytab name: FILE:windows.keytab
KVNO Principal
---- --------------------------------------------------------------------
   3 windows@EXAMPLE.EDU (Triple DES cbc mode with HMAC/sha1)
   3 windows@EXAMPLE.EDU (DES cbc mode with CRC-32)
```

Service OpenAFS User

Samba should have access to the AFS file space of each user in our environment, even though the daemon has no knowledge of OpenAFS and its security system. Having a keytab file allows us to gain a Kerberos ticket for the `windows@EXAMPLE.EDU` principal: it should then be possible to convert the ticket into an AFS token. We need to create an entry in the protection database with the same name as the Kerberos principal, with an ID that will not conflict with any predefined domain IDs (e.g. 512 or 513):

```
# pts createuser windows -id 500
User windows has id 500

# pts listentries
Name                     ID  Owner Creator
anonymous             32766   -204    -204
sysadmin                  1   -204   32766
testuser              10000   -204       1
windows                 500   -204       1
```

Usually low IDs are reserved to system resources, for instance the `root` user has UID 0, and `daemon` has UID 1: the same rule generally applies to Windows domains, so we chose 500 as ID so that `windows` will not be identified with `Domain Admins` or any other default entity.

Now we need to resolve the ID to a valid UNIX user. We have the choice to employ a new LDAP entry—letting the name service switch resolve the numeric ID—or statically enter a new user in /etc/passwd. Our choice is to create a new user in the common UNIX files, with no password and /bin/false as shell—so disallowing any login possibility—and carefully mapping the UID to 500 and its GID to `Domain Users`:

```
# adduser --system --home /tmp --shell /bin/false --uid 500 --gid 513 \
--disabled-password --disabled-login windows

adduser: Warning: The home dir you specified already exists.
Adding system user 'windows'...
Adding new user 'windows' (500) with group 'Domain Users'.
Home directory '/tmp' already exists.
```

The Process Authenticating Group

Any user in a UNIX system has a UID and GID that identifies it in a unique way. The authentication data needed by AFS to identify users is usually stored in a *Process Authentication Group*, or PAG, encoded with the help of two UNIX groups. We can now gain the initial ticket for the `windows` principal using `kinit` and the keytab file:

```
# kinit -k -t /etc/samba/windows.keytab windows

# klist
Ticket cache: FILE:/tmp/krb5cc_0
Default principal: windows@EXAMPLE.EDU

Valid starting       Expires            Service principal
07/07/06 16:13:11  07/08/06 02:13:11  krbtgt/EXAMPLE.EDU@EXAMPLE.EDU

Kerberos 4 ticket cache: /tmp/tkt0
klist: You have no tickets cached
```

Note that `kinit` did not prompt for a password during the authentication process. With the `aklog` command we can then convert the Kerberos ticket to an AFS token:

```
# aklog -setpag

# tokens

Tokens held by the Cache Manager:

User's (AFS ID 500) tokens for afs@example.edu [Expires Jul  8 02:13]
   --End of list--
```

The `-setpag` switch forces the system to create a PAG for the current login session held by `root`: it normally possesses no PAGs since `root` is not an AFS user. The authentication groups will show up in common UNIX tools output:

```
# groups
root id: cannot find name for group ID 34232
34232 id: cannot find name for group ID 40379
40379
```

The **root** user belongs to the GID 0, resolved correctly to the **root** group through **/etc/group**. The two other groups represent the AFS credentials, shown as GID 34232 and 40379. This approach to credential encoding makes it possible for all the processes that will be spawned from the session holding a PAG, to retain the credentials of parent processes. In the following we will modify the Samba script to get the initial ticket and set the PAG before starting the daemon: all the daemons started in the session will be authenticated as the parent process.

Starting Samba with PAG

Debian usually ships services with default settings located in **/etc/default/**, usually named as the service itself. These files are commonly employed to set environment variables before the startup script is executed.

The **/etc/default/samba** contains by default the predefined running mode for the service (i.e. as a daemon). Here we add three new environment variables containing the shell commands to execute in order to obtain the initial ticket for **windows** and then set the PAG for the running service, so that Samba and other processes spawned through the script will inherit the authentication credentials. The third command is used to eliminate the Kerberos ticket when the PAG is defined, since it does no serve any more:

```
RUN_MODE="daemons"

PRE_COMMAND1="/usr/bin/kinit -l 1day -k -t /etc/samba/windows.keytab windows"
PRE_COMMAND2="/usr/bin/aklog -setpag"
POST_COMMAND="/usr/bin/kdestroy"
```

Unfortunately **kinit** has a default hardcoded lifetime for Kerberos tickets, for this reason we had to add the **-l** switch to specify the actual ticket validity period of one day.

The last step is to modify the Samba script using the environment variables set in the **/etc/default/samba** file. Samba is started by the **samba** script located in **/etc/init.d/**, and by default it will be like the following:

```
#!/bin/sh
#
# Start/stops the Samba daemons (nmbd and smbd).
#
#

# Defaults
RUN_MODE="daemons"

# Reads config file (will override defaults above)
[ -r /etc/default/samba ] && . /etc/default/samba

NMBDPID=/var/run/samba/nmbd.pid
SMBDPID=/var/run/samba/smbd.pid

# clear conflicting settings from the environment
unset TMPDIR
```

```
# See if the daemons are there
test -x /usr/sbin/nmbd -a -x /usr/sbin/smbd || exit 0

case "$1" in
      start)
                echo -n "Starting Samba daemons:"

                echo -n " nmbd"
                start-stop-daemon --start --quiet --exec /usr/sbin/nmbd -- -D

                if [ "$RUN_MODE" != "inetd" ]; then
                        echo -n " smbd"
                        start-stop-daemon --start --quiet --exec /usr/sbin/smbd -- -D
                fi

                echo "."
                ;;
      stop)
                echo -n "Stopping Samba daemons: "

                start-stop-daemon --stop --quiet --pidfile $NMBDPID
                # Wait a little and remove stale PID file
                sleep 1
                if [ -f $NMBDPID ] && ! ps h `cat $NMBDPID` > /dev/null
                then
                        # Stale PID file (nmbd was succesfully stopped),
                        # remove it (should be removed by nmbd itself IMHO.)
                        rm -f $NMBDPID
                fi
                echo -n "nmbd"

                if [ "$RUN_MODE" != "inetd" ]; then
                        start-stop-daemon --stop --quiet --pidfile $SMBDPID
                        # Wait a little and remove stale PID file
                        sleep 1
                        if [ -f $SMBDPID ] && ! ps h `cat $SMBDPID` > /dev/null
                        then
                                # Stale PID file (nmbd was succesfully stopped),
                                # remove it (should be removed by smbd itself IMHO.)
                                rm -f $SMBDPID
                        fi
                        echo -n " smbd"
                fi

                echo "."

                ;;
      reload)
                echo -n "Reloading /etc/samba/smb.conf (smbd only)"
                start-stop-daemon --stop --signal HUP --pidfile $SMBDPID

                echo "."
                ;;
      restart|force-reload)
                $0 stop
                sleep 1
                $0 start
                ;;
      *)
                echo "Usage: /etc/init.d/samba {start|stop|reload|restart|force-reload}"
                exit 1
                ;;
esac

exit 0
```

We need to modify the **start)** stanza, requiring the execution of **kinit** and **aklog** obtaining the PAGs, calling the environment variables previously introduced:

```
start)
        $PRE_COMMAND1 ; $PRE_COMMAND2
        echo -n "Starting Samba daemons:"

        echo -n " nmbd"
        start-stop-daemon --start --quiet --exec /usr/sbin/nmbd -- -D

        if [ "$RUN_MODE" != "inetd" ]; then
                echo -n " smbd"
                start-stop-daemon --start --quiet --exec /usr/sbin/smbd -- -D
        fi

        echo "."
        $POST_COMMAND
        ;;
```

The system upon starting the service runs the commands contained in the **PRE_COMMAND1** and **PRE_COMMAND2** variables, and thus obtains the initial ticket and sets the PAGs for the current session. Then it spawns the needed processes with **start-stop-daemon** which inherit the credentials. The last command destroys the obtained Kerberos tickets, affecting only the current session and not the children processes or the AFS tokens.

Note that services run through a keytab with a PAG cannot access the AFS file space after the token expiration. It is then necessary to periodically restart the Samba daemons through a simple scheduled job (e.g. a **cron** job), usually done at nighttime when no user should be using the service.

6.3.5 Testing Samba

Our **testuser** is already in the protection database for OpenAFS, in the Kerberos, and in the LDAP databases. Our objective is to allow the user to login also on Windows clients that joined our domain.

Samba will be authenticated to the AFS file space as **windows** with UID 500, so all the locations where Samba should have access to must be writable to this user. In other words, the profile directory should belong to **windows**:

```
# cd /afs/example.edu/users/testuser/

# ls -ld profile/
drwxr-xr-x  2 windows Domain Users 2048 2006-07-07 16:27 profile/

# fs listacl profile
Access list for profile is
Normal rights:
  system:administrators rlidwka
  windows rlidwka
  testuser rlidwka
```

Note that the profile directory belongs also to the **Domain Users** group. We need now to modify the LDAP entry on the Samba machine for **testuser**, reflecting the home directory in the AFS file space, as well as the new profile location in the Samba configuration files. The new LDAP configuration for `testuser` on the Samba host will be like the following:

```
dn: uid=testuser,ou=Users,dc=win,dc=example,dc=edu
objectClass: top
objectClass: inetOrgPerson
objectClass: posixAccount
objectClass: shadowAccount
objectClass: sambaSamAccount
cn: AFS Testuser
sn: testuser
uid: testuser
loginShell: /bin/bash
gecos: AFS Testuser
description: AFS Testuser
sambaLogonTime: 0
sambaLogoffTime: 2147483647
sambaKickoffTime: 2147483647
vsambaPwdCanChange: 0
displayName: AFS Testuser
sambaSID: S-1-5-21-785093230-3453868100-3778353011-21000
sambaPrimaryGroupSID: S-1-5-21-785093230-3453868100-3778353011-513
sambaLogonScript: testuser.cmd
sambaHomeDrive: Z:
sambaAcctFlags: [U]
sambaPwdLastSet: 1152277354
sambaPwdMustChange: 1160830954
uidNumber: 10000
gidNumber: 513
homeDirectory: /afs/example.edu/users/testuser
sambaProfilePath: \\\%L\profiles\profile
sambaHomePath: \\\%L\homes
```

The `testuser`'s common name, surname, description and GECOS fields have been updated to display the new configuration. In order to automatically create entries akin to `testuser` we need also to modify the `smbldap.conf` Samba-LDAP interaction tool configuration file. Also the Samba configuration must finally match the new profile and home directory paths under AFS, additionally forcing the daemon to use the `windows` user with the `force user` directive:

```
[global]
workgroup = WIN.EXAMPLE.EDU
netbios name = SMBPDC
server string = Samba Domain Master
security = user
ldap passwd sync = yes
passdb backend = ldapsam:ldap://127.0.0.1/
ldap admin dn = cn=ldapadmin,dc=win,dc=example,dc=edu
ldap suffix = dc=win,dc=example,dc=edu
ldap group suffix = ou=Groups
ldap user suffix = ou=Users
ldap machine suffix = ou=Machines
ldap idmap suffix = ou=Idmap
add machine script = /usr/sbin/smbldap-useradd -w '%u'
domain logons = yes
domain master = yes
enable privileges = yes
```

```
[netlogon]
path = /afs/example.edu/users/%U
comment = Samba Domain Login Service
valid users = %S
read only = no
browsable = no

[profiles]
path = /afs/example.edu/users/%U
comment = User Profile Service
valid users = %U
guest ok = no
read only = no
writable = yes
browsable = no
profile acls = yes
inherit permissions = yes
inherit owner = yes
force user = windows

[homes]
path = /afs/example.edu/users/%U
comment = User Home Directory
valid users = %U
guest ok = no
read only = no
writable = yes
browsable = no
inherit permissions = yes
inherit owner = yes
force user = windows
```

Restarting the service is sufficient to make all the changes take effect, and logging on a Windows client as **testuser** we see the home directory contents as in Fig. 6.5.

6.3.6 Backup Domain Controller

A backup domain controller basically is a copy of the primary one, and so it should be a Kerberos and an AFS client as the PDC. This section will outline the main differences between a primary and a backup domain controller installation process. The name of this host should be **smb2.example.edu**.

After installing and configuring a local LDAP server, and removing the entries in the database as we did for the PDC, we need to install Samba and the Samba-LDAP interaction tools. The backup domain controller configuration is slightly different from the previous settings: one obvious change is the NetBIOS name, and the other is the **domain master** field set to **no**. We also decided to change the **server string** to match the new layout:

```
[global]
workgroup = WIN.EXAMPLE.EDU
netbios name = SMBBDC
server string = Samba Domain Slave
security = user
ldap passwd sync = yes
passdb backend = ldapsam:ldap://127.0.0.1/
ldap admin dn = cn=ldapadmin,dc=win,dc=example,dc=edu
```

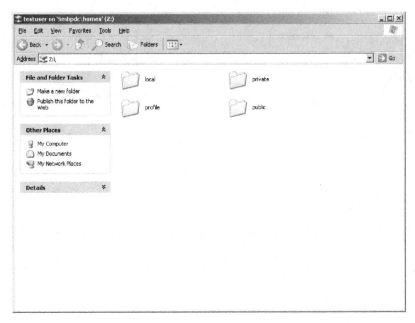

Fig. 6.5. The AFS home directory accessed through Samba

```
ldap suffix = dc=win,dc=example,dc=edu
ldap group suffix = ou=Groups
ldap user suffix = ou=Users
ldap machine suffix = ou=Machines
ldap idmap suffix = ou=Idmap
add machine script = /usr/sbin/smbldap-useradd -w '%u'
domain logons = yes
domain master = no
enable privileges = yes

[netlogon]
path = /afs/example.edu/users/%U
comment = Samba Domain Login Service
valid users = %S
read only = no
browsable = no

[profiles]
path = /afs/example.edu/users/%U
comment = User Profile Service
valid users = %U
guest ok = no
read only = no
writable = yes
browseable = no
profile acls = yes
inherit permissions = yes
inherit owner = yes
force user = windows

[homes]
path = /afs/example.edu/users/%U
comment = User Home Directory
```

```
valid users = %U
guest ok = no
read only = no
writable = yes
browseable = no
inherit permissions = yes
inherit owner = yes
force user = windows
```

Our BDC queries its local LDAP service as specified in the **passdb** backend field. The **testparm** tools correctly shows that our new server acts as a backup controller. After storing the LDAP administrator password with **smbpasswd** as on the PDC, we need to configure the Samba-LDAP tools in **smbladp.conf**:

```
SID="S-1-5-21-785093230-3453868100-3778353011"

slaveLDAP="127.0.0.1"
slavePort="389"

masterLDAP="127.0.0.1"
masterPort="389"

ldapTLS="0"
verify="require"
cafile="/etc/smbldap-tools/ca.pem"
clientcert="/etc/smbldap-tools/smbldap-tools.pem"
clientkey="/etc/smbldap-tools/smbldap-tools.key"

suffix="dc=win,dc=example,dc=edu"
usersdn="ou=Users,${suffix}"
computersdn="ou=Machines,${suffix}"
groupsdn="ou=Groups,${suffix}"
idmapdn="ou=Idmap,${suffix}"

sambaUnixIdPooldn="sambaDomainName=WIN.EXAMPLE.EDU,${suffix}"
scope="sub"
hash_encrypt="SSHA"
crypt_salt_format="%s"

userLoginShell="/bin/bash"
userHome="/afs/example.edu/users/%U"
userGecos="Samba User"
defaultUserGid="513"
defaultComputerGid="515"
skeletonDir="/etc/skel"
defaultMaxPasswordAge="99"

userSmbHome="\\%L\homes"
userProfile="\\%L\profiles\profile"
userHomeDrive="Z:"

userScript="%U.cmd"
mailDomain="example.edu"

with_smbpasswd="0"
smbpasswd="/usr/bin/smbpasswd"
with_slappasswd="0"
slappasswd="/usr/sbin/slappasswd"
```

Note that the SID must correspond to the domain SID on the primary controller. The LDAP binding settings are stored in the **smbldap_bind.conf** file which is a copy of the master configuration, accessible only by `root`. The LDAP database on the backup controller needs to be populated with the entries matching the primary database, an operation that cannot be performed with a sync replica since we need to propagate critical information as user passwords. On the master server we can dump the entire database to an LDIF file and copy the file to the slave with a secure method:

```
# ldapsearch -x -LLL -D "cn=ldapadmin,dc=win,dc=example,dc=edu" -w ldapadmin > all.ldif
```

Once copied the LDIF on the BDC, we need to manually remove the root of the LDAP tree from the file before adding all its contents. Once deleted the root entry, we can import the database with `ldapadd`, authenticating us as administrators:

```
# ldapadd -x -D "cn=ldapadmin,dc=win,dc=example,dc=edu" -w ldapadmin -f all.ldif
adding new entry "sambaDomainName=WIN.EXAMPLE.EDU,dc=win,dc=example,dc=edu"

adding new entry "ou=Users,dc=win,dc=example,dc=edu"
adding new entry "ou=Groups,dc=win,dc=example,dc=edu"
adding new entry "ou=Machines,dc=win,dc=example,dc=edu"
adding new entry "ou=Idmap,dc=win,dc=example,dc=edu"
adding new entry "uid=Administrator,ou=Users,dc=win,dc=example,dc=edu"
adding new entry "uid=nobody,ou=Users,dc=win,dc=example,dc=edu"
adding new entry "cn=Domain Admins,ou=Groups,dc=win,dc=example,dc=edu"
adding new entry "cn=Domain Users,ou=Groups,dc=win,dc=example,dc=edu"
adding new entry "cn=Domain Guests,ou=Groups,dc=win,dc=example,dc=edu"
adding new entry "cn=Domain Computers,ou=Groups,dc=win,dc=example,dc=edu"
adding new entry "cn=Administrators,ou=Groups,dc=win,dc=example,dc=edu"
adding new entry "cn=Print Operators,ou=Groups,dc=win,dc=example,dc=edu"
adding new entry "cn=Backup Operators,ou=Groups,dc=win,dc=example,dc=edu"
adding new entry "cn=Replicators,ou=Groups,dc=win,dc=example,dc=edu"
adding new entry "uid=testuser,ou=Users,dc=win,dc=example,dc=edu"
adding new entry "uid=client1$,ou=Machines,dc=win,dc=example,dc=edu"
```

If the import operation exits successfully, we are able to query the server for all the domain administrators with the `smbldap-groupshow` tool:

```
# smbldap-groupshow "Domain Admins"
dn: cn=Domain Admins,ou=Groups,dc=win,dc=example,dc=edu
objectClass: posixGroup,sambaGroupMapping
gidNumber: 512
cn: Domain Admins
memberUid: Administrator
description: Netbios Domain Administrators
sambaSID: S-1-5-21-785093230-3453868100-3778353011-512
sambaGroupType: 2
displayName: Domain Admins
```

The last steps mimic the primary domain controller, installing and properly configuring the name service switch and allowing the Samba service to access the AFS file space: we need to copy the keytab file and modify the startup script as we have explained earlier. After starting the Samba service, we can test the backup domain controller by detaching the PDC from the network and logging in with a Windows client. We show in Fig. 6.6 that we can successfully perform a domain login, transparently using the backup controller, while SMBPDC is not available. For didactic purposes we left PDC and

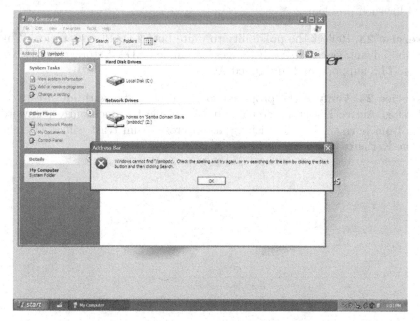

Fig. 6.6. Users perform login on the BDC while the PDC is offline

BDC with a local LDAP service. Of course this is not a solution for production. Since a secure replication in this case can be only achieved by using TLS, to be introduced in the next chapter, we leave this part as an exercise.

Notes on Samba Use

The Samba access to AFS space is determined by the single user **windows**: we prefer to allow **write** access to this user only in a dedicated part of the user volumes, reflected in the previously showed ACLs. Also, an entirely separated volume could be mounted as **profile**, since the final distinction between users is handled by the Samba daemon. Therefore a user can only access the own **profile** but not the one of others.

Practice

Exercise 21. Establish a secure synchronization between the two LDAP servers on the PDC and the BDC: unfortunately the **smbldap-tools** only support plain text authentication. Hence you should disable **ldap://** and enable **ldaps://** with the help of a key and certificate for both of these two servers.

Exercise 22. In the described setup there exist two locations for the user password: one is Kerberos, the other the LDAP servers of PDC and BDC. Write a script which changes both of them, the UNIX `expect` tool is often used for such problems.

Exercise 23. Reflect the possibility to unite both LDAP repositories. What are the advantages and disadvantages? A unified LDAP storage needs Kerberos, TLS support, and fine tuned ACLs.

Exercise 24. Verify if the proposed solution integrates with an already established Active Directory domain. It is possible to synchronize passwords from from both world, establishing also a cross-realm trust, since AD relies on the Kerberos protocol.

## Part II

Pushing the Core Services

7

Further Services

*Always render more and better service than is expected
of you, no matter what your task may be.*
Augustine "Og" Mandino

7.1 DHCP

The assignment of IP addresses on a network is critical, especially in an environment that allows guests to use network services. Originally the BOOTP, the *Bootstrap Protocol* enabled systems to obtain automatically an IP address from a pool of available ones, allowing also systems to load an operating system permitting disk-less workstations. Another application in the past was the operation of "X terminals", which were devices understanding only the X Display Manager Control Protocol. The BOOTP protocol was subsequently obsoleted by the DHCP protocol, which still retains in some implementation a backward compatibility with its ancestor.

DHCP stands for *Dynamic Host Configuration Protocol*, and provides a machine with the necessary information to function on a network: an IP address and the associated network mask, the default gateway address, and DNS servers. A DHCP server will lease a unique IP address to a client, for a fixed amount of time called *lease time*, provided that an address is still available from the pool.

The latest DHCP server provided by Debian, with support also for the legacy BOOTP protocol, is shipped with the `dhcp3-server` package, and as usual Debian configures and starts the service upon a successful installation. For this software, Debian also warns that the server must be configured manually. The configuration file `dhcpd.conf` located in `/etc/dhcp3/` contains all the needed leasing time information and a logging verbosity option. We must manually specify that the DHCP server is the authoritative one in the network[1], with the `authoritative` parameter. The `subnet` stanza provides all the needed information about the IP addresses that the service should handle, offering the configuration parameters required by a client in order to set its network configuration:

---

[1] By default the DHCP server runs as non-authoritative, preventing users to start accidently a valid DHCP server, disturbing the network configuration.

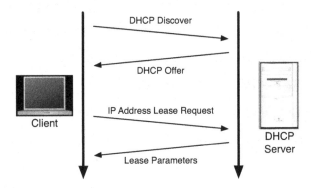

Fig. 7.1. A DHCP service protocol communication outline

```
ddns-update-style none;
default-lease-time 600;
max-lease-time 7200;
authoritative;
log-facility local7;

subnet 192.168.127.0 netmask 255.255.255.0 {
        range 192.168.127.20 192.168.127.200;
        option subnet-mask 255.255.255.0;
        option broadcast-address 192.168.127.255;
        option routers 192.168.127.1;
        option domain-name "example.edu";
        option domain-name-servers 192.168.127.2, 192.168.127.3;
}
```

In our example we restricted the lease time to 10 minutes, allowing a maximum timeframe of 2 hours: after a lease expires the IP address request will be renegotiated. Besides all network parameters, we chose to limit the IP addresses in the pool with the **range** parameter, allowing only addresses 20–200 to be available for lease. Finally in our network we do not make use of dynamic DNS updates. This short configuration suffices to successfully start the server:

```
# /etc/init.d/dhcp3-server start
Starting DHCP server: dhcpd3.
```

To test the availability of our server, we connect a Windows machine to the network with the *automatic* network configuration. Using the command line interface we can inspect the network parameters with the **ipconfig** tool:

```
C:\Documents and Settings\Standard>ipconfig /all

Windows IP Configuration

        Host Name . . . . . . . . . . . . : acer-prozwpnghe
        Primary Dns Suffix  . . . . . . . :
        Node Type . . . . . . . . . . . . : Unknown
        IP Routing Enabled. . . . . . . . : No
```

```
        WINS Proxy Enabled. . . . . . . . : No

Ethernet adapter Local Area Connection:

        Connection-specific DNS Suffix  . : example.edu
        Description . . . . . . . . . . . : Realtek RTL8139/810x
        Physical Address. . . . . . . . . : 00-00-E2-92-CE-7F
        Dhcp Enabled. . . . . . . . . . . : Yes
        Autoconfiguration Enabled . . . . : Yes
        IP Address. . . . . . . . . . . . : 192.168.127.20
        Subnet Mask . . . . . . . . . . . : 255.255.255.0
        Default Gateway . . . . . . . . . : 192.168.127.1
        DHCP Server . . . . . . . . . . . : 192.168.127.7
        DNS Servers . . . . . . . . . . . : 192.168.127.2
                                            192.168.127.3
        Lease Obtained. . . . . . . . . . : Thursday, July 13, 2006 1:52:18 PM
        Lease Expires . . . . . . . . . . : Thursday, July 13, 2006 2:02:18 PM
```

As we can see from the above output, the Windows client has been successfully configured with the DHCP-supplied parameters. On the server side upon a successful DHCP negotiation, the daemon updates the lease data in the dhcpd.leases file under the /var/lib/dhcp3/ location:

```
# cat dhcpd.leases
lease 192.168.127.20 {
  starts 2 2006/07/13 13:52:18;
  ends 2 2006/07/13 14:02:18;
  tstp 2 2006/07/13 14:02:18;
  binding state free;
  hardware ethernet 00:00:e2:92:ce:7f;
  uid "\001\000\000\342\222\316\177";
}
```

Static Hosts

In certain situations it is desirable that a static IP address gets assigned to a specific host. It is possible to provide a fixed IP address to machines based on their MAC address. The MAC address, or *Media Access Control* address, is a unique identifier assigned to any network card, constituted by 6 bytes and regulated by the IEEE MAC address specification, now called MAC-48. Although MAC addresses are physically set on network cards, they can be changed by malicious users: using a per-MAC address setting increases the security level of the service, but it cannot provide resistance to hacking.

In order to allow a particular host to gain a specific IP address we can add a host stanza, specifying the IP address or a DNS name assigned to the machine, and supplying the network card's MAC address as in the following example:

```
host notebook {
  hardware ethernet 00:00:e2:92:ce:7f;
  fixed-address notebook.example.edu;
}
```

The above configuration obviously needs a forward and reverse DNS host mapping.

DHCP Redundancy

DHCP is an important service when clients depend on a dynamic configuration, allowing a great flexibility in host settings and network management: a redundant DHCP server should then be properly configured.

The Debian-provided DHCP server can handle failover situations, specifying the pool of IP addresses managed by the primary and the secondary servers, configuring them with a `failover peer` option that points to the respective partner. A much simpler approach is to configure two DHCP servers to offer exactly the same static IPs, while dynamic addresses can be divided between them in non overlapping ranges.

7.2 Emergency System

In case of a fatal disk crash it can be helpful to boot the failed system in some emergency mode: it is possible to use live CDs to perform emergency repairs or employ a network boot.

During the 90s the Intel Corporation developed a hardware solution to allow new systems to be managed without any previously installed operating system. The effort resulted in the *Wired for Management* platform, which included two major features: the Wake-on-LAN facility and the PXE environment. PXE is the acronym of the *Pre-Boot Execution Environment*, providing hosts with an operating system regardless of any storage devices such as hard drives. The process of booting a system over the network is driven by the internal system firmware as in Fig. 7.2, although almost every system nowadays provides a PXE-enabled firmware. The PXE boot requires the network

Fig. 7.2. The boot menu with the highlighted network boot option

to provide a valid IP address and an operating system image through a DHCP negotiation, and finally the download of the system with a PXE-enabled FTP transfer.

7.2.1 TFTP

The FTP protocol used in PXE-enabled environment is usually the *Trivial File Transfer Protocol* or TFTP, a file transfer protocol defined in early 80s running on the UDP port 69. The FTP protocol—using TCP port 21 and 20—in comparison requires more memory, and offers the user more commands with respect to the TFTP, which for instance cannot list contents of a directory.

In particular, to retrieve a PXE-enabled boot image from the network, we need a PXE-enabled TFTP daemon, included in the `atftpd` package. Debian as usual configures the package, asking whether we want to run the server as an `inetd`-driven service: in our case we run the daemon as a full service and not on-demand. By default Debian uses the `/tftpboot/` root-based directory to store all the TFTP files: it is customary to avoid root-based locations for trivial protocols as TFTP, so our choice falls on another location, `/var/lib/tftpd/`. As a security habit, we will inhibit write-access to all users except `root`:

```
# ls -ld /var/lib/tftpd
drwxr-xr-x  2 root root 4096 2006-07-13 15:23 tftpd/
```

After configuring the package, Debian starts the server: the given permissions guarantee that files can at most be read and not written since the daemon is running under the user `nobody`. To test the system, we create a simple text file and later download it from a TFTP client:

```
# cd /var/lib/tftpd/

# echo 'This is the tftp root directory.' > README

# ls -l
total 4
-rw-r--r--  1 root root 32 2006-07-13 15:25 README
```

On another available system, we install the `atftp` package, the corresponding TFTP client, and test it by downloading the `README` file created earlier:

```
# cd /tmp/

# ls

# atftp tftp.example.edu
tftp> ?
Available command are:
connect         connect to tftp server
mode            set file transfer mode (netascii/octet)
option          set RFC1350 options
put             upload a file to the host
get             download a file from the host
mtftp           set mtftp variables
mget            download file from mtftp server
quit            exit tftp
verbose         toggle verbose mode
trace           toggle trace mode
status          print status information
timeout         set the timeout before a retry
```

```
help            print help message
?               print help message

tftp> get README

tftp> quit

# ls
README

# cat README
This is the tftp root directory.
```

In order to test a real network boot, we can download the RIP distribution, namely *Recovery Is Possible*, a PXE-ready image of a Linux-based operating system. This distribution in form of a zipped file expands into a `tftpboot` directory, as the Debian default. All the contents should be placed into our chosen TFTP root, `/var/lib/tftpd`: the `pxelinux.0` file is our PXE-enabled boot image.

DHCP Configuration

On the DHCP configuration side, we must allow network booting, done in the main stanza adding the `allow booting` parameter, and providing the `filename` boot image and the TFTP `server-name` parameters on a per-subnet basis, or even for specific hosts:

```
allow booting;

host notebook {
   hardware ethernet 00:00:e2:92:ce:7f;
   fixed-address notebook.example.edu;
   filename "pxelinux.0";
   server-name "tftp.example.edu";
}
```

When a client connects to the DHCP server for a network boot, it will receive the RIP Linux system image, as in Fig. 7.3

7.2.2 NFS

In 1984 Sun Microsystems developed a directory sharing protocol over networks called NFS, *Network File System*. Contrary to AFS, the NFS file system provides shared resources, in other words, a NFS server "exports" directories, and clients can mount the shared location knowing the directory name and the NFS host address. NFS does not provide by default any encryption method, all network communications are in clear text, and they are based on a *remote procedure call* protocol RPC which needs an additional open port on the NFS server.

Nevertheless, NFS is often directly compiled into Linux kernels, a handy feature for machine cloning, or once again, for emergency systems. The application of a network boot becomes evident when restoring a system after a

```
                           RIPLinuX

Boot Linux rescue system!
Boot Linux rescue system! (skip keymap prompt)
Boot Linux rescue system to X!
Boot Linux rescue system to X! (skip keymap prompt)
Edit and put 'root=/dev/XXXX' Linux partition to boot!
Boot memory tester!
Boot MBR on first hard drive
Boot partition #1 on first hard drive
Boot partition #2 on first hard drive
Boot partition #3 on first hard drive
Boot partition #4 on first hard drive
```

Fig. 7.3. The PXE RIP Linux boot loader

crash: in this case, we should be able to read a disk image created with tools like dd, tar, or dump, and recreate a previously working situation. An Open-AFS client requires bigger efforts compared to a simple NFS mount point, which is a fast solution to directory sharing problems, and comes with the RIP Linux distribution out of the box. Let us proceed installing the NFS server, provided by the **nfs-kernel-server** package:

```
# apt-get install nfs-kernel-server
Reading Package Lists... Done
Building Dependency Tree... Done
The following extra packages will be installed:
  nfs-common portmap
The following NEW packages will be installed:
  nfs-common nfs-kernel-server portmap
0 upgraded, 3 newly installed, 0 to remove and 0 not upgraded.
Need to get 0B/172kB of archives.
After unpacking 618kB of additional disk space will be used.
Do you want to continue? [Y/n]
Selecting previously deselected package portmap.
(Reading database ... 27786 files and directories currently installed.)
Unpacking portmap (from .../archives/portmap_5-9_i386.deb) ...
Selecting previously deselected package nfs-common.
Unpacking nfs-common (from .../nfs-common_1%3a1.0.6-3.1_i386.deb) ...
Selecting previously deselected package nfs-kernel-server.
Unpacking nfs-kernel-server (from .../nfs-kernel-server_1%3a1.0.6-3.1_i386.deb) ...
Setting up portmap (5-9) ...
Starting portmap daemon: portmap.

Setting up nfs-common (1.0.6-3.1) ...
Starting NFS common utilities: statd.

Setting up nfs-kernel-server (1.0.6-3.1) ...
Not starting NFS kernel daemon: No exports.
```

As shown above Debian starts the **portmap** server, providing the necessary RPC mapping required by NFS in order to work. Our objective is to export two locations through the NFS protocol, subdirectories of **/var/lib/nfs/**, a read-only and a write-enabled location:

```
# cd /var/lib/nfs/

# ls -l
total 8
drwxr-xr-x  2 root root 4096 2006-07-13 16:18 readonly/
drwxrwxrwx  2 root root 4096 2006-07-13 16:18 readwrite/
```

Note that NFS is not a secure and encrypted way of exchanging data, and is used here for recovery, where sensitive data is not transferred. The chosen directories must finally be "exported" publicly in the /etc/exports configuration file, specifying the allowed IP addresses and the access method:

```
/var/lib/nfs/readonly   192.168.127.0/255.255.255.0(ro,sync)
/var/lib/nfs/readwrite  192.168.127.0/255.255.255.0(rw,all_squash,sync)
```

The all_squash option tells the NFS server to map all the remote users to the anonymous user nobody on the server, while ro and rw obviously describe a read-only and write-enabled access, respectively. The sync option is needed by the kernel space daemon, as specified by the NFS documentation. It is then possible to start the NFS daemon allowing clients to mount the exported resources:

```
# /etc/init.d/nfs-kernel-server start
Exporting directories for NFS kernel daemon...done.
Starting NFS kernel daemon: nfsd mountd.
```

Client Configuration

On the client side, with the running RIP distribution employing a BSD-like initialization scripts system, we have to enable the DHCP ethernet configuration by editing the file /etc/rc.d/rc.inet1.conf:

```
IPADDR[0]=""
NETMASK[0]=""
USE_DHCP[0]="yes"
DHCP_HOSTNAME[0]=""
```

After starting the rc.inet1 script, we must enable the portmap service needed by NFS; some services are disabled by default, so we might have to change their execution permission bits prior to starting them:

```
# /etc/rc.d/rc.portmap start
Starting RPC portmapper: /sbin/rpc.portmap
```

At this point we are able to mount the two NFS exported directories, and verify that we are able to write just in one of them. As we previewed, NFS shares directories, without the location transparency allowed by Open-AFS. It is necessary to manually specify the host and directory name—with an optional read-write flag—in the mount command line as in the following output:

```
# cd /var/tmp/

# mkdir ro

# mkdir rw

# mount 192.168.127.154:/var/lib/nfs/readonly ro
# mount 192.168.127.154:/var/lib/nfs/readwrite rw
```

The two mounted NFS mount points will obey to the write-access rules established in the server configuration:

```
# cd ro/

# touch aaa
touch: cannot touch 'aaa': Read-only file system

# cd ../rw

# mkdir ccc

# echo hello > ccc/ddd

# ls -l ccc/
total 4
-rw-r--r-- 1 65534 65534 6 2006-07-13 15:01 ddd
```

On the NFS server we can see that every file and directory created on the client has been assigned to the **nobody** user belonging to the **nogroup** UNIX group:

```
# ls -l /var/lib/nfs/readwrite/
total 4
drwxr-xr-x  2 nobody nogroup 4096 2006-07-13 17:01 ccc/
```

7.3 Certificate Authority

Cryptography, the science studying secrecy in communication, is a key element in a secure environment. Historically an early cryptographic medium was the *"scytale"*, a cylindric rod with a wrapped strip where the message was written: only the one possessing a rod with the same diameter could read the message. This method is known from Ancient Greece, and there is also references to cryptographic systems used by Julius Caesar during his battling campaigns. Modern cryptography distinguishes between two major mechanisms: symmetric and asymmetric cryptographic systems.

The symmetric key cryptosystem is the more intuitive method of sending sensitive data between interlocutors. An individual wishing to send an encrypted message encodes the data with a secret key and sends this encrypted message to the receiver over an insecure communication channel. The message can then be decrypted only with the original secret key, which has to be exchanged between the two parties in a supposedly secure way as in Fig. 7.4.

Kerberos uses such a technique, and among the most famous algorithms employing a symmetric key encryption there are the old *Data Encryption Standard* DES, its variant *Triple DES* or 3DES, and the new Advanced Encryption Standard, or AES, which is to replace DES.

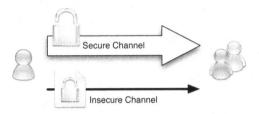

Fig. 7.4. Symmetric key cryptography assumes a method for secure key exchange

Asymmetric cryptography was officially born in 1976 when Bailey Whitfield Diffie and Martin Edward Hellman published a paper describing this methodology, and later in 1977 Ron Rivest, Adi Shamir, and Leonard Adleman invented the renowned algorithm which took name from their initials, RSA. Another algorithm derived from the idea of Diffie and Hellman is the ElGamal encryption scheme, named after the inventor Taher ElGamal, who also worked on a scheme for digital signatures. The key idea in asymmetric cryptographic techniques is that any user possesses two different keys, a "public" and an "private" key. A message encrypted with one of these could only be decrypted by its counterpart, as pictured in Fig. 7.5.

Fig. 7.5. Asymmetric key cryptography encrypts data with one "public" key. Decryption is possible only with the "private" key

The names *public* and *private* become clear when we introduce two individuals trying to exchange data securely.

The sender encrypts the message using the receiver's public key, transmitting the message over the insecure communication channel. The only way to decrypt the message is to possess the counterpart, the "private" key as pictured in Fig. 7.6: in asymmetric systems the hypothesis about a confidential key exchange may be dismissed. The mathematics behind these key pairs is such that they get once generated together but afterwards it is considered to be practically infeasible to calculate one from the other.

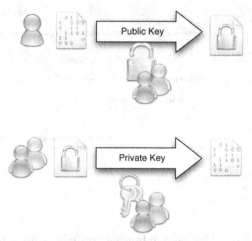

Fig. 7.6. The sender uses the receiver's "public" key to encrypt the message: only the receiver possessing the "private" key will be enabled to decrypt

Another application of public key cryptography is the *digital signature* to confirm the authenticity of a transmission. For this, so called *hash functions* are applied to an arbitrarily long message which produce a *message digest* of a fixed length. Then the message is transferred together with its digest encoded by the private key of the sender. The receiver can decode the digest with the public key of the sender and confront the result with the digest of the actually received message. Examples of hash functions are MD5 or the *Secure Hash Algorithm* SHA. The *Digital Signature Algorithm* DSA, which is a variant of the ElGamal signature scheme, became a standard for digital signatures.

One problem remains to be solved: how can users be sure about the public key of one another? For this a *Public Key Infrastructure* PKI needs to be implemented which relies on a trused third party as in the case of the Kerberos KDC. This trusted entity is called *Certificate Authority*, or simply CA, which has a well known public key. Hence it can digitally sign the public keys of any user, resulting in a *certificate* , and users in turn are able to verify the correctness of a public key with the help of this signature.

Among the most acknowledged certificate authorities we may mention VeriSign and Thawte, offering digital certificate services, and the CAcert and StartCom CA providing the same services, free of charge. A typical CA will issue a digital certificate that contains all the information needed to attest the identity of an individual, such as the name, organization, address, and obviously the user's public key. Usually trusted certificate authorities for digital certificates are hard-wired in a system, as for example in a Web browser like Mozilla Camino pictured in Fig. 7.7.

We need to create our certificate authority CA in order to enable future secure services employing the *Secure Socket Layer*, or SSL, and the *Transport*

Fig. 7.7. The Mozilla Camino web browser trusted CA list with expiry dates

Layer Security, or TLS: these encryption facilities enable secure web or mail servers, as we will see in the next chapters. Our organization will make use of different key lengths for different purposes, using 1024, 2048 and 4096 bits keys for users, hosts, and the CA itself, respectively. Note that laws regarding lengths of encryption keys may significantly vary from one country to another, so it is recommended to comply with the local laws upon CA deployment. Our organization will make use of different key sizes for obvious didactic purposes.

In the following we employ the OpenSSL software for the generation of public/private key pairs, of a self-signed certificate for an in-house certificate authority, and of user or host certificates signed by that authority. For very secure and reliable environments, it is highly recommended to buy certificates from well-known and trusted commercial authorities. As for Kerberos the keytab files encode a secret key of one principal, SSL or TLS need a file for the host certificate and for the host's private key, either in two separated files or combined in a single one.

7.3.1 Installing OpenSSL

First of all we have to install the OpenSSL package along with some commonly known certificate authorities, namely the `openssl` and `ca-certificates` packages, the CA software and trusted certificate authorities as VeriSign and Thawte:

```
# apt-get install openssl ca-certificates
```

Configuring the CA

Debian provides a sample configuration file in `/etc/ssl/`, with the name `openssl.cnf`, which we must edit to suite our needs. We have to store our certificates and private keys in a secure location, accessible only by `root`, so our choice is to place everything in `/etc/ssl/private/`, providing the location with the following restrictive permissions bits:

```
drwx------  2 root root 4096 2005-10-20 12:22 private/
```

In this directory we create the location where we will store all our sensible files, called `CA`, possessing restrictive `root`-only access bits:

```
# ls -al /etc/ssl/private
total 12
drwx------  3 root root 4096 2006-07-18 10:45 ./
drwxr-xr-x  4 root root 4096 2006-07-18 10:45 ../
drwx------  2 root root 4096 2006-07-18 10:45 CA/
```

The next step is to modify the OpenSSL configuration file, referring all the directory and file locations to our CA sensitive data `/etc/ssl/private/CA/`. The file is divided into different sections, such as `CA_default` specifying the predefined properties of issued certificates (e.g. file location, validity period and checksum algorithm), and `req_distinguished_name`, detailing the properties for each field in a digital certificate (e.g. country code, city, organization name, and certificate user name). The following configuration example will issue a certificate for a fictional `ZZ` country, with a default validity period of one year, signing each certificate with the SHA-1 hashing algorithm:

```
[ CA_default ]
dir              = /etc/ssl/private/CA
certs            = $dir/certificates
crl_dir          = $dir/crl
database         = $dir/index.txt
unique_subject   = no
new_certs_dir    = $dir/newcerts
certificate      = $dir/cacert.pem
serial           = $dir/serial
crl              = $dir/crl.pem
private_key      = $dir/cakey.pem
RANDFILE         = $dir/randfile
x509_extensions  = usr_cert
name_opt         = ca_default
cert_opt         = ca_default
default_days     = 365
default_crl_days = 90
default_md       = sha1
preserve         = no
policy           = policy_match

[ policy_match ]
countryName             = match
stateOrProvinceName     = match
localityName            = match
organizationName        = match
organizationalUnitName  = optional
commonName              = supplied
emailAddress            = optional

[ req_distinguished_name ]
countryName                     = Country Name (2 letter code)
```

```
countryName_default                      = ZZ
countryName_min                          = 2
countryName_max                          = 2
stateOrProvinceName                      = State or Province Name (full name)
stateOrProvinceName_default              = Province
localityName                             = Locality Name (eg, city)
localityName_default                     = City
0.organizationName                       = Organization Name (eg, company)
0.organizationName_default               = Example Organization
organizationalUnitName                   = Organizational Unit Name (eg, section)
organizationalUnitName_default           = Central Administration
commonName                               = Common Name (eg, YOUR full name)
commonName_max                           = 64
emailAddress                             = Email Address (optional)
emailAddress_max                         = 64
```

Note that the `req_distinguished_name` contains strings that are the default values for a digital certificate. The fields with the "crl" string refer to the *certificate revocation list*, or CRL, which contains the serial numbers of those certificates which should no longer be valid. Usually a service starts without a revocation list, but adds its use at the moment of the release of a first such list. This list has then to be propagated and hence it is considered as one of the weak points of a PKI: there is an inherent delay before an invalidation becomes active. The above defaults produce a digital certificate with the following subject:

```
C=ZZ, \
ST=Province, \
L=City, \
O=Example Organization, \
OU=Central Administration, \
CN=certificateName
```

As you can imagine such a subject structure is well suited for the storage in a directory service like LDAP.

7.3.2 Creating a CA

We are ready to create the structure with respect to the configuration file, producing the directories needed for the newly-issued certificates, private keys, and revocation list:

```
# cd /etc/ssl/private/CA

# ls -l
total 16
drwx------  2 root root 4096 2006-07-18 11:14 certificates/
drwx------  2 root root 4096 2006-07-18 11:14 crl/
drwx------  2 root root 4096 2006-07-18 11:14 newcerts/
drwx------  2 root root 4096 2006-07-18 11:14 privatekeys/
```

Again the permission bits indicate that all these directories are accessible only for the `root` user. Issuing new certificates requires the creation of a serial number log file, containing the total count of issued certificates, or better, the next certificate serial number: since we have not issued any certificate yet we start with 1 as serial. Additionally, the OpenSSL requires an index file as in the following:

```
# echo "01" > serial

# touch index.txt
```

We are ready to generate our certificate authority's private key using the `openssl` tool with the `genrsa` command, and for our CA we choose strong encryption options, using a 4096 bit key, encrypted with the 256 bit Advanced Encryption Standard symmetric algorithm, which protects the private assymetric key with a *passphrase*:

```
# openssl genrsa -aes256 -out cakey.pem 4096
Generating RSA private key, 4096 bit long modulus
.....................................................................++
........++
e is 65537 (0x10001)
Enter pass phrase for cakey.pem:
Verifying - Enter pass phrase for cakey.pem:
```

The RSA algorithm requires the generation of two random and large prime numbers: the dots above symbolize a search and the plus signs some primality test. The public and private key are calculated from these two numbers which after completed generation will be discarded. The requested `cakey.pem` file, which is a Base64 ASCII format, has been successfully created with restrictive permission bits:

```
# ls -l
total 24
-rw-------  1 root root 3326 2006-07-18 11:24 cakey.pem
drwx------  2 root root 4096 2006-07-18 11:14 certificates/
drwx------  2 root root 4096 2006-07-18 11:14 crl/
-rw-------  1 root root    0 2006-07-18 11:17 index.txt
drwx------  2 root root 4096 2006-07-18 11:14 newcerts/
drwx------  2 root root 4096 2006-07-18 11:14 privatekeys/
-rw-------  1 root root    3 2006-07-18 11:16 serial
```

The next step is then to create the self-signed certificate for our CA containing its public key, using the private key to digitally sign the issued certificate, and storing the resulting certificate in a file, in our case `cacert.pem`. Since a CA is usually of longer use we decide for 10 years as validity period:

```
# openssl req -new -x509 -days 3560 -key cakey.pem -out cacert.pem

Enter pass phrase for cakey.pem:
You are about to be asked to enter information that will be incorporated
into your certificate request.
What you are about to enter is what is called a Distinguished Name or a DN.
There are quite a few fields but you can leave some blank
For some fields there will be a default value,
If you enter '.', the field will be left blank.
-----
```

```
Country Name (2 letter code) [ZZ]:
State or Province Name (full name) [Province]:
Locality Name (eg, city) [City]:
Organization Name (eg, company) [Example Organization]:
Organizational Unit Name (eg, section) [Central Administration]:
Common Name (eg, YOUR full name) []:Certificate Authority
Email Address (optional) []:ca@example.edu
```

The command above issued a new standard digital certificate with the -x509 option[2], with 3560 days of legitimate use to the "Certificate Authority" user, whose email is ca@example.edu. Certificate files are just text files using a Base64 ASCII encoding:

```
# cat cacert.pem
-----BEGIN CERTIFICATE-----
MIIG+jCCBOKgAwIBAgIJAMmxFXMOiAbJMAOGCSqGSIb3DQEBBAUAMIGuMQswCQYD
VQQGEwJaWjERMA8GA1UECBMIUHJvdmluY2UxDTALBgNVBAcTBENpdHkxHTAbBgNV
...
pDv4s92nOjsl3eIODJtKZjROId0cW8w52rfdujwPzrjS8vxSg9/1fqq5/8/xHk8B
3WFOqvQDhSE7R8S6Em8=
-----END CERTIFICATE-----
```

The file name suffixes are defined by the PKI standard determining the actual file format. Both, our private key and certificate end in .pem. Besides these are other suffixes and we want to mention:

.der Binary file encoded with the DER standard, *Distinguished Encoding Rules*, used by OpenLDAP servers;

.pem Text-based Base64 encoded format, used for most daemon configurations;

.p12 Public Key Cryptography Standard 12 format, PKCS12, used for example in Mozilla and formerly Netscape.

Also the private key for our certificate authority is a Base64 encoded text file encrypted symmetrically with a passphrase as can be seen from its content:

```
# cat cakey.pem
-----BEGIN RSA PRIVATE KEY-----
Proc-Type: 4,ENCRYPTED
DEK-Info: AES-256-CBC,6AC2D519F9D4D933D6E598187FDA6408

FOtMkhnXT7M5IFng2OCjnXbxf+jde5VTcrWamDucWhyjireX5X4Mk5JfQH3ZOzIo
D8HRhOunjuxlYcZriUGdfO6q+ujqYssZ81bk8ae3b9gnTJ+A3UzTyqvDn9538ag7
...
h4xWBam8kxZxQ6y8eMyDpHluX99hYYV5MklROfH5wVoj79Z5WdHukuTF1GjcQ2Kc
hGZVaW9+k3Xt13GW83/3Ku75+3Vu+O+yboTCXEqBvHkFKhWEJYhKKHKkH572D2Gm
-----END RSA PRIVATE KEY-----
```

The encoding is obviously suitable for computational purposes, but hardly human-readable. The openssl tool can translate the Base64 encoding into a textual form:

---

[2] PKI and digital certificates are defined by the ITU-T X.509 standard.

```
# openssl x509 -in cacert.pem -noout -text
Certificate:
    Data:
        Version: 3 (0x2)
        Serial Number:
            c9:b1:15:73:34:88:06:c9
        Signature Algorithm: md5WithRSAEncryption
        Issuer: C=ZZ, ST=Province, L=City, O=Example Organization, OU=Central \
Administration, CN=Certificate Authority/emailAddress=ca@example.edu
        Validity
            Not Before: Jul 18 09:30:30 2006 GMT
            Not After : Apr 16 09:30:30 2016 GMT
        Subject: C=ZZ, ST=Province, L=City, O=Example Organization, OU=Central \
Administration, CN=Certificate Authority/emailAddress=ca@example.edu
        Subject Public Key Info:
            Public Key Algorithm: rsaEncryption
            RSA Public Key: (4096 bit)
                Modulus (4096 bit):
                    00:aa:e7:eb:90:3a:10:c1:0f:86:5a:42:a2:47:c5:
                    ...
                    f7:76:1c:dc:dc:e6:d3:9d:2c:d5:70:8b:e4:f8:75:
                    cb:2a:ab
                Exponent: 65537 (0x10001)
        X509v3 extensions:
            X509v3 Subject Key Identifier:
                06:C0:F5:47:F2:DD:22:5B:FD:23:6B:31:9C:76:9B:B2:B7:3C:94:08
            X509v3 Authority Key Identifier:
                keyid:06:C0:F5:47:F2:DD:22:5B:FD:23:6B:31:9C:76:9B:B2:B7:3C:94:08
                DirName:/C=ZZ/ST=Province/L=City/O=Example Organization/OU=\
Central Administration/CN=Certificate Authority/emailAddress=ca@example.edu
                serial:C9:B1:15:73:34:88:06:C9

            X509v3 Basic Constraints:
                CA:TRUE
    Signature Algorithm: md5WithRSAEncryption
        89:aa:c9:d9:86:a2:6f:8e:80:ef:9e:9b:d8:39:91:92:57:73:
        ...
        85:21:3b:47:c4:ba:12:6f
```

Notice that the certificate `Issuer` and the `Subject` coincide since this is a self signed certificate. Their syntax resembles a distinguished name for LDAP. Interestingly, certificates have apart from an expiry date also a latency period for the `Validity`.

7.3.3 Managing Certificates

A certificate authority issues certificates for users, and in special cases, also to non-human entities such as machines. An SSL-enabled service (e.g. a mail or a web server) uses its private key and the public certificate to authenticate the machine as we shall see in the following chapters. In the following we will generate certificates for both hosts and users, storing secret keys and certificates on files. Users may also take advantage of a PKI environment keeping their data in specialized hardware such as security tokens or smart cards.

Machine Certificates

Let us create a certificate for a server, for example our `ldap1.example.edu` server: we do not want to encrypt the private key since a machine, or better a service, should be able to start without providing a passphrase. The first step is to create the private key without any passphrase, omitting the encryption switch as showed earlier:

```
# openssl genrsa -out privatekeys/ldap1.pem 2048
Generating RSA private key, 2048 bit long modulus
.........................................................+++
...................+++
e is 65537 (0x10001)
```

Once the private key has been created, we can generate a certificate request for the LDAP server. A certificate request is nothing but the public key itself plus some information but without the CA digital signature, and is created with the `openssl req` command:

```
# openssl req -new -days 1000 -key privatekeys/ldap1.pem -out ldap1.req
You are about to be asked to enter information that will be incorporated
into your certificate request.
What you are about to enter is what is called a Distinguished Name or a DN.
There are quite a few fields but you can leave some blank
For some fields there will be a default value,
If you enter '.', the field will be left blank.
-----
Country Name (2 letter code) [ZZ]:
State or Province Name (full name) [Province]:
Locality Name (eg, city) [City]:
Organization Name (eg, company) [Example Organization]:
Organizational Unit Name (eg, section) [Central Administration]:
Common Name (eg, YOUR full name) []:ldap1.example.edu
Email Address (optional) []:

Please enter the following 'extra' attributes
to be sent with your certificate request
A good password (min length 4) []:
An optional company name []:
```

For the service we request a validy of 1000 days. Note that in order to employ a machine certificate in future SSL-enabled services, the public certificate, and so the request, must contain the fully qualified domain name `ldap1.example.edu`. Once the request has been created, it can be signed by the certificate authority validating its authenticity. The `openssl ca` command, conforming with the validity period, input and output files, signs the request generating a valid public certificate:

```
# openssl ca -days 1000 -in ldap1.req -out certificates/ldap1.pem
Using configuration from /usr/lib/ssl/openssl.cnf
Enter pass phrase for /etc/ssl/private/CA/cakey.pem:
Check that the request matches the signature
Signature ok
Certificate Details:
        Serial Number: 1 (0x1)
```

```
        Validity
            Not Before: Jul 18 09:55:22 2006 GMT
            Not After : Apr 13 09:55:22 2009 GMT
        Subject:
            countryName             = ZZ
            stateOrProvinceName     = Province
            localityName            = City
            organizationName        = Example Organization
            organizationalUnitName  = Central Administration
            commonName              = ldap1.example.edu
        X509v3 extensions:
            X509v3 Basic Constraints:
                CA:FALSE
            Netscape Comment:
                Example Organization (OpenSSL)
            X509v3 Subject Key Identifier:
                95:EC:4A:DD:66:DB:E0:9C:EE:FA:48:BD:99:D2:16:7C:B2:35:D3:21
            X509v3 Authority Key Identifier:
                keyid:06:C0:F5:47:F2:DD:22:5B:FD:23:6B:31:9C:76:9B:B2:B7:3C:94:08
                DirName:/C=ZZ/ST=Province/L=City/O=Example Organization/OU=\
Central Administration/CN=Certificate Authority/emailAddress=ca@example.edu
                serial:C9:B1:15:73:34:88:06:C9

Certificate is to be certified until Apr 13 09:55:22 2009 GMT (1000 days)
Sign the certificate? [y/n]:y


1 out of 1 certificate requests certified, commit? [y/n]y
Write out database with 1 new entries
Data Base Updated
```

As we can see, by default OpenSSL creates the certificate as we requested on the command line, and another one with the serial number as we specified in the configuration file. These two certificates are identical:

```
# ls newcerts/
01.pem

# ls certificates/
ldap1.pem

# diff newcerts/01.pem certificates/ldap1.pem
```

At this point the file with the request may be erased. The entire procedure creates some new files regarding the certificate attributes, and modifies our old index.txt and serial files:

```
# cat /etc/ssl/private/CA/serial
02

# cat /etc/ssl/private/CA/serial.old
01

# cat /etc/ssl/private/CA/index.txt
V       090413095522Z           01      unknown /C=ZZ/ST=Province/L=City/O=\
Example Organization/OU=Central Administration/CN=ldap1.example.edu

# cat /etc/ssl/private/CA/index.txt.attr
unique_subject = yes

# cat /etc/ssl/private/CA/index.txt.old
```

The `index.txt` file, as we can see from the above output, contains the issued certificates, with the validity flag V, the serial number 01, and the issued distinguished name `ldap1.example.edu`; the `index.txt.old` is empty since this is our first certificate.

User Certificates

Next we want our `testuser` to receive a certificate. Users may apply their certificates and private keys to perform critical procedures, such as logging into a system or digitally sign emails: for this reason we choose to encrypt the private key using a symmetric algorithm, in this case AES. Hence the loss of this private key is a smaller threat since any operation with the key would still require a passphrase. Typically, the private keys of users are smaller than those of services and our choice is to generate a 1024 bits long key. Let us generate the user's private key with the `openssl genrsa` tool, requiring an encryption with the `-aes256` switch:

```
# openssl genrsa -aes256 -out privatekeys/testuser.pem 1024
Generating RSA private key, 1024 bit long modulus
.....................+++++
........+++++
e is 65537 (0x10001)
Enter pass phrase for privatekeys/testuser.pem:
Verifying - Enter pass phrase for privatekeys/testuser.pem:
```

After the creation of the user's private key, encrypted with a passphrase, we issue the certificate request for the "Test User" individual whose email is `testuser@example.edu`:

```
# openssl req -new -key privatekeys/testuser.pem -out testuser.req
Enter pass phrase for privatekeys/testuser.pem:
You are about to be asked to enter information that will be incorporated
into your certificate request.
What you are about to enter is what is called a Distinguished Name or a DN.
There are quite a few fields but you can leave some blank
For some fields there will be a default value,
If you enter '.', the field will be left blank.
-----
Country Name (2 letter code) [ZZ]:
State or Province Name (full name) [Province]:
Locality Name (eg, city) [City]:
Organization Name (eg, company) [Example Organization]:
Organizational Unit Name (eg, section) [Central Administration]:
Common Name (eg, YOUR full name) []:Test User
Email Address (optional) []:testuser@example.edu

Please enter the following 'extra' attributes
to be sent with your certificate request
A good password (min length 4) []:
An optional company name []:
```

The user's passphrase is needed to create the request, and finally we are asked about another "extra" attribute: some password. This can be used by large organization to protect a certificate request, and then send it to the authority: since we want to handle all these steps by ourselves, we can safely leave this password empty. Next, we issue the certificate by signing the request:

```
# openssl ca -in testuser.req -out certificates/testuser.pem
Using configuration from /usr/lib/ssl/openssl.cnf
Enter pass phrase for /etc/ssl/private/CA/cakey.pem:
DEBUG[load_index]: unique_subject = "yes"
Check that the request matches the signature
Signature ok
Certificate Details:
        Serial Number: 2 (0x2)
        Validity
            Not Before: Jul 18 10:30:01 2006 GMT
            Not After : Jul 18 10:30:01 2007 GMT
        Subject:
            countryName               = ZZ
            stateOrProvinceName       = Province
            localityName              = City
            organizationName          = Example Organization
            organizationalUnitName    = Central Administration
            commonName                = Test User
            emailAddress              = testuser@example.edu
        X509v3 extensions:
            X509v3 Basic Constraints:
                CA:FALSE
            Netscape Comment:
                Example Organization (OpenSSL)
            X509v3 Subject Key Identifier:
                10:50:9E:C1:6B:F4:FB:1B:D2:D7:61:BF:9D:46:14:27:F7:F1:C3:FA
            X509v3 Authority Key Identifier:
                keyid:06:C0:F5:47:F2:DD:22:5B:FD:23:6B:31:9C:76:9B:B2:B7:3C:94:08
                DirName:/C=ZZ/ST=Province/L=City/O=Example Organization/OU=\
Central Administration/CN=Certificate Authority/emailAddress=ca@example.edu
                serial:C9:B1:15:73:34:88:06:C9

Certificate is to be certified until Jul 18 10:30:01 2007 GMT (365 days)
Sign the certificate? [y/n]:y


1 out of 1 certificate requests certified, commit? [y/n]y
Write out database with 1 new entries
Data Base Updated
```

At this point, we could erase the request file as we earlier did for the LDAP server. For this certificate the default value of validity applied which is one year.

Publishing Certificates

The whole point about user certificates is that users can use them to sign an electronic mail or receive it in encrypted form. This requires users to store their private keys securely: a system administration might use USB pen-drives, electronic tokens, or smart cards to store this critical information. The public key, as the name itself suggests, should then be made publicly available, a goal easily achieved with our LDAP infrastructure.

OpenLDAP can handle certificates in the DER format, so the first thing to do is to convert the certificate from the PEM standard to DER, using the `openssl` tool:

```
# cd /etc/ssl/private/CA/certificates

# openssl x509 -in testuser.pem -outform DER -out testuser.der

# file testuser.der
testuser.der: data
```

As we can see from the output of the **file** command, the DER format is not human readable. Next, we create an LDIF file that modifies our **testuser** entry adding the **userCertificate** attribute in binary form from the file:

```
dn: uid=testuser,ou=users,dc=example,dc=edu
userCertificate;binary:<file:///etc/ssl/private/CA/certificates/testuser.der
```

Finally we can import the data, provided that we are authenticated as **sysadmin** via Kerberos:

```
# ldapmodify -f testuser.ldif
SASL/GSSAPI authentication started
SASL username: sysadmin@EXAMPLE.EDU
SASL SSF: 56
SASL installing layers
modifying entry "uid=testuser,ou=users,dc=example,dc=edu"
```

The public certificate is now publicly available in the LDAP database, and thus it can be consulted e.g. to verify a digitally signed email:

```
# ldapsearch -LLL "uid=testuser"
SASL/GSSAPI authentication started
SASL username: sysadmin@EXAMPLE.EDU
SASL SSF: 56
SASL installing layers
dn: uid=testuser,ou=users,dc=example,dc=edu
objectClass: top
objectClass: posixAccount
objectClass: shadowAccount
objectClass: inetOrgPerson
cn: Test
sn: User
uid: testuser
uidNumber: 10000
gidNumber: 10000
loginShell: /bin/bash
gecos: Test User,001,555-123,1-123,none
homeDirectory: /afs/example.edu/users/testuser
userCertificate;binary:: MIIF1DCCA3ygAwIBAgIBAjANBgkqhkiG9w0BAQUFADCBrjELMAkGA
 1UEBhMCW1oxETAPBgNVBAgTCFByb3ZpbmN1MQOwCwYDVQQHEwRDaXR5MROwGwYDVQQKExRFeGFtcG
 ...
 LFI70YI3Q==
```

Mozilla and former Netscape can refer to such certificate information provided by directory servers.

7.3.4 Revoking Certificates

For some reasons we may want to revoke a certificate, marking it as invalid. Revoking certificates does not affect the **index.txt** or **serial** files, but generates a list of all revoked certificate numbers: the list should then be exported publicly to ensure that all SSL-enabled services are aware of all invalid certificates.

The list of all available certificates is stored in the `index.txt` file, which contains textual human readable data:

```
# cat index.txt
V        0904130955222Z              01      unknown /C=ZZ/ST=Province/L=City/O=\
Example Organization/OU=Central Administration/CN=ldap1.example.edu
V        070718103001Z               02      unknown /C=ZZ/ST=Province/L=City/O=\
Example Organization/OU=Central Administration/CN=Test User/emailAddress=\
testuser@example.edu
```

A certificate revocation is accomplished with the `openssl` tool with the `-revoke` switch followed by the targeted certificate, an operation that can be performed only by individuals who know the CA passphrase, since the revocation list gets signed by the CA:

```
# openssl ca -revoke certificates/testuser.pem
Using configuration from /usr/lib/ssl/openssl.cnf
Enter pass phrase for /etc/ssl/private/CA/cakey.pem:
Revoking Certificate 02.
Data Base Updated
```

After revoking a certificate for `testuser`, we immediately see the changes in the `index.txt` file, with the certificate marked as `R` "revoked" instead of `V` "valid":

```
# cat index.txt
V        0904130955222Z              01      unknown /C=ZZ/ST=Province/L=City/O=\
Example Organization/OU=Central Administration/CN=ldap1.example.edu
R        070718103001Z  060718120839Z 02     unknown /C=ZZ/ST=Province/L=\
City/O=Example Organization/OU=Central Administration/CN=Test User/emailAddress=\
testuser@example.edu
```

After revoking a certificate, we must create a new revoked certificate list by issuing the `openssl` command with the `-gencrl` switch:

```
# openssl ca -gencrl -out crl/20060718.pem
Using configuration from /usr/lib/ssl/openssl.cnf
Enter pass phrase for /etc/ssl/private/CA/cakey.pem:
```

After revoking a certificate, the generated CRL has to be distributed to the affected applications in order to disallow the usage of the invalidated certificate. As a control check, we can verify that the serial number of the revoked certificate matches the one we really intended to withdraw:

```
# openssl crl -in 20060718.pem -noout -text
Certificate Revocation List (CRL):
        Version 1 (0x0)
        Signature Algorithm: md5WithRSAEncryption
        Issuer: /C=ZZ/ST=Province/L=City/O=Example Organization/OU=Central \
Administration/CN=Certificate Authority/emailAddress=ca@example.edu
```

```
      Last Update: Jul 18 12:14:52 2006 GMT
      Next Update: Oct 16 12:14:52 2006 GMT
Revoked Certificates:
   Serial Number: 02
      Revocation Date: Jul 18 12:08:39 2006 GMT
   Signature Algorithm: md5WithRSAEncryption
      46:50:87:6c:ed:02:9e:b9:a5:0c:e9:6a:4e:1b:80:4d:88:87:
      ...
      19:42:4c:ab:db:a3:1a:f7
```

The serial number 2 was that one of our **testuser**. According to the default settings this CRL is valid for 90 days and within this period a new list has to be created. Attention, since some services referring to expired CRLs might refuse to function.

Practice

Exercise 25. Compare a PGP, OpenPGP, or GnuPG based approach with an S/MIME PKI for secure electronic mail. Remember that PKI data can be stored or even generated on smart-cards. For example there exist small USB based tokens.

Exercise 26. Confront CRLs for revoked certificates with the more recent on-line certificate validation protocol OCSP. Some client software like Mozilla Thunderbird support this protocol. For server daemons this still has to arrive.

Exercise 27. Test some backup procedure over the network with a tool of your choice like **partimage**, **dd**, or **backup**. NFS can be used as one method to store files, while SSH/SCP can be used as a safer alternative for transmission.

Exercise 28. Think of a more scalable solution for a PKI. Ubuntu and the new upcoming release of Debian contain **newpki** packages. This becomes convenient when you have to handle larger amounts of certificates.

Web Server

> *The World Wide Web is the only thing I know of whose*
> *shortened form takes three times longer to say than its*
> *long form.*
> Douglas Adams

8.1 The World Wide Web

The history of networking may be traced back to the ARPANet research
project, *Advanced Research Projects Agency Network*, lead by the United
States Department of Defense, whose objective was to interconnect computers via a network. Since the establishment of ARPANet in mid-60s, the older
NCP protocol was replaced by the more modern TCP/IP network stack, and
in 1980 Timothy John Berners-Lee and Jedda Smith, at the time working
at the CERN[1], created the ENQUIRE, a database project with editing facilities. Later in 1984 Berners-Lee was facing problems when presenting to
his colleagues, all of them physicists, details and results regarding their research projects: he adopted the idea of hypertext documents to solve their
demonstration problems. The concept of "hypertexts", documents containing
links to other objects, dates back to the beginning of the 20th century, with
Theodor Holm Nelson conceiving the "hypertext" word itself in 1965. In 1990
Berners-Lee, aided by Robert Cailliau, developed on a NeXT Cube machine
the first web tools, a server program and a browser with editing capabilities,
on the first web server host named `info.cern.ch`, while the web browser was
simply called `WorldWideWeb`—the original NeXT Cube machine is still exhib-
ited in the public CERN museum. Later in 1991 Berners-Lee posted on the
`alt.hypertext` newsgroup the official public project opening:

"*The WWW project was started to allow high energy physicists to share
data, news, and documentation. We are very interested in spreading the web
to other areas, and having gateway servers for other data. Collaborators wel-
come!*"—Berners-Lee on `alt.hypertext` (excerpt).

The WWW grew faster than anyone expected, rapidly replacing other
hypertext protocols such as Gopher, and increasing its popularity with the
birth of graphical web browsers also on platforms different from the NeXT.
The first graphical browser was the ViolaWWW on X-based UNIX platforms,

---

[1] Conseil Européen pour la Recherche Nucléaire, located in Geneva, Switzerland.

swiftly overtaken by the more famous Mosaic[2] browser, pictured in Fig. 8.1, which gave the start to the WWW boom of the 90s, and changing its name in 1994 to the modern Netscape Navigator.

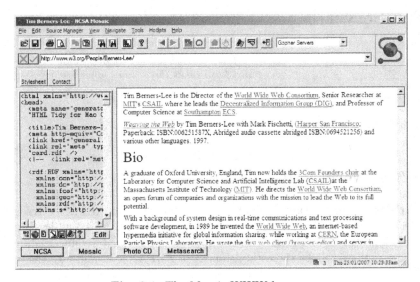

Fig. 8.1. The Mosaic WWW browser

This chapter explains the installation and configuration of a web server, with additional services such as a database and a scripting language to allow the server to manage dynamic web contents. The stack of services is usually referred as "LAMP", the acronym of Linux, Apache, MySQL and PHP, although the latter character is sometimes referring to other languages such as Perl or Python. Moreover, we will enable the web daemon to provide users with WebDAV access and personal web space. The first parts of this chapter abstract from our backbone infrastructure, and can be reproduced on any stand-alone machine. Personal web pages, WebDAV, or deploying the web server pages from the AFS file space, depend on the OpenAFS client as well as Kerberos and OpenLDAP.

8.2 Apache

The first version of the Apache Web Server was developed at the birthplace of the Mosaic Web Browser, the NCSA, by Robert McCool and others with the original name of NCSA HTTPd. The HTTPd server introduced a first version of dynamic web pages handling via Common Gateway Interfaces, or CGI,

---

[2] Mosaic was originally developed by Marc Andreessen and Eric Bina of the NCSA, the US National Center for Supercomputing Applications.

common programs that are run by the server in order to generate HTML code based on some input, usually given by a user through web browser interactions. The official Apache documentation states that the name changed from HTTPd in honor of the Native American Apache tribe, but another common interpretation was given in 1997 stating that the name refers to the fragile development of HTTPd, dubbing the program as "a patchy server".

The latest version of the Apache web server is the second, and it is the most used HTTP server in the open source world, currently being developed by the Apache Software Foundation. Apache is a modular server, supporting modern standards such as DAV, SSL, various scripting languages, and allows great flexibility with respect to authentication methods. Our first machine, called www.example.edu will initially serve web pages created on the local file system, but as we will see, the Apache server can be configured to access the AFS file space as well.

8.2.1 Installing Apache

Debian includes Apache version 2 in its official package repository, but provides also the old Apache 1.3 for legacy applications. Our choice falls to the latest version, distributed via the apache2 package, which automatically includes the SSL support. All the available Apache modules are located in the /usr/lib/apache2/modules/ directory, which for instance contains the mod_ssl.so SSL module:

```
# ls /usr/lib/apache2/modules/
httpd.exp           mod_cgi.so          mod_include.so       mod_speling.so
mod_actions.so      mod_dav_fs.so       mod_info.so          mod_ssl.so
mod_asis.so         mod_dav.so          mod_ldap.so          mod_suexec.so
mod_auth_anon.so    mod_deflate.so      mod_mem_cache.so     mod_unique_id.so
mod_auth_dbm.so     mod_disk_cache.so   mod_mime_magic.so    mod_userdir.so
mod_auth_digest.so  mod_expires.so      mod_proxy_connect.so mod_usertrack.so
mod_auth_ldap.so    mod_ext_filter.so   mod_proxy_ftp.so     mod_vhost_alias.so
mod_cache.so        mod_file_cache.so   mod_proxy_http.so
mod_cern_meta.so    mod_headers.so      mod_proxy.so
mod_cgid.so         mod_imap.so         mod_rewrite.so
```

Configuring Apache

After stopping the service, we can proceed in configuring the Apache daemon. All the configuration files are located in the /etc/apache2/ directory, containing the list of available and enabled modules in mods-available and mods-enabled, plus the list of available and managed web sites in sites-available and sites-enabled:

```
# ls /etc/apache2/
apache2.conf  httpd.conf       mods-enabled/  sites-available/
conf.d/       magic            ports.conf     sites-enabled/
envvars       mods-available/  README         ssl/
```

Both modules and sites can be enabled with Apache's commands **a2enmod** and **a2ensite**, and disabled by their counterparts commands **a2dismod** and **a2dissite**. Debian provides a default configuration file for a site that can be used as an initial setting, so let us copy the file with a name corresponding to our domain:

```
# cd /etc/apache2/sites-available/

# cp default example.edu
```

A site configuration file is an XML-like text, and specifies at the beginning the IP addresses to which the web server name **www.example.edu** is resolved with the **NameVirtualHost** directive. The option allows three different settings: the real IP address, the host name, or the * wildcard, meaning to handle all connections. The latter is chosen since it does not hard-wire any IP address to the WWW server. The configuration for the server is described in the **<VirtualHost>** stanza, setting the web site root location **DocumentRoot** (i.e. where Apache will search for site files), in our case the **/var/www/example.edu/** directory, the server administrator's email **ServerAdmin** and logging facilities (e.g. **ErrorLog** and **LogLevel**). Additionally we define access regulations on a per-directory basis as in the following example:

```
NameVirtualHost *
<VirtualHost *>
        ServerAdmin www@example.edu

        DocumentRoot /var/www/example.edu
        <Directory />
                Options FollowSymLinks
                AllowOverride None
        </Directory>
        <Directory /var/www/example.edu>
                Options All MultiViews
                AllowOverride All
                Order allow,deny
                Allow from all
        </Directory>

        ErrorLog /var/log/apache2/error.log
        LogLevel warn
        CustomLog /var/log/apache2/access.log combined

</VirtualHost>
```

The **<Directory>** stanzas will enable or disable options applied to locations that are contained in the header. The **AllowOverride** option allows or disallows **.htaccess** files which may contain user restrictions to particular locations: in our example **<Directory />** disallows all restrictions with the **AllowOverride None** directive. Obviously the **Options** instruction will consent further settings, such as **FollowSymLinks** which allows Apache to make use of symbolic links within the location and its subdirectories, unless other restrictions are applied by following **<Directory>** sections. Once the main settings are satisfied, Apache will obey to subsequent rules, in this case to all the options regarding the /var/www/example.edu/ directory. In this location we allow all options with Options All included content negotiations with MultiViews[3], allowing for instance multiple language sites. The AllowOverride All directive applies only to subdirectories of the root location, stating that allowance directives have higher priority than denial ones with the Order option, although the default is deny in that case: since our primary objective is to implement a public web server, we will not prevent any host from accessing our site, as specified by the Allow from all option.

Once the options for our site are defined, we create the root location /var/www/example.edu/ enabling all users to access its contents:

```
# mkdir /var/www/example.edu

# ls -l /var/www/
total 8
drwxr-xr-x  2 root root 4096 2006-07-18 14:29 apache2-default/
drwxr-xr-x  2 root root 4096 2006-07-18 14:41 example.edu/
```

It is possible to have the root directory in the AFS file space, but this requires additional configurations that will be explained later, enabling personal web pages for our users. Now we disable the default site, provided by Debian, and enable ours:

```
# a2ensite example.edu
Site example.edu installed; run /etc/init.d/apache2 reload to enable.

# a2dissite default
Site default disabled; run /etc/init.d/apache2 reload to fully disable.
```

The warning can be ignored since we stopped the server. To test our server, we create an index.html file in /var/www/example.org/ directory, which is one of the default files, Apache searches for a location:

```
<html>
<head><title>Example Organization</title></head>
<body>
This is the site for our Example Organization.
</body>
</html>
```

At this point we are ready to start Apache, and use a web browser to reach the http://www.example.edu/ URL as in Fig. 8.2:

---

[3] Apache may serve multiple contents based on language, object types, and other options as defined by the HTTP protocol. For instance browsers may negotiate about languages with an HTTP request as Accept-Language: en; q=1.0, eo; q=0.5, accepting English with higher priority than Esperanto.

```
# /etc/init.d/apache2 start
Starting web server: Apache2.
```

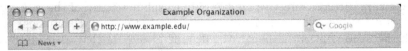

This is the site for our Example Organization.

Fig. 8.2. Browsing the Example Site

Site Information

More information about our web server can be provided for debugging purposes over the network by means of a module called `info`. In the configuration file we have to add a virtual location called for instance `server-info`, and within the `<Location>` stanza we will forward all requests to the Apache `info` service:

```
NameVirtualHost *
<VirtualHost *>
        ServerAdmin www@example.edu

        DocumentRoot /var/www/example.edu
        <Directory />
                Options FollowSymLinks
                AllowOverride None
        </Directory>
        <Directory /var/www/example.edu>
                Options All MultiViews
                AllowOverride All
                Order allow,deny
                Allow from all
        </Directory>

        <Location /server-info>
```

```
         SetHandler server-info
    </Location>

    ErrorLog /var/log/apache2/error.log
    LogLevel warn
    CustomLog /var/log/apache2/access.log combined

</VirtualHost>
```

Once the module has been enabled with the **a2enmod** tool, we can restart Apache to make changes take effect, as indicated by the tool's output:

```
# a2enmod info
Module info installed; run /etc/init.d/apache2 force-reload to enable.

# /etc/init.d/apache2 force-reload
Forcing reload of web server: Apache2.
```

Browsing this specific URL coded in the configuration file, so connecting to http://www.example.edu/server-info, results in a page which shows all available information as in Fig. 8.3. However, in a production environment it is recommended to disable the **info** module.

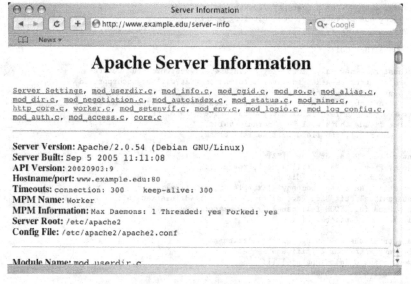

Fig. 8.3. The Apache **info** Module

8.2.2 Secure HTTP

Simple web browsing in a read-only fashion normally does not need to be protected further, but this situation changes if we plan to deploy services requiring some sort of authentication or some other confidential information gets transmitted. In this case the secure protocol HTTPS is used which works like HTTP over an SSL encrypted channel.

Such an SSL-based communication involves both asymmetric and symmetric key encryption methods. The asymmetric encryption is used to securely authenticate the host with its publicly available certificate, and upon a successful verification of the server identity, both client and server establish a symmetrically-encrypted channel, where the secret key has been exchanged with an asymmetric encoding. Nowadays the old SSL protocol is replaced by the modern TLS, which enables clients to negotiate the strength of the encryption algorithm.

SSL Certificate

For such a secured environment we need a certificate for our web server. First, we generate a private key and a certificate request on the machine we are using for our certificate authority. The certificate name must match the FQDN of the server, otherwise SSL-enabled services may complain or even refuse to work:

```
# openssl genrsa -out privatekeys/wwwkey.pem 2048
Generating RSA private key, 2048 bit long modulus
.....................................................................................+++
.......................................................................+++
e is 65537 (0x10001)

# openssl req -new -days 1000 -key privatekeys/wwwkey.pem -out www.req
You are about to be asked to enter information that will be incorporated
into your certificate request.
What you are about to enter is what is called a Distinguished Name or a DN.
There are quite a few fields but you can leave some blank
For some fields there will be a default value,
If you enter '.', the field will be left blank.
-----
Country Name (2 letter code) [ZZ]:
State or Province Name (full name) [Province]:
Locality Name (eg, city) [City]:
Organization Name (eg, company) [Example Organization]:
Organizational Unit Name (eg, section) [Central Administration]:
Common Name (eg, YOUR full name) []:www.example.edu
Email Address (optional) []:

Please enter the following 'extra' attributes
to be sent with your certificate request
A good password (min length 4) []:
An optional company name []:
```

Then we are able to generate the certificate itself, in other words we sign the certificate request with the CA private key so that the authenticity of the issued certificate may be verified by means of the CA public certificate:

```
# openssl ca -days 1000 -in www.req -out certificates/wwwcert.pem
Using configuration from /usr/lib/ssl/openssl.cnf
Enter pass phrase for /etc/ssl/private/CA/cakey.pem:
Check that the request matches the signature
```

```
Signature ok
Certificate Details:
        Serial Number: 3 (0x3)
        Validity
            Not Before: Jul 18 13:18:16 2006 GMT
            Not After : Apr 13 13:18:16 2009 GMT
        Subject:
            countryName             = ZZ
            stateOrProvinceName     = Province
            localityName            = City
            organizationName        = Example Organization
            organizationalUnitName  = Central Administration
            commonName              = www.example.edu
        X509v3 extensions:
            X509v3 Basic Constraints:
                CA:FALSE
            Netscape Comment:
                Example Organization (OpenSSL)
            X509v3 Subject Key Identifier:
                5F:03:99:74:27:37:5B:AA:5D:A4:EC:1B:7A:5F:55:52:88:5D:3B:3D
            X509v3 Authority Key Identifier:
                keyid:06:C0:F5:47:F2:DD:22:5B:FD:23:6B:31:9C:76:9B:B2:B7:3C:94:08
                DirName:/C=ZZ/ST=Province/L=City/O=Example Organization/\
OU=Central Administration/CN=Certificate Authority/emailAddress=ca@example.edu
                serial:C9:B1:15:73:34:88:06:C9

Certificate is to be certified until Apr 13 13:18:16 2009 GMT (1000 days)
Sign the certificate? [y/n]:y


1 out of 1 certificate requests certified, commit? [y/n]y
Write out database with 1 new entries
Data Base Updated
```

Afterwards we have to copy the CA public certificate, the web server certificate, and its private key to the web server machine in **/etc/apache2/ssl/**:

```
# ls -l /etc/apache2/ssl
total 16
-r--r--r--  1 root root 2480 2006-07-18 15:22 cacert.pem
-r--r--r--  1 root root 6441 2006-07-18 15:24 wwwcert.pem
-r--------  1 root root 1679 2006-07-18 15:24 wwwkey.pem
```

The permission bits as shown for the private key file and for the certificates are important for their protection: certificates are world-readable, while the secret key for the web server may be read only by the **root** user.

Apache Configuration

The HTTP and HTTPS protocol work on different TCP ports, and it is useful for didactic purposes to create a new site handled by Apache, working only on the encrypted channel. In our example we start to distinguish the incoming port:

```
NameVirtualHost *
<VirtualHost *:80>
        ServerAdmin www@example.edu

        DocumentRoot /var/www/example.edu
```

```
    <Directory />
            Options FollowSymLinks
            AllowOverride None
    </Directory>
    <Directory /var/www/example.edu>
            Options All MultiViews
            AllowOverride All
            Order allow,deny
            Allow from all
    </Directory>

    ErrorLog /var/log/apache2/error.log
    LogLevel warn
    CustomLog /var/log/apache2/access.log combined

</VirtualHost>
```

By default, the `example.edu` location will be served on the unencrypted HTTP port 80 by our `www.example.edu` host. The new HTTPS port must be then added to the `ports.conf` file, that tells Apache which ports it should listen to: we have to enable the port 443 which corresponds to HTTPS:

```
Listen 80
Listen 443
```

At this point we can start from the insecure web server configuration file to create the new SSL-enabled location. This new file contains the configuration for our secured site, pointing at a different directory in the file system, in our example to `/var/www/example.edu_ssl/`. In addition to the new port specification in the `<VirtualHost>` section, we must enable the SSL engine, allowing high and medium security level for encryption, and permitting only SSL version 3 and TLS communications with the `SSLProtocol` directive. It is then mandatory to specify the SSL certificates for the server and the issuing CA, along with the `www.example.edu` private key as in the following:

```
<VirtualHost *:443>
        ServerAdmin www@example.edu

        SSLEngine on
        SSLCipherSuite HIGH:MEDIUM
        SSLProtocol -all +SSLv3 +TLSv1
        SSLCaCertificateFile /etc/apache2/ssl/cacert.pem
        SSLCertificateFile /etc/apache2/ssl/wwwcert.pem
        SSLCertificateKeyFile /etc/apache2/ssl/wwwkey.pem

        DocumentRoot /var/www/example.edu_ssl
        <Directory />
                Options FollowSymLinks
                AllowOverride None
        </Directory>
        <Directory /var/www/example.edu_ssl>
                Options All MultiViews
                AllowOverride All
                Order allow,deny
                Allow from all
        </Directory>

        ErrorLog /var/log/apache2/error_ssl.log
```

```
        LogLevel warn
        CustomLog /var/log/apache2/access_ssl.log combined

</VirtualHost>
```

A brief list of SSL-related options are described in Table 8.1, but for a complete index it is recommended to refer to the official Apache documentation. The first part of the global configuration is the same as in our previous site like the `ServerAdmin` option, while the `DocumentRoot` is set to a different directory, and for better debugging the logging information is sent to different files than the logging archives of our principal unencrypted site. Now we can

Table 8.1. Apache SSL options (excerpt)

Option	Meaning
SSLCACertificateFile	The CA public certificate file
SSLCARevocationFile	The optional revoked certificates list
SSLCertificateFile	The web server public certificate file
SSLCertificateKeyFile	The web server private key file
SSLCipherSuite	Enforces encryption methods for SSL negotiations
SSLEngine	Enable or disable SSL/TLS
SSLProtocol	Configures allowed SSL protocols
SSLVerifyClient	Require the verification of the client's certificate

create `/var/www/example.edu_ssl/`, the root directory for our secure site, and put there a sample index file:

```
<html>
<head><title>Example Organization</title></head>
<body>
This is the site for our Example Organization with SSL.
</body>
</html>
```

Finally we have to enable the `ssl` module for our web server and restart it in order to allow the daemon to listen on both ports:

```
# a2enmod ssl
Module ssl installed; run /etc/init.d/apache2 force-reload to enable.

# /etc/init.d/apache2 restart
Stopping web server: Apache2.
Starting web server: Apache2.
```

The `nmap` tool shows that the host is currently listening on the 80 and 443 TCP ports, and we can browse the new site `https://www.example.edu/` as in Fig. 8.4:

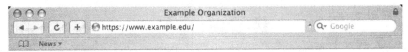

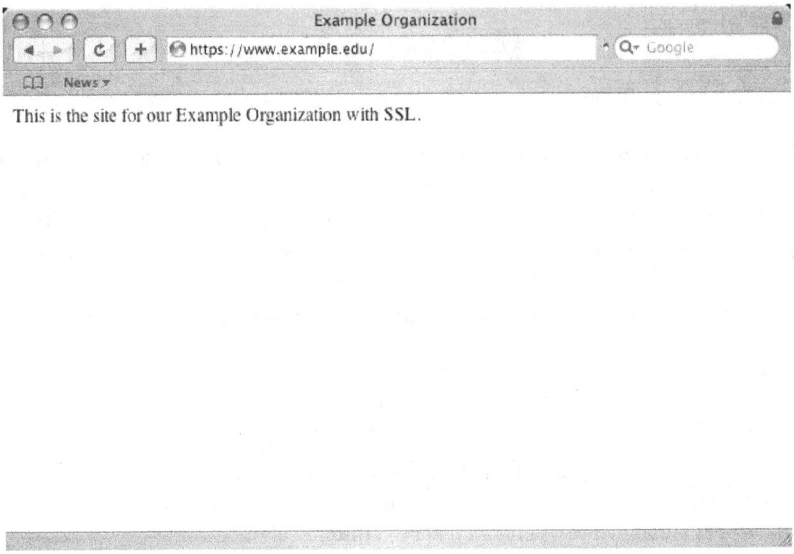

This is the site for our Example Organization with SSL.

Fig. 8.4. Browsing the Secure Example web site

```
# nmap localhost

Starting nmap 3.81 ( http://www.insecure.org/nmap/ ) at 2006-07-18 15:44 CEST
Interesting ports on localhost.localdomain (127.0.0.1):
(The 1660 ports scanned but not shown below are in state: closed)
PORT    STATE SERVICE
80/tcp  open  http
443/tcp open  https

Nmap finished: 1 IP address (1 host up) scanned in 0.510 seconds
```

At a first visit, a web browser might complain that the certificate from the web server is not trusted, or known, since it is not signed by any of the well-known certificate authorities. Certificates from our CA are not considered as valid as those released by third-party companies trusted by default. A good practice is to make our CA certificate publicly available, for example by providing it on the web site itself: clients can download the certificate, if the organization and the web site is believed to be authentic, and then import it in their system, permanently trusting all certificates signed by that CA.

8.3 MySQL

MySQL is probably the most used database in the free software world, becoming popular with the de facto standardization of the LAMP stack. MySQL is a lightweight database developed and maintained by the MySQL AB, a Swedish company established in the mid-90s. This multi-threaded and multi-user database is usually employed in dynamic web page generation, and is currently available free of charge to the public, and with commercial licenses, too. Well known users of this product are the free online encyclopedia *Wikipedia* and the *WordPress* personal blogging software; among the commercial users we may mention the online travel agency *Travelocity* and the NASA with their NASA Acquisition Internet Service (NAIS).

Currently Debian includes MySQL in their distribution, providing MySQL 4.1 along with the legacy 4.0 version. Our choice falls on the most up-to-date version contained in the `mysql-server-4.1` package. The default configuration locally binds the database to the host, making the service available for only `localhost`. By default MySQL under Debian has a user called `root` with administrative rights inside the database without a password, which can be employed in a first to create a new administrative entity. We can then proceed connecting to the data base server with the client tool `mysql`, and create a new administrator, protected with a password[4]:

```
# mysql -u root
Welcome to the MySQL monitor.  Commands end with ; or \g.
Your MySQL connection id is 5 to server version: 4.1.11-Debian_4sarge5-log

Type 'help;' or '\h' for help. Type '\c' to clear the buffer.

mysql> connect mysql;
Reading table information for completion of table and column names
You can turn off this feature to get a quicker startup with -A

Connection id:    6
Current database: mysql

mysql> select Host,User from user;
+-----------+------------------+
| Host      | User             |
+-----------+------------------+
| localhost | debian-sys-maint |
| localhost | root             |
| www       | root             |
+-----------+------------------+
3 rows in set (0.00 sec)
```

Note that the `mysql` tool has been started specifying the `root` user with the –u option to gain administrative privileges; moreover, the users currently available to MySQL contain `debian-sys-maint`, which will be described shortly. Using the `grant` command we create a user `admin` granting all administrative privileges and binding its usage to the `localhost` machine:

```
mysql> grant all privileges on *.* to 'admin'@'localhost' identified by 'mypasswd' \
with grant option;
Query OK, 0 rows affected (0.01 sec)
```

The password, in this case `mypasswd`, is provided in clear-text on the command line, so it is advisable that nobody is looking at the screen while per-

---

[4] A complete description of MySQL and the SQL language used to manipulate the database is out of the scope of this book.

forming this operation. We can now safely use this new administrative user
by quitting MySQL and reconnecting with the client:

```
# mysql -u admin -p
Enter password:
Welcome to the MySQL monitor.  Commands end with ; or \g.
Your MySQL connection id is 7 to server version: 4.1.11-Debian_4sarge5-log

Type 'help;' or '\h' for help. Type '\c' to clear the buffer.

mysql> connect mysql;
Reading table information for completion of table and column names
You can turn off this feature to get a quicker startup with -A

Connection id:    8
Current database: mysql

mysql> select user,host from user;
+------------------+-----------+
| user             | host      |
+------------------+-----------+
| admin            | localhost |
| debian-sys-maint | localhost |
| root             | localhost |
| root             | www       |
+------------------+-----------+
4 rows in set (0.00 sec)
```

MySQL stores internally users and the encrypted version of their password,
and having added the new **admin** user we may remove the previous user **root**:

```
mysql> delete from user where user = 'root';
Query OK, 2 rows affected (0.01 sec)

mysql> flush privileges;
Query OK, 0 rows affected (0.00 sec)

mysql> select user,host,password from user;
+------------------+-----------+------------------+
| user             | host      | password         |
+------------------+-----------+------------------+
| debian-sys-maint | localhost | 35171d6b5e02839a |
| admin            | localhost | 7d02d4862a143836 |
+------------------+-----------+------------------+
2 rows in set (0.00 sec)
```

In case of losing the **admin** password, Debian provides a superuser called
debian-sys-maint, with the password stored in a file located in **/etc/mysql/**
called **debian.cnf**:

```
# Automatically generated for Debian scripts. DO NOT TOUCH!
[client]
host     = localhost
user     = debian-sys-maint
password = qkWyfZVJC7mYrINd
socket   = /var/run/mysqld/mysqld.sock
```

The permission bits for this file allow only the **root** user:

```
# ls -l
total 16
-rw-------  1 root root  185 2006-07-18 16:04 debian.cnf
-rw-r--r--  1 root root  610 2006-07-10 21:43 debian-log-rotate.conf
-rwxr-xr-x  1 root root  559 2006-07-10 21:43 debian-start*
-rw-r--r--  1 root root 3315 2006-07-10 21:42 my.cnf
```

Non-administrative Users

As a practical security habit, administrative users should not be used for
daily work, and the same rule applies to MySQL users. We want to create a
non-administrative user allowing it to interact with MySQL on a personalized
database. Every web-based project will have a dedicated user with a dedicated database, and to simplify maintenance, we choose to have their names
coincide. For the moment as an example, we add a database **testdb** and simultaneously create a new user **testuser**, granting all the privileges to that
new database:

```
# mysql -u admin -p
Enter password:
Welcome to the MySQL monitor.  Commands end with ; or \g.
Your MySQL connection id is 12 to server version: 4.1.11-Debian_4sarge5-log

Type 'help;' or '\h' for help. Type '\c' to clear the buffer.

mysql> connect mysql;
Reading table information for completion of table and column names
You can turn off this feature to get a quicker startup with -A

Connection id:    13
Current database: mysql

mysql> create database testdb;
Query OK, 1 row affected (0.00 sec)

mysql> grant all privileges on testdb.* to 'testuser' identified by 'testpw';
Query OK, 0 rows affected (0.00 sec)
```

The **grant** command as a side effect creates a new user, connecting in the
db table the new user and the database:

```
mysql> select user,host from user;
+-----------------+-----------+
| user            | host      |
+-----------------+-----------+
| testuser        | %         |
| admin           | localhost |
| debian-sys-maint | localhost |
+-----------------+-----------+
3 rows in set (0.00 sec)

mysql> select host,db,user from db;
+------+--------+----------+
| host | db     | user     |
+------+--------+----------+
| %    | testdb | testuser |
+------+--------+----------+
1 row in set (0.01 sec)
```

This new `testuser` is not to be confused with the corresponding user of AFS or UNIX: they are completely distinct entities. As we can see from the output above the database `testdb` can be managed by `testuser` regardless of the host where the user connects from, if MySQL permits such connection.

Testing Users

We can finally test this new user connecting to the MySQL server with the `mysql` client tool and verifying that `testuser` cannot perform any operation on the MySQL private `mysql` administrative database:

```
# mysql -u testuser -p
Enter password:
Welcome to the MySQL monitor.  Commands end with ; or \g.
Your MySQL connection id is 14 to server version: 4.1.11-Debian_4sarge5-log

Type 'help;' or '\h' for help. Type '\c' to clear the buffer.

mysql> connect mysql;
ERROR 1044 (42000): Access denied for user 'testuser'@'%' to database 'mysql'
```

Our normal user can connect to its own personal database `testdb`, which at this point contains no tables:

```
mysql> connect testdb;
Connection id:    16
Current database: testdb

mysql> show tables;
Empty set (0.00 sec)
```

We granted all privileges to `testuser` in its sandbox, so we can test writing permissions by creating a new table and inserting new values:

```
mysql> create table testtable (i int);
Query OK, 0 rows affected (0.00 sec)

mysql> select * from testtable;
Empty set (0.00 sec)

mysql> insert into testtable values (0);
Query OK, 1 row affected (0.00 sec)

mysql> insert into testtable values (1);
Query OK, 1 row affected (0.00 sec)

mysql> select * from testtable;
+------+
| i    |
+------+
|    0 |
|    1 |
+------+
2 rows in set (0.00 sec)

mysql> quit
Bye
```

8.4 Adding PHP

Since the introduction of CGIs in the historical web server HTTPd, simple programs, that generated HTML pages dynamically provided with particular input, stimulated, that dynamic scripting languages and tools have prospered. One of the first processing languages used in GCIs, apart from plain C, was Perl[5], a programming language originally developed by Larry Wall in 1987.

The last letter in the LAMP acronym was originally referred to another scripting language called PHP, a recursive abbreviation standing for *PHP Hypertext Preprocessor*. In the beginning PHP, developed in C by Rasmus Lerdorf in 1994, was intended as a replacement of Perl scripts, whose language parser was later rewritten by Zeev Suraski and Andi Gutmans, who also changed the name from the original "Personal Home Page Tools" to the contemporary acronym. As a side-note, the LAMP stack is also known to be associated to other languages, such as the Python object-oriented programming language besides Perl.

The stable version of the Debian GNU/Linux distribution includes packages for the version 4 of the PHP scripting language, provided in form of a module for Apache, and contained in the `libapache2-mod-php4` package. The Debian configuration script installs the necessary files and also enables the Apache module:

```
# ls mods-available/*php*
mods-available/php4.conf  mods-available/php4.load

# a2enmod php4
This module is already enabled!
```

After the installation of the package Apache is already configured to execute PHP scripts since a restart has been forced. To test the server interaction with the PHP language, we create a very basic script called `test.php` calling a PHP function that gives us PHP-related information:

```
<? phpinfo(); ?>
```

We place a copy of this file in our HTTP document root, and also in the HTTPS location. Connecting to `http://www.example.edu/test.php` on the unencrypted site, we will be shown a web page, generated by the `phpinfo()` function, as in Fig. 8.5. The same script run from the encrypted site, shows a similar page as the unencrypted version, showing also the server root directory pointing to the SSL-based web service as in Fig. 8.6.

---

[5] The original name was meant to be "Pearl", but the name conflicted with the PEARL programming language. The acronym "Practical Extraction and Report Language" is a later non-official invention.

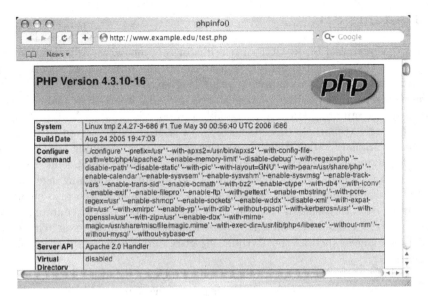

Fig. 8.5. The PHP informative page

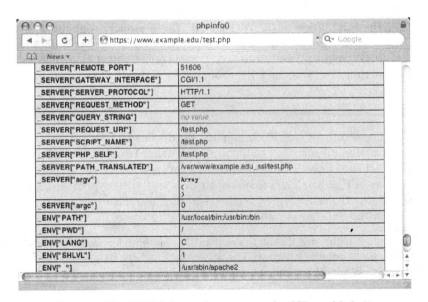

Fig. 8.6. The PHP informative page on the SSL-enabled site

Sample MySQL-PHP Interaction

As an example for the interaction between MySQL and PHP, we will install and configure the web-based MySQL administration tools called phpMyAdmin, distributed by Debian with the homonymous package. After installing the contents of the package and properly configuring it, we need to restart the web service in order to have changes take effect. The default configuration file for the software is located in **/etc/apache2/conf.d/** and is called **phpmyadmin.conf**. In order to enable phpMyAdmin to function properly we should allow all directives contained in **.htaccess** files for the locations where the software is installed to:

```
<Directory /usr/share/phpmyadmin/>
    AllowOverride All
</Directory>

<Directory /var/www/phpmyadmin/>
    AllowOverride All
</Directory>
```

To make phpMyAdmin accessible on the web server, we need to create a symbolic link in the HTTPS site. The MySQL administration package will necessarily send loggin information over the network, and thus the SSL-encrypted channel is critical to avoid sending passwords in clear-text:

```
# cd /var/www/example.edu_ssl/

# ln -s /usr/share/phpmyadmin
```

The **/usr/share/phpmyadmin/** directory contains all the necessary scripts to administer a MySQL installation and upon login we are presented a web page as in Fig. 8.7.

PHP Exploits

Unfortunately PHP runs with Apache credentials, and this may lead to malicious scripts that can affect the security of our web site, especially when dealing—as we will shortly see—with personal web pages.

Securing PHP scripting is beyond the scope of this book, and should be taken care of when deploying a PHP-based web infrastructure. Examples of PHP-based solutions to this problem are *suPHP* and *Safe mode*. The same problem occours for CGIs where Apache provides the *suEXEC* mechanism. As for almost all problems, each solution has advantages and drawbacks which should be carefully weighted by the organization.

8.5 Apache with Kerberos and AFS

As we already previewed, we want to enable our users to have personal web space in their AFS home directories: this requires Apache to fully access,

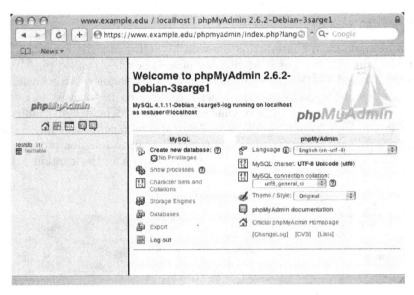

Fig. 8.7. The phpMyAdmin page for `testuser`

with read and occasionally write permissions, in a user AFS file space. Unfortunately Apache is not AFS-aware, so out of the box it cannot perform any action on AFS volumes, but using the same procedure as we did on the Samba server, it is possible to provide Apache with a valid token so that it can easily access users home pages, and of course, enable the web site root to reside on an AFS volume. In the following we assume the web server host to be a full Kerberos, LDAP and AFS client, so that the system can resolve user and group names to UIDs and GIDs, and retrieve home directory locations.

8.5.1 Web Server Principal

The procedure we are going to perform mirrors the one conducted on the Samba server in order to allow user profiles in the AFS space: we will create a Kerberos principal and modify the Apache startup script to provide the web server with a valid AFS token. Let us proceed then creating the Kerberos principal for our web server machine, remembering that host principals need the FQDN in the name:

```
kadmin:  add_principal -randkey host/www.example.edu
WARNING: no policy specified for host/www.example.edu@EXAMPLE.EDU; defaulting to no policy
Principal "host/www.example.edu@EXAMPLE.EDU" created.

kadmin:  ktadd host/www.example.edu
Entry for principal host/www.example.edu with kvno 3, encryption type \
Triple DES cbc mode with HMAC/sha1 added to keytab WRFILE:/etc/krb5.keytab.
Entry for principal host/www.example.edu with kvno 3, encryption type \
DES cbc mode with CRC-32 added to keytab WRFILE:/etc/krb5.keytab.
```

After exporting the host principal to the default keytab file, we create the web service principal and export it to a keytab different from the default one. The service principal name for web service has the prefix HTTP followed by the host name, and it will be exported to a http.keytab file located in the default Apache configuration directory /etc/apache2/:

```
kadmin:  add_principal -randkey HTTP/www.example.edu
WARNING: no policy specified for HTTP/www.example.edu@EXAMPLE.EDU; defaulting to no policy
Principal "HTTP/www.example.edu@EXAMPLE.EDU" created.

kadmin:  ktadd -k /etc/apache2/http.keytab HTTP/www.example.edu
Entry for principal HTTP/www.example.edu with kvno 3, encryption type \
Triple DES cbc mode with HMAC/sha1 added to keytab WRFILE:/etc/apache2/http.keytab.
Entry for principal HTTP/www.example.edu with kvno 3, encryption type \
DES cbc mode with CRC-32 added to keytab WRFILE:/etc/apache2/http.keytab.
```

In order to let Apache access to the AFS file space, we need to create the equivalent of the windows user in our OpenAFS protection database. As we could have more than one web server, and all of them should access the AFS space with different keytabs, we choose to create a group that will contain all the AFS-enabled web servers in our organization:

```
# pts creategroup webservers -id -400
group webservers has id -400

# pts listentries -groups
Name                       ID   Owner  Creator
system:administrators    -204   -204   -204
system:backup            -205   -204   -204
system:anyuser           -101   -204   -204
system:authuser          -102   -204   -204
system:ptsviewers        -203   -204   -204
testgroup              -10000      1      1
webservers               -400      1      1
```

Remember to be extremely careful choosing the IDs, as you could encounter problems with existing users and groups. Next, we create the AFS user and add it to the webservers group, noting as the principal name HTTP/hostname corresponds to the PTS entry http.hostname:

```
# pts createuser http.www.example.edu -id 501
User http.www.example.edu has id 501

# pts adduser http.www.example.edu webservers

# pts membership webservers
Members of webservers (id: -400) are:
  http.www.example.edu

# pts membership http.www.example.edu
Groups http.www.example.edu (id: 501) is a member of:
  webservers
```

It is a good practice to test the keytab file gaining the initial ticket and next convert it to an AFS token with the aklog command:

```
# kinit -k -t /etc/apache2/http.keytab HTTP/www.example.edu

# aklog

# klist
Ticket cache: FILE:/tmp/krb5cc_0
Default principal: HTTP/www.example.edu@EXAMPLE.EDU

Valid starting       Expires             Service principal
07/20/06 11:27:00   07/20/06 21:26:59   krbtgt/EXAMPLE.EDU@EXAMPLE.EDU
07/20/06 11:27:06   07/20/06 21:26:59   afs/example.edu@EXAMPLE.EDU


Kerberos 4 ticket cache: /tmp/tkt0
klist: You have no tickets cached

# tokens

Tokens held by the Cache Manager:

User's (AFS ID 501) tokens for afs@example.edu [Expires Jul 20 21:26]
   --End of list--
```

The final step to combine Apache with AFS is to modify the startup
script exactly the same way we did for Samba, since the web server is not
AFS aware. In /etc/default/ you can find the file **apache2** containing the
initial environment variables used in the daemon starting shell script, so let
us modify it adding three variables with commands we need, symmetrically
to those used for Samba:

```
PRE_COMMAND1="/usr/bin/kinit -l 1day -k -t /etc/apache2/http.keytab HTTP/www.example.edu"
PRE_COMMAND2="/usr/bin/aklog -setpag"
POST_COMMAND="/usr/bin/kdestroy"
```

Finally the **start** section in the /etc/init.d/apache2 file has to be altered as follows, calling the Kerberos and AFS commands through the environment variables **PRE_COMMAND1** and **PRE_COMMAND2**, before starting the web
server program:

```
       start)
               [ -f /etc/apache2/httpd.conf ] || touch /etc/apache2/httpd.conf
               #ssl_scache shouldn't be here if we're just starting up.
               [ -f /var/run/apache2/ssl_scache ] && rm -f /var/run/apache2/*ssl_scache*
               echo -n "Starting web server: Apache2"
               $PRE_COMMAND1 ; $PRE_COMMAND2
               $APACHE2CTL startssl
               $POST_COMMAND
               echo "."
       ;;
```

In this way a PAG is set before starting the web server daemon and before leaving the script, the Kerberos authentication ticket is removed with
POST_COMMAND, thus lessening any security concern about the Kerberos file-
based credential cache. As we can see from the **kinit** command line, this
combination provides a valid authentication for just one day: after this period Apache needs to be restarted, for instance with a **cron** job. The Apache

daemon can now access the AFS file space provided that ACLs permit the
`webservers` group to perform operations on certain locations.

8.5.2 Personal Web Pages

Once Apache has been enabled to access the AFS space, it is straightforward
to provide users with their personal web space. Since usually home pages are
publicly visible, we choose to create a new directory `html` under the `public`
location dedicated to the web. Let us create the `html` directory providing it
with the necessary write access to the `webservers` PTS group since we foresee
DAV, too:

```
# cd /afs/example.edu/users/testuser/public

# mkdir html

# fs setacl html webservers write

# fs setacl html anonymous none

# fs listacl html/
Access list for html/ is
Normal rights:
  webservers rlidwk
  system:administrators rlidwka
  testuser rlidwka
```

In large environments we could dedicate a specific AFS volume to personal web spaces, such that it is convenient to backup all the volumes with
automated scheduled jobs. The example shows the setup for our `testuser`.
Since Apache enables users to control the access to their personal space with
`.htaccess` files[6], we choose not to expose the user web location to the public `system:anyuser` group: a user may wish to restrict the access to some
locations under its own personal space. Let us now create in AFS a sample
`index.html` file for our `testuser`:

```
<html>
<head><title>Test User</title></head>
<body>
This is the site of our testuser.
</body>
</html>
```

Note that we gave our web server group full write access to this location:
in the following we will enable the WebDAV an alternative way of accessing
the AFS file space. To instruct Apache to look also at our users personal web
pages, we must modify the configuration for our `example.edu` site adding
a new location. The `UserDir` directive tells the Apache server to read also
user home directories, as the `http://www.example.edu/~username/` URL.

---

[6] The `.htaccess` mechanism is provided by Apache on a per-directory basis—as
AFS ACLs—and is enabled with the `AllowOverride` in the Apache configuration.

Additionally we will specify access options for the home directories with the standard `<Directory>` directive as in the following example:

```
NameVirtualHost *
<VirtualHost *:80>
        ServerAdmin www@example.edu

        DocumentRoot /var/www/example.edu
        <Directory />
                Options FollowSymLinks
                AllowOverride None
        </Directory>
        <Directory /var/www/example.edu>
                Options All MultiViews
                AllowOverride All
                Order allow,deny
                Allow from all
        </Directory>

        ErrorLog /var/log/apache2/error.log
        LogLevel warn
        CustomLog /var/log/apache2/access.log combined

        <Directory /afs/example.edu/users>
                Options All MultiViews
                AllowOverride All
                Order allow,deny
                Allow from all
        </Directory>
        UserDir /afs/example.edu/users/*/public/html
</VirtualHost>
```

Then the `http://www.example.edu/~testuser/` URL will be translated to the `/afs/example.edu/users/testuser/public/html` home directory location with the help of the NSS contacting LDAP, and it obeys to restrictions detailed in the `<Directory>` stanza.

8.6 WebDAV

Until this point the web space is a read-only world, allowing users to share documents, but denying any modification on them. The IETF worked to produce a series of standard documentations on an extension to the HTTP protocol enabling writing access to web pages, resulting in the WebDAV specification, the acronym of *Web-based Distributed Authoring and Versioning*. This feature is already available on commercial systems: the Apple iDisk and Microsoft's *Web Folder* are both based on the WebDAV extension. As a read-write entry point, WebDAV is a viable replacement for users to access the AFS file space, while the client cannot be employed or for mobile users.

Since the access to the AFS file space may expose personal documents to the network traffic, it is highly recommended to make use of a secure communication channel with the SSL-enabled web location. By default Apache ships with the WebDAV extension, provided by two modules named `dav` and `dav_fs`:

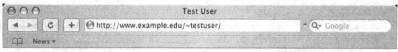

This is the site of our testuser.

Fig. 8.8. Browsing the `testuser`'s site

```
# a2enmod dav_fs
Module dav_fs installed; run /etc/init.d/apache2 force-reload to enable.

# a2enmod dav
Module dav installed; run /etc/init.d/apache2 force-reload to enable.
```

Furthermore, Apache needs to contact the Kerberos server for authenticating all the connecting users, a functionality provided by the Debian `libapache2-mod-auth-kerb` package: user passwords are transmitted in cleartext, so the use of HTTPS is obligatory. By default Apache treats all files starting with `.ht` in a special way since this prefix is used for access control: an example of these files is the well known `.htaccess`. Since it can be useful to modify these special files over WebDAV too, we choose to use a different file name for access control. Therefore in our SSL-enabled site `example.edu_ssl`, we specify the `.davacl` for access control over a user home directory with the `AccessFileName` directive:

```
<VirtualHost *:443>
        ServerAdmin www@example.edu

        SSLEngine on
        SSLCipherSuite HIGH:MEDIUM
        SSLProtocol -all +SSLv3 +TLSv1
        SSLCaCertificateFile /etc/apache2/ssl/cacert.pem
        SSLCertificateFile /etc/apache2/ssl/wwwcert.pem
        SSLCertificateKeyFile /etc/apache2/ssl/wwwkey.pem

        DocumentRoot /var/www/example.edu_ssl
        <Directory />
                Options FollowSymLinks
```

```
            AllowOverride None
        </Directory>
        <Directory /var/www/example.edu_ssl>
                Options All MultiViews
                AllowOverride All
                Order allow,deny
                Allow from all
        </Directory>

        ErrorLog /var/log/apache2/error_ssl.log
        LogLevel warn
        CustomLog /var/log/apache2/access_ssl.log combined

        AccessFileName .davacl
        <Files ~ "^\.ht">
                Order allow,deny
                Allow from all
        </Files>
        <Directory /afs/example.edu/users>
                Options All MultiViews
                AllowOverride All
                Order allow,deny
                Allow from all
                Dav On
                DavDepthInfinity On
        </Directory>
        UserDir /afs/example.edu/users/*/public/html

</VirtualHost>
```

On the users home directories stanza we added the necessary `Dav On` directive to enable WebDAV. With these simplified settings all control is delegated to our users who have to take care of a suitable setting in their `public/html` directory. On DAV access Apache is not running as `root` anymore: as a consequence it cannot read the keytab file with the previous permission bits. For this we will allow the group called `www-data` to read the keytab file, since Apache is running as user `www-data` belonging to the homonymous group:

```
-rw-r----- 1 root www-data 144 2006-07-20 11:22 /etc/apache2/http.keytab
```

To set properly a WebDAV ACL may not be easy for users, so it is advisable to provide a template with the appropriate configuration to all users in the organization. WebDAV requires the specification of the authentication method with the `AuthType` directive, in our case `Kerberos`, the Kerberos realm and service names, `KrbAuthRealms` and `KrbServiceName` respectively, along with the complete keytab file path. Since write-enabled access should be restricted to the web space owner, we require a specific principal to be authenticated in order to establish a DAV connection:

```
AuthType Kerberos
KrbMethodNegotiate off
AuthName "Please enter your EXAMPLE.EDU credentials."
KrbAuthRealms EXAMPLE.EDU
KrbServiceName HTTP
Krb5Keytab /etc/apache2/http.keytab
require user testuser@EXAMPLE.EDU
```

The `AuthName` string will appear on the connecting client, while the method negotiation setting is needed when connecting from Windows machines via WebDAV to avoid Windows related authentication attempts. The access to the web space of our `testuser` over DAV is granted just to this very user who has to authenticate against Kerberos. To enable this new service all we need is to restart Apache:

```
# /etc/init.d/apache2 start
Starting web server: Apache2.
```

At this point it is possible to test the connection using a DAV-enabled web browser. Windows provides Internet Explorer, a DAV-aware browser that can open WebDAV connections using the "Open as Web Folder" option with results similar to those pictured in Fig. 8.9.

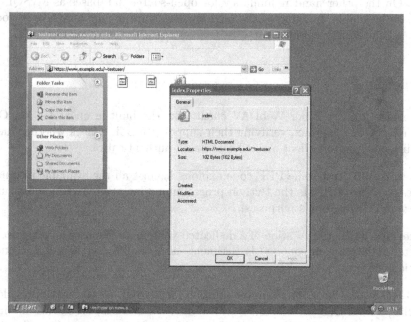

Fig. 8.9. Opening a "Web Folder"

8.7 Redundant Web Server

As all the services provided by our organization, the web server should be redundant. As we have already seen, DNS provides the ability to assign multiple IP addresses to a single name, in this case `www.example.edu`, providing also a simple load balancing[7] facility. For web server replication all is needed is to install the same Apache modules and configure it exactly as the first server. The only difference could exist in the site configuration files, where the `VirtualHost` stanza might refer to a specific IP address.

If the `example.edu` and `example.edu_ssl` sites have their web root in AFS space then the configuration will not need any further modification: remember that keytab and certificate files have to be copied as well. A simple Apache configuration can be tuned in such a way that no modification is necessary. Be aware that this proposed redundancy might not work with all web browsers: it depends on the specific implementation if use is made of several IPs offered for one name.

A last word should be spent on MySQL since it can save some state for dynamic web pages. On the one hand database services cannot reside on AFS since they need some byte-level locking which is unsupported by OpenAFS yet. On the other hand redundancy for open-source databases as MySQL is already available, but due to the lengthy procedure it might involve it does not get further developed here.

Practice

Exercise 29. Try other WebDAV clients like the built-in client for MacOS X or `cadaver` for Linux, verifying their support for SSL. Check whether they additionally permit client a certificate-based authentication.

Exercise 30. Test some PHP code exploits against all the available alternatives to secure PHP. Is the Python programming language a valid substitute for your organization's purposes?

Exercise 31. Is the creation of a dedicated volume for the user's web space a better option in your context? Experiment suitable quota settings and backup options.

Exercise 32. Check for a failover solution for MySQL based on the provided packages from Debian. The documentation contains a chapter about building a cluster which needs two nodes and an additional management host. Special SQL commands are provided to make use of such a cluster.

---

[7] If you plan to have heavy load web sites you should consider installing a real load balancing software.

9

Electronic Mail

> *The Americans have need of the telephone, but we do not. We have plenty of messenger boys.*
> William Henry Preece

9.1 The Electronic Mail System

Electronic mail, or the more famous abbreviation *email* nowadays has become a daily experience. The electronic mailing system is at the origin of networking environments, dating back to the 60s, starting at the Massachusetts Institute of Technology, and rapidly spreading on the ARPANet computer network, the predecessor of modern Internet. The first implementation of an emailing system is attributed to Raymond Tomlinson in 1971, where the @ sign was used to indicate the machine where the user had an email box.

The emailing system is comparable to the current physical mail distributing organization. A user located on some machine writes a text using a mail program (e.g. Apple Mail, Microsoft Outlook, Mozilla Thunderbird), specifying the destination user: email addresses still retain the ARPANet @ sign to separate the username from the following domain name. The client upon a user command contacts its domain outgoing mail server and transfers the email text along with the necessary delivery information: in the electronic mail terminology, the client program is called the *Mail User Agent*, MUA, while the outgoing mail server is called *Mail Tranfer Agent* or MTA.

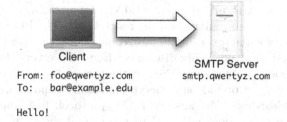

Client
From: foo@qwertyz.com
To: bar@example.edu

SMTP Server
smtp.qwertyz.com

Hello!

Fig. 9.1. A client sending an email contacts its SMTP server

The MTA acts exactly as a mailing office in the real world: it temporarily stores the email from the client, and delivers it to the destination post office contacting the addressee's MTA. Optionally the post office provides the service of delivering mails directly into the user's mailbox, which in the electronic mail world is done by a program called *Mail Delivery Agent* or MDA.

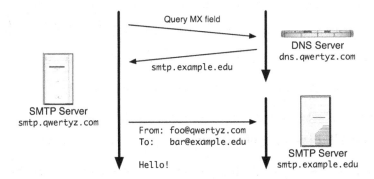

Fig. 9.2. The email is delivered to the addressee via the SMTP protocol. The destination server is retrieved by a DNS query

The de facto standard communication protocol for MTAs in the Internet world is SMTP, the *Simple Mail Transfer Protocol*, originally conceived as a companion of the historical UUCP protocol, *UNIX to UNIX Copy*, used on machines that were not permanently connected to a network. The SMTP as the name itself suggests, is a simple protocol, based on a clear text communication between two servers, and strongly relying on the DNS service. When a SMTP server receives an email to `bar@example.edu`, it contacts the DNS server of the `example.edu` domain for the `MX` service record. If the query is fulfilled, it will contact the DNS-provided destination SMTP server, and transfers the email to the destination. Exactly as the standard mail, the SMTP provides additional services as priority mails and return receipts: unfortunately these two features are not used in every emailing system.

The mail reading system currently uses two different protocols, the *Post Office Protocol* or POP, and the newer IMAP, *Internet Message Access Protocol*, at their third and fourth versions, respectively. The POP protocol was designed to access email texts with dial-up connections: the client would download all the messages and finally disconnect from the server. Moreover, since dial-up connections were slow and costly, the protocol was extremely simple, and originally did not provide any encryption facility, sending usernames and passwords in clear-text. The modern IMAP protocol, first implemented by Mark Crispin in 1986, does not need to retrieve all the email text at once, downloading only the informative context (i.e. the mail headers, containing the addressee, sender, dates and additional contents such as the SMTP transaction log), fetching the whole email only upon request. Additional features of

IMAP with respect to POP, are on-server mailboxes and email flagging (e.g. "read", "unread", "replied", and "forwarded").

Storage of emails, which as a matter of fact are simple text messages, have been historically realized with a single file per mailbox. This format is referred with the common `mbox` name. There are several drawbacks to the use of such a storage format, the most relevant are the necessity of locking the whole file when receiving new emails (usually appended to the mailbox file), and another is the progressive slowness in retrieving a particular email as the file size grows. An alternative to the `mbox` format is the more modern `Maildir` format which stores emails in separate files. This per-email format overcomes the limitations of `mbox` discarding the need for file locking when receiving new emails.

This chapter describes the setup of an infrastructure for electronic mail employing secure solutions, and which integrates well with our backbone based on Kerberos, LDAP, and AFS. In comparison with the web server, which has Apache as the favorite candidate, the setup of a mail system has many possible solutions. For MTAs there are currently several SMTP servers, such as Exim, Postfix, qmail, and the historical `sendmail` program, the first MTA ever available to the public. Reading emails is also possible with different servers, where we may mention IMAP/POP products as Courier, Cyrus, and the implementation from the University of Washington.

9.2 Mail Transport with Postfix

Historically `sendmail` is the classical MTA, dating back to the ARPANet implementation of mailing system named `delivermail`. In the 80s Eric Allman wrote the `sendmail` program which replaced the legacy program in the BSD UNIX distribution 4.1c released in 1983 including TCP/IP support.

The original `sendmail` program is still one of the most used SMTP daemons on the Internet, but it is hard to understand the precise configuration procedure and several security issues in the past do not make it the best option in our case. Our choice falls on the MTA implementing the SMTP protocol written by a team under Wietse Venema called `postfix`. The Postfix server has several additional features that will be employed in the following, such as an easy to use LDAP connection, the support for encrypted channels, and the `Maildir` format for mailboxes.

DNS Entries

Before installing an SMTP server, we have to prepare the DNS service according to the SMTP protocol, creating the special `MX` record that indicate the domain MTA host:

```
example.edu.    MX    0 smtp.example.edu.
```

The third field indicates the priority of each SMTP machine, with lower numbers indicating higher preferences. A strong constraint to the way this name is resolved is that it cannot be an alias, so it should not be a CNAME entry: MX records must be simple A entries in the DNS zone description. As for other service fields, it is possible to specify several MX records, so that if one fails, the next one will be used. As a drawback to this simple replicated service, all the load is given to the entry in the DNS database with the lowest preference number, a circumstance avoided by reusing the same number, as we will see later.

9.2.1 Installing Postfix

Debian provides us with the second version of the Postfix daemon, and includes an extension with SASL and TLS support, too. We choose to install the extended postfix-tls package, since we intend to provide a secure authentication to our users, avoiding sending clear-text authentication data over the network. During installation Debian configures the daemon. We can safely choose a typical Internet configuration, since afterwards we are going to modify the generated configuration. The Debian system configures the package after a successful installation, and as the list of destinations Postfix should accept mail for, one of the Debian questions to the user, we can include localhost besides our DNS domain. Before the actual configuration, we install further additional packages to enhance the map support for the various lookup tables. One commonly used extension is postfix-pcre allowing for Perl-compliant regular expressions, and another important addition is postfix-ldap package: we will allow our users to have email aliases, storing the information inside the LDAP tree. After installing the packages we stop the daemon in order to proceed with the configuration:

```
# /etc/init.d/postfix stop
Stopping mail transport agent: Postfix.
```

Configuring Postfix

The configuration files for the Postfix daemon are stored in the /etc/postfix/ directory, and the main file is called main.cf. The default configuration file provided by Debian can be left almost untouched, except for the domain-specific values listed below:

```
biff = no
append_dot_mydomain = no
delay_warning_time = 4h

myhostname = smtp.example.edu
```

```
myorigin = /etc/mailname
mydestination = example.edu, localhost
mynetworks = 127.0.0.0/8

mailbox_size_limit = 0
alias_maps = hash:/etc/aliases,ldap:/etc/postfix/ldap.cf
alias_database = hash:/etc/aliases
```

The first block of values regards the old UNIX mail notification program biff, which is not used on our systems, and sets general properties of mail handling: append_dot_mydomain sets whether Postfix should append missing domain name parts, while the delay_warning_time affects notification messages sent to the user if an email could not be delivered within a certain amount of time. The second block of settings configures the local SMTP host service, setting the host name, the destination domains and networks which Postfix is allowed to receive emails from. The myorigin field indicate a text file containing the domain name of our SMTP server, example.edu, in our case. The third block permits unlimited mailbox size and provides settings for the resolution of email aliases.

Email Aliases

Usernames are not always suitable mail addresses, since they rarely allow long and meaningful strings indicating name and surname of users; moreover, users may wish to receive emails to a particular address completely unrelated to the real name. Having installed the LDAP extension, Postfix can consult the LDAP database, and the classic UNIX file /etc/aliases, to resolve addresses that are not actual users in our system.

The LDAP configuration file is placed in the same location as the main one, and it is called ldap.cf, as specified in the alias_maps line of main.cf. It contains all the needed information to resolve email aliases, such as the server name and port and the LDAP sub-tree where aliases are stored:

```
server_host = ldap.example.edu
server_port = 389
search_base = ou=aliases,dc=example,dc=edu
query_filter = (sn=%s)
result_attribute = mail
bind = no
```

Our aliases are to be stored in the ou=aliases subtree, with the actual user name placed in the attribute specified by the result_attribute field. As an example, our first alias is for the testuser, who wants to receive emails as name.surname@example.edu instead of the classic and less meaningful testuser@example.edu. The LDIF file to create such an alias, is as follows:

```
dn: cn=name.surname,ou=aliases,dc=example,dc=edu
objectClass: pilotPerson
cn: name.surname
```

```
sn: name.surname
mail: testuser
```

Here the predefined object class `pilotPerson` is used, which just contains sufficient elements `cn`, `sn`, and the actual email address entry in `mail`. Note that an alias does not affect any login parameter. The `testuser` user name and its password need always be used to authenticate in any case, whereas the alias is just a fictional email address that can be used instead of the username. To test that the alias works, we can use the `postmap` tool to query a specific email address for the given specific Postfix configuration file:

```
# postmap -q name.surname ldap:/etc/postfix/ldap.cf
testuser
```

9.2.2 Testing Postfix

To test our first instance of this mail delivery agent, we use the legacy UNIX text-only client `mail`. By default, Postfix delivers all emails in the `/var/spool/mail/` storage directory, using the `mbox` format, with one file for every user:

```
# cd /var/spool/mail

# ls -l
total 4
-rw-rw----  1 admin mail 1001 2006-06-15 13:06 admin
```

Right now there is only one mailbox of the user which has been created during the Debian installation besides `root`. This is the moment to start Postfix and check all the open ports, as a good security practice:

```
# /etc/init.d/postfix start
Starting mail transport agent: Postfix.

# nmap localhost

Starting nmap 3.81 ( http://www.insecure.org/nmap/ ) at 2006-07-20 16:49 CEST
Interesting ports on localhost.localdomain (127.0.0.1):
(The 1661 ports scanned but not shown below are in state: closed)
PORT   STATE SERVICE
25/tcp open  smtp

Nmap finished: 1 IP address (1 host up) scanned in 0.520 seconds
```

Let us use the `mail` tool by first specifying the user name and the subject of the email we want to send with the `-s` option. The end of the message is indicated by a single line with just a dot: as we have previewed, `mail` is a legacy tool, and its user interface is very simple, but serves our testing purposes. At this point `mail` asks for a carbon-copy email address which can be left blank:

```
# mail testuser -s test1
hello world!
.
Cc:
```

We can see in the spool that the mailbox file for **testuser** has been successfully created, and inside we find the full body of our sent email:

```
# ls -l
total 8
-rw-rw----  1 admin    mail 1001 2006-06-15 13:06 admin
-rw-------  1 testuser mail  427 2006-07-20 16:51 testuser

# cat testuser
From root@example.edu  Thu Jul 20 16:51:28 2006
Return-Path: <root@example.edu>
X-Original-To: testuser
Delivered-To: testuser@example.edu
Received: by smtp.example.edu (Postfix, from userid 0)
        id AE57E2FEA8; Thu, 20 Jul 2006 16:51:28 +0200 (CEST)
To: testuser@example.edu
Subject: test1
Message-Id: <20060720145128.AE57E2FEA8@smtp.example.edu>
Date: Thu, 20 Jul 2006 16:51:28 +0200 (CEST)
From: root@example.edu (root)

hello world!
```

Next we test the **testuser** alias: we should be able to receive another email using the previously defined **name.surname@example.edu** email alias:

```
# mail name.surname@example.edu -s test2
hello alias!
.
Cc:
```

We can verify that the delivery worked by inspecting the user mailbox, finding the second email at the bottom of the file:

```
# cat testuser
From root@example.edu  Thu Jul 20 16:51:28 2006
Return-Path: <root@example.edu>
X-Original-To: testuser
Delivered-To: testuser@example.edu
Received: by smtp.example.edu (Postfix, from userid 0)
        id AE57E2FEA8; Thu, 20 Jul 2006 16:51:28 +0200 (CEST)
To: testuser@example.edu
Subject: test1
Message-Id: <20060720145128.AE57E2FEA8@smtp.example.edu>
Date: Thu, 20 Jul 2006 16:51:28 +0200 (CEST)
From: root@example.edu (root)

hello world!

From root@example.edu  Thu Jul 20 16:54:49 2006
Return-Path: <root@example.edu>
X-Original-To: name.surname@example.edu
Delivered-To: testuser@example.edu
Received: by smtp.example.edu (Postfix, from userid 0)
        id B885B2FEA9; Thu, 20 Jul 2006 16:54:49 +0200 (CEST)
```

```
To: name.surname@example.edu
Subject: test2
Message-Id: <20060720145449.B885B2FEA9@smtp.example.edu>
Date: Thu, 20 Jul 2006 16:54:49 +0200 (CEST)
From: root@example.edu (root)

hello alias!
```

9.2.3 Secure Delivery

As for the web server we want to permit secure connections when an external server prefers to deliver emails in this way for our domain. This is done via *Transport Layer Security* or TLS. Unlike the *Secure Socket Layer*, or SSL, where the communication gets encrypted immediately, TLS allows for an initial negotiation of whether to use cryptography and the chosen encoding algorithm. The first step is to produce a certificate for our server as we did for Apache and store both the private key and public certificate, along with our CA certificate, in a secure location available to Postfix. We choose to store all these files in a new subdirectory of /etc/postfix/ called ssl/:

```
# ls -l /etc/postfix/ssl
total 16
-r--r--r--  1 root root 2480 2006-07-20 17:02 cacert.pem
-r--r--r--  1 root root 6441 2006-07-20 17:02 smtpcert.pem
-r--------  1 root root 1679 2006-07-20 17:02 smtpkey.pem
```

Note the permission bits which allow the private key to be readable by root only. The next step is to enable TLS in the main Postfix configuration file. Our main.cf has to be modified as follows:

```
biff = no
append_dot_mydomain = no
delay_warning_time = 4h

myhostname = stmp.example.edu
myorigin = /etc/mailname
mydestination = example.edu, localhost
mynetworks = 127.0.0.0/8

mailbox_size_limit = 0
alias_maps = hash:/etc/aliases,ldap:/etc/postfix/ldap.cf
alias_database = hash:/etc/aliases

smtpd_tls_cert_file = /etc/postfix/ssl/smtpcert.pem
smtpd_tls_key_file = /etc/postfix/ssl/smtpkey.pem
smtpd_tls_CAfile = /etc/postfix/ssl/cacert.pem
smtpd_use_tls = yes
smtpd_enforce_tls = no
smtpd_tls_loglevel = 1

smtp_tls_cert_file = /etc/postfix/ssl/smtpcert.pem
smtp_tls_key_file = /etc/postfix/ssl/smtpkey.pem
smtp_tls_CAfile = /etc/postfix/ssl/cacert.pem
smtp_use_tls = yes
smtp_enforce_tls = no
smtp_tls_loglevel = 1
```

As we can see, we added two more configuration sections, smtpd_* and smtp_*. In this way we enable users to encrypt their transmission when sending email, setting the smtpd_* parameters to match the certificate files and using TLS by default as indicated by smtpd_use_tls. These parameters affect also transmissions incoming by other servers, as the SMTP is used as a medium to transport emails from user clients to the addressee's SMTP server: for this reason we do not enforce an encrypted communication by setting smtpd_enforce_tls to no, since the communication between MTAs may be unencrypted due to legacy servers not supporting TLS. The analogous smtp_* parameters are used by Postfix when sending email to other external servers, in other words when delivering emails sent by our users. Again, we cannot enforce the use of TLS since other SMTP servers might not be able to use it. In order to activate these new settings the daemon has to be restarted.

9.2.4 Testing TLS with Postfix

To test the TLS layer we need a client that can talk over an encrypted channel: for this test we choose the Apple Mail program configuring it to use SSL as shown in Fig. 9.3. For the test a mail to name.surname@example.edu has

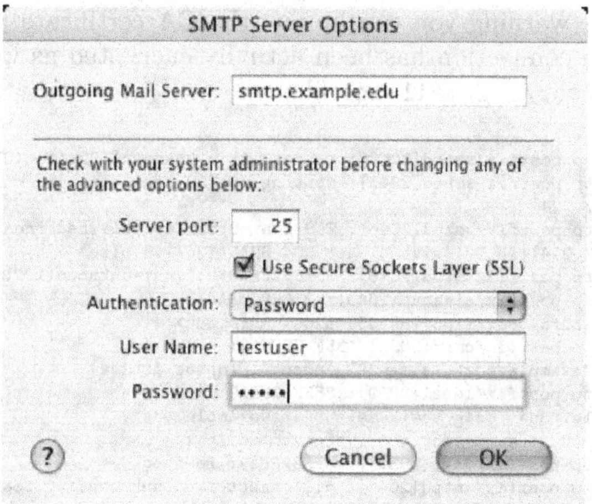

Fig. 9.3. Apple Mail configuration panel for SMTP

been composed and correctly delivered as we can see from the contents of our testuser's mailbox file:

```
From name.surname@example.edu  Thu Jul 20 17:25:10 2006
Return-Path: <name.surname@example.edu>
X-Original-To: name.surname@example.edu
Delivered-To: testuser@example.edu
Received: from [192.168.127.224] (unknown [192.168.127.224])
```

```
          by smtp.example.edu (Postfix) with ESMTP id 35FF82FEA9
          for <name.surname@example.edu>; Thu, 20 Jul 2006 17:24:12 +0200 (CEST)
Mime-Version: 1.0 (Apple Message framework v624)
To: name.surname@example.edu
Message-Id: <c2639e2b2f51c8a2ff1e878a9e5599a2@example.edu>
Content-Type: multipart/alternative; boundary=Apple-Mail-4--991818294
From: Test User <name.surname@example.edu>
Subject: Test TLS
Date: Thu, 20 Jul 2006 17:24:00 +0200
X-Mailer: Apple Mail (2.624)


--Apple-Mail-4--991818294
Content-Transfer-Encoding: 7bit
Content-Type: text/plain;
      charset=US-ASCII;
      format=flowed

Hello tls!
--Apple-Mail-4--991818294
Content-Transfer-Encoding: 7bit
Content-Type: text/enriched;
      charset=US-ASCII

<bigger><bigger><x-tad-bigger>Hello tls!</x-tad-bigger></bigger></bigger>
--Apple-Mail-4--991818294--
```

It is also possible that the mail program warns about the certificate not
being known to the system, due to the fact that we produced our own authority: to avoid the warning you can import the CA certificate permanently in
the system. The connection has been actually encrypted as we can see from
the logs in the /var/log/mail.log file:

```
Jul 20 17:24:11 smtp postfix/smtpd[2046]: connect from unknown[192.168.127.224]
Jul 20 17:24:11 smtp postfix/smtpd[2046]: setting up TLS connection from \
unknown[192.168.127.224]
Jul 20 17:24:12 smtp postfix/smtpd[2046]: TLS connection established from \
unknown[192.168.127.224]: TLSv1 with cipher RC4-SHA (128/128 bits)
Jul 20 17:24:12 smtp postfix/smtpd[2046]: 35FF82FEA9: client=unknown[192.168.127.224]
Jul 20 17:24:12 smtp postfix/cleanup[2048]: 35FF82FEA9: \
message-id=<c2639e2b2f51c8a2ff1e878a9e5599a2@example.edu>
Jul 20 17:24:12 smtp postfix/qmgr[2032]: 35FF82FEA9: \
from=<name.surname@example.edu>, size=892, nrcpt=1 (queue active)
Jul 20 17:25:10 smtp postfix/local[2049]: 35FF82FEA9: \
to=<testuser@example.edu>, orig_to=<name.surname@example.edu>, \
relay=local, delay=58, status=sent (delivered to mailbox)
Jul 20 17:25:10 smtp postfix/qmgr[2032]: 35FF82FEA9: removed
Jul 20 17:25:12 smtp postfix/smtpd[2046]: disconnect from unknown[192.168.127.224]
```

9.2.5 Authenticated Mail Relay

So far our server accepts mail to be delivered to our domain possibly encrypting the communication; furthermore it permits localhost to send mail
anywhere allowing for TLS if applicable. This configuration actually denies
any external user to send email through our service: we would like to extend
this *mail relay* to all our users, so that they can send emails from any location
and host they wish.

In the early days of the Internet such mail relay used to be open until the advent of *spam*, unsolicited electronic mail, which took its name from a notable sketch from the Monty Python. Hence we need to restrict this relaying to just authenticated users, avoiding casual spammers to use our SMTP as an *open relay* server. Postfix uses SASL, the *Simple Authentication and Security Layer*, to authenticate clients, a software that we have seen in use with our LDAP service. Here SASL gets combined with TLS to guarantee a secure data transmission.

To fine tune mail relay settings we need to modify the corresponding `smtpd_recipient_restrictions` parameter in the Postfix main configuration file. Besides `localhost` and the destination being our domain, we will permit all authenticated users to user the SMTP service. For these users we can safely enforce the usage of TLS, since almost all email clients currently support the TLS/SSL protocol:

```
biff = no
append_dot_mydomain = no
delay_warning_time = 4h
myhostname = stmp.example.edu
myorigin = /etc/mailname
mydestination = example.edu, localhost
mynetworks = 127.0.0.0/8
mailbox_size_limit = 0

alias_maps = hash:/etc/aliases,ldap:/etc/postfix/ldap.cf
alias_database = hash:/etc/aliases

smtpd_tls_cert_file = /etc/postfix/ssl/smtpcert.pem
smtpd_tls_key_file = /etc/postfix/ssl/smtpkey.pem
smtpd_tls_CAfile = /etc/postfix/ssl/cacert.pem
smtpd_use_tls = yes
smtpd_enforce_tls = no
smtpd_tls_loglevel = 1

smtp_tls_cert_file = /etc/postfix/ssl/smtpcert.pem
smtp_tls_key_file = /etc/postfix/ssl/smtpkey.pem
smtp_tls_CAfile = /etc/postfix/ssl/cacert.pem
smtp_use_tls = yes
smtp_enforce_tls = no
smtp_tls_loglevel = 1

smtpd_tls_auth_only = yes
smtpd_sasl_auth_enable = yes
smtpd_recipient_restrictions = permit_mynetworks \
permit_sasl_authenticated reject_unauth_destination
smtpd_sasl_application_name = smtp
smtpd_sasl_security_options = noanonymous
broken_sasl_auth_clients = yes
```

The `smtpd_sasl_security_options` setting denies all anonymous authentication methods, while the `smtpd_recipient_restrictions` allows all local users (i.e. logged on the SMTP server itself) and SASL-authenticated ones to utilize our MTA. The `broken_sasl_auth_clients` setting permits inter-operability with some obsolete SMTP authentication implementations as found in older Microsoft products. It is critical to set the value for the smtpd_sasl_application_name parameter, since that is a key component for the cooperation between SASL and Postfix.

SASL Configuration

Besides the SASL activation on the SMTP server side, the SASL authentication packages sasl2-bin must be installed, providing the saslauthd authentication daemon. Our objective is to utilize SASL to authenticate users as pictured in Fig. 9.4: users send their authentication parameters—user name and password—to the SMTP via a secure TSL channel, and SASL will locally redirect the authentication process to PAM. The PAM stack will finally use the pam_krb5.so module which authenticates securely over Kerberos. After

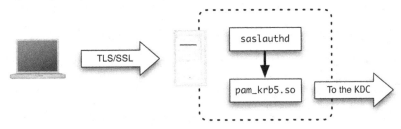

Fig. 9.4. Clients use TLS to authenticate over SASL which redirects the process to Kerberos via PAM

installation Debian makes the daemon available as a service at boot time, but contrary to many servers, it does not get started. Next we install the libsasl2-modules that enable us to use different authentication methods, among them we have the previously introduced PAM mechanism. After that we modify the default SASL settings in /etc/default/saslauthd as follows:

```
START=yes
MECHANISMS="pam"
```

This setting enables PAM as the method for authentication. This means that our SMTP server locally authenticates with the help of SASL that itself uses PAM for greater flexibility. All communications are *local* and are not transmitted over the network. The last step is to enable the PAM module corresponding to our SASL configuration. In /etc/pam.d/ we have to create a configuration file for the authentication service we are going to request from SASL. In other words, when asking SASL to authenticate, our SMTP server asks for a service called smtp as we specified in the smtpd_sasl_application_name in our Postfix configuration file. This service name matches with the proper PAM configuration file with the name smtp that enables our Kerberos authentication:

```
auth            required        pam_krb5.so
account         required        pam_permit.so
password        required        pam_permit.so
session         required        pam_permit.so
```

SASL uses its plaintext method to contact the underlying PAM: hence the transmission of the password over the network had to be protected by TLS. The Kerberos PAM module is provided by the `libpam-krb5` package, as we have seen earlier in the Kerberos chapter. At this point we can safely start the SASL authentication daemon:

```
# /etc/init.d/saslauthd start
Starting SASL Authentication Daemon: saslauthd.
```

We finally try to authenticate our `testuser` for the service `smtp`, with a password which is in clear-text using `testsaslauthd` tool:

```
# testsaslauthd -u testuser -p password -s smtp
0: OK "Success."
```

The success indicates that the combination of SASL and PAM is working correctly.

Configuring Postfix

According to the Debian defaults some components of Postfix are configured to run in a `chroot` environment: this means that they cannot access anything outside the directory where the `chroot` call placed them. On the one hand this can provide more security, on the other hand it can become troublesome if interaction with special device files, sockets, or libraries is needed. To keep the entire configuration simple we drop the `chroot` jail for the `smtpd` component to permit easy interaction with the `saslauthd` daemon. To share the session information between multiple `smtpd` processes we use the `tlsmgr` credential cache session manager. These configuration parameters are present in the Postfix configuration directory inside the `master.cf` file:

```
# ==========================================================================
# service type  private unpriv  chroot  wakeup  maxproc command + args
#               (yes)   (yes)   (yes)   (never) (100)
# ==========================================================================
smtp      inet  n       -       n       -       -       smtpd
tlsmgr    fifo  -       -       n       300     1       tlsmgr
```

These two lines are a good example of an externally available service and an internal service. The first one operates publicly over an TCP/IP port, does not need `root` permissions, and does not operate in a `chroot`-ed environment. The second one, operated over a named pipe, is private, does not need `root` permissions either, and does also not operate under `chroot`. The other fields define a possible wakeup time in seconds and a maximum number

of simultaneous processes. At the end comes the command for the daemon
followed by possible arguments. An example of such an argument could be -o
smtpd_enforce_tls=yes to enforce encrypted operation of smtpd, like SMTP
over SSL on port 465.

To enable Postfix to use the SASL mechanism, we have to tell SASL that
the service we want to use for Postfix, that is smtp, uses a plain authentication
over PAM. This is done in the /etc/postfix/sasl/ directory with a file
having the same service name, so smtpd.conf:

```
pwcheck_method: saslauthd
mech_list: plain
```

The service is then configured to use the saslauthd daemon for authentication, passing a plain-text password as its parameter, as indicated by the
mech_list value. The last step is to add the postfix user, used by our daemon, to the sasl group in order to interact with SASL. The authentication
daemon uses a socket file located in /var/run/saslauthd/ called mux, with
the following permissions:

```
srwxrwxrwx  1 root root 0 2006-07-25 14:24 mux=
-rw-------  1 root root 0 2006-07-25 14:24 mux.accept
-rw-------  1 root root 5 2006-07-25 14:24 saslauthd.pid
```

Finally add the postfix user to the sasl group using the Debian adduser
tool.

9.2.6 Local Delivery with Procmail

Right now the local delivery of email for our users is done in a single mbox
file storing all users mailboxes in the default directory, /var/spool/mail/,
as we have previously seen. This specific directory resides on the local file
system of the host smtp.example.edu. We want to overcome this single point
of failure and use AFS for mail spooling, storing users mailboxes in the AFS
file space. As outlined at the beginning, the Maildir format is suited for
AFS, since OpenAFS does not support byte-range file locking yet. Postfix
supports delivery to Maildir folders too, but there exist subtle problems with
atomic operations in the file system like link(), unlink(), and rename().
In order to deliver emails correctly we need procmail as the MDA, since its
implementation is compatible with AFS operation, and also supports both
mailbox formats.

Procmail, currently developed by Stephen van den Berg and Philip Guenther, is a very flexible MDA that could be programmed to do some mail
preprocessing as spam and antivirus checks. We choose to deliver user emails
using Procmail to a subdirectory under the user's home in AFS file space, as
we will shortly see. So le us start by installing the procmail package:

```
# apt-get install procmail
```

In the following we are going to enable Procmail for AFS operation: we need to install then all the necessary Kerberos and AFS client packages, configuring them as we already did for other services.

Procmail and AFS

The `procmail` tool is not AFS-aware, so we have to create again a keytab file and get AFS credentials at the activation of the program. We start creating a group for our mail servers with an ID that is not used, as we did for the web servers, using the `pts` tool:

```
# pts creategroup mailservers -id -401
group mailservers has id -401
```

The next step is to create an AFS user for our mail servers, and add it to our `mailservers` group:

```
# pts createuser procmail -id 504
User procmail has id 504

# pts adduser procmail mailservers

# pts membership mailservers
Members of mailservers (id: -401) are:
  procmail
```

Last, we have to create a Kerberos principal with `kadmin` and export the entry in a keytab file, in our case **/etc/postfix/smtp.keytab**:

```
kadmin:  add_principal -randkey procmail
WARNING: no policy specified for procmail@EXAMPLE.EDU; defaulting to no policy
Principal "procmail@EXAMPLE.EDU" created.

kadmin:  ktadd -k /etc/postfix/smtp.keytab procmail
Entry for principal procmail with kvno 3, encryption type \
Triple DES cbc mode with HMAC/sha1 added to keytab WRFILE:/etc/postfix/smtp.keytab.
Entry for principal procmail with kvno 3, encryption type \
DES cbc mode with CRC-32 added to keytab WRFILE:/etc/postfix/smtp.keytab.
```

Configuring Procmail

The global Procmail configuration file is **/etc/procmailrc**, and it is divided into section called "recipes": each stanza processes emails identified by a particular regular expression starting with the * character. First, we wish all email for **root** to be delivered to the local spool in **/var/spool/mail/**; all other users should receive their mail in the **email** subdirectory of their home directory in **Maildir** format:

```
:0 Wic
* !^Delivered-To: root@
| /usr/bin/kinit -k -t /etc/postfix/procmail.keytab procmail

:0 Wic
* !^Delivered-To: root@
| /usr/bin/aklog

:0 Wic
* !^Delivered-To: root@
| /usr/bin/kdestroy

:0
* !^Delivered-To: root@
$HOME/email/

DROPPRIVS=yes

:0:
* ^Delivered-To: root@
/var/spool/mail/$USER
```

The first three recipes are related to authentication: since the first part of this file, until the line that drops all `root` privileges with `DROPPRIVS=yes`, is executed with the rights of `root`[1] it is possible to read the Procmail keytab file. After obtaining Kerberos credentials and transforming them into the AFS token for the user `procmail` these credentials are immediately deleted with `kdestroy`: the AFS token remains unaffected. The fourth recipe forces mail delivery for all users except `root` into a named `Maildir` subdirectory recognizable by the trailing slash "/". Afterwards all privileges are dropped. Observe that the authentication related commands can not be combined into a longer shell line, since a sub-shell gets invoked with the rights of the receiver.

Note that these rules are triggered by regular expressions: the ^ character refers to the beginning of a line and the ! character negates a regular expression. Since these two cases are complementary and all mail gets delivered, no user-defined `.procmailrc` gets invoked. For this delivery to work we have to create a subdirectory `email` in every home directory, or create a dedicated volume mounting it as `email`. The ACL of this directory should be set to `write` for the `mailservers` group, enabling Procmail to write in the location.

Finally, Postfix has to be configured in such a way to deliver mail with the help of Procmail: although Postfix supports `Maildir` too, only the use of Procmail is considered to be AFS-safe. The link between Procmail and Postfix is a single line in the Postfix `main.cf` file:

```
mailbox_command = /usr/bin/procmail -a "$EXTENSION"
```

As usual, the Postfix service must be restarted to enable the change.

---

[1] Debian installs `procmail` with the setuid bit set and owner `root`.

Testing Procmail

In order to test Procmail, in the local email spool directory **/var/spool/mail/**
we truncate all the mailboxes to start our tests:

```
# ls -l
total 0
-rw-rw----  1 admin    mail 0 2006-07-25 15:21 admin
-rw-------  1 testuser mail 0 2006-07-25 14:39 testuser
```

When sending an email to **testuser@example.edu**, Postfix runs the
procmail tool that delivers all the incoming emails to the correct location
in the AFS file space, thus leaving the **testuser** mailbox under the directory
/var/spool/mail/ intact:

```
# mail -s test4 testuser@example.edu
ddd
.
Cc:

# ls -l
total 0
-rw-rw----  1 admin    mail 0 2006-07-25 15:21 admin
-rw-------  1 testuser mail 0 2006-07-25 15:33 testuser

# mail -s test5 name.surname@example.edu
eee
.
Cc:

# ls -l
total 0
-rw-rw----  1 admin    mail 0 2006-07-25 15:21 admin
-rw-------  1 testuser mail 0 2006-07-25 15:33 testuser
```

Nothing happened in the local spool since mail got delivered to the **email**
subdirectory in our user's home in the **Maildir** format:

```
# cd /afs/example.edu/users/testuser/email

# ls
cur/  new/  tmp/

# find .
.
./new
./new/1153834883.4435_0.smtp
./new/1153834903.4445_0.smtp
./cur
./tmp
```

Our Postfix configuration states that a mailbox has no maximum size, but
since our users have their own mailboxes on the AFS space, the usual AFS
quota mechanism applies. Please note that Postfix imposes a message size
limit of 10 MB by default, but these settings can be easily changed according
to your organizational needs.

9.3 Reading Mail with Courier

It remains to provide a way for the users to consult their email, and as we have introduced earlier, this is done over two possible protocols: IMAP or POP. The use of the `Maildir` format for the user's mailbox restricts the choice of possible daemons considerably, and needing AFS compatibility only the Courier implementation remains as a free of charge product. Courier provides an IMAP and POP server that enables our users to read their email with a client of their choice. Our aim is to enable both protocols in a secure fashion, and inhibit any unencrypted communication.

9.3.1 Installing Courier

Since we do not want unencrypted connections, we just install the SSL-enabled packages `courier-pop-ssl` and `courier-imap-ssl`, which also install their own authentication daemon. Debian's installer script creates during the installation two keys and certificates for these servers, referenced in the server configuration files: in the following we will replace those with our self generated files.

The above Debian package by default enables both secure and unencrypted versions POP and IMAP daemons, so with a tool like `rcconf` remove the non SSL-enabled daemons from the boot services list. Before continuing with the configuration the daemons have to be stopped:

```
# /etc/init.d/courier-imap-ssl stop
Stopping Courier IMAP-SSL server: imapd-ssl.

# /etc/init.d/courier-pop-ssl stop
Stopping Courier POP3-SSL server: pop3d-ssl.

# /etc/init.d/courier-authdaemon stop
Stopping Courier authdaemon: done.
```

Remember to stop the non-SSL daemons, too, since disabling a service does not imply that it should be immediately stopped. The Courier-provided authentication service `courier-authdaemon` plays a similar role as the `saslauthd` for Postfix; the respective authentication daemons need to be started before the application accessing it.

In the following we assume a dedicated host with the name, not an alias, `mail.example.edu` for the installation of Courier. As we did for Postfix, we create a certificate for our mail server. We need one certificate for POP, and one for IMAP service, with their private keys in the same file[2]:

```
-rw-------  1 root root 8120 2006-07-25 16:28 imapd.pem
-rw-------  1 root root 8120 2006-07-25 16:28 pop3d.pem
```

---

[2] If both POP and IMAP services run on the same host, the files can be identical.

Note the permission bits that restrict all accesses to the **root** user, since we are creating a single file for both public and private certificate keys:

```
# cat /etc/courier/imapd.pem
-----BEGIN RSA PRIVATE KEY-----
MIIEpQIBAAKCAQEAxLEU4f/+l+Wglymvq7zsHUdm5P7YNpF/nB1P2jo1tXY3WV9l
...
eRLqiouErlXR7c8G/F5l+XJzSNE7dP/2fySWTmuvA6tx+ieVrlauSbA=
-----END RSA PRIVATE KEY-----
-----BEGIN CERTIFICATE-----
MIIF+TCCA+GgAwIBAgIBBDANBgkqhkiG9w0BAQUFADCBrjELMAkGA1UEBhMCW1ox
...
LLc2zqwF2ZP7nBmG1zXDEIqUKRkBM+bfQapjALcdXPOEu39itS/s6v4rVOGo
-----END CERTIFICATE-----
```

9.3.2 Configuring Courier

The following configuration process will mimic Apache's settings by modifying Courier's startup scripts; it will also mirror the Postfix settings, enabling a Kerberos authentication via PAM as in Fig. 9.4, replacing the SASL authentication daemon with Courier's **courier-authdaemon**.

Configuring the Authentication

Courier with its authentication daemon uses PAM to authenticate users reading the service names **imap** and **pop3**. So in **/etc/pam.d/** we have to create two files with names matching these services, configuring them to authenticate against Kerberos:

```
# cat /etc/pam.d/imap
auth         required      pam_krb5.so
account      required      pam_permit.so
password     required      pam_permit.so
session      required      pam_permit.so

# cat /etc/pam.d/pop3
auth         required      pam_krb5.so
account      required      pam_permit.so
password     required      pam_permit.so
session      required      pam_permit.so
```

The configuration of Courier's authentication daemon is in **/etc/courier/**, using a file called **authdaemonrc**. Debian default values are fine for us, since they point to a PAM-based authentication mechanism, as we can see from the **authmodulelist** field:

```
authmodulelist="authpam"
authmodulelistorig="authcustom authcram authuserdb authldap authpgsql authmysql authpam"
daemons=5
version=""
authdaemonvar=/var/run/courier/authdaemon
```

Courier and AFS

Courier is not yet AFS-ready, so we have to create the correct group and users as we did before for Apache and Postfix. We choose to put Courier in the already created **mailservers** group, since Courier needs write-enabled access to users mailboxes, so all we need is to create the AFS **pts** entry:

```
# pts createuser courier -id 505
User courier has id 505

# pts adduser courier mailservers

# pts membership mailservers
Members of mailservers (id: -401) are:
  procmail
  courier
```

Again we have to create the Kerberos principal matching the AFS entry and export its credentials to a keytab file:

```
kadmin: add_principal -randkey courier
WARNING: no policy specified for courier@EXAMPLE.EDU; defaulting to no policy
Principal "courier@EXAMPLE.EDU" created.

kadmin: ktadd -k /etc/courier/courier.keytab courier
Entry for principal courier with kvno 3, encryption type \
Triple DES cbc mode with HMAC/sha1 added to keytab WRFILE:/etc/courier/courier.keytab.
Entry for principal courier with kvno 3, encryption type \
DES cbc mode with CRC-32 added to keytab WRFILE:/etc/courier/courier.keytab.
```

Exporting the principal and creating a keytab file readable only by **root** should work as before:

```
# klist -ke /etc/courier/courier.keytab
Keytab name: FILE:/etc/courier/courier.keytab
KVNO Principal
---- --------------------------------------------------------------------------
   3 courier@EXAMPLE.EDU (Triple DES cbc mode with HMAC/sha1)
   3 courier@EXAMPLE.EDU (DES cbc mode with CRC-32)

# ls -l /etc/courier/courier.keytab
-rw------- 1 root root 116 2006-07-25 16:47 /etc/courier/courier.keytab
```

In **/etc/default** we have a file called **courier** which is used by the startup script to set some default environment variables. As we did for Apache, we create first a Kerberos ticket and then gain the AFS token via **aklog**:

```
MAILDIR="email"

PRE_COMMAND1="/usr/bin/kinit -l 1day -k -t /etc/courier/courier.keytab courier"
PRE_COMMAND2="/usr/bin/aklog -setpag"
POST_COMMAND="/usr/bin/kdestroy"
```

The first line tells which directory should Courier look for in each user's home to read the email in **Maildir** format. Remember that this daemon like Apache has to be restarted every day, which can easily be done with a simple **cron** job.

IMAP Configuration

The IMAP server configuration is located in Courier's configuration directory
/etc/courier/ and is named imapd-ssl. The important change which should
be made to this file is the last line, MAILDIRPATH, indicating which directory
holds the mailbox directory:

```
SSLPORT=993
SSLADDRESS=0
SSLPIDFILE=/var/run/courier/imapd-ssl.pid
IMAPDSSLSTART=YES
IMAPDSTARTTLS=YES
IMAP_TLS_REQUIRED=1
COURIERTLS=/usr/bin/couriertls
TLS_PROTOCOL=SSL3
TLS_STARTTLS_PROTOCOL=TLS1
TLS_CERTFILE=/etc/courier/imapd.pem
TLS_VERIFYPEER=NONE
TLS_CACHEFILE=/var/lib/courier/couriersslcache
TLS_CACHESIZE=524288

MAILDIRPATH=email
```

The SSL-enabled service will automatically start a TLS communication as
stated by the IMAPDSTARTTLS, supporting the encrypted channel on port 993;
the TLS_CERTFILE points to the certificate file that contains both private and
public key for our server, used to establish the authenticity of our host. Note
that we force users to use secure communications with the IMAP_TLS_REQUIRED
value set to 1: non encrypted connections will then be discarded.

Some values such as the Trash name are set in the non-encrypted configuration file imapd, as we can see from the init script itself. This file contains some
other useful configuration variables such as the **sendmail** command Courier
should use: Postfix is designed as a complete Sendmail replacement, and no
change is needed. Although the non-encrypted version is not implemented in
our system, we show its configuration file for completeness:

```
ADDRESS=0
PORT=143
MAXDAEMONS=40
MAXPERIP=20
PIDFILE=/var/run/courier/imapd.pid
TCPDOPTS="-nodnslookup -noidentlookup"
AUTHMODULES="authdaemon"
AUTHMODULES_ORIG="authdaemon"
DEBUG_LOGIN=0
IMAP_CAPABILITY="IMAP4rev1 UIDPLUS CHILDREN NAMESPACE THREAD=ORDEREDSUBJECT \
THREAD=REFERENCES SORT QUOTA IDLE"
IMAP_KEYWORDS=1
IMAP_CAPABILITY_ORIG="IMAP4rev1 UIDPLUS CHILDREN NAMESPACE THREAD=ORDEREDSUBJECT \
THREAD=REFERENCES SORT QUOTA AUTH=CRAM-MD5 AUTH=CRAM-SHA1 IDLE"
IMAP_IDLE_TIMEOUT=60
IMAP_CAPABILITY_TLS="$IMAP_CAPABILITY AUTH=PLAIN"
IMAP_CAPABILITY_TLS_ORIG="$IMAP_CAPABILITY_ORIG AUTH=PLAIN"
IMAP_DISABLETHREADSORT=0
IMAP_CHECK_ALL_FOLDERS=0
IMAP_OBSOLETE_CLIENT=0
IMAP_ULIMITD=65536
```

```
IMAP_USELOCKS=1
IMAP_SHAREDINDEXFILE=/etc/courier/shared/index
IMAP_ENHANCEDIDLE=0
IMAP_TRASHFOLDERNAME=Trash
IMAP_EMPTYTRASH=Trash:7
IMAP_MOVE_EXPUNGE_TO_TRASH=0
SENDMAIL=/usr/sbin/sendmail
HEADERFROM=X-IMAP-Sender
IMAPDSTART=YES

MAILDIRPATH=email
```

POP Configuration

The same approach is used to configure the POP server: the principal modification is the mailbox name, which matches the default one, and as for IMAP, some default values are set in the unencrypted version of our configuration file. For additional security the POP3_TLS_REQUIRED option guarantee that a potential server running on the conventional port requires an encrypted communication:

```
# cat /etc/courier/pop3d-ssl
SSLPORT=995
SSLADDRESS=0
SSLPIDFILE=/var/run/courier/pop3d-ssl.pid
POP3DSSLSTART=YES
POP3_STARTTLS=YES
POP3_TLS_REQUIRED=1
COURIERTLS=/usr/bin/couriertls
TLS_PROTOCOL=SSL3
TLS_STARTTLS_PROTOCOL=TLS1
TLS_CERTFILE=/etc/courier/pop3d.pem
TLS_VERIFYPEER=NONE
TLS_CACHEFILE=/var/lib/courier/couriersslcache
TLS_CACHESIZE=524288

MAILDIRPATH=email

# cat /etc/courier/pop3d
PIDFILE=/var/run/courier/pop3d.pid
MAXDAEMONS=40
MAXPERIP=4
AUTHMODULES="authdaemon"
AUTHMODULES_ORIG="authdaemon"
DEBUG_LOGIN=0
POP3AUTH=""
POP3AUTH_ORIG="LOGIN CRAM-MD5 CRAM-SHA1"
POP3AUTH_TLS=""
POP3AUTH_TLS_ORIG="LOGIN PLAIN"
PORT=110
ADDRESS=0
TCPDOPTS="-nodnslookup -noidentlookup"
POP3DSTART=YES

MAILDIRPATH=email
```

Modifying the Startup Script

As the last step of our configuration we have to modify `courier-imap-ssl` and `courier-pop3-ssl`, startup scripts located in `/etc/init.d/` to gain the

correct AFS token from the Kerberos keytab. The modifications are similar
to what we did for Apache, thus the **start)** stanza looks like the following
for our IMAP script:

```
start)
    echo -n "Starting $PROGRAM:"
    AUTHMODULELIST=""
    for f in $AUTHMODULES
    do
      if [ -e $libexecdir/authlib/$f ]; then
          AUTHMODULELIST="$AUTHMODULELIST $libexecdir/authlib/$f"
          fi
    done
    AUTHMODULELIST="`echo $AUTHMODULELIST`"

    ulimit -d $IMAP_ULIMITD
    /usr/bin/env - /bin/sh -c " . ${sysconfdir}/imapd ; \
               . ${sysconfdir}/imapd-ssl ; \
               IMAP_TLS=1 ; export IMAP_TLS ; \
               $PRE_COMMAND1 ; $PRE_COMMAND2; \
               `sed -n '/^#/d;/=/p' <${sysconfdir}/imapd | \
                    sed 's/=.*//;s/^/export /;s/$/;/'`
               `sed -n '/^#/d;/=/p' <${sysconfdir}/imapd-ssl | \
                    sed 's/=.*//;s/^/export /;s/$/;/'`
               $TCPD -address=$SSLADDRESS \
                    -stderrlogger=${sbindir}/courierlogger \
                    -stderrloggername=imapd-ssl \
                    -maxprocs=$MAXDAEMONS -maxperip=$MAXPERIP \
                    -pid=$SSLPIDFILE $TCPDOPTS \
                    $SSLPORT $COURIERTLS -server -tcpd \
                    ${libexecdir}/courier/imaplogin $AUTHMODULELIST \
                         ${bindir}/imapd $MAILDIR"
    echo " $DAEMON."
    $POST_COMMAND
        ;;
```

Note the calls to **PRE_COMMAND1**, **PRE_COMMAND2** and **POST_COMMAND**; the
corresponding POP server startup script will look similar to the previous one.
Now we are ready to start all servers to make these settings take effect:

```
# /etc/init.d/courier-authdaemon start
Starting Courier authdaemon: done.

# /etc/init.d/courier-imap-ssl start
Starting Courier IMAP-SSL server: imapd-ssl.

# /etc/init.d/courier-pop-ssl start
Starting Courier POP3-SSL server: pop3d-ssl.
```

Remember that both IMAP and POP daemons have to be restarted every
day: the frequency depends on the life time of the corresponding AFS token.
However, there should be no need to restart the authentication daemon.

9.3.3 Testing Courier

As a first test, we check all the available open ports with **nmap**, confirming
that the server has no insecure open ports:

```
# nmap localhost

Starting nmap 3.81 ( http://www.insecure.org/nmap/ ) at 2006-07-25 17:38 CEST
Interesting ports on localhost.localdomain (127.0.0.1):
(The 1659 ports scanned but not shown below are in state: closed)
PORT    STATE SERVICE
993/tcp open  imaps
995/tcp open  pop3s

Nmap finished: 1 IP address (1 host up) scanned in 0.507 seconds
```

Using a modern mail client, such as the Apple Mail pictured in Figs. 9.5 and 9.6, you should be able to access the `testuser` mailbox securely.

Fig. 9.5. Apple Mail settings for TLS-enabled IMAP access

9.4 Redundant Mail System

One way to achieve redundancy for the SMTP server is to have several MX records in the DNS with the same preference number: this would try to balance the load over all the MTA servers. Another way is to have several A records in the DNS with the same name and different IPs. Again, the DNS would try to balance loads on every IP address.

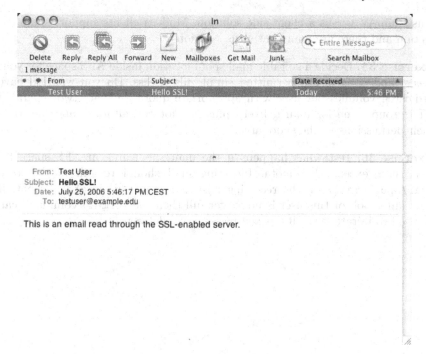

Fig. 9.6. The results reading an email via TSL connection

In the first case we need two different names, their reverse DNS mappings, and obviously different certificates. In the second case the host names are the same, the reverse DNS mapping giving the same name for different IPs, but certificates remain the same—host names do not change. Additionally the second way gives us more control over the load balancing since the DNS server takes care of that and not every single client.

Keeping it in symmetry with the solution for the web server we prefer the second method: in that case the entire client configuration is identical on two or more hosts except their IP address. The rest of the work is handled by the redundancy of the core services Kerberos, LDAP, and AFS file system.

Practice

Exercise 33. Compare other possible MTAs with respect to their suitability in the context of Kerberos, LDAP, and AFS. The Carnegie Mellon University, the birth place of AFS, decided in the meantime not to use AFS file space in its Cyrus mailing system.

Exercise 34. Confront the advantages and disadvantages of a centralized anti-spam and antivirus system like SpamAssasin combined with AMaViS plus ClamAV versus a client-side solution. Modern clients support spam detection and there are many antivirus solutions.

Exercise 35. Decide a suitable mail spool location inside AFS space for your needs, and if users are permitted simple file access. Do you want to have dedicated volumes per user with appropriate quotas? Create two separated PTS groups, one for mail delivery plus one for consultation, and fine tune their permissions to the spool area.

Exercise 36. Test what happens if the mail spool area in AFS space for some user exceeds its quota. Incoming mail should remain in the local `/var/spool/mail/` on the receiving host as a single file in `mbox` format. If the mail spool for this user is no longer full then the `formail` command can be used to iterate over all blocked messages to deliver them.

10

Newsgroups

The man who reads nothing at all is better educated than the man who reads nothing but newspapers.
Thomas Jefferson

10.1 The Usenet

Before the web became publicly available, users all over the world used a community-based system called *User Network*, or simply Usenet[1], as a way of sharing files and messages. It was first originally conceived at the Duke University and the University of North Carolina-Chapel Hill by Tom Truscott and Jim Ellis in 1979, using the UUCP protocol to offer an email-like system where users could publicly "post" articles using a news client.

Usenet is organized in newsgroups with a name describing its "on-topic" articles, and threaded in a tree-based hierarchy. Originally there were seven major topics named the "Big 7", described in Table 10.1, and all the newsgroups were sub-topics of these ones, with the dot "." separating each subject name (e.g. `comp.lang.c` relates with computers "`comp`", then languages "`lang`", and finally with the C programming language, "`c`").

Table 10.1. The "Big 7" newsgroup hierarchies

Hierarchy	Example	Topics
comp	comp.answers	Discussion groups about computers
misc	misc.fitness.aerobics	General discussions
news	news.admin.announce	Usenet-related topics
rec	rec.windsurfing	Recreational discussion boards
sci	sci.engr.biomed	Debates on science
soc	soc.history.medieval	Society-related arguments
talk	talk.environment	Arguable topics

Each article was posted to a particular newsgroup where it could be on-topic and thus made publicly available. People could respond to a "post" on

---

[1] The name was intended to attract the USENIX community the *Advanced Computing Technical Association* focused on the UNIX operating system.

a newsgroup, organizing the discussion in a simple tree-based hierarchy of articles called "threads", the same way email threads are commonly displayed on modern clients. Prior to the "Great Renaming" of the mid-80s, where the "Big 7" were created, Usenet had only the net hierarchy, with vivid debate on whether highly controversial topics should be allowed. The conflict resulted in the creation of the alt chain, the "alternative" newsgroup hierarchy, where all discussions were permitted: such a freedom lead to a complete alt-based newsgroup hierarchy that mirrored the others in a much more anarchic way (e.g. alt.comp.lang.php and the comp.lang.php newsgroups). The "Big 7" became the "Big 8" with the growth of the new humanities tree (e.g. humanities.classics), and all the major hierarchies were collectively known as the "Big 8 and alt". Generally, newsgroup posts are supposed to be written in English, thus language-based hierarchies were created such as it.comp.lang.c and de.comp.lang.c. Nowadays newsgroups are also handled by companies and institutions, for instance yale.general dealing with the Yale University , and microsoft.public.fortran held by the Microsoft Corporation; an historical archive of Usenet is currently a service free of charge offered by Google Inc.

The original UUCP protocol, employed in the early implementation, was replaced in the late 80s by the *Network News Transfer Protocol*, or NNTP, that mimics the SMTP, with later specifications allowing secure and encrypted solutions. This chapter shows the setup of a Usenet bulletin board system open only to users of our organization, providing also a secure channel for authentication employing the TLS/SSL protocol for NNTP, sometimes referred to as NNTPS. Our news server will have the real name nntp.example.edu, meaning no CNAME alias.

10.2 INN

InterNetNews INN was the first available news server, programmed by Rich Salz and released in 1991. It became renowned at the USENIX conference of 1992, being the first available news server supporting the NNTP protocol. Debian provides the older version, along with a more recent one, and clearly our decision falls on the newer inn2-ssl package, which also provides SSL support. The INN software needs some MTA which can be exim in a minimal Debian default installation: this is needed for moderated newsgroups[2] to contact the moderator. Since we already got familiar with Postfix, we stop exim4 and replace it with a minimal Postfix configuration.

During the Postfix installation Debian removes the exim mail agent, which is normal behavior when there are two packages able to perform the same task as daemon and thus considered potentially conflicting software. Here we are

---

[2] Some newsgroups may enforce an etiquette about topics and expressions: posts may be analyzed and edited by a human or an automatic moderator program.

going to configure a "satellite system" that forwards mails to our relay host
smtp.example.edu. The configuration file for the Postfix daemon, located at
/etc/postfix/main.cf, should be like the following:

```
inet_interfaces = loopback-only
relayhost = smtp.example.edu

biff = no
append_dot_mydomain = no

myhostname = nntp.example.edu
mydestination = nntp.example.edu, localhost
mynetworks = 127.0.0.0/8

mailbox_size_limit = 0
alias_maps = hash:/etc/aliases
alias_database = hash:/etc/aliases
```

The first two lines differ from previous Postfix configurations in that they
restrict SMTP to just listen to its local lo interface and forward all mail
to smtp.example.edu: this SMTP server is not visible from outside the nntp
host. We have to add the IP address of nntp.example.edu to the mynetworks
option on the principal mail relay host, such that mail relay is permitted without authentication from the nntp machine. For the news host no myorigin
option is needed, since it defaults to the myhostname setting. All administrative emails are, by default, redirected to root as we can see from the settings
in /etc/aliases:

```
# cat /etc/aliases
mailer-daemon: postmaster
postmaster: root
nobody: root
hostmaster: root
usenet: root
news: root
webmaster: root
www: root
ftp: root
abuse: root
noc: root
security: root
root: admin
```

10.2.1 Configuring INN

After installation stop the daemon inn2 in order to modify the INN configuration files located in /etc/news/. We start to modify the inn.conf file, setting
our organization name in the organization fields, and telling INN to track
all the senders of posts in the headers which is set by the nnrpdauthsender
line, here an excerpt:

```
mta:                "/usr/sbin/sendmail -oi -oem %s"
organization:       "Example Organization Newsgroups"
nnrpdauthsender:    true
```

All other Debian default settings should be fine. Postfix installed a replacement for /usr/sbin/sendmail, therefore the above mta configuration is correct. All our newsgroups need a root, a common prefix, such as the famous public comp.* newsgroups have comp as root. Following the ongoing habit of naming the newsgroup root with the company or the organization name, we decide for the prefix example. This can be anything suitable for your organization, but should not be in conflict with any global newsgroup if you wish to propagate news to the global Usenet infrastructure. This prefix will later be necessary for restricting accesses to our service. The next configuration regards the expiration of articles, in other words the lifetime of posts on our server. Our choice is to keep posts for one year, except for all testing newsgroups ending in .test which have an expiration period of one day. The file that handles these settings is expire.ctl:

```
/remember/:10
*:A:1:10:never
example.*:A:365:365:365
*.test:A:1:1:1
```

The remember tag defines how long the service will keep the history of expired articles. The specification for article lifetime is constituted of 5 fields separated by colons. The first field indicates the newsgroup string pattern, followed by a flag for further limitation to the applied rule: A for all groups, M for moderated ones, U to apply the rule only to unmoderated newsgroups, and X to immediately remove articles posted on all newsgroups it was sent to. Then follows the description of expiration dates in the format keep:default:purge, where the default value will be used in most occasions, expressing a lifetime in days. The other values, keep and purge will be used only in case an article requests a specific expiration period, restricted by the minimum and maximum lifetime expressed by keep and purge, respectively.

As next step for conducting some tests, we enable all the local networks to read and post to our news server: note that this procedure is intended to show and test INN, our final configuration will permit only authenticated users to submit articles. The file that determines the news reading and writing access is called readers.conf:

```
auth "localhost" {
    hosts: "localhost, 127.0.0.1, stdin"
    default: "<localhost>"
}
auth "network" {
    hosts: "192.168.127.0/24"
    default: "<network>"
}
access "localhost" {
    users: "<localhost>"
    newsgroups: "*"
    access: RPA
}
access "network" {
    users: "<network>"
```

```
    newsgroups: "example.*"
    access: RP
}
```

First a client host gets classified with respect to the authentication groups `auth`: both groups define a `default` value between angular parentheses, indicating the relative access rule. Here `localhost` can read R, post P, and approve A articles for moderated newsgroups. Users from our network can read and post articles for groups under the `example` hierarchy, and clients outside the network cannot contact this news server, because they do not occur in the above settings. Another configuration file is `news2mail.conf` that forwards posts to a possible mailing list. Just comment the mail forwarding line, which is there just for illustration, as follows:

```
### news-software@localhost.our.domain.com      news-software@real-host.somewhere.com
```

Creating Newsgroups

Right now there are no newsgroups except some default administrative ones. These predefined groups are needed by INN for its internal operations, so in order to proceed in creating our groups, we have to start the INN daemon first:

```
# /etc/init.d/inn2 start
Starting news server: done.
```

We want to create our first newsgroup, called `example.test`: note that any organization, and almost all news hierarchy, provides a newsgroup dedicated to tests, such that users can check their news clients. The tool that controls INN is `ctlinnd`, and the subcommand `newgroup` creates a new group:

```
# ctlinnd newgroup example.test
Ok
```

The counterpart of this subcommand is `rmgroup` which deletes a newsgroup. Another important subcommand could be `cancel` to remove a specific message from a newsgroup, using its unique identifier called `Message-ID`. This might be necessary to delete undesired contents before its expiration date.

10.2.2 Testing INN

To test our current INN daemon we make use of the Mozilla Thunderbird program, which is also an NNTP client. After configuring the software to utilize our `nntp.example.edu` host, we post an article and read the results as in Fig. 10.1. On either client or server side we can see the full header of a posted article with some useful information:

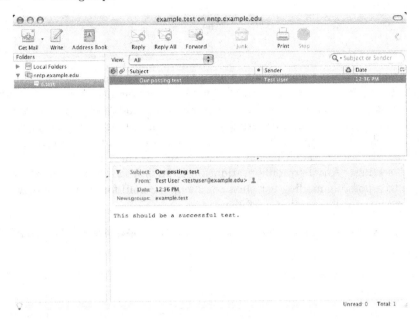

Fig. 10.1. Posting and reading articles to the `example.test` newsgroup

```
Path: unknown!not-for-mail
From: Test User <testuser@example.edu>
Newsgroups: example.test
Subject: Our posting test
Date: Tue, 01 Aug 2006 12:36:26 +0200
Organization: Example Organization Newsgroups
Lines: 1
Message-ID: <eanas1$467$1@nntp.example.edu>
NNTP-Posting-Host: 192.168.127.224
Mime-Version: 1.0
Content-Type: text/plain; charset=ISO-8859-1; format=flowed
Content-Transfer-Encoding: 7bit
X-Trace: nntp.example.edu 1154428609 4295 192.168.127.224 (1 Aug 2006 10:36:49 GMT)
X-Complaints-To: usenet@nntp.example.edu
NNTP-Posting-Date: Tue, 1 Aug 2006 10:36:49 +0000 (UTC)
User-Agent: Thunderbird 1.5.0.5 (Macintosh/20060719)
Xref: unknown example.test:1

This should be a successful test.
```

The line `Message-ID`[3] is unique on the NNTP server and can serve to
delete unwanted messages with the command `ctlinnd cancel` followed by
the `Message-ID`.

---

[3] The real `Message-ID` includes the angular parentheses.

10.3 Posting with Authentication

As the next step we want to restrict postings only to authenticated users enforcing the use of an encrypted communication channel. As we previewed, NNTP supports the TLS and SSL protocols, so before proceeding we need to create a key and certificate for our NNTP host:

```
# openssl genrsa -out privatekeys/nntp.pem 2048

# openssl req -new -days 1000 -key privatekeys/nntp.pem -out nntp.req

# openssl ca -days 1000 -in nntp.req -out certificates/nntp.pem
```

These files must be copied securely on the NNTP machine, in a private subdirectory ssl/ of /etc/news/ that contains the private key and the public certificates of the server and our authority:

```
# ls -ld ssl
drwxr-x---  2 root news 4096 2006-08-01 14:23 ssl/

# ls -l ssl/
total 16
-r--r--r--  1 news news 2480 2006-08-01 14:22 cacert.pem
-r--r--r--  1 news news 6446 2006-08-01 14:22 nntpcert.pem
-r--------  1 news news 1675 2006-08-01 14:23 nntpkey.pem
```

INN runs under user and group **news**. For accessing the file containing the private key this user needs access to it. This is reflected by the actual permission bits.

10.3.1 Authentication with FreeRADIUS

A commonly available authentication mechanism is the *Remote Authentication Dial In User Service*, or simply RADIUS, originally designed and developed by Livingston Enterprises as an AAA protocol: "authentication, authorization, accounting". Its main usage is for dial-up connections and mobile solutions such as wireless LANs, but because of its flexibility it can be employed for different usages. There are several RADIUS implementations on the market, but we focus on the free of charge server called FreeRADIUS. The procedure, we are going to explain, will once again make use of an authentication server, bounded to the local host, which then diverts the process to the Kerberos infrastructure via PAM as we have already seen for the email system. So let us proceed installing the server provided by the **freeradius** package:

```
# apt-get install freeradius
```

We configure the RADIUS daemon on the same host as INN, binding it just to the **localhost**, such that it remains invisible to external users and less prone to possible attacks. Internally, RADIUS uses a symmetric cryptography, with a shared secret key for client and server which is used to encode the communication between them: in this case, it is used to encrypt the communication between RADIUS and INN, which reside on the same host.

The configuration file for the FreeRADIUS daemon is located in the /etc/freeradius/ directory inside radiusd.conf. One option to modify is authenticate, specifying PAM as a valid authentication module and inhibiting the classic UNIX /etc/passwd file. Additionally bind_address is set in such a way that only the local host can contact the server:

```
bind_address = 127.0.0.1
...
authenticate {
...
        pam
#       unix
}
```

The next FreeRADIUS configuration file to edit is users, such that the default authentication mechanism is set to PAM:

```
DEFAULT Auth-Type = Pam
```

As we have already seen, FreeRADIUS uses a secret password, stored in the clients.conf file, in order to authenticate its clients; the value is used to encrypt the traffic between the daemon and the network client:

```
client 127.0.0.1 {
        secret        = testing123
        shortname     = localhost
        nastype       = other
}
```

The daemon contacts PAM with a service name called radiusd, so as we did for the email system, we have to create a file with this name in /etc/pam.d/. As the previous authentication daemons it redirects to Kerberos with the pam_krb5.so:

```
auth        required      pam_krb5.so
account     required      pam_permit.so
password    required      pam_permit.so
session     required      pam_permit.so
```

It is then necessary to install the Kerberos PAM module and configure our host to access the EXAMPLE.EDU realm. At this point the daemon is ready to be started, and you should verify immediately that only ports on localhost are opened:

```
# /etc/init.d/freeradius start
Starting FreeRADIUS daemon: Tue Aug  1 14:54:15 2006 : Info: \
Starting - reading configuration files ...
freeradius.
```

The RADIUS server can be tested with the `radtest` tool, providing a username, a password, the host, the port number, and shared secret, exactly in this order; in our case the port number is meaningless, so a any value, for example 0, is valid:

```
# radtest testuser password 127.0.0.1 0 testing123
Sending Access-Request of id 11 to 127.0.0.1:1812
        User-Name = "testuser"
        User-Password = "password"
        NAS-IP-Address = nntp
        NAS-Port = 0
rad_recv: Access-Accept packet from host 127.0.0.1:1812, id=11, length=20
```

The `Access-Accept` packets represents a successful authentication attempt on the RADIUS port 1812. If a wrong password is used, the authentication will be correctly rejected encoded by a `Access-Reject` packet after some delay:

```
# radtest testuser WrongPassword 127.0.0.1 0 testing123
Sending Access-Request of id 15 to 127.0.0.1:1812
        User-Name = "testuser"
        User-Password = "WrongPassword"
        NAS-IP-Address = nntp
        NAS-Port = 0
Re-sending Access-Request of id 15 to 127.0.0.1:1812
        User-Name = "testuser"
        User-Password = "\002\021\336\\:8\354\025\250i\364\210\266\t\311A"
        NAS-IP-Address = nntp
        NAS-Port = 0
rad_recv: Access-Reject packet from host 127.0.0.1:1812, id=15, length=20
```

10.3.2 Secure INN

To configure an SSL-enabled INN server, we start restricting the daemon running on the unencrypted port to the outer world in the `readers.conf` INN configuration file: any configuration except for `localhost` is removed. The default behavior is then to deny any access:

```
auth "localhost" {
    hosts: "localhost, 127.0.0.1, stdin"
    default: "<localhost>"
}
access "localhost" {
    users: "<localhost>"
    newsgroups: "*"
    access: RPA
}
```

Remember that these settings for `localhost` are necessary for the operation of INN: at least the daemon itself has to reach its internal groups for server administration. Next we prepare another configuration file for readers connecting over SSL that we choose to call `readers.sasl`. Here we enforce authentication with the help of the predefined method `radius`. Setting a pattern for the newsgroups restricts reading and posting just to all groups starting with **example**, and it avoids to expose the internal administrative groups of the server:

```
auth "world" {
    hosts: "*"
    auth: "radius"
}
access "world" {
    users: "*"
    newsgroups: "example.*"
    access: RP
}
```

Since there is no **default** stanza, non authenticated users are not permitted to access the service. Next we have to adapt our certificate configuration file for INN, that is **/etc/news/sasl.conf**, pointing to the right location where the private key and the public certificates are stored:

```
tls_cert_file:     /etc/news/ssl/nntpcert.pem
tls_key_file:      /etc/news/ssl/nntpkey.pem
tls_ca_path:       /etc/news/ssl
tls_ca_file:       /etc/news/ssl/cacert.pem
```

Now INN needs to be started on the SSL-enabled port, too: as seen for the Kerberos replication, we let the **xinetd** daemon take care of this part. Hence we have to install the corresponding suer-server package. The NNTPS service has to be configured in the **/etc/xinetd.d/** configuration directory, with a file called **nntps** according to the naming in **/etc/services**:

```
service nntps
{
        disable       = no
        socket_type   = stream
        protocol      = tcp
        user          = news
        wait          = no
        server        = /usr/lib/news/bin/nnrpd-ssl
        server_args   = -S -f -c /etc/news/readers.sasl
}
```

The program specified in **server** is part of the **inn2-ssl** package, and activates the SSL enabled NNTP daemon for requests with the **readers.sasl** configuration, given after the **-c** option, for client access. The option **-S** forces INN to start a SSL negotiation for client connections.

The last step is to link INN and FreeRADIUS. This is done by modifying the **radius.conf** file in **/etc/news/**, where we have to provide the RADIUS host and port, together with the shared secret:

```
server radiusserver {
radhost:       127.0.0.1
radport:       1812
lochost:       127.0.0.1
```

```
secret:        testing123
ignore-source: false
}
```

This configuration reflects that INN and RADIUS reside on the same host
127.0.0.1, and the setting of the `ignore-source` option checks that the
answer comes indeed from the RADIUS authenticator on `localhost`. To activate this new configuration stop the INN server, and next start both INN
and `xinetd`. Since this `xinetd` setting requires INN to work, we have to start
if after the news server:

```
# /etc/init.d/inn2 start
Starting news server: done.

# /etc/init.d/xinetd start
Starting internet superserver: xinetd.
```

As we can see, from the outside we can reach both NNTP ports, encrypted
and unencrypted, nevertheless the configuration will drop connections from
the outside to the unencrypted port. On the encrypted port, the authentication is enforced:

```
# nmap nntp.example.edu

Starting nmap 3.81 ( http://www.insecure.org/nmap/ ) at 2006-08-01 15:23 CEST
Interesting ports on nntp.example.edu (192.168.127.237):
(The 1660 ports scanned but not shown below are in state: closed)
PORT    STATE SERVICE
119/tcp open  nntp
563/tcp open  snews

Nmap finished: 1 IP address (1 host up) scanned in 0.507 seconds
```

Another time Thunderbird is used for testing, and its setup has to require
the use of SSL and user authentication since otherwise the news server rejects
the communication. The application might complain about an unknown certificate authority, but afterwards the username and password dialog starts.
Successful reading after a posting is shown in Fig.10.2 and the name of the
authenticated user appears in the `Sender:` field.

Practice

Exercise 37. Decide if INN is the right choice for your organizational needs:
there might exist other simpler web based newsgroup servers. Also the *Really
Simple Syndication* RSS standard could be of interest in this context.

Exercise 38. Design a newsgroup hierarchy suitable for your organization,
deciding also suitable expiration dates. What is a sensible setting for unauthenticated access?

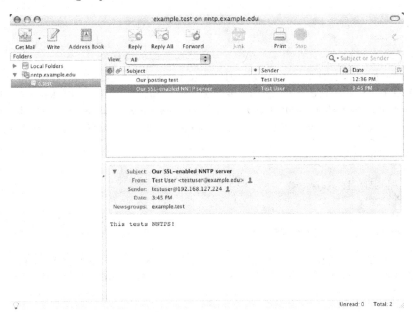

Fig. 10.2. Posting and reading articles via NNTPS

Exercise 39. The demonstrated RADIUS server directed all authentication requests towards Kerberos with the help of PAM. Explore other possibilities to use a RADIUS server.

Exercise 40. Try some backup procedure for net news in AFS space assuming that the `tradspool` and the `tradindexed` methods are used. The FAQs about INN suggest to make a backup of all the files in `$patharticles`, `$pathdb`, and `$pathetc`. These can be restored on an accordingly compiled and configured INN server in combination with the commands `makehistory` and `makedbz` for reproducing the previous state.

11

PostgreSQL Database

> *As a general rule the most successful man in life is the man who has the best information.*
> Benjamin Disraeli

11.1 Database Software

Commonly a database is a software that handles information, organizing it under a suitable form so that data retrieval can be fast, as well as permitting complex queries on its contents. The *Database Management Systems*, or DBMS, became renowned applications in the 60s, and were formally defined in their relational form by Edgar Frank Codd at IBM in 1970, but the first commercial products were not available until the 80s, with notable products as dBASE, Oracle, and DB2. During the 90s there was an explosion of object-oriented database management systems, which paved the way to the XML-based DBMS of later years.

The topic of DBMS can easily fill entire book shelves, and cannot be explained in details here, being far beyond the scope of this book. Nevertheless, so far we have seen the MySQL database, used in the context of dynamic web applications. For this purpose it is sufficient that it is just available for the web server, while in this chapter we want to provide our users with a personal database. Note that if you need a mission-critical DBMS with Kerberos capability, and high-bandwidth usage, it is strongly advisable to look for other solutions, for example the Oracle RDBMS (i.e. Relational DBMS) which is a commercially available Kerberized database software.

The PostgreSQL DBMS

PostgreSQL is an object-rational DBMS, available free of charge from the PostgreSQL Global Development Group, which is one example of a Kerberos-enabled database software. It was developed in 1986 by Prof. Michael Stonebrake to replace its ancestor Ingres: in fact the name was initially "Postgres", later changing the name to PostgreSQL and starting as an open source project from the initial academic concept.

It uses the *Structured Query Language* SQL for data manipulation respecting the ANSI standards SQL 92/99, and for the support of *transactions* it has been a forerunner in the world of open source databases. As we mentioned, PostgreSQL is also capable of using Kerberos credentials to allow users to manipulate their records.

The database server host will be called psql.example.edu and should not be an alias. Since we will run a Kerberized service, we need the machine to operate with our infrastructure as there are NTP, DNS, and Kerberos. As for the news server, we do not need any LDAP or AFS client configuration: the AFS file system is not an option for the location of the data base files, since DBMSs need direct file access, sometimes even at the level of a raw device.

11.2 PosgreSQL Installation

We start with the installation of the postgresql package, setting up both server and client programs. An advantage of this Debian-provided package is that it is compiled in such a way to be ready for Kerberos and SSL right out of the box. Debian asks for the preferred location for the database files. We can leave the default location, remembering to make sure that the chosen directory is not in the AFS file space. After installation we stop the service immediately: unlike MySQL which is not available over the public network, the PostgreSQL service needs to be reachable from the outside.

11.2.1 Configuring PostgreSQL

The configuration files for this DBMS are located in the /etc/postgresql/ directory. We start modifying the main configuration file postgresql.conf. For security reasons we want to log errors verbosely, and make sure to track also the connecting hosts; here is an excerpt of postgresql.conf:

```
#ssl = false
password_encryption = true
#krb_server_keyfile = ''
syslog = 0
log_error_verbosity = verbose
silent_mode = false
log_connections = true
log_duration = true
log_timestamp = true
log_hostname = true
datestyle = 'ISO,European'
```

Note the commented line for SSL and Kerberos support, which are going to be modified later on. The setting of password_encryption forces the encryption of internal stored passwords, while the datestyle option does some localization for the presentation of dates.

11.2.2 PostgreSQL with Kerberos

Next we have to create an administrative user that will be used in connection with Kerberos. By default there is a UNIX user **postgres** which is granted all administrative rights coming from `localhost`, so let us start the PostgreSQL server and proceed administering it:

```
# /etc/init.d/postgresql start
Starting PostgreSQL database server: postmaster.
```

We get the rights of the **postgres** user with the help of the **su** command, and connect to the default database created during installation time called `template1` with the client `psql`:

```
# su - postgres
postgres@psql:~$ psql template1
Welcome to psql 7.4.7, the PostgreSQL interactive terminal.

Type:  \copyright for distribution terms
       \h for help with SQL commands
       \? for help on internal slash commands
       \g or terminate with semicolon to execute query
       \q to quit

template1=#
```

Notice the typical prompt showing the database name of the connection, and the "#" sign that indicates an administrative user. This auxiliary database `template1` is needed for the operation of PostgreSQL and should not be deleted. The next step is to create a user in the internal PostgreSQL user database that has full administrative privileges: our choice is that **sysadmin** becomes PostgreSQL superuser, too, which is achieved by the option **createuser**. After that, just exit the DBMS and stop the daemon:

```
template1=# create user sysadmin createuser;
CREATE USER

template1=# select * from pg_user;
 usename  | usesysid | usecreatedb | usesuper | usecatupd |  passwd  | valuntil |
----------+----------+-------------+----------+-----------+----------+----------+...
 postgres |        1 | t           | t        | t         | ******** |          |
 sysadmin |      100 | t           | t        | t         | ******** |          |
(2 rows)

template1=# \q
```

The **pg_user** table above is an internal PostgreSQL system table, similar to `/etc/passwd`, reflecting the users known to the DBMS which have nothing to do with the underlying operating system.

On the KDC we have to create the PostgreSQL service principal, similarly to the LDAP service; the DBMS needs a principal called **postgres/hostname**, so in our case it will be **postgres/psql.example.edu**. We finally need to export its credentials to a keytab file on the database server:

```
# klist -ke /etc/postgresql/postgres.keytab
Keytab name: FILE:postgres.keytab
KVNO Principal
---- --------------------------------------------------------------------
   3 postgres/psql.example.edu@EXAMPLE.EDU (Triple DES cbc mode with HMAC/sha1)
   3 postgres/psql.example.edu@EXAMPLE.EDU (DES cbc mode with CRC-32)
```

Note that here the keytab file should be readable by the `postgres` group or user in order to make the Kerberos authentication work:

```
-rw-r----- 1 root postgres 154 2006-08-01 17:07 postgres.keytab
```

We are ready to make a first modification to the `postgresql.conf` file which refers to the keytab file:

```
...
#ssl = false
password_encryption = true
krb_server_keyfile = '/etc/postgresql/postgres.keytab'
...
```

To enable all Kerberized hosts to connect to PostgreSQL with the `sysadmin` user we have to modify the `pg_hba.conf` file containing access permissions. The first three lines are default settings, in particular the first line permitted the earlier operation as the `postgres` user, whereas the second and third line allow connections via sockets or `localhost` with coinciding database and user name:

```
local   all   postgres    ident sameuser
local   all   all         ident sameuser
host    all   all         127.0.0.1    255.255.255.255 ident sameuser
host    all   sysadmin    0.0.0.0      0.0.0.0         krb5
host    all   all         0.0.0.0      0.0.0.0         reject
```

This file lists in order type, database, user, optionally an IP address, and method with possible options for client authentication. The lines are examined from top to bottom and the first matching line decides the authentication method. Now we can start PostgreSQL service and proceed testing it:

```
# /etc/init.d/postgresql start
Starting PostgreSQL database server: postmaster.
```

11.2.3 Testing Kerberos Authentication

As a test we can try to connect to our DBMS from a machine without any Kerberos ticket. To test our configuration we must install the PostgreSQL client package called `postgresql-client`, and we expect to be rejected by the database server:

```
# klist
klist: No credentials cache found (ticket cache FILE:/tmp/krb5cc_0)


Kerberos 4 ticket cache: /tmp/tkt0
klist: You have no tickets cached

# psql -h psql.example.edu template1
psql: FATAL:  no pg_hba.conf entry for host "192.168.127.145", user "root", \
database "template1", SSL off
```

The next test is to gain the **sysadmin** Kerberos credentials and to retry the connection to the server:

```
# kinit sysadmin
Password for sysadmin@EXAMPLE.EDU:

# psql -h psql.example.edu template1
Welcome to psql 7.4.7, the PostgreSQL interactive terminal.

Type:  \copyright for distribution terms
       \h for help with SQL commands
       \? for help on internal slash commands
       \g or terminate with semicolon to execute query
       \q to quit

template1=#
```

Note that it worked using a single sign on since we were not asked any password; moreover from the prompt we know to have administrative rights.

11.2.4 Securing PostgreSQL

At the moment all our connections work over an unencrypted channel, except for the Kerberos authentication. Since we wish to have secure services, we will encrypt our traffic on the network via SSL. As for all SSL-enabled services, we need to create a certificate and a private key for our PostgreSQL host **psql.example.edu**:

```
# openssl genrsa -out privatekeys/psql.pem 2048

# openssl req -new -days 1000 -key privatekeys/psql.pem -out psql.req

# openssl ca -days 1000 -in psql.req -out certificates/psql.pem
```

Next, we have to copy the private key and public certificate to the PostgreSQL server with the file names specified by the DBMS software. These files must be called **server.key** and **server.crt** in **/var/lib/postgres/data/**, with the following permissions and ownership:

```
-r--r--r--  1 postgres postgres 6446 2006-08-01 17:37 server.crt
-r--------  1 postgres postgres 1679 2006-08-01 17:37 server.key
```

Note that only the public certificate is world-readable. You can also opt for symbolic links placing the files under /etc/postgresql/ as Debian normally does: in any case, PostgreSQL will refuse to start if it cannot find them in /var/lib/postgres/data/. At this point we can enable SSL connections in postgresql.conf:

```
...
ssl = true
password_encryption = true
krb_server_keyfile = '/etc/postgresql/postgres.keytab'
...
```

PostgreSQL distinguishes between open or SSL-encrypted channels for client authentication, achieved by substituting host with the hostssl directive in the pg_hba.conf configuration file. With the following configuration the sysadmin user is allowed from everywhere provided that the connection is SSL encrypted, and the user is authenticated by Kerberos:

```
local    all    postgres    ident sameuser
local    all    all         ident sameuser
host     all    all         127.0.0.1    255.255.255.255 ident sameuser
hostssl  all    sysadmin    0.0.0.0      0.0.0.0         krb5
host     all    all         0.0.0.0      0.0.0.0         reject
```

The server has to be restarted so that these new setting take effect, and besides the sysadmin user all other connection attempts will be rejected. To test, gain sysadmin credentials and connect to the database server to see that an SSL connection has been started:

```
# psql -h psql.example.edu template1
Welcome to psql 7.4.7, the PostgreSQL interactive terminal.

Type:  \copyright for distribution terms
       \h for help with SQL commands
       \? for help on internal slash commands
       \g or terminate with semicolon to execute query
       \q to quit

SSL connection (cipher: DHE-RSA-AES256-SHA, bits: 256)

template1=#
```

As it appears in the output, SSL explicitly reports the settings for the opened channel.

11.3 PostgreSQL Users

So far we connected to PostreSQL by means of a Kerberos authentication, but this does not mean that the DBMS automatically knows about our users: in fact we needed to add the sysadmin entry in the internal administrative database. Every user has to be created for PostgreSQL as well and, to simplify administration, we choose to prepare a database for every user with

the identical name. The change of connectivity permissions is reflected in the
pg_hba.conf file, enabling our Kerberos authenticated users for connections
from everywhere to a database which matches their principal name with the
sameuser option. The configuration file looks like the following:

```
local    all    postgres    ident sameuser
local    all    all         ident sameuser
host     all    all         127.0.0.1       255.255.255.255 ident sameuser
hostssl  all    sysadmin    0.0.0.0         0.0.0.0         krb5
hostssl  all    all         0.0.0.0         0.0.0.0         krb5 sameuser
host     all    all         0.0.0.0         0.0.0.0         reject
```

Note that we reject all insecure connections over the network using the
hostssl directive instead of the host one.

11.3.1 User Privileges

Our user database name has to match the user name, so for instance our
testuser will posses a database called testuser: of course this is a choice
that eases the administration, but other decisions might be suitable as well.
Remember that, as database administrators, we have to create users and provide them with a dedicated database. We need to connect to the database
server as an administrator from a client system: first we create the user and
give optionally a password which is used later, and next make a database
granting all the privileges to just that user:

```
# kinit sysadmin

# psql -h psql.example.edu template1
Welcome to psql 7.4.7, the PostgreSQL interactive terminal.

Type:  \copyright for distribution terms
       \h for help with SQL commands
       \? for help on internal slash commands
       \g or terminate with semicolon to execute query
       \q to quit

SSL connection (cipher: DHE-RSA-AES256-SHA, bits: 256)

template1=# create user testuser password 'initialpw';
CREATE USER

template1=# create database testuser owner testuser;
CREATE DATABASE
```

Now it is possible to test the new PostgreSQL user testuser connecting to
the corresponding database, and without any Kerberos credential the access
should be denied:

```
# klist
klist: No credentials cache found (ticket cache FILE:/tmp/krb5cc_0)

Kerberos 4 ticket cache: /tmp/tkt0
```

```
klist: You have no tickets cached

# psql -h psql.example.edu testuser
psql: Kerberos 5 authentication failed

# psql -h psql.example.edu -u testuser
psql: Warning: The -u option is deprecated. Use -U.
User name: testuser
Password:
psql: Kerberos 5 authentication failed
```

The last example using the -u switch shows that our database password "initialpw" does not work for connections. Gaining the initial ticket we are allowed to issue any command we have the privilege for. Note that the prompt differs from the previous one, since **testuser** is not a superuser:

```
# kinit testuser
Password for testuser@EXAMPLE.EDU:

# klist
Ticket cache: FILE:/tmp/krb5cc_0
Default principal: testuser@EXAMPLE.EDU

Valid starting     Expires           Service principal
08/03/06 10:25:45  08/03/06 20:25:43 krbtgt/EXAMPLE.EDU@EXAMPLE.EDU


Kerberos 4 ticket cache: /tmp/tkt0
klist: You have no tickets cached

# psql -h psql.example.edu testuser
Welcome to psql 7.4.7, the PostgreSQL interactive terminal.

Type:  \copyright for distribution terms
       \h for help with SQL commands
       \? for help on internal slash commands
       \g or terminate with semicolon to execute query
       \q to quit

SSL connection (cipher: DHE-RSA-AES256-SHA, bits: 256)

testuser=>
```

Our user is not able to create new databases, neither there are permissions to access other databases, but any operation is granted to operate in the sandbox of its own database over the safe and encrypted channel:

```
testuser=> create table test(i int);
CREATE TABLE

testuser=> insert into test values(1000);
INSERT 17145 1

testuser=> insert into test values(2000);
INSERT 17146 1

testuser=> insert into test values(3000);
INSERT 17147 1

testuser=> select * from test;
  i
```

```
------
1000
2000
3000
(3 rows)

testuser=> \q
```

11.3.2 Access from Web Scripts

Our objective is to allow the web server to connect to these personal Post-greSQL databases. We have to enable all of our web servers with the help of their IP addresses to connect to the DBMS, using the password we have set in the user creation process, which internally is encoded with the MD5 algorithm. In the `pg_hba.conf` configuration file we add our web servers, and due to the stack-like property of PostgreSQL host settings, it is mandatory that these lines come before the Kerberos authentication, and after `sysadmin`, which has higher priority.

The web server has an AFS token but no Kerberos ticket, therefore it needs to authenticate with the help of a password which can occur in scripts, too. This procedure guarantees that every user has an own password for access to the personal data base:

```
local    all    postgres      ident sameuser
local    all    all           ident sameuser
host     all    all           127.0.0.1        255.255.255.255 ident sameuser
hostssl  all    sysadmin      0.0.0.0          0.0.0.0         krb5
hostssl  all    all           192.168.127.145  255.255.255.255 md5 sameuser
hostssl  all    all           192.168.127.230  255.255.255.255 md5 sameuser
hostssl  all    all           0.0.0.0          0.0.0.0         krb5 sameuser
host     all    all           0.0.0.0          0.0.0.0         reject
```

Two web server with the IPs `192.168.127.145` and `192.168.127.230`, occour in this configuration repectively. Be aware that every user can change this personal web-only password by the following command from the SQL interaction when authenticated either via Kerberos or also from a web server host via the old password:

```
testuser=> alter user testuser with password 'webpasswd';
ALTER USER
```

The new password can be tested from one web server by installing there the PostgreSQL client and connecting to the database server with the modified web password for `testuser`:

```
# klist
klist: No credentials cache found (ticket cache FILE:/tmp/krb5cc_0)


Kerberos 4 ticket cache: /tmp/tkt0
klist: You have no tickets cached
```

```
# ifconfig eth0
eth0      Link encap:Ethernet  HWaddr 00:10:5A:C4:93:37
          inet addr:192.168.127.145  Bcast:192.168.127.255  Mask:255.255.255.0
          UP BROADCAST RUNNING MULTICAST  MTU:1500  Metric:1
          RX packets:11979 errors:0 dropped:0 overruns:0 frame:0
          TX packets:682 errors:0 dropped:0 overruns:0 carrier:0
          collisions:0 txqueuelen:1000
          RX bytes:1075115 (1.0 MiB)  TX bytes:81461 (79.5 KiB)
          Interrupt:10 Base address:0xd000

# psql -h psql.example.edu -u testuser
psql: Warning: The -u option is deprecated. Use -U.
User name: testuser
Password:
Welcome to psql 7.4.7, the PostgreSQL interactive terminal.

Type:  \copyright for distribution terms
       \h for help with SQL commands
       \? for help on internal slash commands
       \g or terminate with semicolon to execute query
       \q to quit

SSL connection (cipher: DHE-RSA-AES256-SHA, bits: 256)

testuser=>
```

To benefit from the personal database for web applications we have to enable PostgreSQL support in the relative scripting language. On our web server we decide to add the PHP-PostgreSQL connector and restart the web server, such that the extension gets loaded:

```
# apt-get install php4-pgsql

# tail -2 php.ini
extension=mysql.so
extension=pgsql.so

# /etc/init.d/apache2 stop
Stopping web server: Apache2.

# /etc/init.d/apache2 start
Starting web server: Apache2.
```

To check that the connection is working we create a simple PHP script to show the fields of the table we have created before:

```php
<?php
  $db_connection = pg_connect("host=psql.example.edu " .
                              "dbname=testuser " .
                              "user=testuser " .
                              "password=webpasswd")
                 or die('Could not connect to database: ' .
                        pg_last_error());
  $query = "SELECT * FROM test";
  $result = pg_query($query) or die('Query failed: ' . pg_last_error());
  echo "<html>\n";
  echo "<head><title>PostgreSQL Test</title></head>\n";
  echo "<body>\n";
  echo "<table>\n";
  while ($row = pg_fetch_row($result, null)) {
    echo "<tr>\n";
```

```
 foreach ($row as $column) {
   echo "<td>$column</td>\n";
 };
 echo "</tr>\n";
};
echo "</table>\n";
echo "</body>\n";
echo "</html>\n";
pg_free_result($result);
pg_close($db_connection);
?>
```

This script has to be stored in a file with the .php suffix, for instance psql.php. The http://www.example.edu/~testuser/psql.php web location should show the previously created entries as in Fig. 11.1. Analogously

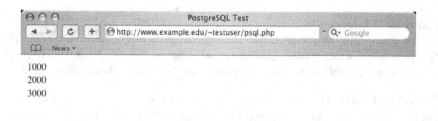

Fig. 11.1. PHP Script Using PostgreSQL

to the phpMyAdmin package there exists the PostgreSQL counterpart phpP-gAdmin. The installation is very similar to the version for MySQL and it provides a web interface for PostgreSQL. Although the web server authenticates with the help of the simple password, the actual access to these administrative web pages could be additionally protected by Kerberos to avoid data base break in attempts over the web server.

PHP Security Issue

Again this PHP script can be an entry point for malicious users: the password is stored in clear text inside the scripts, and since PHP works at the same level as Apache, a user could use another PHP script to discover passwords of others. Please refer to the web server chapter for possible solutions to this problem.

Practice

Exercise 41. Judge on the base of your user requests if *Open Database Connectivity*, the ODBC, is a desirable option to connect to databases from UNIX. There exist packages for Debian, too, as unixodbc. Additionally there are library files for MySQL and PostgreSQL plus the connector for PHP.

Exercise 42. Check the presented authentication methods. Do they fit your needs? How would your pg_hba.conf look like?

Exercise 43. Does your activity often require statistical analysis? In this case the programming language GNU R inspired by S might be of interest. Try the package r-cran-rodbc providing database access for R or the package postgresql-plr allowing for a language interface from PostgreSQL to R.

Exercise 44. For the redundancy of PostgreSQL there is the SLONY-I project as a master-slave setting with the possibility of fail-over. A second solution is to implement *high availability* with a second node in stand-by: the support for such a two-node cluster can be found in the package heartbeat.

12

Further Web Applications

> *There are no such things as applied sciences, only applications of science.*
> Louis Pasteur

12.1 Web Application

Web applications are a special form of the general client-server architecture: on the client side they require a web browser and on the server side a web server. These two sides communicate with the help of the standardized protocol HTTP over an unencrypted or encrypted channel .depending on the settings. Usually a web application is organized as a "three-tiered" service, as pictured in Fig. 12.1. The client performs an operation on the web browser, and sends the necessary data to the server: this is the first tier or "presentation" level. The second level, the "logic" tier, is a dynamic content manager as ASP, JSP, or PHP which can translate the requested operation to a permanent data management system such as DBMS, which constitute the third "data" tier along with the actual storage medium. Although for the client

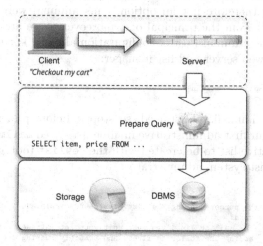

Fig. 12.1. A three-tier architecture

any specific application can be substituted conveniently with general browser software, nevertheless the standards to be supported by the client are several, such as *JavaScript* or *Flash*: JavaScript can be found in most browser software by default independently of the underlying platform, while the other technology usually requires an add-on for the browser in use.

This chapter presents some examples of web applications. We will show a mailing list management system, a groupware software, an e-Learning system, and simple calendaring. Only the first steps in the setup process are shown up to the point when the rest of the configuration can be handled with the help of a web interface.

12.2 Mailman Mailing List Manager

Mailing lists are a method to distribute email messages to many recipients simultaneously, where users normally subscribe or unsubscribe to a specific mailing list. Here we present a commonly used mailing list software Mailman, developed by a community that releases the software under the GPL license. The Mailman software has the option to synchronize mailing lists with a newsgroup server: in order to simplify the entire setup we choose to install this package on the same machine running INN which is `nntp.example.edu`.

12.2.1 Installing Mailman

We start with the installation of the `mailman` package: the software depends on a web server which has to be installed on the same host, thus all cooperating servers Apache, INN, Mailman, and Postfix are on the `nntp` machine. Additionally, some form of indexing is used in the mailing list management system: AFS is therefore not an option. This minimal web server installation is separated from the principal one, moreover as we are acting on `nntp` there exists some minimal Postfix configuration already. Let us then proceed installing both web server and list manager:

```
# apt-get install apache2 mailman
```

Apache gets immediately started, so stop it before proceeding. Now we have to create our first administrative mailing list called `mailman` as a mandatory administrative list to be created with the `newlist` tool, giving the email of the mailing list system administrator:

```
# newlist mailman
Enter the email of the person running the list: testuser@example.edu
Initial mailman password:
To finish creating your mailing list, you must edit your /etc/aliases (or
equivalent) file by adding the following lines, and possibly running the
'newaliases' program:
```

```
## mailman mailing list
mailman:              "|/var/lib/mailman/mail/mailman post mailman"
mailman-admin:        "|/var/lib/mailman/mail/mailman admin mailman"
mailman-bounces:      "|/var/lib/mailman/mail/mailman bounces mailman"
mailman-confirm:      "|/var/lib/mailman/mail/mailman confirm mailman"
mailman-join:         "|/var/lib/mailman/mail/mailman join mailman"
mailman-leave:        "|/var/lib/mailman/mail/mailman leave mailman"
mailman-owner:        "|/var/lib/mailman/mail/mailman owner mailman"
mailman-request:      "|/var/lib/mailman/mail/mailman request mailman"
mailman-subscribe:    "|/var/lib/mailman/mail/mailman subscribe mailman"
mailman-unsubscribe:  "|/var/lib/mailman/mail/mailman unsubscribe mailman"

Hit enter to notify mailman owner...
```

At the moment we have to append manually the last lines to /etc/aliases and run the newaliases command as requested. Be aware, that without this list Mailman will refuse to work. For all non-administrative mailing lists we will not need to modify this alias file, but all the changes will happen with the help of a web interface and operate on a separated file. The last installation step is to set the mailing lists administrator and creator passwords with the proper command mmsitepass:

```
# mmsitepass sitepassword
Password changed.

# mmsitepass -c listpassword
Password changed.
```

The first command is for the site administrator, and can be used in any situation that an authentication is required by Mailman. The second command defines the password for the list creator, the user that can initialize new lists through the Mailman web interface. Remember that the site password is a then passe-partout to administer all mailing lists and to create new ones.

12.2.2 Postfix Configuration

We tune our previous Postfix configuration done for NNTP, preferring that the host nntp.example.edu handles all mail relay by itself: mailing lists could provoke a very heavy load for the machines involved, because they send copies to potentially thousands of different email addresses, and we do not want this load to harm our principal mailing system. The changes to our previous Postfix configuration includes the setup of a Mailman-only alias file as seen in alias_maps, handled by the software via the web interface:

```
inet_interfaces = all

biff = no
append_dot_mydomain = no

myhostname = nntp.example.edu
mydestination = nntp.example.edu, localhost
mynetworks = 127.0.0.0/8
```

```
mailbox_size_limit = 0
alias_maps = hash:/etc/aliases, hash:/var/lib/mailman/data/aliases
alias_database = hash:/etc/aliases
```

In comparison with the previous configuration all the network interfaces have been enabled, as the **inet_interfaces** field clearly shows; furthermore the mail relay has been removed. The alias file dedicated to Mailman still has to be created with the right ownership and permissions:

```
# cd /var/lib/mailman/data/

# touch aliases

# ls -l aliases
-rw-rw---- 1 www-data list 0 2006-08-03 12:29 aliases
```

We prepare settings that assume the addresses for our mailing lists to look like **listname@nntp.example.edu**, therefore our main SMTP servers have to pass on the entire subdomain **nntp.example.edu** to **nntp**. The Postfix settings in **main.cf** have to contain the following new line on the central servers:

```
masquerade_domains = !nntp.example.edu, example.edu
```

This means, that the subdomain **nntp.example.edu** will not be treated as the domain **example.edu**, and the mail is forwarded to the **nntp** host which takes care of all mailing list addresses. Therefore all mailing list related mail is principally handled by the dedicated host.

12.2.3 Mailman Configuration

Mailman is programmed in the Python scripting language and some more global modifications have to be done. The main configuration file is called **mm_cfg.py**, hinting the language, and located in the **/etc/mailman/** directory. We want to activate Mailman only on the SSL-enabled web server, since we avoid our passwords to travel the network unencrypted. Mailman can additionally send periodically reminders containing the user's password, but we inhibit this behavior since sending unencrypted emails containing passwords is clearly a security threat. Another configuration parameter is the default NNTP host for newsgroup synchronization which we set to **localhost**:

```
from Defaults import *
MAILMAN_SITE_LIST = 'mailman'
DEFAULT_URL_PATTERN = 'https://%s/mailman/'
PRIVATE_ARCHIVE_URL = '/mailman/private/'
IMAGE_LOGOS = '/images/'
DEFAULT_EMAIL_HOST = 'nntp.example.edu'
DEFAULT_URL_HOST = 'nntp.example.edu'
add_virtualhost(DEFAULT_URL_HOST, DEFAULT_EMAIL_HOST)
DEFAULT_SERVER_LANGUAGE = 'en'
USE_ENVELOPE_SENDER = 0
DEFAULT_SEND_REMINDERS = 0
```

```
MTA='Postfix'
DEFAULT_NNTP_HOST = 'localhost'
```

These settings refer to the site list **mailman** for management, furthermore they define default URLs and hosts. For the moment we have created just one mailing list, necessary for internal administrative purposes of Mailman. To verify the existence of this list we call the **list_lists** tool:

```
# list_lists
1 matching mailing lists found:
   Mailman - [no description available]
```

12.2.4 Apache Configuration

We have already created the SSL certificates for **nntp.example.edu**, therefore we can copy key and certificates into **/etc/apache2/ssl/**:

```
# ls -l /etc/apache2/ssl
total 16
-r--r--r--  1 root root 2480 2006-08-03 12:49 cacert.pem
-r--r--r--  1 root root 6446 2006-08-03 12:49 nntpcert.pem
-r--------  1 root root 1675 2006-08-03 12:49 nntpkey.pem
```

Then we have to enable the SSL module with **a2enmod**, in order to be able to serve **https://** requests:

```
# a2enmod ssl
Module ssl installed; run /etc/init.d/apache2 force-reload to enable.
```

Again, we avoid using insecure protocols, since users have to subscribe and unsubscribe using web forms. Then we need to create the configuration for both encrypted and unencrypted sites, redirecting any HTTP connection to the SSL-based HTTPS protocol. Our site files are called **nntp.example.edu** and **nntp.example.edu_ssl**, where the SSL-enabled site has its document root in **/var/www/nntp.example.edu_ssl**:

```
<VirtualHost 192.168.127.237:443>
        ServerAdmin www@example.edu

        SSLEngine on
        SSLCipherSuite HIGH:MEDIUM
        SSLProtocol -all +SSLv3 +TLSv1
        SSLCaCertificateFile /etc/apache2/ssl/cacert.pem
        SSLCertificateFile /etc/apache2/ssl/nntpcert.pem
        SSLCertificateKeyFile /etc/apache2/ssl/nntpkey.pem

        DocumentRoot /var/www/nntp.example.edu_ssl
        <Directory />
                Options FollowSymLinks
                AllowOverride None
        </Directory>
        <Directory /var/www/nntp.example.edu_ssl>
                Options All MultiViews
```

```
            AllowOverride All
            Order allow,deny
            Allow from all
    </Directory>

    ErrorLog /var/log/apache2/error_ssl.log
    LogLevel warn
    CustomLog /var/log/apache2/access_ssl.log combined

    ScriptAlias /mailman/ /usr/lib/cgi-bin/mailman/
    Alias /images/ /usr/share/images/mailman/
    Alias /pipermail/ /var/lib/mailman/archives/public/

    <Directory "/usr/lib/cgi-bin/mailman/">
            Options ExecCGI
            AllowOverride None
            Order allow,deny
            Allow from all
    </Directory>

    <Directory "/usr/share/images/mailman/">
            AllowOverride None
            Order allow,deny
            Allow from all
    </Directory>

    <Directory "/var/lib/mailman/archives/public/">
            Options All
            AddDefaultCharset Off
            AllowOverride None
            Order allow,deny
            Allow from all
    </Directory>

</VirtualHost>
```

The `Alias` and `ScriptAlias` instructions redirect all URLs pointing to `mailman/`, `images/`, and `pipermail/` to the correct Mailman directories as indicated by the software documentation. Note that GCI execution is enabled for all `mailman` web locations as indicated by the `Options ExecCGI` directive. Our non-SSL site shall redirect all communication to the secure server: one way to achieve this is using an Apache module that rewrites URLs. So let us enable the `rewrite` module:

```
# a2enmod rewrite
Module rewrite installed; run /etc/init.d/apache2 force-reload to enable.
```

Then our site configuration for the normal port 80 should redirect everything to port 443 with the `RewriteEngine` instruction enabled. According to `Redirect` the root locations is rewritten immediately:

```
<VirtualHost 192.168.127.237:80>
    ServerAdmin www@example.edu

    DocumentRoot /var/www/nntp.example.edu
    <Directory />
            Options FollowSymLinks
            AllowOverride None
    </Directory>
```

```
        <Directory /var/www/nntp.example.edu>
                Options All MultiViews
                AllowOverride All
                Order allow,deny
                Allow from all
        </Directory>

        ErrorLog /var/log/apache2/error.log
        LogLevel warn
        CustomLog /var/log/apache2/access.log combined

        RewriteEngine On
        Redirect / https://nntp.example.edu/

</VirtualHost>
```

Remember to create the site directories in **/var/www/**, and to enable Apache to listen to HTTPS in **/etc/apache2/ports.conf**:

```
Listen 80
Listen 443
```

The last step is to enable these two sites and to remove the default one from the installation:

```
# a2ensite nntp.example.edu
Site nntp.example.edu installed; run /etc/init.d/apache2 reload to enable.

# a2ensite nntp.example.edu_ssl
Site nntp.example.edu_ssl installed; run /etc/init.d/apache2 reload to enable.

# a2dissite default
Site default disabled; run /etc/init.d/apache2 reload to fully disable.
```

12.2.5 Starting Mailman

At this point we are ready to start all our services in order: first comes the MTA Postfix, then the Mailman list manager, and finally the Apache web server:

```
# /etc/init.d/postfix start
Starting mail transport agent: Postfix.

# /etc/init.d/mailman start
Starting Mailman's master qrunner.

# /etc/init.d/apache2 start
Starting web server: Apache2.
```

It is helpful that the SSL site contains an **index.html** file in order to make browsers load directly the Mailman overview web page:

```
# cat /var/www/nntp.example.edu_ssl/index.html
<html>
<head>
```

```
<META HTTP-EQUIV="Refresh" CONTENT="0;
    URL=https://nntp.example.edu/mailman/listinfo">
</head>
<body>
</body>
</html>
```

This way any browser gets directed to the information about mailing lists, and any insecure connection is forced to the secure port which lists all visible lists. All administrative tasks can be handled via the web interface, as we see in Fig. 12.2.

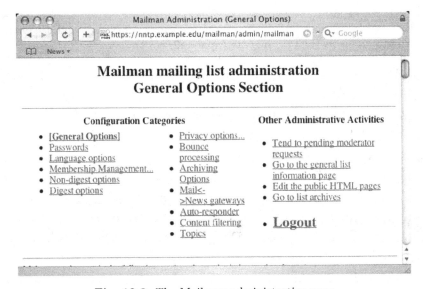

Fig. 12.2. The Mailman administrative page

Some aspects of a user's configuration can be handled by sending specially crafted mail messages too, which is a remainder of previous list software like `listserv` or `majordomo`. Remember that in case of a forgotten list administrator password one can always use the site administrator's password. A mailing list can be manually removed by issuing the `rmlist` command, where the `-a` switch forces the removal of the archives, too:

```
# rmlist testlist
Not removing archives.  Reinvoke with -a to remove them.
Removing list info

# rmlist -a testlist
No such list: testlist.  Removing its residual archives.
Removing private archives
Removing private archives
Removing public archives
testlist public archives not found as /var/lib/mailman/archives/public/testlist.mbox
```

```
# list_lists
1 matching mailing lists found:
   Mailman - [no description available]
```

In the rare circumstance that the site's password is lost, it is still possible to reset this password directly with the `mmsitepass` command.

12.3 Horde Groupware

In this section we present the Horde web based groupware system developed by the Horde Project as an open source and free of charge project. Essentially Horde is a framework of a web-based application, on the top of which it is possible to add supplementary services in order to provide an environment where users may interactively collaborate. Horde, based on the LAMP stack that we have already implemented, provides users with easy web interfaces to email system, calendaring, sketch notes, and address books; a complete list of Horde projects is in Table 12.1. In the following we assume that Horde is

Table 12.1. Horde Projects

Project	Description
Chora	Source code repository viewer
DIMP	Dynamic IMP based on AJAX[1]
Gollem	Web-based file manager
IMP	Access to POP and IMAP email
Ingo	Mail filter manager
Kronolith	Calendaring system
MIMP	Mobile version of IMP for PDAs
Mnemo	Sketch note manager
Nag	Task manager
Sork	Account management (e.g. forwarding and vacation)
Trean	Bookmark manager
Turba	Address book
Whups	Bug tracking system

installed on a host prepared with the LAMP stack as seen in the chapter about the Apache web server. For simplicity we configure everything on a local file system but it could be in AFS space as well. Remember that the web server needs write access to the installation area, at least until the configuration is finished, since much of the settings can be changed by a web interface as for Mailman.

12.3.1 Installing Horde

We download directly the latest version from the Internet, which at the time of writing this book is 3.1.3, so the current version can differ. Here the `wget` command line tool is used, which can fetch a specific URL:

```
# wget ftp://ftp.horde.org/pub/horde/horde-3.1.3.tar.gz
```

Since Horde requires passwords over the network, too, we install Horde in the SSL enabled site. First uncompress the Horde archive and make a symbolic link to the directory such that you can smoothly change it, if a new version is released:

```
# cd /var/www/example.edu_ssl/

# tar zxf /var/www/src/horde-3.1.3.tar.gz

# ln -s horde-3.1.3 horde

# ls -l /var/www/example.edu_ssl/
total 4
lrwxrwxrwx   1 root root   11 2006-09-05 11:36 horde -> horde-3.1.3/
drwxr-xr-x  14 root root 4096 2006-08-17 15:28 horde-3.1.3/
```

Horde needs PEAR, the *PHP Extension and Application Repository*, which is a PHP code repository library:

```
# apt-get install php4-pear php4-pear-log
```

Next, we have to install all the PHP components needed by Horde with the `pear` tool, which acts in a similar way as the `apt` program:

```
# pear install -o Log Mail Mail_Mime DB Date File
downloading Log-1.9.8.tgz ...
Starting to download Log-1.9.8.tgz (38,841 bytes)
.........done: 38,841 bytes
Package 'Mail' already installed, skipping
downloading Mail_Mime-1.3.1.tgz ...
Starting to download Mail_Mime-1.3.1.tgz (16,481 bytes)
...done: 16,481 bytes
Package 'DB' already installed, skipping
downloading Date-1.4.6.tgz ...
Starting to download Date-1.4.6.tgz (53,535 bytes)
...done: 53,535 bytes
downloading File-1.2.2.tgz ...
Starting to download File-1.2.2.tgz (15,796 bytes)
...done: 15,796 bytes
skipping Package 'log' optional dependency 'DB'
skipping Package 'log' optional dependency 'MDB2'
Package 'PEAR' already installed, skipping
install ok: Date 1.4.6
install ok: Mail_Mime 1.3.1
install ok: File 1.2.2
Optional dependencies:
package 'MDB2' version >= 2.0.0RC1 is recommended to utilize some features.
'sqlite' PHP extension is recommended to utilize some features
install ok: Log 1.9.8
```

Now we are ready to configure Horde according to its installation instructions. In the `config` subdirectory of the Horde distribution we have to copy all the configuration files removing the `.dist` suffix:

```
# for f in *.dist; do cp $f `basename $f .dist`; done

# ls
conf.php        hooks.php.dist       motd.php.dist   prefs.php.dist
conf.php.dist   mime_drivers.php     nls.php         registry.php
conf.xml        mime_drivers.php.dist nls.php.dist   registry.php.dist
hooks.php       motd.php             prefs.php
```

Besides PEAR, Horde requires some more PHP components contained in several Debian packages, and belong to the *PHP Extension Community Library* or PECL library. We need to intall them before proceeding:

```
# apt-get install php4-domxml php4-mcrypt php4-gd imagemagick php-mail-mime
```

Horde relies on the complete LAMP stack, so our system must contain MySQL, too, symmetrically to the host `www.example.edu`. This has to be accessible from PHP as seen in a previous chapter:

```
# tail -5 /etc/php4/apache2/php.ini
extension=mysql.so
extension=pgsql.so
extension=domxml.so
extension=mcrypt.so
extension=gd.so
```

The inclusion of these extensions is the result of the installation of several PECL components.

12.3.2 Configuring Horde

In the following we assume, that MySQL is already configured and running on the same host as the Horde installation, since the groupware software needs a dedicated database for its own internal use. Unfortunately the scripts shipped with Horde pretend, that you are the DBMS administrator since they operated directly on the system database `mysql`:

```
# cd ../scripts/sql/

# head -30 create.mysql.sql
-- $Horde: horde/scripts/sql/create.mysql.sql,v 1.4.6.9 2006/07/05 15:53:10 jan Exp $
--
-- If you are installing Horde for the first time, you can simply
-- direct this file to mysql as STDIN:
--
-- $ mysql --user=root --password=<MySQL-root-password> < create.mysql.sql
--
-- If you are upgrading from a previous version, you will need to comment
-- out the the user creation steps below, as well as the schemas for any
-- tables that already exist.
```

```
--
-- If you choose to grant permissions manually, note that with MySQL, PEAR DB
-- emulates sequences by automatically creating extra tables ending in _seq,
-- so the MySQL ''horde'' user must have CREATE privilege on the ''horde''
-- database.
--
-- If you are upgrading from Horde 1.x, the Horde tables you have from
-- that version are no longer used; you may wish to either delete those
-- tables or simply recreate the database anew.

USE mysql;

REPLACE INTO user (host, user, password)
    VALUES (
        'localhost',
        'horde',
-- IMPORTANT: Change this password!
        PASSWORD('horde')
);
```

We prefer to be more cautious and do not run such script as the MySQL administrator acting directly on system tables. Instead, we execute some preparatory statements in order to create a dedicated user and database for Horde: this user will be just allowed to operate on the corresponding database, so connect to MySQL with an administrative identity:

```
# mysql -u admin -p
Enter password:
Welcome to the MySQL monitor.  Commands end with ; or \g.
Your MySQL connection id is 17 to server version: 4.1.11-Debian_4sarge7-log

Type 'help;' or '\h' for help. Type '\c' to clear the buffer.

mysql> create database horde;
Query OK, 1 row affected (0.00 sec)

mysql> grant all privileges on horde.* to 'horde'@'localhost' identified by 'hordepasswd';
Query OK, 0 rows affected (0.00 sec)

mysql> quit
Bye
```

The above defines a user **horde** and a database **horde** for the Horde framework. The user got all privileges for that database. It is good practice that only such restricted user is used to initialize the database using the MySQL **source** command:

```
# mysql -u horde -p
Enter password:
Welcome to the MySQL monitor.  Commands end with ; or \g.
Your MySQL connection id is 22 to server version: 4.1.11-Debian_4sarge7-log

Type 'help;' or '\h' for help. Type '\c' to clear the buffer.

mysql> connect horde;
Connection id:    23
Current database: horde

mysql> source create.mysql.sql;
```

Note that some commands do fail: this is not harmful since all those state-ments are related to database creation and privilege settings, which has been taken care of before. A verification executed in the **horde** database shows all the created tables:

```
mysql> show tables;
+----------------------------+
| Tables_in_horde            |
+----------------------------+
| horde_datatree             |
| horde_datatree_attributes  |
| horde_histories            |
| horde_prefs                |
| horde_sessionhandler       |
| horde_tokens               |
| horde_users                |
| horde_vfs                  |
+----------------------------+
8 rows in set (0.00 sec)

mysql> quit
Bye
```

At this point we are ready to test Horde, first granting Apache all privileges to the Horde directories and restart it:

```
# chown -R www-data.www-data horde-3.1.3

# /etc/init.d/apache2 stop
Stopping web server: Apache2.

# /etc/init.d/apache2 start
Starting web server: Apache2.
```

Finally, we can connect with a web browser to the web server at the horde/test.php location as in Fig. 12.3. The final step is to connect di-rectly to the administrative section and define the database connection: browse to https://www.example.edu/horde/ and set up the MySQL connection as seen in Fig. 12.4. As a good practice the test link should be disabled or deleted after successfully completing the installation.

12.3.3 Additional Packages

So far we have just installed the basic Horde framework: in the following it has to be enhanced by further components. Therefore we download some other Horde packages, including IMP, the web-based email access system:

```
# wget ftp://ftp.horde.org/pub/imp/imp-h3-4.1.3.tar.gz

# wget ftp://ftp.horde.org/pub/turba/turba-h3-2.1.2.tar.gz

# wget ftp://ftp.horde.org/pub/ingo/ingo-h3-1.1.1.tar.gz

# wget ftp://ftp.horde.org/pub/kronolith/kronolith-h3-2.1.2.tar.gz
```

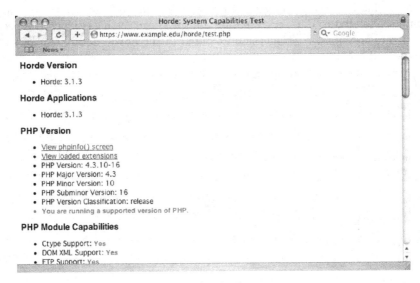

Fig. 12.3. The Horde test page

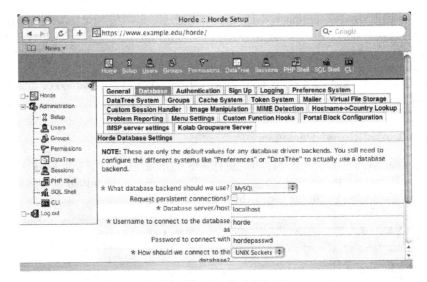

Fig. 12.4. The Horde administration pages

```
# wget ftp://ftp.horde.org/pub/nag/nag-h3-2.1.1.tar.gz

# wget ftp://ftp.horde.org/pub/mnemo/mnemo-h3-2.1.tar.gz

# wget ftp://ftp.horde.org/pub/mimp/mimp-h3-1.0.tar.gz

# wget ftp://ftp.horde.org/pub/chora/chora-h3-2.0.1.tar.gz

# wget ftp://ftp.horde.org/pub/gollem/gollem-h3-1.0.2.tar.gz
```

We focus on the IMP package for IMAP mail access over the web, because
it is one of the most complex ones, since all other packages follow the same
style of setup. We show the most difficult part since IMP requires additional
configuration steps to handle the SMTP and IMAP protocols. The first step
is to uncompress the `imp` archive in the `horde` subdirectory; again make a
symbolic link to the relative directory, such that an upgrade will be easy in
the future:

```
# cd /var/www/example.edu_ssl/horde/

# tar zxf /var/www/src/imp-h3-4.1.3.tar.gz

# ln -s imp-h3-4.1.3 imp
```

To work as a web-based email system, IMP requires PHP to be able to
handle mail via the IMAP protocol, so we have to install the `php4-imap`
package, another part of the PECL library:

```
# apt-get install php4-imap
```

By default Debian allows uploading of files setting the maximum size in the
`php.ini` configuration file with the parameters shown below. These settings
have to be tuned if you wish users to send larger attachments, caring also
about the restrictions on `post_max_size`, since this limits the size for the
HTTP POST method:

```
file_uploads = On
upload_max_filesize = 2M
```

Next we have to create the configuration files for IMP the same way we
did for Horde, removing the trailing `.dist` suffix:

```
# cd imp/config/

# for f in *.dist; do cp $f `basename $f .dist`; done

# ls
conf.xml          menu.php          motd.php.dist     trailer.txt
filter.txt        menu.php.dist     prefs.php         trailer.txt.dist
filter.txt.dist   mime_drivers.php  prefs.php.dist
header.php        mime_drivers.php.dist  servers.php
header.php.dist   motd.php          servers.php.dist
```

```
# cd ../..

# chown -R www-data.www-data imp-h3-4.1.3/
```

The last command is necessary, since the web server will try to write modifications directly into this space, and thus it needs a write-enabled access. We prefer to manually enumerate the IMAP servers, our users can connect to: this is done inside the `servers.php` file within the `config` subdirectory of IMP. Our servers require SSL but their certificate is signed by our non-official certificate authority, so we need to disable any CA validation. For our Example organization then, the configuration file contains the following:

```
$servers['_prompt'] = array(
    'name' => _("Choose a mail server:")
);

$servers['imap'] = array(
    'name' => 'IMAP Server',
    'server' => 'mail.example.edu',
    'hordeauth' => true,
    'protocol' => 'imap/ssl/novalidate-cert',
    'port' => 993,
    'maildomain' => 'example.com',
    'smtphost' => 'smtp.example.edu',
    'smtpport' => 25,
    'realm' => '',
    'preferred' => '',
);
```

Setting `hordeauth` to `true` makes IMP use the credentials already provided by a user during the Horde login process. Restart Apache to enable the last configuration steps over the web, and test that IMP actually works reaching the location under `horde/imp/test.php`, mirrored by the URL `https://www.example.edu/horde/imp/test.php`. The final setup is tuned over the web interface, in particular the Horde authentication can coincide with the IMP authentication, as in Fig. 12.5: with these settings the user has to authenticate only once since the entire Horde authentication is delegated to the IMP module which on its part contacts the IMAP server. Before enabling the authentication, do not forget to define an administrator for Horde: in case that something went wrong there is always a backup file with the suffix `.bak` located in the `config` directory of Horde which can be used to overwrite the freshly created settings. The IMP interface can be tested with the `testuser` shown in Fig. 12.6.

Security

For security reasons, it is a good practice to deny all users the web access to those Horde subdirectories not necessary for direct browsing. Horde already provides `.htaccess` files in its distribution, so we need to enable this feature in the Apache configuration:

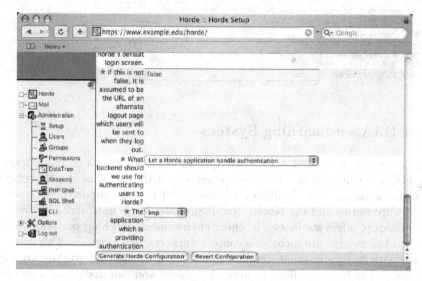

Fig. 12.5. Setting IMP to use the Horde login credentials

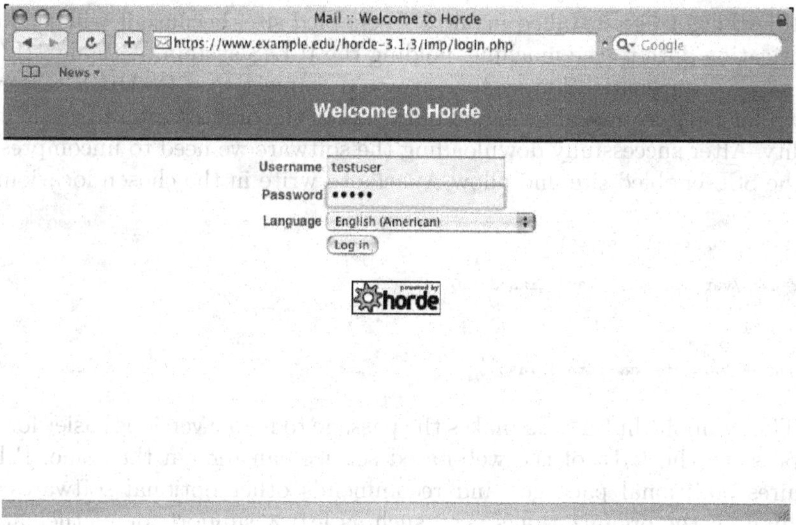

Fig. 12.6. The IMP login page

```
# find horde-3.1.3/ -name .htaccess -print
horde-3.1.3/config/.htaccess
horde-3.1.3/lib/.htaccess
horde-3.1.3/locale/.htaccess
horde-3.1.3/po/.htaccess
horde-3.1.3/scripts/.htaccess
horde-3.1.3/templates/.htaccess
```

12.4 ILIAS e-Learning System

The last example for a bigger LAMP application is ILIAS, a web based learning management system. The development of ILIAS started at the University of Cologne under Prof. Wolfgang Leidhold and is also supported by several other universities and the Novell, Inc. It provides every user with a personalized desktop, offers students a learning environment, teaching personnel with class tests services, and includes a content authoring for lecturers. This system comes with its own internal communication features and supports the work in groups. It has been localized to many languages and can make use of several authentication mechanisms; furthermore it is aware of several standards in the context of e-Learning like SCORM, AICC, and LOM. Again, we suppose a fully-functional LAMP-based system as we did for Horde.

Let us start the installation of this software by downloading it from the official site:

```
# wget http://www.ilias.de/download/src/ilias-3.7.0.tar.gz
```

ILIAS has to be installed in the SSL-enabled site, because it will send authentication data to the machine, holding the ILIAS system. Although ILIAS has an own authentication system, it could connect to a RADIUS server as shown for newsgroups, allowing all our users in the organization to access this facility. After successfully downloading the software we need to uncompress it on the SSL-enabled site and allow Apache to write in the chosen location:

```
# cd /var/www/example.edu_ssl/

# tar zxf /var/www/src/ilias/ilias-3.7.0.tar.gz

# ln -s ilias3 ilias

# chown -R www-data.www-data ilias3
```

The symbolic link ilias makes the passage to newer versions easier for our users, since the URL of the web-based service can remain the same. ILIAS requires additional packages and recommends other optional softwares depending on the organization's need such as LaTeX support for mathematical coding. This application has similar requirements as Horde with the following additional packages:

```
# apt-get install zip unzip sablotron php-auth php-xslt htmldoc php-imagick
```

Moreover, ILIAS requires a Java SDK to be installed in the system which has to be downloaded from Sun's web site. At the time of writing this book the recommended version is JSDK 1.4.2. Take care of setting the necessary environment variables like PATH such that the java command can be found. Additionally ILIAS requires some PEAR-provided components:

```
# pear install Auth HTML_Template_IT Net_URL Net_Socket

# pear upgrade Net_Socket

# pear install HTTP_Request
```

ILIAS makes use of the uploading facility via PHP as Horde, and has to be granted a long session lifetime for allowing users to answer questions, for instance in class tests. The following parameters might have to be tuned for an individual setting, and are considerably larger than the settings for Horde:

```
memory_limit = 50M
session.gc_maxlifetime = 3600
max_execution_time = 600
post_max_size = 50M
upload_max_filesize = 50M
```

As the next step ILIAS, based on LAMP, requires a database for its own purposes. Proceeding as for Horde, a dedicated user and database get created by the MySQL administrator:

```
# mysql -u admin -p
Enter password:
Welcome to the MySQL monitor.  Commands end with ; or \g.
Your MySQL connection id is 32 to server version: 4.1.11-Debian_4sarge7-log

Type 'help;' or '\h' for help. Type '\c' to clear the buffer.

mysql> create database ilias;
Query OK, 1 row affected (0.11 sec)

mysql> grant all privileges on ilias.* to 'ilias'@'localhost' identified by 'iliaspasswd';
Query OK, 0 rows affected (0.23 sec)

mysql> quit
Bye
```

Another directory is needed for ILIAS to store all documents for the courses and related data, which is required to be located outside the web space. Our choice is /var/spool/ilias/ for the purpose of demonstration, and the web server is allowed full write access:

```
# cd /var/spool

# mkdir ilias

# chown www-data.www-data ilias/
```

A further package, which should be considered for installation is `mimetex`, which provides a way for converting LaTeX or TeX code to images, a software that is particularly handy when dealing with mathematical courses and exams. We will then install this package and copy the installed binary to a directory reachable over the web; we choose to have the same ILIAS installation directory handle this binary as a CGI script:

```
# apt-get install mimetex

# cd /var/www/example.edu_ssl/ilias

# cp /usr/bin/mimetex mimetex.cgi
```

To make Apache aware of CGIs apart from the default `cgi-bin` subdirectory, we activate a handler in the `apache2.conf` file, a setting that will become active as we restart the service:

```
AddHandler cgi-script .cgi
```

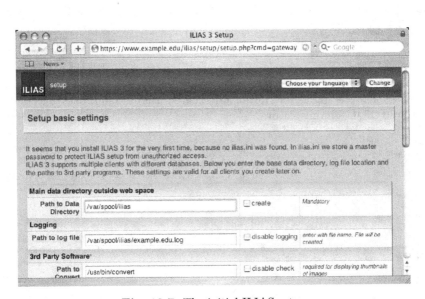

Fig. 12.7. The initial ILIAS setup

At this point we can configure ILIAS over the web by connecting to `ilias/setup/setup.php` as we can see in Fig. 12.7, and follow all the instructions provided by the web-driven setup process. After the setup you are provided with a login screen for Ilias: the very first time we have to login as `root` with password `homer`, which is stored by default in the MySQL backend of Ilias.

The application of an e-Learning platform needs some initial training on how to map your ideas to the specific platform. In case of ILIAS, it is usual to start defining role templates and roles for users which will be handy for creating users. Next it is useful to create some `categories` in the global repository with access rights, such that a lecturer has read-write access, while students are only allowed to read.

12.5 Calendaring

Sharing schedules may be quite useful in large teams, posting publicly and updating appointments. The iCalendar is the standard IETF specification based on the historical vCalendar standard provided by the Internet Mail Consortium. There are already many iCalendar-aware clients such as Apple iCal, Lotus Notes from IBM, Microsoft Outloook, and Mozilla Sunbird. As the last example for a very simple web application we show a calendaring system, which does not require the complete LAMP stack, but only the WebDAV support. Calendar data is stored in text-based files with suffix `.ics`, in the standardized iCalendar format, sometimes abbreviated as iCal.

In the chapter about the web server we have already prepared all necessary components: users can access their personal web space with the help of WebDAV over HTTPS providing their credentials. Thereafter the uploaded files appear in their home page. Our goal is to provide a facility to our users for sharing public calendars via web: this works right out of the box with our WebDAV-enabled web site, where a calendaring software such as Mozilla Sunbird export the calendar file to a web location, and the same location is used by another user using a WebDAV-aware calendaring software to subscribe to the exported schedule. In Fig. 12.8 we used the Apple iCal software to subscribe a public iCalendar schedule. Note that calendar updates occour by the owner via WebDAV, handled over the secure SSL-enabled HTTPS protocol.

Practice

Exercise 45. Confront the mailing list and newsgroup approach with respect to your needs. Are they both needed, and to which degree do they have to be synchronized? Is the Mailman software sufficient for your needs or would you investigate other solutions, such as for example the Sympa mailing list manager?

Exercise 46. Verify if the Horde framework is sufficient for your situation: which components are needed by your users? Check for possible helper applications to visualize Windows documents in the UNIX world.

Exercise 47. Ilias is just one example of an e-Learning system. Confront it with other solutions, such as the Moodle software, also provided by a Debian package. A further software making use of the LAMP stack is ATutor.

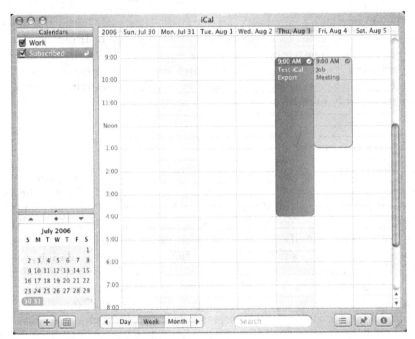

Fig. 12.8. The Apple iCal with a subscribed calendar

Exercise 48. What about other possible solutions besides Horde's IMP and the shown iCalendar sharing? Courier contains, together with its own web interface `sqwebmail`, the `courier-pcp` package supporting the personal calendaring protocol PCP. For the sake of completeness it has to be mentioned that Courier has some form of mailing list handling offered by `courier-mlm`, too.

Part III

Applications

13

Client Systems

All things are difficult before they are easy.
Thomas Fuller

13.1 Server-side Configuration

This chapter is dedicated to client setup using different platforms and operating systems, allowing users to log into the system using their common password, with home directories located under the AFS file space. All clients will be connected to our environment, becoming Kerberos, LDAP, and Open-AFS clients, or on the Windows side, joining our WIN.EXAMPLE.EDU domain.

We will first configure the client from a server-side point of view. For the client machine we will make use of the name client.example.edu, using a fixed IP address given on a per-host basis by the DHCP service using the client MAC address. Note that MAC addresses change on each machine with a different card, but we will show a prototype configuration for just the first Ethernet card.

DNS and DHCP

Each client has a host name that needs to be resolved by the DNS service, with both direct and reverse queries. Hence the zone files contain entries like the following:

```
client          A       192.168.127.237

237             PTR     client.example.edu.
```

Restarting the bind9 daemon is sufficient to make changes take effect. On the client machine, we need to retrieve the Ethernet card MAC address in order to configure the DHCP server. Each client gets a special stanza that matches its MAC address to a fixed host name, as in the following example from the dhcpd.conf file:

```
host client {
  hardware ethernet 00:b0:d0:20:f2:e3;
  fixed-address client.example.edu;
}
```

Kerberos Host Principal

In order to identify each machine it is a good practice to create a host principal in the Kerberos database. Additionally, some services as SSH will require such a principal and need its keys to be exported to a file on the client machine. Let us use the kadmin interface to create a new principal for the client machine called host/client.example.edu@EXAMPLE.EDU with a random password:

```
# kadmin -p sysadmin
Authenticating as principal sysadmin with password.
Password for sysadmin@EXAMPLE.EDU:

kadmin:  add_principal -randkey host/client.example.edu
WARNING: no policy specified for host/client.example.edu@EXAMPLE.EDU; \
defaulting to no policy
Principal "host/client.example.edu@EXAMPLE.EDU" created.
```

For other hosts just the FQDN part of this principal has to be modified for the creation of its service principal.

13.2 Ubuntu Linux

In this section we focus on setting up a client running Linux Ubuntu version 6.10. This distribution is very similar to Debian, so all the commands, tools and locations are compatible with the ones described in previous chapters. The advantage of using this distribution is, that it ships up-to-date packages and also commercial ones, including closed source applications (e.g. the Adobe Acrobat Reader, the Flash Player and plugin, or the Opera web browser). The installation is driven by a graphical user interface using the Gnome Desktop Environment, and usually it is suitable for workstations. We should mention the previous Ubuntu version 6.06 since it comes with long term support of 3 years for the desktop version and 5 years for servers. The Ubuntu distribution, with respect to Debian, can be considered more desktop-oriented, while the other retains a server-prone attitude. Installation of software packages is identical to Debian, using the **apt-get** tool or **dpkg**. Furthermore, Ubuntu provides a graphical front-end to this command line interface, called *Synaptic* and pictured in Fig. 13.1. In order to be allowed to install all kinds of software, we need to manually enable all repositories in the Synaptic configuration. By default Ubuntu activates a DHCP-based networking setting, as we can see from the /etc/network/interfaces configuration file:

```
auto lo
iface lo inet loopback

auto eth0
iface eth0 inet dhcp
```

It is seldom required to manually set the host name, given a valid DHCP server-side configuration. Contrary to Debian, Ubuntu ships with no **root**

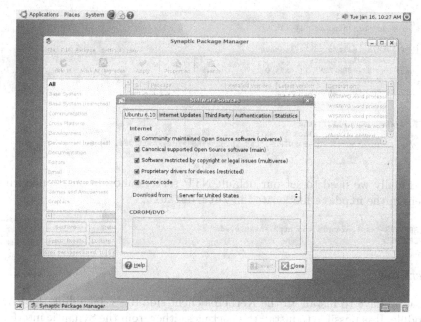

Fig. 13.1. The Synaptic package manager

user available for login, and uses the `sudo` package to obtain administrative privileges from the user added during the installation process:

```
$ sudo -s
Password:
#
```

That user has to provide its own password another time in order to become `root` or perform commands as `root`.

Time Synchronization

Since the machine becomes a Kerberos and OpenAFS client it needs its clock to be synchronized with our NTP servers. It is possible to install the NTP server on the client, thus opening a port on the machine, or use the predefined services in the Ubuntu system based on the `ntpdate` client program. The default setting in the last release is to use an `if-up` script: a daemon will monitor the network cable link, and start all the scripts contained in the `/etc/network/if-up.d/` directory when the link is brought up. The location contains a script `ntpdate` that will be executed each time the network is enabled:

```
#!/bin/sh

[ "$IFACE" != "lo" ] || exit 0
```

```
test -f /usr/sbin/ntpdate || exit 0

if [ -f /etc/default/ntpdate ]; then
    . /etc/default/ntpdate
    test -n "$NTPSERVERS" || exit 0
else
    NTPSERVERS="ntp.ubuntu.com"
fi

if [ "$VERBOSITY" = 1 ]; then
    echo "Synchronizing clock to $NTPSERVERS..."
    /usr/sbin/ntpdate -b -s $NTPOPTIONS $NTSERVERS >/dev/null 2>&1 || true
fi
```

Finally we need to set our default NTP servers and options, configuring them in the ntpdate file located in /etc/default:

```
NTPSERVERS="ntp1.example.edu ntp2.example.edu"
NTPOPTIONS="-u"
```

Kerberos

Now we have to install all the Kerberos client-side tools, including the PAM module. It is possible to install the packages either from the Synaptic interface or with the usual apt-get tools:

```
# apt-get install krb5-config krb5-user libpam-krb5
```

Ubuntu, deriving from Debian, configures the packages upon a successful installation, using a command line interface or a graphical front-end depending on how we installed the software. After setting up the realm and Kerberos servers, the /etc/krb5.conf file looks like the following:

```
[libdefaults]
        default_realm = EXAMPLE.EDU
        krb4_config = /etc/krb.conf
        krb4_realms = /etc/krb.realms
        kdc_timesync = 1
        ccache_type = 4
        forwardable = true
        proxiable = true
        v4_instance_resolve = false
        v4_name_convert = {
                host = {
                        rcmd = host
                        ftp = ftp
                }
                plain = {
                        something = something-else
                }
        }

[realms]
EXAMPLE.EDU = {
        kdc = kdc1.example.edu
        kdc = kdc2.example.edu
        admin_server = krb.example.edu
```

```
}

[domain_realm]
        .example.edu = EXAMPLE.EDU
        example.edu = EXAMPLE.EDU
```

It is a good practice before proceeding to test the new configuration by obtaining the initial ticket for a Kerberos principal:

```
# kinit testuser
Password for testuser@EXAMPLE.EDU:

# klist
Ticket cache: FILE:/tmp/krb5cc_0
Default principal: testuser@EXAMPLE.EDU

Valid starting       Expires              Service principal
07/27/06 11:41:36  07/27/06 21:41:32  krbtgt/EXAMPLE.EDU@EXAMPLE.EDU


Kerberos 4 ticket cache: /tmp/tkt0
klist: You have no tickets cached
```

We can then safely continue with the export of the host principal keys to the default keytab file from the client using the kadmin interface:

```
# kadmin -p sysadmin
Authenticating as principal sysadmin with password.
Password for sysadmin@EXAMPLE.EDU:

kadmin:  ktadd host/client.example.edu
Entry for principal host/client.example.edu with kvno 3, encryption type \
Triple DES cbc mode with HMAC/sha1 added to keytab WRFILE:/etc/krb5.keytab.
Entry for principal host/client.example.edu with kvno 3, encryption type \
DES cbc mode with CRC-32 added to keytab WRFILE:/etc/krb5.keytab.
```

Finally we add Kerberos to the PAM authentication stack in the configuration file common-auth, enabling the use of the previously entered password with the use_first_pass option:

```
auth     sufficient     pam_unix.so
auth     sufficient     pam_krb5.so use_first_pass
auth     required       pam_deny.so
```

LDAP

Since Kerberos user passwords are now enabled, we can proceed in permitting the retrieval of user information from our LDAP servers. We should install the LDAP client tools shipped with the ldap-utils package, the name service switch plugin libnss-ldap, and the GSSAPI library for the SASL layer libsasl2-gssapi-mit, so that users can modify and retrieve data from the LDAP server with a secure authentication method. As for other packages, we may choose the graphical interface or the command line, being completely equivalent, and as usual the system configures the installed softwares asking for server names and search base.

The GSSAPI mechanism is not enabled by default after installing these packages, so we have to modify the `ldap.conf` file in `/etc/ldap/` adding the SASL_MECH option:

```
BASE       dc=example,dc=edu
URI        ldap://ldap1.example.edu ldap://ldap2.example.edu
SASL_MECH GSSAPI
```

After configuring the client-side LDAP tools we are able to test both: simple anonymous authentication and SASL-based authentication.

```
# ldapsearch -x -LLL "uid=testuser"
dn: uid=testuser,ou=users,dc=example,dc=edu
objectClass: top
objectClass: posixAccount
objectClass: shadowAccount
objectClass: inetOrgPerson
cn: Test
sn: User
uid: testuser
uidNumber: 10000
gidNumber: 10000
loginShell: /bin/bash
gecos: Test User,001,555-123,1-123,none
homeDirectory: /afs/example.edu/users/testuser
userCertificate;binary:: MIIF1DCCA3ygAwIBAgIBAjANBgkqhkiG9w0BAQUFADCBrjELMAkGA
 1UEBhMCW1oxETAPBgNVBAgTCFByb3ZpbmN1MQOwCwYDVQQHEwRDaXR5MROwGwYDVQQKExRFeGFtcG
 ...
 Qv/GouuJjzOx/81oD75/gfeDCqsP8iWDGspHIvKGK1qpNOo3JWpWOJ8sbMF/ClwQXdNO6AcIZ4u55
 LFI70YI3Q==

# kinit testuser
Password for testuser@EXAMPLE.EDU:

# ldapsearch -LLL "uid=testuser"
SASL/GSSAPI authentication started
SASL username: testuser@EXAMPLE.EDU
SASL SSF: 56
SASL installing layers
dn: uid=testuser,ou=users,dc=example,dc=edu
objectClass: top
objectClass: posixAccount
objectClass: shadowAccount
objectClass: inetOrgPerson
cn: Test
sn: User
uid: testuser
uidNumber: 10000
gidNumber: 10000
loginShell: /bin/bash
gecos: Test User,001,555-123,1-123,none
homeDirectory: /afs/example.edu/users/testuser
userCertificate;binary:: MIIF1DCCA3ygAwIBAgIBAjANBgkqhkiG9w0BAQUFADCBrjELMAkGA
 1UEBhMCW1oxETAPBgNVBAgTCFByb3ZpbmN1MQOwCwYDVQQHEwRDaXR5MROwGwYDVQQKExRFeGFtcG
 ...
 Qv/GouuJjzOx/81oD75/gfeDCqsP8iWDGspHIvKGK1qpNOo3JWpWOJ8sbMF/ClwQXdNO6AcIZ4u55
 LFI70YI3Q==
```

Finally we can enable the system to map group and user IDs with the help of entries in our LDAP database. For this we need to modify the `nsswitch.conf` file first, enabling LDAP as a valid source for a map, and next the mapping configuration file `libnss-ldap.conf`:

```
# cat nsswitch.conf
passwd:          compat ldap
group:           compat ldap
shadow:          compat ldap

hosts:           files dns
networks:        files
protocols:       db files
services:        db files
ethers:          db files
rpc:             db files
netgroup:        nis

# cat libnss-ldap.conf
host ldap1.example.edu ldap2.example.edu
base dc=example,dc=edu
ldap_version 3
timelimit 30
bind_timelimit 30
bind_policy hard
idle_timelimit 60

nss_base_passwd ou=users,dc=example,dc=edu
nss_base_shadow ou=users,dc=example,dc=edu
nss_base_group  ou=groups,dc=example,dc=edu
```

These changes take effect immediately, hence we can test the system with standard UNIX tools:

```
# groups testuser
testuser : testgroup

# echo ~testuser
/afs/example.edu/users/testuser
```

OpenAFS

As for Debian, the Ubuntu Linux distribution does not provide an OpenAFS pre-compiled binary kernel module, and we need to create one on our own. Installing the `openafs-modules-source` usually includes Linux kernel headers, but no symbolic link `linux` pointing at the current kernel version as in the following:

```
# uname -a
Linux client 2.6.17-10-generic #2 SMP Tue Dec 5 22:28:26 UTC 2006 i686 GNU/Linux

# ls -l
total 4356
lrwxrwxrwx  1 root src        31 2007-01-16 11:01 linux -> linux-headers-2.6.17-10-generic
drwxr-xr-x 19 root root     4096 2007-01-16 08:53 linux-headers-2.6.17-10
drwxr-xr-x  4 root root     4096 2007-01-16 08:53 linux-headers-2.6.17-10-generic
-rw-r--r--  1 root root 4436150 2007-01-11 22:41 openafs.tar.gz
```

Once uncompressed the OpenAFS module sources, we can invoke the `make-kpkg` tool from the `linux` directory, obtaining a Debian package in

/usr/src/, which can be easily installed by dpkg. It is a good practice to load the module with modprobe in order to test it, and successively remove it from the kernel space with the rmmod tool. It might be necessary to use the depmod program to generate the module dependencies for the new kernel. Note that if your system is running any file system other than ext2 or ext3, the OpenAFS client complains about its cache. Either use a dedicated partition for this cache or create an on-file ext2 file system and mounting it in the cache directory as shown before.

After installing and testing the kernel module we can proceed installing the OpenAFS client openafs-client, configuring the package as the system requests. Additionally we need the Kerberos-OpenAFS interaction tools openafs-krb5 and the PAM session library libpam-openafs-session in order to allow an integrated login on the client. The configuration files for our OpenAFS client, and for the common PAM authentication and session, are as shown the in the following output:

```
# cd /etc/openafs/

# head CellServDB
>example.edu          #Example Organization
192.168.127.154              #afs1.example.edu
192.168.127.230              #afs2.example.edu
>grand.central.org    #GCO Public CellServDB 27 Jan 2005
18.7.14.88                   #grand-opening.mit.edu
128.2.191.224                #penn.central.org
130.237.48.87                #andrew.e.kth.se
>wu-wien.ac.at        #University of Economics, Vienna, Austria
137.208.3.33                 #afsdb1.wu-wien.ac.at
137.208.7.4                  #afsdb2.wu-wien.ac.at

# cat ThisCell
example.edu

# cat /etc/pam.d/common-auth
auth    sufficient     pam_unix.so nullok_secure
auth    sufficient     pam_krb5.so use_first_pass
auth    required       pam_deny.so

# cat /etc/pam.d/common-session
session required       pam_unix.so
session optional       pam_krb5.so
session optional       pam_openafs_session.so
```

After starting manually the OpenAFS client—or simply rebooting the system—we can login with our Kerberos testuser, obtaining both Kerberos and AFS credentials as in Fig. 13.2.

13.3 Apple MacOS X

Apple released the first version of its UNIX-based operating system in 1999, after the Mac System 9: the X is the Roman numeral standing for 10, and also a hint on the UNIX heritage. In fact, Apple's operating system directly derives

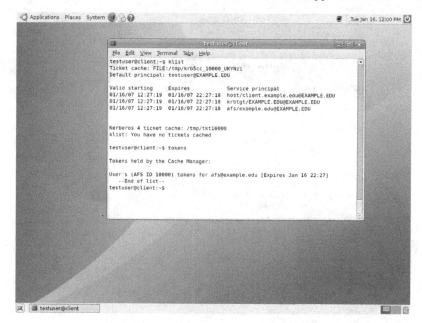

Fig. 13.2. The Ubuntu 6.10 desktop after a login, and cached credential

from NeXT, a microkernel operating system released by NeXT Software Inc. founded by Steve Jobs in 1985—also founder of Apple Computer Inc., now Apple Inc.—based on the Mach kernel and having its UNIX roots in the BSD implementation of NeXTSTEP. We focus in this section on the latest release of Apple's operating system, the MacOS X version 10.4 "Tiger".

Much of the configuration can be easily done by graphical interactions, and in the following we will show some of the settings with graphical images, as well as textually describe the procedure. The first operation regards the time synchronization with our NTP servers, which is easily configured with the System Preferences application as shown in Fig. 13.3.

Kerberos

The graphical Kerberos configuration is preceded by a command line interaction. Opening the Terminal application, we need to gain **root** privileges with the **sudo** tool and create the standard **krb5.conf** file. The password for **sudo** is the same as for the first user created during system installation.

```
$ sudo -s

We trust you have received the usual lecture from the local System
Administrator. It usually boils down to these three things:

    #1) Respect the privacy of others.
    #2) Think before you type.
```

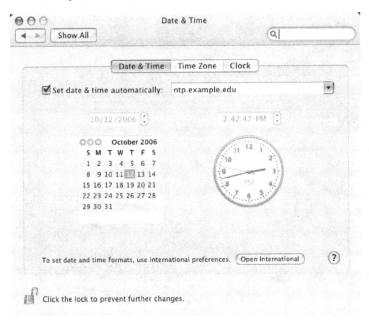

Fig. 13.3. The MacOS X 10.4 time synchronization control panel

```
    #3) With great power comes great responsibility.

Password:
# touch /etc/krb5.conf

# ln -s /etc/krb5.conf /Library/Preferences/edu.mit.Kerberos
```

Notice that we created an empty file, since the actual configuration is done graphically with the Kerberos application. The last line creates a symbolic link `edu.mit.Kerberos` which might be useful for some rare applications. The Kerberos tool can be reached under `/System/Library/CoreServices/` under the boot volume, and it can be used to modify all the configuration parameters as well as obtaining the initial ticket. The application, shown in Fig. 13.4, can also renew expiring tickets automatically and destroy existing ones. After configuring and testing the realm, we can use the `kadmin` interface to export the host key to the default keytab file:

```
# kadmin -p sysadmin
Authenticating as principal sysadmin with password.
Password for sysadmin@EXAMPLE.EDU:

kadmin:  ktadd host/client.example.edu
Entry for principal host/client.example.edu with kvno 4, encryption type \
Triple DES cbc mode with HMAC/sha1 added to keytab WRFILE:/etc/krb5.keytab.
Entry for principal host/client.example.edu with kvno 4, encryption type \
DES cbc mode with CRC-32 added to keytab WRFILE:/etc/krb5.keytab.
```

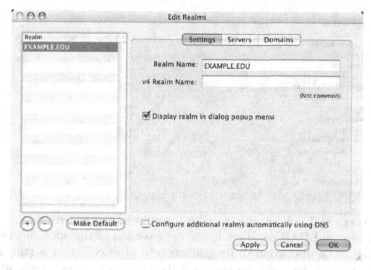

Fig. 13.4. The MacOS X 10.4 Kerberos configuration tool

Observe that MacOS X is Kerberos aware, where there are several clients compiled and configured with Kerberos support.

LDAP

MacOS X inherits a legacy configuration database from the NeXTSTEP called NetInfo. It is used to store system information such as users, groups, services, and machines, replacing the common UNIX files. Its contents can be queried via the `niutil` tool, as we can see from the following interaction:

```
# niutil -list . /
1       users
2       groups
3       machines
4       networks
5       protocols
6       rpcs
7       services
8       aliases
9       mounts
10      printers

# niutil -list . /users
11      nobody
12      root
13      daemon
14      unknown
15      lp
16      postfix
17      www
18      eppc
19      mysql
20      sshd
21      qtss
```

```
22        cyrusimap
23        mailman
24        appserver
25        clamav
26        amavisd
27        jabber
28        xgridcontroller
29        xgridagent
30        appowner
31        windowserver
32        tokend
33        securityagent
92        installuser

# niutil -list . /machines
72        localhost
73        broadcasthost
```

Its usage will not be supported in future releases, and it is going to be replaced by an LDAP database in the next version of the operating system. Although to be discontinued, its utilization in MacOS X 10.4 is still critical for user information, and we shall use the Directory Access application to enable LDAP for both services and authentication settings, as in Fig. 13.5. Remember that the LDAP version is 3 and that UNIX mappings are defined by the RFC 2307, using our LDAP search base dc=example,dc=edu. We need

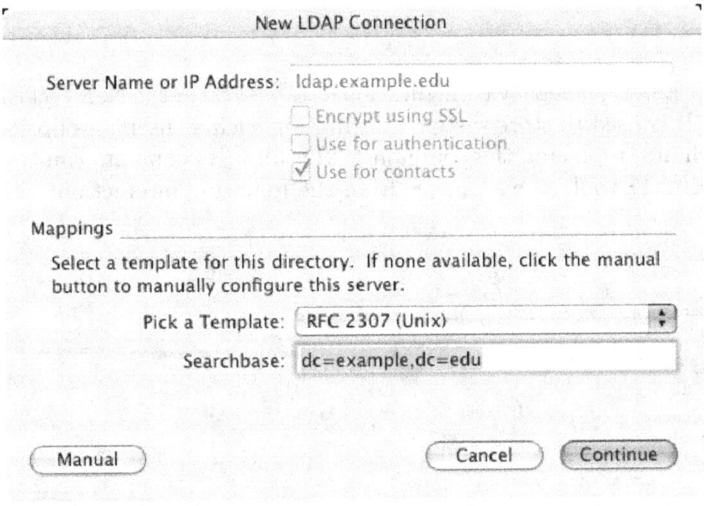

Fig. 13.5. The NetInfo-LDAP binding settings

to prevent the system from performing an automatic login in the Accounts pane of the System Preferences. Furthermore it should not display the login window asking for user name and password by displaying all available users in the system. After configuring the NetInfo subsystem to use LDAP mappings, we can test it asking for all users and groups in the tree with the dscl tool:

```
# dscl localhost list /LDAPv3/ldap.example.edu/Users
testuser

# dscl localhost list /LDAPv3/ldap.example.edu/Groups
testgroup
```

Kerberos Login

Apple's MacOS X has a PAM-like mechanism to handle login authentication requests, driven by a single file called /etc/authorization. This file, contrary to most UNIX configurations, is an XML file, where each section can be compared to a service file in the /etc/pam.d/ directory. The <key>authenticate</key> section is the equivalent to the /lib/security/ directory on a Linux system: on Linux it contains all the available plugins, while on MacOS X it lists all the possible authentication mechanisms. Since Kerberos is bundled in the operating system, we simply need to add a new <string> field for the builtin:krb5authnoverify mechanism, with the privileged option as in the following excerpt:

```
<key>authenticate</key>
<dict>
        <key>class</key>
        <string>evaluate-mechanisms</string>
        <key>mechanisms</key>
        <array>
                <string>builtin:authenticate</string>
                <string>builtin:krb5authnoverify,privileged</string>
                <string>authinternal</string>
        </array>
</dict>
```

The same consideration applies to the login mechanisms available to the login service. On Linux we had to modify a file called login in the PAM configuration directory, while on MacOS X we simply add a new <string> field to the <key>system.login.console</key> stanza for the builtin:krb5authnoverify mechanism:

```
<key>system.login.console</key>
<dict>
        <key>class</key>
        <string>evaluate-mechanisms</string>
        <key>comment</key>
        <string>Login mechanism based rule.</string>
        <key>mechanisms</key>
        <array>
                <string>builtin:auto-login,privileged</string>
                <string>loginwindow_builtin:login</string>
                <string>builtin:krb5authnoverify,privileged</string>
                <string>builtin:reset-password,privileged</string>
                <string>authinternal</string>
                <string>builtin:getuserinfo,privileged</string>
                <string>builtin:sso,privileged</string>
                <string>HomeDirMechanism:login,privileged</string>
                <string>HomeDirMechanism:status</string>
                <string>MCXMechanism:login</string>
```

```
                  <string>loginwindow_builtin:success</string>
                  <string>loginwindow_builtin:done</string>
        </array>
</dict>
```

OpenAFS

The installation of the OpenAFS client, which can be downloaded from the official site, is guided by a wizard, and requires administrative privileges as any other software with an impact on the operating system. After the installation we need to configure as usual the cell name and the database server list: ThisCell and CellServDB, respectively. These configuration files are located in the /var/db/openafs/etc/ directory, and after restarting the machine, we can easily test it obtaining a valid ticket and AFS token with an administrative user:

```
# kinit testuser
Please enter the password for testuser@EXAMPLE.EDU:

# klist
Kerberos 5 ticket cache: 'API:Initial default ccache'
Default principal: testuser@EXAMPLE.EDU

Valid Starting      Expires             Service Principal
10/12/06 16:12:52  10/13/06 02:12:52  krbtgt/EXAMPLE.EDU@EXAMPLE.EDU
        renew until 10/19/06 16:12:52

klist: No Kerberos 4 tickets in credentials cache

# aklog

# klist
Kerberos 5 ticket cache: 'API:Initial default ccache'
Default principal: testuser@EXAMPLE.EDU

Valid Starting      Expires             Service Principal
10/12/06 16:12:52  10/13/06 02:12:52  krbtgt/EXAMPLE.EDU@EXAMPLE.EDU
        renew until 10/19/06 16:12:52
10/12/06 16:13:00  10/13/06 02:12:52  afs/example.edu@EXAMPLE.EDU
        renew until 10/19/06 16:12:52

klist: No Kerberos 4 tickets in credentials cache

# tokens

Tokens held by the Cache Manager:

User's (AFS ID 10000) tokens for afs@example.edu [Expires Oct 13 02:12]
    --End of list--

# ls /afs/example.edu/
services        software        users
```

Note that we had full access to the AFS file space, but we still need to obtain a valid token upon a successful login in order to let users work within their AFS home directories. The equivalent of a PAM session on the MacOS X system is a *login hook*, easily done via a shell script that directly calls aklog.

Therefore in the `/Applications/Scripts/` folder we create the `login.sh` shell script with the following contents and permissions:

```
# cat /Applications/Scripts/login.sh

#!/bin/bash
/usr/bin/sudo -u "$1" /usr/bin/aklog &> /dev/null
exit 0

# ls -l /Applications/Scripts/login.sh
-rwsr-sr-x 1 root root 69 2006-10-29 12:20 /Applications/Scripts/login.sh
```

Verify that the system has the SUID bit set for the `sudo` command itself which has to be owned by `root`. The login process calls the login hook script with the user name as a parameter, such that the `sudo` program authenticates as the given user name through the parameter `$1`, running `aklog` that obtains a valid AFS token. Obviously the script must be owned by root in order to let `sudo` work with any user in the system. A reference to the login hook must be set system-wide using the `defaults` tool, which handles all the user and system properties. On MacOS X settings are organized in "domains", identified by a DNS-like string as in the following example:

```
# defaults read com.apple.loginwindow LoginHook
2006-10-17 11:27:57.225 defaults[408]
The domain/default pair of (com.apple.loginwindow, LoginHook) does not exist
```

The `com.apple.loginwindow` entry contains attributes that describe the behavior of the login process, and is actually a binary file with the same name located in the `/Library/Preferences/` folder:

```
# ls /Library/Preferences
DirectoryService/                    com.apple.dockfixup.plist
Network/                             com.apple.iDVD.plist
Soundtrack/                          com.apple.iLifeMediaBrowser.plist
SystemConfiguration/                 com.apple.iMovie.plist
Systems/                             com.apple.iWork.plist
com.apple.ARDAgent.plist             com.apple.iWork06.Installer.plist
com.apple.BezelServices.plist        com.apple.iWork06.plist
com.apple.ByteRangeLocking.plist     com.apple.loginwindow.plist
com.apple.HIToolbox.plist            com.apple.networkConfig.plist
com.apple.QuickTime.plist            com.apple.security.plist
com.apple.RemoteManagement.plist     com.apple.sharing.firewall.plist
com.apple.SetupAssistant.plist       com.apple.windowserver.plist
com.apple.SoftwareUpdate.plist       com.apple.xgrid.agent.plist
com.apple.audio.DeviceSettings.plist com.apple.xgrid.controller.plist
```

These files are another NeXTSTEP heritage, convertible to a textual XML file through the `plutil` tool. If we choose to install the Apple's Developer Tools we are able to open property list files, or shortly `plist` files, with a graphical front-end. An example of a `plist` file is as follows:

```
# plutil -convert xml1 /Library/Preferences/com.apple.networkConfig.plist -o a.txt

# cat a.txt
```

```
<?xml version="1.0" encoding="UTF-8"?>
<!DOCTYPE plist PUBLIC "-//Apple Computer//DTD PLIST 1.0//EN"
                       "http://www.apple.com/DTDs/PropertyList-1.0.dtd">
<plist version="1.0">
<dict>
        <key>NetworkingConfigured</key>
        <integer>1</integer>
</dict>
</plist>
```

Let us now update the login settings with the **LoginHook** attribute pointing at our new shell script:

```
# defaults write com.apple.loginwindow LoginHook '/Applications/Scripts/login.sh'

# defaults read com.apple.loginwindow
{LoginHook = "/Applications/Scripts/login.sh"; }
```

Finally, it is possible to login for our Kerberos users, having their home directory mounted at login time with a valid AFS token thanks to the login hook, as we can see in Fig. 13.6.

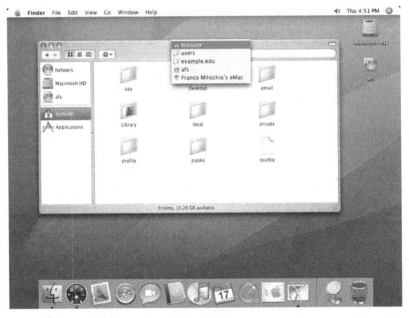

Fig. 13.6. The desktop of MacOS X 10.4 after a login

13.4 Microsoft Windows XP

Microsoft Windows XP is for many realities probably the most used desktop operating system, and Samba in our environment acts as a gateway between the two major worlds: the UNIX world with MacOS X or Linux and the Windows world. Windows XP, released in 2001, is the natural successor of Windows 2000, and like its ancestor has its root in the NT operating system. It has the ability, in its Professional version, to join NT or Active Directory domains.

Like MacOS X, configuring a Windows operating system is commonly done by means of the graphical user interface, and in the following paragraphs we describe the procedures to enable full AFS access along with pictures of the operation in progress. We start with Fig. 13.7 showing the NTP synchronization settings, where the "Internet Time" tab is clearly visible.

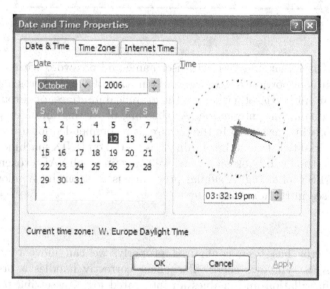

Fig. 13.7. The Windows XP time settings window

Kerberos

We assume the `client` machine to be installed with Windows XP Professional, and after the necessary reboot we need to login as an administrator in order to install the Kerberos software. As we already previewed, Kerberos is at the core of the authentication system, and it is also supported by Microsoft but with some modifications. Therefore we stick with the the official Kerberos for Windows package from the MIT, enabling the automatic ticket retrieval as in Fig. 13.8. This setting enables the Kerberos manager to obtain the initial

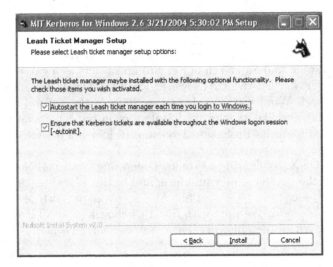

Fig. 13.8. The Kerberos for Windows installation process

ticket for a user that matches both user name and password with a Kerberos principal. It is important to test the configuration of the Kerberos manager by obtaining an initial ticket, either via the graphical interface, or through `kinit` with a command line interaction. At the time of writing an older version of the MIT software, as shown in the picture, is recommended for use with AFS.

If the initial ticket could be obtained, as we did on UNIX machines through PAM or via the login hook on a Mac, we can gain a valid AFS token through the OpenAFS tool `aklog`. A similar procedure is done on the Windows client, as we will see in the following.

OpenAFS

Once Kerberos has been configured properly, we can move on installing the OpenAFS Windows client. The client correctly handles a pre-existing Kerberos installation and enables an integrated login, a setting pictured in Fig. 13.9: we obtain an AFS token for the current user if Kerberos could acquire the initial ticket, i.e. if user name and password coincide with the principal name and password. This means that Kerberos password and Samba password have to coincide, otherwise this procedure fails, assuming that the host joined our Windows domain.

The OpenAFS client can automatically mount the AFS file space as a network shared drive, similar to the [homes] share in a Samba domain. It is useful to configure a system-wide shared drive such that all users can access their AFS space seamlessly.

Recently the client has been added the useful functionality of accessing the AFS file space with a UNC \\afs: this convenient solution makes it pos-

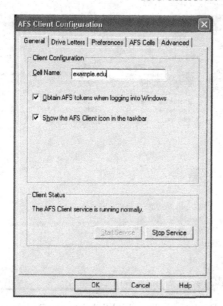

Fig. 13.9. The OpenAFS for Windows integrated login setting

sible to point directly to the AFS cell with the standard Windows notation
\\afs\example.edu.

Domain Join

Now we are ready to join the WIN.EXAMPLE.EDU Windows domain, having all
our users obtain a Kerberos ticket and an AFS token at login time, since our
Samba password coincides with the Kerberos password.

As previously detailed, Windows XP Professional can join a Samba domain
in case we set the RequireSignOrSeal property to 0. This key of the registry,
which is the main Windows database containing system and user settings, is
located under the following path:

```
[HKEY_LOCAL_MACHINE\SYSTEM\CurrentControlSet\Services\Netlogon\Parameters]
requiresignorseal=dword:00000000
```

We can manually set the value by using the Registry Editor, as in
Fig. 13.10, running the regedit tool from the Start menu—or locating it
under the Windows root folder. An easier way to immediately set this key in
the registry on multiple machines, is to use the same Registry Editor for modifying the entry on a host, and then export the entire \Netlogon\Parameters
to a file. Exported registry entries are actually text files that can also be
modified with a text editor:

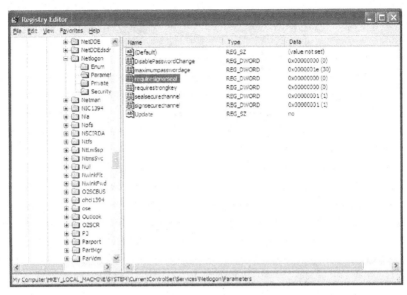

Fig. 13.10. The Registry Editor highlighting the `RequireSignOrSeal` key

```
Windows Registry Editor Version 5.00

[HKEY_LOCAL_MACHINE\SYSTEM\CurrentControlSet\Services\Netlogon\Parameters]
"DisablePasswordChange"=dword:00000000
"maximumpasswordage"=dword:0000001e
"requiresignorseal"=dword:00000000
"requirestrongkey"=dword:00000000
"sealsecurechannel"=dword:00000001
"signsecurechannel"=dword:00000001
"Update"="no"
```

We can then remove all the unnecessary entries and leave only the `RequireSignOrSeal` item as in the following example:

```
Windows Registry Editor Version 5.00

[HKEY_LOCAL_MACHINE\SYSTEM\CurrentControlSet\Services\Netlogon\Parameters]
"requiresignorseal"=dword:00000000
```

By using the modified registry file on each client, we merge the only key contained in the file with the machine registry content, actually overwriting the host `RequireSignOrSeal` entry. Once the system has been enabled to join a Samba domain, we can use the control panel and provide a `WIN.EXAMPLE.EDU` administrative password in order to join the domain, as in Fig. 13.11: remember that the `Administrator` user in this procedure is the domain administrator, and not the local Windows user. If the join succeeds then we are welcomed to the domain and we are asked to reboot the machine: on the next boot we

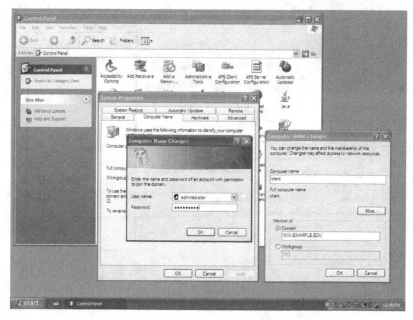

Fig. 13.11. The Windows domain joining procedure

are able to use our domain users, for example the `testuser` as in Fig. 13.12, and one should automatically obtain Kerberos and AFS credentials.

User Profiles

We have seen in the chapter regarding Samba that user profiles, the analogous of users home directories, are stored on the Samba server:

```
Application Data/   Favorites/      NTUSER.DAT*     PrintHood/   Start Menu/
Cookies/            My Documents/   NTUSER.DAT.LOG* Recent/      Templates/
Desktop/            NetHood/        ntuser.ini      SendTo/
```

Windows upon login creates a local copy of the profile on the client, and then synchronizes the profile with the domain controller. Since a profile contains the `My Documents` folder, it might grow in size as Windows user are used to save personal file in this location, or even on the Desktop which is again part of the profile. This means that Samba gets used intensively instead of employing the OpenAFS service, which scales better than Samba or NFS from small to big companies. Hence it is a good practice to instruct users to set the path of `My Documents` to their AFS space to seamlessly employ the distributed file system architecture, for instance our `testuser` should point its personal folder to the `\\afs\example.edu\users\testuser`, or a subdirectory of its choice.

Local profiles may be left on machines, or if this fact raises security or privacy concerns, Windows XP can be instructed to purge the local copy

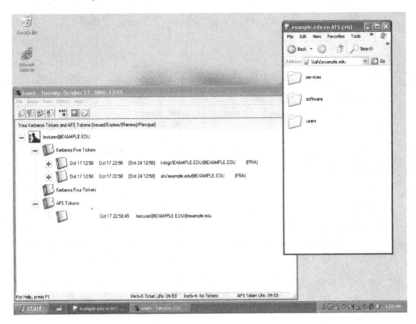

Fig. 13.12. The Windows integrated login provides both Kerberos ticket and AFS token, with a full AFS file space access

upon a successful logout. This configuration can be set on a per-host basis on the client itself with the Group Policy Editor gpedit.msc tool, modifying the "Delete cached copies of roaming profiles" property as in Fig 13.13:

```
[Computer Configuration\Administrative Templates\System\User Profiles]
Delete cached copies of roaming profiles="Enabled"
```

Practice

Exercise 49. Exploit PAM to introduce further restrictions for login on an Ubuntu host, convenient for hosts dedicated to a group of users. Make use of the central LDAP service.

Exercise 50. Introduce similar restrictions for a Mac OS X client, referring again to the LDAP service. As before, the best would be to define a group.

Exercise 51. Explore the possibilities of the netlogon share, opening the client configuration for scripting. To some extend one should be able to re-semble "group policies" of Active Directory.

Exercise 52. Are the here presented client systems sufficient for your purposes? Do you need support for other architectures? Verify the availability of a client with the OpenAFS site.

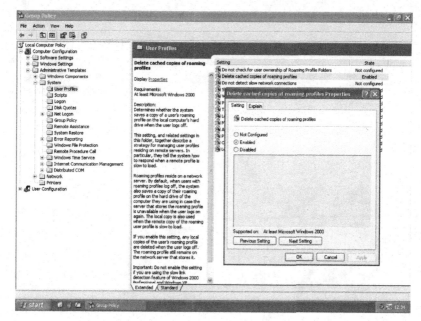

Fig. 13.13. The roaming profile settings in the Group Policy Editor tool

Clustering

Suum Cuique ("To each his own").
Marcus Tullius Cicero

14.1 Introduction

Computer clusters are basically groups of computers working on a common task, and their birth may be traced back in history to the time when one computer occupied an entire room, and often was not enough powerful to fulfill the requested jobs. Suddenly it appeared clear that more than one machine could increase productivity by splitting jobs on each host, and in 1967 Gene Amdahl of IBM paved the way to modern clustering introducing the paper *"Validity of the Single Processor Approach to Achieving Large-Scale Computing Capabilities"* in the proceedings of the American Federation of Information Processing Societies Conference. The research paper presented a mathematical explanation of the supposed speedup allowed by parallelizing tasks with respect to a simple serial execution; later this mathematical model become famous as Amdahl's law.

Clusters are usually constituted by networked computers, although this is not true for all environments. Historically, cluster development was coupled with the growth of networking solutions. After the first commercialization of ARCnet by Datapoint, the first cluster based on PDP-11, several solutions were available as DEC's VAXcluster and IBM's S/390 Parallel Sysplex.

Different products were later introduced, with an affordable clustering solution proposed by the Parallel Virtual Machine, or PVM, a joint effort from the Oak Ridge National Laboratory, the University of Tennessee, and Emory University. Later the Message Passing Interface, MPI, became available as a standard communication library specification for both the C and Fortran programming languages. Using both PVM and MPI in different software, the NASA then developed the Beowulf project, a cluster of homogeneous reduced-cost computers running a Linux system. Another notable project was started in 1981 at the Hebrew University of Jerusalem by a team lead by Prof. Amnon Barak, providing a transparent clustering software (i.e. no ad-hoc code is virtually needed) called MOSIX.

In the following of this chapter we are going to install and configure a cluster constituted by two nodes called **node01** and **node02**, employing MPI, PVM, and MOSIX. Since communication between nodes on a network is a crucial operation, we will introduce the Secure Shell software SSH which avoids any unencrypted communications among hosts, and can use Kerberos authentication though the GSSAPI layer.

14.2 Secure Shell

The Secure Shell is an encrypted network protocol that uses public key authentication in order to allow secure communication between hosts. The first version was developed by Tatu Ylönen at the Helsinki University of Technology with the objective to replace remote login protocols such as **rlogin**, **rsh**, and **telnet**, which did not provide any encryption facility. The original author released the software free of charge, and founded the SSH Communications Security to commercialize SSH. The second version of this protocol was developed in 1996 and standardized by the IEFT in 2006, improving security and integrity check features. The implementation shipped with Debian is OpenSSH, a free and open source implementation started by the OpenBSD team. The SSH servers in our network, as well as clients, have to become Kerberos clients, with name service switch using the LDAP plugin for user information, and the AFS file system for users home directories. These prerequisites then imply that the time on each host is synchronized with the NTP servers.

In order to allow the Single Sign-On, that is the ability to authenticate once and use the obtained credentials for further services—as for our LDAP service through SASL—the SSH server needs a manual intervention of a system administrator. The SSH server makes use of the host principal keys exported to the default keytab file in order to enable Kerberos logins.

Debian provides a Kerberized version of SSH with the package **ssh-krb5**, and after installing it, the system configures the daemon as usual: the first SSH protocol version should be avoided if possible, since it is vulnerable by design and considered obsolete. After stopping the daemon, we can proceed configuring it by modifying the **sshd_config** file, located under **/etc/ssh/**. The critical settings to enable Kerberos authentication and dealing with the GSS-API layer, are the **GSSAPIAuthentication** and **KerberosAuthentication** options. It is important to notice that some older systems may require the **GSSAPINoMICAuthentication** to be enabled, allowing an old GSSAPI authentication method inherently vulnerable to man in the middle attacks. A full detail of all OpenSSH configuration options is out of the scope of this book, here we illustrate the main concepts to employ the remote login service. The resulting configuration file looks like the following:

```
Port 22
Protocol 2
HostKey /etc/ssh/ssh_host_rsa_key
HostKey /etc/ssh/ssh_host_dsa_key
UsePrivilegeSeparation no
KeyRegenerationInterval 3600
ServerKeyBits 768
SyslogFacility AUTH
LogLevel INFO
LoginGraceTime 600
PermitRootLogin yes
StrictModes yes
RSAAuthentication yes
PubkeyAuthentication yes
IgnoreRhosts yes
RhostsRSAAuthentication no
HostbasedAuthentication no
PermitEmptyPasswords no
PasswordAuthentication no

KerberosAuthentication yes
KerberosTicketCleanup yes

GSSAPIAuthentication yes
GSSAPINoMICAuthentication yes
GSSAPICleanupCredentials yes

X11Forwarding yes
X11DisplayOffset 10
PrintMotd no
PrintLastLog yes
KeepAlive yes

Subsystem      sftp    /usr/lib/sftp-server

UsePAM yes
```

The ServerKeyBits define the length of the key which can be changed and all keys in /etc/ssh/ are freshly generated when removed. Enabling PAM allows us to permit local users upon login to gain a valid AFS token through the pam_openafs_session.so plugin. Restarting the service activates the changes. The corresponding script is /etc/init.d/ssh-krb5.

The client-side configuration file is located in the same directory as for the server, named ssh_config. OpenSSH permits a host-based configuration by declaring a Host stanza followed by the host name specification. In our case we enable GSSAPI for all our example.edu machines, delegating the issued credential to the server in order to allow Single Sign-On:

```
Host *.example.edu
        GSSAPIAuthentication yes
        GSSAPIDelegateCredentials yes
```

To test the credential forwarding, and actually establishing a remote connection utilizing the issued tickets via the ssh program, we start a SSH session between two nodes in the cluster system. First, let us check for valid tickets on the originating host node01:

```
testuser@node01:~$ klist
Ticket cache: FILE:/tmp/krb5cc_10000_8Yvjas
Default principal: testuser@EXAMPLE.EDU

Valid starting     Expires              Service principal
08/03/06 17:20:23  08/04/06 03:20:23    host/node01.example.edu@EXAMPLE.EDU
08/03/06 17:20:23  08/04/06 03:20:23    krbtgt/EXAMPLE.EDU@EXAMPLE.EDU
08/03/06 17:20:23  08/04/06 03:20:23    afs/example.edu@EXAMPLE.EDU


Kerberos 4 ticket cache: /tmp/tkt10000
klist: You have no tickets cached

testuser@node01:~$ tokens

Tokens held by the Cache Manager:

User's (AFS ID 10000) tokens for afs@example.edu [Expires Aug  4 03:20]
  --End of list--
```

Then we can connect to the **node02** system, using the **-v** switch to increase the verbosity level:

```
testuser@node01:~$ ssh -v node02.example.edu
OpenSSH_3.8.1p1  Debian-krb5 3.8.1p1-7, OpenSSL 0.9.7e 25 Oct 2004
debug1: Reading configuration data /etc/ssh/ssh_config
debug1: Applying options for *.example.edu
debug1: Connecting to node02.example.edu [192.168.127.145] port 22.
debug1: Connection established.
debug1: identity file /afs/example.edu/users/testuser/.ssh/identity type -1
debug1: identity file /afs/example.edu/users/testuser/.ssh/id_rsa type -1
debug1: identity file /afs/example.edu/users/testuser/.ssh/id_dsa type -1
debug1: Remote protocol version 2.0, remote software version OpenSSH_3.8.1p1 \
Debian-krb5 3.8.1p1-7
debug1: match: OpenSSH_3.8.1p1  Debian-krb5 3.8.1p1-7 pat OpenSSH*
debug1: Enabling compatibility mode for protocol 2.0
debug1: Local version string SSH-2.0-OpenSSH_3.8.1p1  Debian-krb5 3.8.1p1-7
debug1: Mechanism encoded as toWM5Slw5Ew8Mqkay+al2g==
debug1: Mechanism encoded as A/vx1jAEU54gt9a48EiANQ==
debug1: SSH2_MSG_KEXINIT sent
debug1: SSH2_MSG_KEXINIT received
debug1: kex: server->client aes128-cbc hmac-md5 none
debug1: kex: client->server aes128-cbc hmac-md5 none
debug1: Calling gss_init_sec_context
debug1: Delegating credentials
debug1: Received GSSAPI_COMPLETE
debug1: Calling gss_init_sec_context
debug1: Delegating credentials
debug1: SSH2_MSG_NEWKEYS sent
debug1: expecting SSH2_MSG_NEWKEYS
debug1: SSH2_MSG_NEWKEYS received
debug1: SSH2_MSG_SERVICE_REQUEST sent
debug1: SSH2_MSG_SERVICE_ACCEPT received
...
debug1: channel 0: new [client-session]
debug1: Entering interactive session.

testuser@node02:~$
```

The remote login session has been successfully established without prompting for any further password, and with the help of PAM **node02** enabled the user to gain the correct AFS token upon authentication:

```
testuser@node02:~$ klist
Ticket cache: FILE:/tmp/krb5cc_10000_ym2150
Default principal: testuser@EXAMPLE.EDU

Valid starting      Expires             Service principal
08/03/06 17:21:18   08/04/06 03:20:23   krbtgt/EXAMPLE.EDU@EXAMPLE.EDU
08/03/06 17:21:18   08/04/06 03:20:23   afs/example.edu@EXAMPLE.EDU


Kerberos 4 ticket cache: /tmp/tkt10000
klist: You have no tickets cached

testuser@node02:~$ tokens

Tokens held by the Cache Manager:

User's (AFS ID 10000) tokens for afs@example.edu [Expires Aug  4 03:20]
  --End of list--
```

By default the clustering software, MPI and PVM, use an unencrypted channel with rsh. In the following section we will install both packages instructing them to use the SSH protocol encrypting the communication between nodes. In any case Debian installs ssh as a substitution for rsh employing a mechanism of alternatives configured under /etc/alternatives/.

14.3 MPI and PVM

The Message Passing Interface along with the Parallel Virtual Machine are commonly used to implement parallel and distributed computations, often on computer clusters. MPI is actually a description of APIs, implemented by independent projects that are not bound to a single specification, such as a particular network protocol, although the majority of MPI libraries employ TCP/IP and socket connections. Such a library allows developers to write programs relying on general functions, such as sending data to a process, without caring about the physical location of any of these. The Parallel Virtual Machine is an analogous software, allowing transparency about the location of processes and providing high-level functions to the programmer. Contrary to MPI, which is a specification, PVM is a concrete implementation. The complete transparency from the developer point of view is achieved by a MOSIX cluster which is based on the "fork and forget" principle: this kernel extension itself distributes processes to different nodes.

14.3.1 Message Passing Interface

The MPI specification reached the second version, and from its original C and Fortran version, bindings were made available for other languages such as Java, OCaml, and Python. There are various implementations of the MPI specification, among these we want to mention MPICH, LAM-MPI, and Open-MPI. We prefer the LAM-MPI library, distributed with the lam4-dev and lam-runtime Debian packages:

```
# apt-get install lam4-dev lam-runtime
```

LAM-MPI uses by default the remote shell program rsh; or by setting
the LAMRSH environment variable to ssh, the MPI library is forced to use
the secure shell instead of the unencrypted remote shell. All what is needed
to start a program on multiple machines, such as our node01 and node02
hosts, is to create a node configuration file containing the host names—or
IP addresses—of all the nodes that will constitute the cluster. Note that the
localhost name cannot be used since it would be resolved to 127.0.0.1
regardless of the actual IP address of a host and hence it is not suitable for
Kerberos:

```
$ export LAMRSH=ssh

$ cat machinefile
node01.example.edu
node02.example.edu
```

A simple MPI example coded in the programming language C is the following:

```
1   #include <stdio.h>
    #include <string.h>
3   #include "mpi.h"

5   #define MSG_LEN 1024

7   int main(int argc, char *argv[])
    {
9       int         ntasks, whoami, len, i;
        char        host[MPI_MAX_PROCESSOR_NAME];
11      char        message[MSG_LEN];
        MPI_Comm    handle;
13      MPI_Status  status;

15      memset(host, 0, MPI_MAX_PROCESSOR_NAME);

17      /* Initialize MPI */
        MPI_Init(&argc, &argv);
19      handle = MPI_COMM_WORLD;
        /* Get the total number of processes,
21          process rank and host name*/
        MPI_Comm_size(handle, &ntasks);
23      MPI_Comm_rank(handle, &whoami);
        MPI_Get_processor_name(host, &len);
25      /* If we are the root, aka process rank 0 */
        if (!whoami)
27      {
            for (i = 1; i < ntasks; i++)
29          {
                /* Initialize the buffer */
31              memset(message, 0, MSG_LEN);
                /* Receive strings in order
33                  and print the output */
                MPI_Recv(message, MSG_LEN, MPI_CHAR,
35                      i, 0, MPI_COMM_WORLD, &status);
                puts(message);
37          }
        }
39      else
```

```
     {
41          /* Initialize the buffer */
            memset(message, 0, MSG_LEN);
43          printf("%d: starting snprintf\n", whoami);
            snprintf(message, MSG_LEN - 1,
45                  "Hello from host %s, process %d, total processes %d!",
                    host, whoami, ntasks);
47          /* Send to the rank 0 process */
            MPI_Send(message, MSG_LEN, MPI_CHAR,
49                  0, 0, MPI_COMM_WORLD);
     }
51     printf("Finally done.");
       MPI_Finalize();
53     return 0;
}
```

After compiling and linking this code with the gcc compiler wrapper mpicc, LAM-MPI has to be started with the lamboot command providing the machine file as a command line parameter:

```
$ mpicc -Wall -pedantic -ansi mpi-example.c -o mpi-example

$ lamboot -v machinefile

LAM 7.1.1/MPI 2 C++/ROMIO - Indiana University

n-1<1549> ssi:boot:base:linear: booting n0 (node01.example.edu)
n-1<1549> ssi:boot:base:linear: booting n1 (node02.example.edu)
n-1<1549> ssi:boot:base:linear: finished
```

The lamboot tool starts the LAM-MPI daemon on all the cluster nodes, and thereafter we can run the MPI-based program with the starter tool mpirun specifying the number of processes to be spawned in the cluster with the -np switch:

```
$ mpirun -np 10 mpi-example
Finally done.
Finally done.
Hello from host node01, process 1, total processes 10!
Hello from host node02, process 2, total processes 10!
Hello from host node01, process 3, total processes 10!
Hello from host node02, process 4, total processes 10!
Finally done.
Finally done.
Finally done.
Hello from host node01, process 5, total processes 10!
Hello from host node02, process 6, total processes 10!
Finally done.
Hello from host node01, process 7, total processes 10!
Hello from host node02, process 8, total processes 10!
Finally done.
Finally done.
Hello from host node01, process 9, total processes 10!
Finally done.
Finally done.
```

14.3.2 Parallel Virtual Machine

Historically the Parallel Virtual Machine is a predecessor of MPI, developed in 1989 by the Oak Ridge National Laboratory, and its functionalities are similar to its counterpart. Its last stable release was made available in 1994, and is currently being lively maintained and supported by the PVM community. The Parallel Virtual Machine software has several bindings, such as the R statistical programming language, Java, PERL and common LISP. PVM is distributed by Debian with the **pvm** and **pvm-dev** packages:

```
# apt-get install pvm pvm-dev
```

As for MPI, we need to force PVM to use SSH instead of the RSH protocol, again using an environment variable. Providing a machine file, which indicates all the hosts in the cluster, is optional with the PVM software since it uses a command line interface similar to the **kadmin** tool:

```
$ export PVM_RSH=ssh

$ cat machinefile
node01.example.edu
node02.example.edu
```

The C program we are going to test on the machines is the following:

```
   #include <stdio.h>
2  #include "pvm3.h"

4  int main(int argc, char *argv[])
   {
6    int whoami;

8    /* Get the ID */
     whoami = pvm_mytid();
10   /* Print it */
     printf("My PVM ID is %d\n", whoami);
12   /* Ask PVM to exit gently */
     pvm_exit();

14
     return 0;
16 }
```

After compiling and linking the source code file with the **gcc** tool, we can start the PVM console program **pvm**:

```
$ gcc -Wall pvm-example.c -o pvm-example -lpvm3

$ pvm
pvm> help
help
help        Print helpful information about a command
Syntax: help [ command ]
Commands are:
   add        Add hosts to virtual machine
   alias      Define/list command aliases
   conf       List virtual machine configuration
   delete     Delete hosts from virtual machine
   echo       Echo arguments
   export     Add environment variables to spawn export list
   halt       Stop pvmds
   help       Print helpful information about a command
   id         Print console task id
```

```
jobs        Display list of running jobs
kill        Terminate tasks
mstat       Show status of hosts
names       List message mailbox names
ps          List tasks
pstat       Show status of tasks
put         Add entry to message mailbox
quit        Exit console
reset       Kill all tasks, delete leftover mboxes
setenv      Display or set environment variables
sig         Send signal to task
spawn       Spawn task
trace       Set/display trace event mask
unalias     Undefine command alias
unexport    Remove environment variables from spawn export list
version     Show libpvm version

pvm> version
version
3.4.2

pvm> quit
quit

Console: exit handler called
pvmd still running.
```

It is possible, as we can see in the output above, to add manually new hosts with the add command, or feed a machine file to the pvm tools, so that all the hosts are automatically added to the cluster host list. Running a PVM program is done via the PVM console with the spawn command, indicating the number of tasks and the PVM program:

```
$ pvm machinefile
pvm> conf
conf
2 hosts, 1 data format
                HOST    DTID    ARCH    SPEED      DSIG
    node01.example.edu  40000   LINUX   1000  0x00408841
    node02.example.edu  80000   LINUX   1000  0x00408841

pvm> spawn -5 -> /afs/example.edu/users/testuser/local/pvm/pvm-example
spawn -5 -> /afs/example.edu/users/testuser/local/pvm/pvm-example
[2]
5 successful
t80004
t80005
t80006
t40007
t40008

pvm>
[2:t40007] My PVM ID is 262151
[2:t40008] My PVM ID is 262152
[2:t40007] EOF
[2:t40008] EOF
[2:t80004] My PVM ID is 524292
[2:t80005] My PVM ID is 524293
[2:t80004] EOF
[2:t80005] EOF
[2:t80006] My PVM ID is 524294
[2:t80006] EOF
[2] finished
```

```
pvm> halt
halt
Terminated
```

14.4 MOSIX Cluster Management

MOSIX is a cluster management system capable of automatic job distribution among machines on a network. Contrary to MPI or PVM a cluster based on the MOSIX software acts transparently to a user, as if they were part of a symmetric multi-processor host, a strategy mentioned before as "fork and forget". Of course this assumes that a program makes use of several communicating processes, as it is common in the world of UNIX.

The software was developed in 1981 at the Hebrew University of Jerusalem by Prof. Amnon Barak and his research team. Originally the Multicomputer OS or MOS, was developed on a cluster of PDP-11 machines with Bell Lab Unix 7, and later ported to UNIX flavors as Unix System V and BSD. MOSIX in 1999 turned its efforts to the Linux kernel, providing both a kernel patch and maintenance tools. A parallel program was started in 2001 by Moshe Bar to comply with the GPL software license, called OpenMOSIX, although the latest version according to the official home page is of December 2004. In this section we focus on the MOSIX package, showing how to configure a cluster based on this software with just two machines **node01** and **node02**. Note that MOSIX is not certified to run on the AFS file system, and deployment of MOSIX-based clusters on AFS clients should be carefully planned, especially running jobs that access the OpenAFS file space. Anyway, the process we are going to show does not depend on files located in AFS file space.

14.4.1 Patching the Kernel

We describe in this section a typical installation process on the **node01** machine, a host that is already a Kerberos, LDAP, and OpenAFS client with synchronized time. Again, we stress that programs run by MOSIX and accessing the AFS file space are not guaranteed to function correctly, and may result in unexpected behaviors.

MOSIX is basically a patch to the Linux kernel, and as a patch it must be applied to the exact version of the kernel it was developed for. The clustering system is released only for the official Linux kernel source, also known as "vanilla" kernel, with a package called MOSKRN, and with user tools MOSIX. Let us start then downloading the kernel sources, and both MOSIX packages:

```
# wget http://www.kernel.org/pub/linux/kernel/v2.4/linux-2.4.33.tar.gz

# wget http://www.mosix.org/moskrn/MOSKRN-1.13.4.tar.bz2

# wget http://www.mosix.org/mosultp/MOSIX-1.13.4.tar.bz2
```

Note that we downloaded a specific kernel version, since MOSIX version 1.13.4 was developed for the Linux kernel version 2.4.33, and the installation may fail on subversions as 2.4.33.3. Proceed with uncompressing the MOSIX packages by the `bzip2` compression tool, provided by Debian with the homonymous package:

```
# cd /usr/src/

# tar zxf ~/linux-2.4.33.tar.gz

# tar jxf ~/MOSKRN-1.13.4.tar.bz2

# tar jxf ~/MOSIX-1.13.4.tar.bz2
```

The next steps, in order to create a full MOSIX node, are to apply the kernel patch, and then to recompile it with the `gcc` compiler, which should be already installed on machines that are AFS clients and needed to compile the AFS kernel module before. As usual, we create a symbolic link to the Linux kernel source in `/usr/src/` called simply `linux`:

```
# rm -f linux

# ln -s linux-2.4.33 linux

# ls -l linux
lrwxrwxrwx  1 root src 14 2006-09-06 11:00 linux -> linux-2.4.33/
```

Next we have to apply the MOSIX patch with the `patch` tool, and proceed configuring the Linux kernel with the standard vanilla `make menuconfig` command.

```
# cd linux

# patch -p0 < /usr/src/MOSKRN-1.13.4/patches.2.4.33

# make menuconfig
```

A kernel configuration description is out of the scope of this book, and it is highly dependent on the hardware configuration of the machine. The basic requirements for MOSIX to work are usually met[1], leaving the hardware, network, and disk access configuration to the system administrator. As required by the MOSIX documentation, we need to remove the Linux `version.h` header file and create a symbolic link to the clustering software in `/usr/include/`:

```
# rm -f include/linux/version.h

# ls -l /usr/include/mos
lrwxrwxrwx  1 root root 26 2006-09-06 14:26 /usr/include/mos -> \
/usr/src/linux/include/mos/
```

---

[1] MOSIX requires an ELF binary image for the kernel, and the `procfs`, two standard options often enabled on all Linux systems.

Having successfully configured the Linux kernel we can proceed compiling it with the standard **make** tool. Another possibility, which is the preferred option on Debian systems, is to create packages the same way we did for the OpenAFS kernel module with the **make-kpkg** tool. We first clean the source tree from any binaries residue of preceding compilations, then configure the kernel source tree, and finally produce the binary kernel image and module packages:

```
# make-kpkg clean

# make-kpkg configure

# make-kpkg --initrd kernel_image

# make-kpkg modules_image
```

The **--initrd** option creates an initial RAM disk that is mounted as the preliminary root file system containing the necessary modules to access file systems and hardware devices. The resulting binary files are created in /usr/src/, and as we can see from the following output, all preceding packages have not been removed by the process:

```
# ls /usr/src/*.deb
/usr/src/kernel-image-2.4.33_10.00.Custom_i386.deb
/usr/src/openafs-modules-2.4.27-3-686_1.3.81-3sarge1+2.4.27-10sarge3_i386.deb
/usr/src/openafs-modules-2.4.33_1.3.81-3sarge1+10.00.Custom_i386.deb

# dpkg -i kernel-image-2.4.33_10.00.Custom_i386.deb

# dpkg -i openafs-modules-2.4.33_1.3.81-3sarge1+10.00.Custom_i386.deb
```

After installing the two packages, Debian will automatically update the boot loader so that at the next boot we can choose the newly compiled kernel, or in case of failure, boot with an older and working version. Before actually rebooting, we need to proceed with some further configuration explained in the following.

14.4.2 Configuring MOSIX

We have introduced MOSIX as a transparent clustering software, capable of migrating processes from one host to another according to necessity. This relocation may result in catastrophic results if crucial system processes are migrated to a different machine, thus all critical processes should be locked on the machine where they got started. The MOSIX userspace tools provide such a vital facility.

MOSIX contains two additional archives: one for manuals and the other for user programs. The latter archive is named **user.tar**, and includes a **Makefile** that runs with **make** and the **install** target to copy all the necessary files for the user space commands to their correct locations:

```
# tar xf /usr/src/MOSIX-1.13.4/user.tar

# ls
bin/  lib/  Makefile  Rules.make  sbin/  usr.bin/

# make install
```

All critical daemons should be locked on the machine, and these MOSIX
user tools provide a program called **mosrun** that with the **-h** switch locks a program to the host starting the process. We need to modify the **/etc/inittab**
file so that all the scripts in all run-levels become non-relocatable, as in the
following configuration file:

```
id:2:initdefault:

si::sysinit:/bin/mosrun -h /etc/init.d/rcS
~~:S:wait:/bin/mosrun -h /sbin/sulogin

10:0:wait:/bin/mosrun -h /etc/init.d/rc 0
11:1:wait:/bin/mosrun -h /etc/init.d/rc 1
12:2:wait:/bin/mosrun -h /etc/init.d/rc 2
13:3:wait:/bin/mosrun -h /etc/init.d/rc 3
14:4:wait:/bin/mosrun -h /etc/init.d/rc 4
15:5:wait:/bin/mosrun -h /etc/init.d/rc 5
16:6:wait:/bin/mosrun -h /etc/init.d/rc 6

z6:6:respawn:/bin/mosrun -h /sbin/sulogin
ca:12345:ctrlaltdel:/bin/mosrun -h /sbin/shutdown -t1 -a -r now
pf::powerwait:/bin/mosrun -h /etc/init.d/powerfail start
pn::powerfailnow:/bin/mosrun -h /etc/init.d/powerfail now
po::powerokwait:/bin/mosrun -h /etc/init.d/powerfail stop

1:2345:respawn:/sbin/getty 38400 tty1
2:23:respawn:/sbin/getty 38400 tty2
3:23:respawn:/sbin/getty 38400 tty3
4:23:respawn:/sbin/getty 38400 tty4
5:23:respawn:/sbin/getty 38400 tty5
6:23:respawn:/sbin/getty 38400 tty6
```

Note that all run-levels are prefixed by **mosrun -h**, and remember that
if a node runs services through the **xinetd** daemon or with **cron** jobs, such
services may require the host-locking command, too. On the other hand the
terminal sessions are not bount to the local host. Now that all vital services are
bound to the running host, we can install the MOSIX service in **/etc/init.d/**,
copying the script from the **MOSIX** user package, and creating the needed links
to the run-level directories to ensure MOSIX is started as the last service, and
stopped before any other:

```
# cp /usr/src/MOSIX-1.13.4/mosix.init /etc/init.d/mosix

# chmod a+x /etc/init.d/mosix

# ls -l /etc/init.d/mosix
-rwxr-x--x  1 root root 3022 2006-09-06 15:27 mosix*

# cd /etc/rc2.d/
```

```
# ln -s ../init.d/mosix S95mosix

# ln -s ../init.d/mosix K05mosix
```

To ensure that MOSIX is stopped before halting the network services, thus avoiding possible kernel panics, make sure to link the script also in run-levels 0, 1, and 6. Finally we can configure the cluster nodes in the `mosix.map` file located in the `/etc/` directory. The syntax of this configuration file is similar to the machine file list used for PVM and MPI, with lines indicating the node configuration: the first parameter specifies the node number, followed by the IP address of the host, and finally by the number of consecutive IP addresses to include in the cluster. Since our hosts have non-contiguous IP addresses, we need to describe them individually, with a single IP address on each line:

```
1 192.168.127.141 1
2 192.168.127.103 1
```

After configuring the host list we can safely reboot the machine with our new MOSIX enabled kernel. The next section assumes that in the meantime the other host `node02` got prepared with the MOSIX kernel, too.

14.4.3 Testing MOSIX

Once logged in, we can test immediately the functionality of the MOSIX cluster using the provided monitor program `mon`, which graphically represents the load on each node:

For a simple test to show how MOSIX automatically migrates processes, we can start a sequence of `awk` commands in background, as suggested in the MOSIX documentation:

```
$ awk 'BEGIN {for (i=0;i<10000;i++) for (j=0;j<10000;j++);}' &
[1] 898
$ awk 'BEGIN {for (i=0;i<10000;i++) for (j=0;j<10000;j++);}' &
[2] 899
$ awk 'BEGIN {for (i=0;i<10000;i++) for (j=0;j<10000;j++);}' &
[3] 900
$ awk 'BEGIN {for (i=0;i<10000;i++) for (j=0;j<10000;j++);}' &
[4] 901
$ awk 'BEGIN {for (i=0;i<10000;i++) for (j=0;j<10000;j++);}' &
[5] 902
$ awk 'BEGIN {for (i=0;i<10000;i++) for (j=0;j<10000;j++);}' &
[6] 903
$ awk 'BEGIN {for (i=0;i<10000;i++) for (j=0;j<10000;j++);}' &
[7] 904
$ awk 'BEGIN {for (i=0;i<10000;i++) for (j=0;j<10000;j++);}' &
[8] 905
$ awk 'BEGIN {for (i=0;i<10000;i++) for (j=0;j<10000;j++);}' &
[9] 906
$ awk 'BEGIN {for (i=0;i<10000;i++) for (j=0;j<10000;j++);}' &
[10] 907
$ awk 'BEGIN {for (i=0;i<10000;i++) for (j=0;j<10000;j++);}' &
[11] 908
$ awk 'BEGIN {for (i=0;i<10000;i++) for (j=0;j<10000;j++);}' &
[12] 909
```

These one line `awk` scripts just simulate a computation intensive job without further input or output. The processes are started on one specific host, but seamlessly they get relocated on another node by the underlying MOSIX system according to the local load of the machine. This can be nicely seen from the `mon` output:

Practice

Exercise 53. Check out the latest version of SSH. What is the current support for Kerberos and AFS? Are there situations where you need user keys instead of Kerberos?

Exercise 54. Try the combination of MPI and Mosix. In this case MPI initializes the processes on determined nodes. Mosix takes care of load balancing between them.

Exercise 55. Try the graphical interface for monitoring PVM. It is contained in the xpvm package. POV-Ray is a ray tracer program which can benefit from PVM and hence is suitable for testing.

Exercise 56. MOSIX works with the Linux kernel 2.4, but in the meantime MOSIX2 is available for the new kernel 2.6. Test the new version which combines support for cluster and grid computing. Compare this approach with the Condor and BOINC projects.

Laboratories

I am among those who think that science has great beauty. A scientist in his laboratory is not only a technician: he is also a child placed before natural phenomena which impress him like a fairy tale.
Marie Curie

15.1 Foreword

In a previous chapter we have employed the PXE system for an emergency operating system obtainable from the network. Workstations are an integral part of a company or organization, and it might arise the need for a specific client or groups of machines, to have different boot options and to show or hide installed operating systems: the Pre-Boot Execution Environment could be used as a medium to provide a specific client with a particular boot option, as we shall describe soon. Another problem often present in large environments is constituted by the installation of several workstation providing them with an operating system. PXE could once again become a useful tool to build a customized operating system to suite our needs. In the following we will modify the RIP Linux distribution, as we have already got accustomed with, but the same procedure can be applied to any Linux distribution, such as Debian itself, to automatically clone machines or even start an unattended installation process. The last section will be dedicated to the process of installing a client that has to work as a kiosk, a public computer that is used by several guests often offering just one predefined program such as a web browser. In the following we assume that a simple client `client1.example.edu` is installed, with a known MAC address and already configured to run one or more operating systems.

15.2 Multiboot Clients

We have already introduced PXE to have a rescue operating system on our network. In this section we make use of the same infrastructure to boot clients with multiple installed operating systems into a specific one, letting the system administrator specify a choice, or even providing the user a selection of boot options from a specific list.

Client configuration

Let us first analyze our example client and the installed operating systems: in our client we installed both Debian Linux and Microsoft Windows operating systems, as we can see from the partition list:

```
# fdisk -l

Disk /dev/hda: 40.0 GB, 40060403712 bytes
255 heads, 63 sectors/track, 4870 cylinders
Units = cylinders of 16065 * 512 = 8225280 bytes

   Device Boot      Start         End      Blocks   Id  System
/dev/hda1   *           1        3187    25599546    7  HPFS/NTFS
/dev/hda2            3188        3190       24097+  83  Linux
/dev/hda3            3191        3299      875542+  82  Linux swap / Solaris
/dev/hda4            3300        4870    12619057+  83  Linux
```

The first partition is used by Windows and it is formatted with NTFS, meaning that Linux cannot have a write-enabled access to the data stored in the /dev/hda1 partition. The third partition is necessary for Linux swap space, used by the operating system as additional virtual memory device[1]. The second and forth partitions are /boot/ and / for Linux, respectively. Our objective is to enable the network boot as the default boot device, done by acting on the firmware, EFI, or BIOS depending on the client. On the server, supporting the PXE boot, we want to decide which one of the two systems has to boot, possibly avoiding any manual intervention like the choice from a list at boot time.

15.2.1 Machine-specific Boot

Once the client has been enabled to boot from the network, we need to specify the DHCP settings regarding the PXE environment, such as the TFTP server and the boot image, as we have previously done in order to enable the emergency operating system boot:

```
host client1 {
  hardware ethernet 00:0b:6a:84:09:93;
  fixed-address client1.example.edu;
  filename "pxelinux.0";
  server-name "tftp.example.edu";
}
```

Besides mapping the given MAC address to the host name client1, there are the reference to the TFTP server and the boot image pxelinux.0, passed to the machine upon client request. On the TFTP server, we have to modify the already installed RIP Linux in order to allow a machine-specific configuration: in /var/lib/tftpd/ we have a configuration directory called

---

[1] Linux needs a raw swap partition, while other operating systems such as Apple MacOS X and Microsoft Windows make use of a file-based solution.

pxelinux.cfg, where right now just the default boot is present. Each host can have a specific configuration file with a name containing its MAC address in the format 01-MAC, in our case, being 00:0b:6a:84:09:93 the machine MAC address, it is the following:

```
# cat /var/lib/tftpd/pxelinux.cfg/01-00-0b-6a-84-09-93
DEFAULT local
PROMPT 0
TIMEOUT 10

LABEL local
LOCALBOOT 0
SAY Booting from local disk.
```

These settings correspond to those of PXELinux, starting the client with the configuration detailed in the DEFAULT field without showing a PROMPT, and booting the system with the default medium upon a timeout of TIMEOUT in tenths of a second, in our case then, 1 second. The default boot setting local then displays a message indicated by the SAY directive. The LOCALBOOT option specifies the default boot mechanism: a value of 0 sets the client to operate normally. We have to restart the DHCP service, such that it can consult the new configuration, whereas the TFTP service just accesses the new files without further interventions. Test, if the client boots correctly over the network showing the "Booting from local disk." message: in this case the host boots from *Master Boot Record* or MBR which is the first sector of the primary hard drive.

15.2.2 Customized GRUB

GRUB, the *Grand Unified Boot Loader* from the GNU Project, is a universal boot loader used in many distributions, and allows a greater flexibility in its configuration than its historical counterpart LILO, the *Linux Loader*. One of the major differences between the two is that LILO hardwires the configuration in the MBR, meaning that any change in the system settings need a reinstallation of the LILO loader. GRUB overcomes this barrier by directly accessing the boot sequence stored into files in a particular disk partition: as a consequence GRUB can be employed only on file systems[2] it is aware of.

In the following we recompile GRUB on the TFTP server in order to send a customized boot loader to our client machine, which is able to boot just a specific partition of our choice. For this we download the GRUB source code, uncompress it, and create a directory where we will store customized boot menus:

---

[2] Currently GRUB supports several file systems, among which we may mention ext2, ext3, fat, jfs, reiser, and xfs.

```
# cd grub-0.97/

# mkdir menus
```

In this directory we create two menu files, one for each operating system installed on our client, that is Windows and Linux. GRUB is compiled with a default menu which we are going to set to one of these two:

```
# cat menu.windows
default         0
timeout         0

title           Microsoft Windows XP Professional
root            (hd0,0)
makeactive
chainloader     +1

# cat menu.linux
default         0
timeout         0

title           Debian GNU/Linux, kernel 2.6.8-3-686
root            (hd0,3)
kernel          /boot/vmlinuz-2.6.8-3-686 root=/dev/hda4 ro
initrd          /boot/initrd.img-2.6.8-3-686
boot
```

As we can see, a GRUB boot menu list contains initial values such as the **default** boot item, with increasing numbers starting at 0, and the automatic boot **timeout**. Then we need to specify all the stanzas that describe each boot option, with a **title** and the necessary **root** partition. The Linux configuration specifies also the Linux kernel and an optional initial RAM disk used by Debian to start the Linux system.

The following steps show how to compile GRUB with a given default menu, assuming that at least the development packages **make** and **gcc** are installed:

```
# ./configure --enable-preset-menu=menus/menu.windows --enable-sis900 --enable-diskless

# make
```

Note that we also compile a network device driver into GRUB which optionally permits further network operation: the choice of that driver depends on the system at hand, checking with **configure --help** for all the possible options. The **--enable-diskless** option prevents that GRUB consults any menu file on the hard disk, and uses directly the provided default. The compilation will create a PXE-specific file located in the **stage2/** subdirectory of the source code, and it should be copied into the TFTP root directory:

```
# ls -l stage2/pxegrub
-rw-r--r--  1 root root 122688 2006-10-09 11:48 stage2/pxegrub

# cp stage2/pxegrub /var/lib/tftpd/pxegrub.windows
```

We repeat the same steps adapted for the Linux system, so that we end up with two different PXE boot images, one for Windows and one for Linux:

```
# cd /var/lib/tftpd/

# ls -l pxegrub.*
-rw-r--r--  1 root root 122752 2006-10-09 11:55 pxegrub.linux
-rw-r--r--  1 root root 122688 2006-10-09 11:52 pxegrub.windows
```

All we need now for selecting the default boot image, is to create a symbolic link called **pxegrub.0** to the image of our choice, in our example we will use Windows, and then modify the machine specific configuration to match the new configuration:

```
# ls -l pxegrub.0
lrwxrwxrwx  1 root root 15 2006-10-09 11:56 pxegrub.0 -> pxegrub.windows

# cat pxelinux.cfg/01-00-0b-6a-84-09-93
DEFAULT pxegrub.0
APPEND -
TIMEOUT 0
```

Note that the file name suffix .0 is critical for a correct configuration which derives from PXELinux. Now the system is ready to boot directly with Microsoft Windows, without any query to the user, getting the decision which image to boot from the network. The `client1` machine can be booted now, checking that it directly boots with Microsoft Windows: the entire process can be easily customized to provide several choices and allowing users to select a boot option.

15.3 PC Cloning

Another possibility, offered by this network boot procedure, is to create an automated PC cloning facility. There are already several cloning solutions on the market, for instance NetBackup from Symantec Corporation or the NovaBACKUP software from NovaStor Corporation. In the following we will modify the RIP Linux distribution such that NFS gets started automatically and used to store or fetch disk images over the network. As for other solutions, if you need a high-load backup solution it is strongly advisable to research for commercial products.

15.3.1 Customizing RIP Linux

NFS has already been introduced as a way of sharing resources in case of some emergency situation; the support for NFS is included in the RIP Linux system and can be employed for automatic machine cloning. We modify the startup scripts of RIP Linux to start networking and mount our previously exported NFS partitions, here we recall the corresponding exports:

```
/var/lib/nfs/readonly   192.168.127.0/255.255.255.0(ro,sync)
/var/lib/nfs/readwrite  192.168.127.0/255.255.255.0(rw,all_squash,sync)
```

We wish now to modify the operation of RIP Linux: for this we leave the kernel untouched but change the initial RAM disk, a temporary file system used at boot time. Let us copy the RIP initial RAM disk and mount it in a valid mount point:

```
# cd /tmp

# cp /var/lib/tftpd/initrd.gz .

# gunzip initrd.gz

# mkdir initrd.mount

# mount -o loop initrd initrd.mount
```

The last mount command uses a `loop` device, permitting to mount as if it were a regular file system. At the time of writing this RIP initial ramdisk contains a compressed root filesystem `rootfs.tgz` which we uncompress in order to modify it below the directory `root.mount`:

```
# ls initrd.mount/
bin/   dev/   lib/      mnt/    root/        sbin/  usr/
boot/  etc/   linuxrc*  proc/   rootfs.tgz   tmp/   var/

# cp initrd.mount/rootfs.tgz .

# mkdir root.mount

# cd root.mount

# tar zxf ../rootfs.tgz

# ls
acpi/           genpowerd.conf  lvm/           pcmcia/       shells
adjtime         group           magic          ppp/          skel/
apmd_proxy      gshadow         mailcap        profile       smartd.conf
at.deny         host.conf       modprobe.conf  profile.d/    ssh/
cron.daily/     hosts           modules.conf   protocols     ssmtp/
cron.hourly/    inittab         modules.devfs  raidtab       sudoers
cron.monthly/   inputrc         mtab           rc.d/         sysctl.conf
cron.weekly/    issue           mtools.conf    rpc           syslog.conf
dhcpc/          ld.so.cache     networks       samba/        termcap
dialogrc        ld.so.conf      nntpserver     securetty     vche.conf
DIR_COLORS      localtime       nsswitch.conf  serial.conf   vga/
exports         login.access    partimaged/    services      wgetrc
fstab           login.defs      passwd         shadow        whois.conf
```

We start with a modification of the `/etc/rc.d/rc.inet1.conf` file that drives the network interfaces known to the system, enabling the network at boot time with DHCP support:

```
IPADDR[0]=""
NETMASK[0]=""
USE_DHCP[0]="yes"
DHCP_HOSTNAME[0]=""
```

Additionally we act on the last script that is started in the RIP system `rc.local` in order to mount the NFS exports:

```
#!/bin/sh
/etc/rc.d/rc.inet1 start
/etc/rc.d/rc.portmap start
cd /tmp
mkdir ro
mkdir rw
mount -o ro 192.168.127.154:/var/lib/nfs/readonly /tmp/ro
mount -o rw 192.168.127.154:/var/lib/nfs/readwrite /tmp/rw
```

Note that `rc.inet1` and `rc.portmap` must have the executable bit set in order to work, which might not be the default case. It is at this point where other commands could be appended for further customization, starting an automated process as cloning: we will not use an unmanned script other than mounting the NFS exports for didactic reasons, anyway all the process can be easily handled by an unsupervised procedure. Once that the system configuration is finished, we need to recreate the compressed root file system, and copy it into the mounted initial RAM disk directory:

```
# cd /tmp/root.mount

# tar czf ../rootfs.tgz *

# cp ../rootfs.tgz ../initrd.mount/
```

The compressed `rootfs.tgz` archive has to be created in its mount point so that it contains only relative paths, and not absolute ones. Now we can unmount the `initrd`, compress it, and finally move it into the TFTP directory:

```
# cd /tmp

# umount /tmp/initrd.mount

# gzip initrd

# cp initrd.gz /var/lib/tftpd/newinitrd.gz
```

To test the modified system, we just have to modify the `APPEND` parameter with respect to the default RIP configuration of PXE for the machine we want to use, adding the string `initrd=newinitrd.gz`. Booting into the modified RIP system, we should see, after entering as `root` without password, that it correctly mounted the NFS exports:

```
# cd /tmp

# ls -l
total 12
drwxr-xr-x  2 root root 4096 Jul 13 14:18 ro
drwxrwxrwx  2 root root 4096 Oct  9 13:31 rw
-rw-r--r--  1 root root   11 Oct  9 15:30 skip_tmpfs
```

```
# mount
...
192.168.127.154:/var/lib/nfs/readonly on /tmp/ro type nfs (ro,addr=192.168.127.145)
192.168.127.154:/var/lib/nfs/readwrite on /tmp/rw type nfs (rw,addr=192.168.127.145)
```

15.3.2 Partition Images

There are many tools to store and recover disk images, one of the easiest is the classic UNIX dd command, which operates just on a data stream: it has no further knowledge about a concrete file system. More sophisticated is the dump and restore combination, permitting a full and incremental backup solution, unfortunately limited to ext2 and ext3 file systems. Another option is the rsync program which can be combined with ssh: both are included in RIP and allow for a synchronization of the local system with respect to a remote reference system. Only the differences between files are propagated over the network, allowing also the synchronization of special file types (e.g. symbolic links, device files), and having the advantage of a complete transparency with respect to the underlying file system[3].

Here we show the partimage tool which acts on one entire partition, but with the useful knowledge of the underlying file system: currently it has full support for ext2, ext3, fat, hpfs, jfs, reiser, and xfs, while in the future also ufs, hfs, ntfs will be supported. This command allows us to create partition images and split them into files of a fixed size, useful in case of NFS (with a 2GB file size limit) or with other file systems that do not allow large file support. Although the procedure we are going to show could be completely automated in a startup script, for purpose of explanation we start using the commands interactively.

As example we create a dump of the Windows partition from our client machine. The partimage tool can be used either interactively or with a command line. Interactively we can choose many options in a semi-graphic fashion, such as the dump file name, the compression method to use, the maximum file size, and a human-readable description:

```
+-------------------- Partition Image 0.6.4 --------------------+
| * Partition to save/restore                                  |
|   hda1                         ntfs        24.41 GiB          |
|   hda2                         ext2fs      23.53 MiB   #      |
|   hda3                         swap (v1)   855.02 MiB         |
|   hda4                         ext3fs      12.03 GiB          |
|                                                              |
|                                                              |
|                                                             |-
|                                                              |
| * Image file to create/use                                   |
|   /tmp/rw/windows_____ |
```

---

[3] The rsync tool may also synchronize owner, group and permission bits, although such features may not be functional on some implementations such as the fat file system.

```
|                                                                      |
|  Action to be done:                             <Next (F5)>          |
|  (*) Save partition into a new image file                           |
|  ( ) Restore partition from an image file       <About>             |
|  ( ) Restore an MBR from the imagefile                              |
|                                                 <Exit (F6)>         |
|  [ ] Connect to server                                              |
|      IP/name of the server: _____ Port: 4025__ |
|      SSL disabled at compile time                                   |
+----------------------------------------------------------------------+
```

Just the first screen of user interaction is shown, where we use the NFS mounted file space under /tmp/rw/, and it guides the user with a wizard through the setting of all the needed parameters such as the already mentioned file size split limit. Additionally, the partimage command has a dedicated SSH-aware server which can be installed on a central host: in this case we have to guarantee, that the client and server versions are exactly the same.

Using the presented combination of PXE boot and NFS mountable dump files created by partimage, it is possible to easily deploy an automated and completely unattended machine cloning, easily extendable to handle several computers at once.

15.4 Kiosks

It is nowadays a common practice to provide guest users with public available computers only supporting a single operation, such as browsing the web, called kiosks. These computers include a limited minimal graphical interface running a program, in our case, a web browser. Moreover, the browser should be locked up, so that it does not store sensible informative contents. This section shows how to modify a locally installed Debian Linux to grant only a minimal access, allowing interaction through the Mozilla Firefox web browser, running on top of a minimal X Windows system under a restricted user. Such settings could provide a public Internet web access point, but it is also helpful for online exams too, maybe with the introduction of additional constraints, such as allowing selective connections with the use of a firewall.

15.4.1 Configuring a Kiosk

Our kiosk needs a minimal graphic interface and a web browser, hence we will install the XFree86 server first, distributed via the x-window-system package. The configuration of an X-based system is out of the scope of this book, since it is highly dependent on the provided hardware. Afterwards we install the mozilla-firefox package such that all the needed libraries for Firefox are downloaded: the actual browser we prefer is the more recent Mozilla Firefox version 1.5, downloaded from the official site and correctly unpacked in /usr/local/src/. For kiosk mode we need this up to date version making it available in /usr/local/bin/:

```
# cd /usr/local/bin/

# ln -s /usr/local/src/firefox/firefox
```

To enhance kiosk security we create a local user **kiosk**, adding it to the **audio** and **video** groups, so that the public computer will be enabled to such contents:

```
# adduser kiosk

# adduser kiosk audio

# adduser kiosk video
```

Immediately we try to login as the **kiosk** user, testing the recent Firefox version. This has to be done with a running X windows environment which is provided through the **xinit** tool, feeding it with the program to run, in our case, the web browser:

```
$ xinit /usr/local/bin/firefox
```

As an additional feature, as **kiosk** user we browse to the Mozilla site and search for Add-ons for Firefox: the web browser still needs to be enabled in kiosk-mode. One possible add-on for kiosk-mode browsing is the R-kiosk Plugin for Firefox, which can be easily downloaded and installed so that it will become active immediately after restarting the browser. This plugin forces a full-screen mode, and reduces the browser interface to a bare minimum (e.g. it disables windows borders, program menus, and status bar). In order to remove the plugin, Firefox has to be run in "safe mode" with the **-safe-mode** option, yet it does not restrict the destination reachable by the browser.

15.4.2 Stand-alone Kiosks

To enhance security, we make our kiosk host a pure stand-alone machine, enabling the web browser at startup, and inhibiting the user login process. First we lock down our **kiosk** user, such that there is no valid login shell to execute commands, furthermore we exclude any kind of interactive login on a console by creating the **/etc/nologin** file, which inhibits interactive logins except for **root**:

```
# usermod -s /bin/false -L kiosk

# touch /etc/nologin
```

All the textual consoles should be turned off in the **/etc/inittab** file, which is responsible for all tasks to be activated at boot time. Hence all **getty**-related lines should be commented out:

```
id:2:initdefault:
si::sysinit:/etc/init.d/rcS
~~:S:wait:/sbin/sulogin

10:0:wait:/etc/init.d/rc 0
11:1:wait:/etc/init.d/rc 1
12:2:wait:/etc/init.d/rc 2
13:3:wait:/etc/init.d/rc 3
14:4:wait:/etc/init.d/rc 4
15:5:wait:/etc/init.d/rc 5
16:6:wait:/etc/init.d/rc 6
z6:6:respawn:/sbin/sulogin

ca:12345:ctrlaltdel:/sbin/shutdown -t1 -a -r now

pf::powerwait:/etc/init.d/powerfail start
pn::powerfailnow:/etc/init.d/powerfail now
po::powerokwait:/etc/init.d/powerfail stop

#1:2345:respawn:/sbin/getty 38400 tty1
#2:23:respawn:/sbin/getty 38400 tty2
#3:23:respawn:/sbin/getty 38400 tty3
#4:23:respawn:/sbin/getty 38400 tty4
#5:23:respawn:/sbin/getty 38400 tty5
#6:23:respawn:/sbin/getty 38400 tty6
```

It is also possible to ignore the famous key combination CTRL+ALT+DEL by commenting the line starting with the ca: string: this restricts users from forcing a reboot from a virtual terminal. It is advisable for public kiosks to turn off all unnecessary services: the X Font Server xfs, and some administrative daemons like the cron service are sufficient. To activate our kiosk at boot time, we decide to create our own startup script in /etc/init.d/ called kiosk, with symbolic links in all the necessary run-level directories called S99kiosk, so that it is the last script to be called: startup scripts will be loaded in the order specified by the number contained in their names. This script contains an infinite loop which starts the browser as the kiosk user by means of the sudo command. Therefore install the sudo package first, and next proceed creating the shell script:

```
#!/bin/bash
trap "" SIGHUP SIGINT SIGTERM
url=http://www.google.com/

while true;
do
  /usr/bin/sudo -u kiosk -H /usr/bin/X11/xinit \
  /usr/local/bin/firefox $url -- -nolisten tcp
  /usr/bin/pkill -u kiosk
  /bin/sleep 3
done

/sbin/reboot
```

The X server is started without opening TCP/IP ports for security reasons by the option -nolisten tcp, while the initial trap instruction prevents user interrupts such as the CTR+C key combination. As the last step any local user should be allowed to use the X server including kiosk, done by instructing the

X server with the `allowed_users` directive in the `Xwrapper.config` located in the `/etc/X11/` directory:

```
allowed_users=anybody
nice_value=0
```

After rebooting the machine, it will automatically run in kiosk mode. Killing the X server with the `CTRL+ALT+BACKSPACE` key combination will simply restart the kiosk mode after three seconds waiting, as indicated by the script with the `sleep` command. In normal operation there is no way to login into this host: this assumes that no daemons, for instance `sshd`, is running. Maintenance still can be done done from the UNIX "single user mode", hence protect your firmware, boot loader, and the `root` user with suitable passwords.

Practice

Exercise 57. Confront RIP with PXELinux and ISOLinux. Can RIP be sufficient for your requirements, or do you have to produce an own Linux version?

Exercise 58. Do you need cloning and to which extent? Does the described procedure scale for your case? Compare with commercial solutions and investigate recent multicast possibilities.

Exercise 59. Look for other kiosk modes. Ubuntu contains now Opera, which includes by default a kiosk mode, too.

Exercise 60. Benefit from an AFS configuration such that all laboratory clients could have a BSD like `rc.local` script to be executed as the very last one during startup. If the client is enabled for AFS, then this script could copy some global `rc.global` script from the AFS file space and execute it.

16

Collaborative Software

No one wants advice, only collaboration.
John Ernst Steinbeck

16.1 Foreword

The field of collaborative software combines various methods to let teams communicate, share information, and exchange files. This chapter will deal with this topic, introducing some of the most used ways of interaction on a network, apart from the email: the instant messaging. Actively there are several different protocols and software available on the market, some of which are distributed free of charge, such as AIM, ICQ, Skype, and WLM; or on the commercial side the IBM collaborative software Lotus Notes, based on a client-server architecture, include an instant messaging platform called Lotus Sametime. The other side of team collaboration presented in this chapter regards software development. Large companies and universities employ software version control systems to allow multiple developers to work on the same code without incurring into conflictual changes, or in case, resolve modification problems tracking each change. In the following we are going to introduce a secure instant messaging solution based on an open standard protocol, and successively configure two of the most used software version control, allowing also anonymous source code download, a usual facility provided by open projects.

16.2 Instant Messaging

The instant messaging, similarly to the email system, has a long history, tracing its root in the UNIX commands as `write` that could send a message to a user on a particular console, in a one-way only fashion. The first form of a real instant messaging software, allowing two users to have a conversation, was the `talk` command, which paired with the `talkd` daemon provided an earlier form of an IM infrastructure, with a textual interface as pictured in Fig. 16.1.

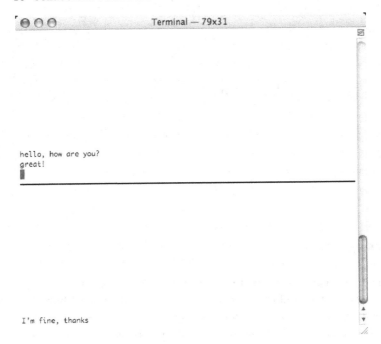

Fig. 16.1. A `talk` session

Successively in the 90s there was an explosion of graphical IM programs, with the renowned ICQ program, intended to sound as "I seek you", and immediately after America Online Inc., released the AIM program and eventually acquired the Mirabilis software company that developed ICQ. Later there were other clients available such as Yahoo! Messenger, and Microsoft's MSN Messenger, now known as Windows Live Messenger. Among other historical quick communication mediums we may mention the Internet Relay Chat, granting users a conferencing environment based on channels focused on a topic (e.g. `#debian`, `#clanguage`) and multi-user communication.

In 1998 Jeremie Miller started the development of the Jabber protocol, which later became an IETF standard named XMPP, the *Extensible Messaging and Presence Protocol*. The specification supports XML-based transmissions of instant messages between peers, and being designed as extensible, it can provide also voice capabilities as the Skype program. The XMPP protocol is already used in other products, such as Google Talk, and provides also support for SSL-encrypted communications. Jabber functions as a decentralized networking service comparable to SMTP: two users can communicate through their respective Jabber servers, which take care of exchanging the actual data. In the following we are going to create a Jabber server for our organization employing secure connections and authenticating over our Kerberos infrastructure: we assume then that a Kerberos client `jabber.example.edu` has been already properly configured.

16.2.1 Using Backports

The Debian stable distribution contains many well integrated packages, with a security team guaranteeing fast response times for discovered security problems. On the downside several packets might become outdated during the usually long lifetime of the stable version. To overcome this problem there exists a repository of software ported back to the current stable Debian distribution called Backports. This back-ported software repository can simply be activated by modifying the configuration file `sources.list` of the `apt` tool which is located in `/etc/apt/`:

```
deb http://www.backports.org/debian/ sarge-backports main
```

In general, it is advisable to use packages from the stable branch only, but occasionally we wish to get a software from the Backports in order to install newer services, such as the Jabber server version 2, not included in the current Debian stable branch. In order to avoid conflicts with newer packages, provided by the new source, we set a low priority to packages from the back-ported repository by adding the `/etc/apt/preferences` file with the following lines:

```
Package: *
Pin: release a=sarge-backports
Pin-priority: 200
```

Before proceeding, we need to update the current list of known packages, such that also the new repository is consulted by the `apt` tools:

```
# apt-get update
Get:1 http://www.backports.org sarge-backports/main Packages [484kB]
Hit http://mirror.switch.ch stable/main Packages
Hit http://mirror.switch.ch stable/main Release
Hit http://mirror.switch.ch stable/main Sources
Hit http://mirror.switch.ch stable/main Release
Get:2 http://www.backports.org sarge-backports/main Release [119B]
Get:3 http://security.debian.org stable/updates/main Packages [372kB]
Get:4 http://security.debian.org stable/updates/main Release [110B]
Fetched 856kB in 8s (100kB/s)
Reading Package Lists... Done
```

From this moment on, all software from the main Backports repository is available, too; nevertheless the Debian stable branch is preferred.

16.2.2 Installing Jabber

As message storage Jabber provides different backends like MySQL, PostgreSQL, and Berkeley DB: our choice is to use the last one, since it provides a straightforward installation, remembering that files related to Berkeley database have to stay outside AFS space due to locking problems. Let us proceed with installing the `jabberd2-bdb` package and stopping the Jabber daemon immediately:

```
# apt-get install jabberd2-bdb

# /etc/init.d/jabberd2-bdb stop
Stopping Jabber Services: c2s s2s sm resolver router.
```

The configuration files for the Jabber service are stored in the `jabberd2/` subdirectory of `/etc/` in XML files. We are going to modify the `c2s.xml` file settings first, which is the file that determines all client-to-server connections. In the `local` stanza, we set the correct host name to `jabber.example.edu` and enable `pam` as the authentication module in the `authreg` stanza. Next we have to remove from the `register` stanza the `enable` and `password` entries: this means to deny the change of passwords via Jabber since it will use our Kerberos-enabled facilities, and also external users are denied to register freely on our server, since we did not intend to open our Jabber service to the public. So the `c2s.xml` file will look like the following:

```
<c2s>
  ...
  <local>
    <id>jabber.example.edu</id>
    <ip>0.0.0.0</ip>
    <port>5222</port>
  </local>
  ...
  <authreg>
    <module>pam</module>
    <register>
      <instructions>Enter your username and password.</instructions>
    </register>
  ...
  </authreg>
</c2s>
```

Next we have to change the session manager configuration file `sm.xml`: as on the previous file we have to set our host name in the main stanza called `sm`, and we want to enable our users to use Jabber without any further system administration approval, so in the `user` stanza enable the `auto-create` entry. The file should then look like the following:

```
<sm>
  <id>jabber.example.edu</id>
  ...
  <storage>
    <driver>db</driver>
    <db>
      <path>/var/lib/jabberd2/db</path>
      <sync/>
    </db>
  </storage>
  <aci>
```

```
      <acl type='all'>
        <jid>sysadmin@example.edu</jid>
      </acl>
      <acl type='broadcast'>
        <jid>sysadmin@example.edu</jid>
      </acl>
      <acl type='disco'>
        <jid>sysadmin@example.edu</jid>
      </acl>
   </aci>
   ...
   <user>
     <auto-create/>
     <template>
     </template>
   </user>
</sm>
```

From the example above we notice as we set also the `sysadmin` user
to have administrative rights over the Jabber service: a Jabber user is
then identified by the username followed by our organization domain, as in
`sysadmin@example.edu`. With the help of PAM our users can be authenticated using Kerberos, symmetrically to the settings we provided to Postfix and
Courier, without any intermediate authentication daemon. The corresponding
Jabber 2 service, called `jabberd`, will make use of the PAM Kerberos module
`pam_krb5.so`:

```
auth       required       pam_krb5.so
account    required       pam_permit.so
password   required       pam_permit.so
session    required       pam_permit.so
```

16.2.3 Securing Jabber

Jabber uses plain text passwords to authenticate, hence we want our connections to be established over a secure channel, such that these passwords
can not be easily intercepted. As usual, create a certificate for the host
`jabber.example.edu` and put both, private key and public certificate, together in a single file as needed by Jabber. Make sure that this file is readable
by the `jabber` user, since Jabber does not run as `root`, a fact that ensures
additional security:

```
# ls -l /etc/jabberd2/server.pem
-rw-------  1 jabber nogroup 8123 2006-08-04 15:33 server.pem
```

To enable SSL for Jabber, we have to make further modifications to the
configuration file `c2s.xml` where we have to specify the location of the certificate file inside the `local` network stanza. Old Jabber clients start directly
an SSL connection on the port 5223 without any TLS handshake, and if
you want to support them too, you should enable the `ssl-port` entry in the
`local` stanza. The last step is, to insist on a TLS connection by enabling the

`require-starttls` entry, denying any insecure connections, thus the `c2s.xml` file will now look like the following:

```
<c2s>
  ...
  <local>
    <id>jabber.example.edu</id>
    <ip>0.0.0.0</ip>
    <port>5222</port>
    <pemfile>/etc/jabberd2/server.pem</pemfile>
    <require-starttls/>
    <ssl-port>5223</ssl-port>
  </local>
  ...
</c2s>
```

From the above configuration, we observe that TSL is required on port 5222, while port 5223 directly starts an encrypted communication. After this preparation the daemon can be safely started:

```
# /etc/init.d/jabberd2-bdb start
Starting Jabber Services: router resolver sm s2s c2s.
```

We verify that Jabber is using SSL by looking at the log file located in the `/var/log/jabberd2/` directory:

```
# cat c2s.log
Fri Aug  4 15:44:13 2006 [notice] starting up
Fri Aug  4 15:44:13 2006 [info] process id is 3357, written to /var/run/jabberd2/c2s.pid
Fri Aug  4 15:44:13 2006 [notice] initialised auth module 'pam'
Fri Aug  4 15:44:13 2006 [notice] [jabber.example.edu] configured; realm=(null)
Fri Aug  4 15:44:13 2006 [notice] attempting connection to router at 127.0.0.1, port=5347
Fri Aug  4 15:44:13 2006 [notice] connection to router established
Fri Aug  4 15:44:13 2006 [notice] [0.0.0.0, port=5222] listening for connections
Fri Aug  4 15:44:13 2006 [notice] [0.0.0.0, port=5223] listening for SSL connections
Fri Aug  4 15:44:13 2006 [notice] ready for connections
```

Port 5222 accepts only TLS enabled connections and port 5223 requires immediately SSL, and both will accept connections from any host.

Closing All Ports

Jabber version 2 by default enables external server-to-server networking and router connections, which are recent new features. This means that on our server we have more than these two open ports. This can be seen by the **nmap** tool using the host's IP address:

```
# nmap jabber.example.edu -p5000-6000

Starting nmap 3.81 ( http://www.insecure.org/nmap/ ) at 2006-08-04 15:45 CEST
Interesting ports on jabber.example.edu (192.168.127.237):
(The 997 ports scanned but not shown below are in state: closed)
PORT     STATE SERVICE
5222/tcp open  unknown
5223/tcp open  unknown
```

```
5269/tcp open   unknown
5347/tcp open   unknown

Nmap finished: 1 IP address (1 host up) scanned in 0.372 seconds
```

Since we do not want to supply these features publicly, the last two ports should be restricted to `localhost`. In the `resolver.xml` file the use of port 5347 has to be bound to `localhost`:

```
<resolver>
  <id>resolver</id>
  ...
  <router>
    <ip>127.0.0.1</ip>
    <port>5347</port>
    <user>jabberd</user>
    <pass>secret</pass>
    <retry>
       <init>3</init>
       <lost>3</lost>
       <sleep>2</sleep>
    </retry>
  </router>
  ...
</resolver>
```

Here the IP address `127.0.0.1` is used for `localhost`. The same modification should be done to the `router.xml` file, restricting it to `localhost`, too:

```
<router>
  <id>router</id>
  ...
  <local>
    <ip>127.0.0.1</ip>
    <port>5347</port>
    <users>/etc/jabberd2/router-users.xml</users>
    <secret>secret</secret>
  </local>
  ...
  <aci>
    <acl type='all'>
       <user>jabberd</user>
       <user>sysadmin@example.edu</user>
    </acl>
  </aci>
</router>
```

The last file to modify is the server-to-server connection `s2s.xml`, closing the 5269 port to all but the `localhost` machine:

```
<s2s>
  <id>s2s</id>
  ...
  <router>
    <ip>127.0.0.1</ip>
    <port>5347</port>
    <user>jabberd</user>
    <pass>secret</pass>
```

```
  <retry>
    <init>3</init>
    <lost>3</lost>
    <sleep>2</sleep>
  </retry>
</router>
...
<local>
  <ip>127.0.0.1</ip>
  <port>5269</port>
  <resolver>resolver</resolver>
</local>
  ...
</s2s>
```

After these modifications the Jabber 2 daemon has to be restarted to consult the new setup, and the **nmap** tool should report only two open Jabber related ports now: 5222 and 5223. In order to test our Jabber server we chose the **testuser** and a new **sambauser** created for the occasion, with results pictured in Fig. 16.2 on the Windows XP operating system running the Jabber-aware free client GAIM.

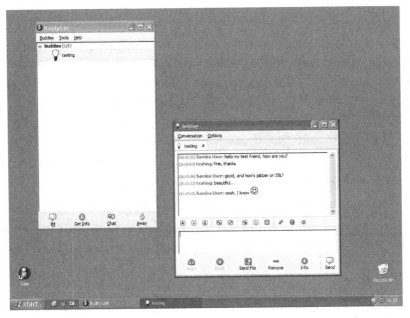

Fig. 16.2. A Jabber IM conversation session

16.3 Collaborative Development

This section shows two applications that support code management also known as revision control: these applications back the maintenance of source code for complex software development. An early system has been SCCS, the *Source Code Control System*, originally developed by the Bell Labs for the IBM System/370 system, and later ported on the PDP-11 machine under UNIX. Later this got replaced by RCS, the *Revision Control System*, developed by by Walter Tichy at the Purdue University.

Two more recent tools are CVS and Subversion, produced by Dick Grune (as the original developer), and the CollabNet Inc., respectively. The *Concurrent Versions System*, or CVS, overcomes the restrictions of RCS now supporting work on multiple files concurrently, while Subversion, or SVN, adds further features to CVS, such as atomic operations, fine-grained file locking, and native support for binary files.

Both these systems aid the development of software, and rely on a centralized server that resolves conflicts between concurrent submits trying to merge both versions, and not by just locking the files for exclusive access. The purpose of versioning software is to initialize a file set for a common project in some central repository: a developer can "check out" a working copy of the file set, modify it locally, and then "commit" all changes after finishing work. On this occasion a merge might be necessary with the work of another developer. In some situations one wants to grant access to the developed software to everybody: in this case we need on the one hand some kind of anonymous access. On the other hand this should not compromise the security of the entire system. So let us start to prepare a host called `src.example.edu` which has to be synchronized with respect to our network time server, a Kerberos client, and with active LDAP name service switch. Additionally it needs an active SSH daemon with Kerberos support provided by the `ssh-krb5` package, as we have previously seen. A complete description of CVS and Subversion, their usage and terminology is out of the scope of this book, which provide a possible solution to software managing for readers already accustomed with such software products.

16.3.1 Anonymous Users

A versioning system that provides source code access to users other than developers should enable some sort of anonymous user, and in the context of AFS it is sometimes handy to create such a user with UID 32766, since this reflects the PTS entry for unauthenticated users. So let us create a local anonymous user, with a simple password:

```
# adduser anonymous
Adding user 'anonymous'...
Adding new group 'anonymous' (1001).
Adding new user 'anonymous' (1001) with group 'anonymous'.
```

```
Creating home directory '/home/anonymous'.
Copying files from '/etc/skel'
Enter new UNIX password:
Retype new UNIX password:
passwd: password updated successfully
Changing the user information for anonymous
Enter the new value, or press ENTER for the default
        Full Name []:
        Room Number []:
        Work Phone []:
        Home Phone []:
        Other []:
Is the information correct? [y/N] y
```

It is usual to provide anonymous users with the password matching the username. Now, an anonymous user should not be able to do anything except what is explicitly permitted: this means that such user cannot have a full access to a normal shell. A tool called *Restricted Shell* provides such restrictions, therefore we install the **rssh** package with the usual **apt** tool:

```
# apt-get install rssh
```

Now we can edit the configuration file **/etc/rssh.conf**, and allow for example only the operation of secure copy **scp**:

```
logfacility = LOG_USER
allowscp
umask = 022
```

To activate these restrictions we have to change the default shell for the the **anonymous** user to this specific shell **rssh**:

```
# usermod -s /usr/bin/rssh anonymous
```

To test the setup, we try to open an SSH connection to the **src** host, which should not be possible because of the constraints imposing a secure copy as the only available action:

```
$ ssh anonymous@src.example.edu
Password:
Last login: Thu Sep 21 13:14:01 2006 from client1.example.edu

This account is restricted by rssh.
Allowed commands: scp

If you believe this is in error, please contact your system administrator.

Connection to src.example.edu closed.
```

Instead, an **scp** command should be allowed, and as example we transfer a file which got copied during the creation of the user account:

```
$ scp anonymous@src.example.edu:.bashrc .
Password:
.bashrc                            100% 1834    288.1KB/s   00:00
```

16.3.2 Concurrent Versions System

CVS is the first of two presented applications to allow for several users to collaborate on a set of files. It provides a dedicated server for public remote access called **pserver**, but since it opens a new port, we prefer to employ the secure SSH protocol permitting the **anonymous** user to access the repository with the help of the restricted shell. We start with installing the **cvs** package and choose a directory, where to store the project files, for instance the /home/cvs/ location:

```
# apt-get install cvs
```

All CVS users have to belong to a common group, which we call **src**, hence make sure that all users with write access to the repository belong to this group:

```
# ls -ld /home/cvs
drwxrwsr-x  3 root src 4096 2006-09-21 13:30 /home/cvs/

# groups testuser
testuser : testgroup src
```

New projects can be immediately initiated, securely via SSH, for example our **testuser** can "import" the previous MPI example with the help of the **cvs** command, which consults the environment variables CVSROOT and CVS_RSH:

```
$ klist
Ticket cache: FILE:/tmp/krb5cc_10000_Ywe67f
Default principal: testuser@EXAMPLE.EDU

Valid starting      Expires            Service principal
09/21/06 12:46:26  09/21/06 22:46:26  host/client1.example.edu@EXAMPLE.EDU
09/21/06 12:46:26  09/21/06 22:46:26  krbtgt/EXAMPLE.EDU@EXAMPLE.EDU
09/21/06 12:46:27  09/21/06 22:46:26  afs/example.edu@EXAMPLE.EDU


Kerberos 4 ticket cache: /tmp/tkt10000
klist: You have no tickets cached

$ ls
machinefile  mpi-example.c

$ export CVSROOT=:ext:testuser@src.example.edu:/home/cvs
$ export CVS_RSH=ssh

$ cvs import MPI-Example main start
N MPI-Example/machinefile
N MPI-Example/mpi-example.c

No conflicts created by this import
```

```
$ ls -l /home/cvs/
total 8
drwxrwsr-x  3 root     src 4096 2006-09-21 13:30 CVSROOT/
drwxrwsr-x  2 testuser src 4096 2006-09-21 13:38 MPI-Example/
```

CVSROOT defines an external method to connect to the repository, expressing the username followed by the CVS server and the repository directory; the CVS_RSH environment variable sets the underlying protocol to ssh. So far we did not provide outsiders the ability to check out our projects, as we can see from the following attempt by the user anonymous:

```
$ export CVSROOT=:ext:anonymous@src.example.edu:/home/cvs
$ export CVS_RSH=ssh

$ cvs co MPI-Example
Password:

This account is restricted by rssh.
Allowed commands: scp

If you believe this is in error, please contact your system administrator.

cvs [checkout aborted]: end of file from server (consult above messages if any)
```

Therefore in the restricted shell configuration CVS has to be enabled and SCP can be disabled:

```
logfacility = LOG_USER
allowcvs
umask = 022
```

In this case CVS needs a lock directory accessible even by users not belonging to the src group, done by editing the config file in the repository's CVSROOT directory:

```
# cat /home/cvs/CVSROOT/config
LockDir=/tmp
LogHistory=TMAR
```

The last line tells CVS to log only write operations such that the anonymous user can check out any project, which is a read-only action:

```
$ export CVSROOT=:ext:anonymous@src.example.edu:/home/cvs
$ export CVS_RSH=ssh

$ cvs co MPI-Example
Password:
cvs checkout: Updating MPI-Example
U MPI-Example/machinefile
U MPI-Example/mpi-example.c
```

16.3.3 Subversion

The Subversion software, unlike CVS, allows each project to have its own repository, and as CVS, it provides a dedicated daemon for remote access. Again we prefer the use of SSH instead of a plain-text communication. The current Subversion release from the Debian stable branch uses a Berkeley DB back-end as default, which is not suitable for AFS. As the first step install the administrative and client-side subversion tools:

```
# apt-get install subversion subversion-tools
```

Unfortunately the restricted shell does not support Subversion, hence anonymous access will not be possible over SSH. For remote connections we have to enable SSH tunneling in the /etc/subversion file:

```
[auth]

[helpers]

[tunnels]
ssh = ssh

[miscellany]
```

Symmetrically to CVS we create in /home/ a svn/ directory for the repositories with owner and permissions similar to CVS:

```
# ls -ld cvs svn
drwxrwsr-x  5 root src 4096 2006-09-21 13:40 cvs/
drwxrwsr-x  2 root src 4096 2006-10-05 12:08 svn/
```

Again all developers need to belong to the same src group. Now, to create a new project, we have to make a corresponding directory and initialize its repository with the svnadmin command:

```
$ mkdir MPI-Example

$ svnadmin create MPI-Example
```

The structure of the resulting subversion repository is quite complex, as we can see from the following output:

```
$ ls -al MPI-Example/
total 36
drwxr-sr-x  7 testuser src 4096 2006-10-05 12:15 ./
drwxrwsr-x  3 root     src 4096 2006-10-05 12:14 ../
drwxr-sr-x  2 testuser src 4096 2006-10-05 12:15 conf/
drwxr-sr-x  2 testuser src 4096 2006-10-05 12:15 dav/
drwxr-sr-x  2 testuser src 4096 2006-10-05 12:15 db/
-r--r--r--  1 testuser src    2 2006-10-05 12:15 format
drwxr-sr-x  2 testuser src 4096 2006-10-05 12:15 hooks/
drwxr-sr-x  2 testuser src 4096 2006-10-05 12:15 locks/
-rw-r--r--  1 testuser src  379 2006-10-05 12:15 README.txt
```

On a client our **testuser** can issue an "import" command for **svn**, specifying the URL of the remote repository. Subversion uses a simple syntax similar to web addresses starting with **svn://** or **svn+ssh://** for SSH-tunneled operations:

```
$ ls
machinefile    mpi-example.c

$ svn import svn+ssh://testuser@src.example.edu/home/svn/MPI-Example -m "Project start"
Adding         mpi-example.c
Adding         machinefile

Committed revision 1.
```

The syntax for a checkout is similar to the respective CVS command:

```
$ svn checkout svn+ssh://testuser@src.example.edu/home/svn/MPI-Example
A  MPI-Example/mpi-example.c
A  MPI-Example/machinefile
Checked out revision 1.
```

Note that the restricted shell does not currently allow to use subversion commands, therefore an anonymous access should be provided by different means, for instance via a web access.

Practice

Exercise 61. Verify the demand for *Voice Over IP*, or VOIP, in your context: can a specific Jabber client satisfy these needs?

Exercise 62. Test a CVS repository in AFS with write permissions for a specific PTS group of developers. Granting **system:anyuser** read permissions should allow for anonymous access as for the local file system. Anonymous access should be possible with SSH as shown before.

Exercise 63. Test a Subversion repository in AFS space: more recent versions of Subversion can use the FSFS back-end instead of the classic Berkeley DB.

Exercise 64. Weigh the benefits of "distributed" revision control as offered by packages related to the GNU arch project, as **archway**, **bazaar**, and **tla**.

Where To Go From Here

I never think of the future—it comes soon enough.
Albert Einstein

This book presented an implementation of many fundamental services, as they are needed today by institutions ranging from small to large companies or universities, focusing on security and reliability while offering a completely networked IT infrastructure. On the one hand the concrete realization for the support of client systems like Linux, MacOS X, and Windows XP has been performed with the help of the Debian GNU/Linux distribution. On the other hand we believe that the most important aspect of this work is *the chosen combination* of Kerberos, LDAP, and OpenAFS to approach an enterprise infrastructure, which actually is an *OS-independent method*: the whole infrastructure could be easily implemented on other UNIX operating systems, such as the BSD-family.

Once that a core infrastructure is in place, organization becomes easier, having configuration files centrally stored in AFS, making further services benefit from Kerberos authentication and LDAP information, and additionally monitoring the server performance. Although major topics have been covered, there are still several points that could be enhanced.

We have to mention one notable omission which is printing that has not been included in the list of services. Printers nowadays support several standards for network printing, however the communication usually is in clear-text and there is no mutual authentication. Kerberos support for CUPS is on the way, the *Common UNIX Printing System*, as it exists for LPRng, the new generation of the legacy *Line Printer Daemon*, and it will hopefully soon find its way in commercial systems: only then the offered solution would be satisfactory from our point of view. Windows hosts could print in this case with the help of Samba, and hence all platforms are then supported. We outline in the following paragraphs other topics that should be considered for further development.

Servers

Organizations sharing a common objective may trust each other's Kerberos infrastructure, with a *cross-realm* trust; enabling users from one realm to be trusted on another allows also AFS *cross-cell* authentication. Additionally, as we have seen, some applications require certificates for authentication, therefore it would be helpful to have an integration of Kerberos with a public key infrastructure and some implementations of such a service are already available and applied.

Unfortunately the possibility for delegating administrative rights is quite coarse-grained in OpenAFS at the moment. With suitable scripting one should overcome this obstacle which is definitely useful in larger environments.

A last note on the ongoing development of the OpenAFS project. The current roadmap indicates, among other important enhancements, that the underlying Rx AFS protocol will support multiple encryption types as well as full IPv6, the successor of IPv4.

Clients

Instead of a thick-client approach as used in this book, one could imagine a thin-client approach, which has often been realized by NFS. A switch to Open-AFS can raise the number of clients connected simultaneously with respect to an NFS-based solution.

For an automated client installation procedure, there exist several solutions, one of those is *Fully Automatic Installation*, or FAI, distributed by Debian with the `fai` package. Among its strong features is the ability to handle unattended installations of several clients in heterogeneous contexts.

Finally the KNOPPIX distribution, bootable from CD or DVD, allows for remastering with an own choice of preinstalled applications. It could be customized to provide a test bed for a small example AFS installation.

A

Technical Summary

Table A.1. Kerberos administrative ACL (MIT)

Allow	Deny	Operation
a	A	Add principals or policies
d	D	Delete principals or policies
m	M	Modify principals or policies
c	C	Change passwords
i	I	Inquiry the database
l	L	List principals or policies
s	S	Set key for principals
* or x		Allow all privileges

Table A.2. Kerberos `kadmin` password policies (MIT)

Option	Meaning
-history	Minimum count of unusable old passwords
-maxlife	Maximum allowed lifetime
-minclasses	Minimum character classes
-minlength	Minimum password length
-minlife	Minimum lifetime

Table A.3. LDAP access control list levels

Level	Privilege Coding	Explanation
none	=0	No access at all
auth	=x	Permits authentication attempt
compare	=cx	Permits comparison
search	=scx	Permits search filter application
read	=rscx	Permits search result inspection
write	=wrscx	Permits modification or deletion

Table A.4. The OpenAFS access control list attributes

Permission	Meaning
l	List contents (lookup)
i	Create new files or directories (insert)
d	Delete files or directories
a	Change ACL attributes of directories (administer)
r	Read contents of files
w	Modify contents of files (write)
k	Lock files for reading
read	Equivalent to rl
write	Equivalent to rlidwk (no administrative rights)
all	Equivalent to rlidwka
none	Remove all ACL permissions

Table A.5. The OpenAFS @sys names (excerpt)

@sys	Architecture
alpha_dux40	Digital UNIX 4 on an Alpha
alpha_dux50	Digital UNIX 5 on an Alpha
i386_linux24	Linux Kernel 2.4 on Intel and compatible
i386_linux26	Linux Kernel 2.6 on Intel and compatible
i386_nt40	Microsoft Windows NT and later on Intel and compatible
ppc_darwin70	Apple MacOS X 10.3 on a PowerPC Macintosh
ppc_darwin80	Apple MacOS X 10.4 on a PowerPC Macintosh
ppc_darwin90	Apple MacOS X 10.5 on a PowerPC Macintosh
rs_aix52	IBM AIX 5.2 on a pSeries
rs_aix53	IBM AIX 5.3 on a pSeries
sgi_65	SGI Irix 6.5 on a MPIS
x86_darwin80	Apple MacOS X 10.4 on an Intel Macintosh
x86_darwin90	Apple MacOS X 10.5 on an Intel Macintosh

Table A.6. New OpenAFS extensions (excerpt)

Command	Option or Subcommand	Comment
afsd	-afsdb	DB lookup in DNS
	-backuptree	Prefer backup volumes
	-dynroot	Construct root dynamically
	-fakestat	Avoid blocking ls for cross-cell mounts
	-fakestat-all	Avoid blocking ls for all mounts
	-nomount	Do not mount /afs
fs	getcalleraccess	Show context permissions
	getcrypt	Show encryption flag
	getfid	Show file location
	listaliases	Show cell aliases
	newalias	Set new cell alias
	rxstatpeer	Rx peer statistics
	rxstatproc	Rx process statistics
	setcbaddr	Set call back address
	setcrypt	Set encryption flag
vos	changeloc	Set new RW location
	clone	Make a volume clone
	convertROtoRW	Convert RO volume to RW
	copy	Make a volume copy
	offline	Set volume offline (hidden from help)
	online	Set volume online (hidden from help)
	setfields	Set information fields
	shadow	Make a shadow volume
	size	Show size information

Table A.7. OpenAFS 1.4.2 characteristics (excerpt)

Feature	Value Limitation
Access Control List	Maximum 20 entries per directory
BOS Server	Optionally restricted mode
Cache Size	Gigabyte order of magnitude possible
Data Encryption	Optionally with fcrypt()
Directory Entries	For short file names maximal about 64000
Clone DB Servers	Together with database servers, up to 20
Database Servers	Minimum 1, recommended 3 or 5, maximum 8
File Server Type	namei, iname, optional accelerated start
File Size	More than 2GB possible (for Windows in 1.5 series)
Group Membership	Optionally other groups allowed
Kerberos Support	Moving from Kerberos IV to V
Partitions	Up to 255 /vicepX per file server
Size Unit	Kilobyte
Time Skew Allowed	Up to 10 minutes
Volume Name	Maximum 22 characters
Volume Sites	Up to 13, hence at most 11 RO sites
Volume Size	Theoretically up to Terabytes (OS-dependent)
Volume Types	RW, RO, backup, clone

Table A.8. Brief OpenAFS terminology

Name	Meaning
#	Normal mount point
%	Force RW volume
.backup	Backup volume extension
.readonly	RO volume extension
apropos	In most commands available
help	In most commands available
BosConfig	Server configuration for bos
CellAlias	Aliases for cells
CellServDB	List of DB servers for cells
KeyFile	Server keytab file
NetInfo	IP addresses to use
NetRestrict	IP addresses not to use
ThisCell	Name of the local cell
UserList	AFS administrative user (for a server)

Table A.9. AFS and Kerberos/OpenAFS

AFS	OpenAFS
bos addkey	asetkey add
bos listkeys	asetkey list
bos removekey	asetkey delete
kas	kadmin
kaserver	fakeka, ka-forwarder
klog	aklog
uss	

Table A.10. Variable substitution in the Samba configuration file (excerpt)

Variable	Substitution
%D	Domain or workgroup name for the current user
%h	Internet host name of the Samba server
%L	NetBIOS Samba server name
%m	NetBIOS client name
%M	Internet host name of the client
%S	Current requested service name
%U	Session username as indicated by the client

Table A.11. Samba account flags

Flag	Description
D	Disabled account
H	Account requires a home directory
I	Inter-domain account trust
L	The account has been locked
M	A Microsoft Network Service (MSN) account
N	No password is required
S	Server trust account
T	A temporarily duplicated account
U	Normal user account
W	Workstation trust account
X	Password does not expire

Table A.12. Apache SSL options (excerpt)

Option	Meaning
SSLCACertificateFile	The CA public certificate file
SSLCARevocationFile	The optional revoked certificates list
SSLCertificateFile	The web server public certificate file
SSLCertificateKeyFile	The web server private key file
SSLCipherSuite	Enforces encryption methods for SSL negotiations
SSLEngine	Enable or disable SSL/TLS
SSLProtocol	Configures allowed SSL protocols
SSLVerifyClient	Require the verification of the client's certificate

References

[Ait05]   Ronald G. F. Aitchison. *Pro DNS and BIND*. Apress, 2005.

[AL06]   Paul Albitz and Cricket Liu. *DNS and BIND*. O'Reilly, 2006. 5th Edition.

[Bau05]   Michael D. Bauer. *Linux Server Security*. O'Reilly, 2005. 2nd Edition.

[BC02]   Daniel P. Bovet and Marco Cesati. *Understanding the Linux Kernel*. O'Reilly, 2002. 2nd Edition.

[BM06]   Heiko Bauke and Stephan Mertens. *Cluster Computing*. Springer, 2006. German.

[BSB05]   Daniel J. Barret, Richard E. Silverman, and Robert G. Byrnes. *SSH, The Secure Shell: The Definitive Guide*. O'Reilly, 2005. 2nd Edition.

[Buc03]   W. J. Buchanan. *The Complete Handbook of the Internet*. Springer, 2003.

[Cam98]   Richard Campbell. *Managing AFS: The Andrew File System*. Prentice Hall, 1998.

[Car03]   Gerald Carter. *LDAP System Administration*. O'Reilly, 2003.

[Den03]   Kyle D. Dent. *Postfix: The Definitive Guide*. O'Reilly, 2003.

[DHS06]   Rolf Dietze, Tatjana Heuser, and Jörg Schilling. *OpenSolaris für Anwender, Administratoren und Rechenzentren*. Springer, 2006. German.

[Don06]   Taylor Dondich. *Network Monitoring with Nagios*. O'Reilly, 2006.

[Fou95]   Open Software Foundation. *OSF DCE DFS Administration Guide and Reference*. Prentice Hall, 1995. Release 1.1.

[GA05]   Peter H. Ganten and Wulf Alex. *Debian GNU/Linux - PowerPack*. Springer, 2005. 2nd Edition, German.

[Gar03]   Jason Garman. *Kerberos: The Definitive Guide*. O'Reilly, 2003.

[Has02]   Jonathan Hassell. *RADIUS: Securing Public Access to Private Resources*. O'Reilly, 2002.

[Jac05]   Tom Jackiewicz. *Deploying OpenLDAP*. Apress, 2005.

[KHP05]   Yanek Korff, Paco Hope, and Bruce Potter. *Mastering FreeBSD and OpenBSD Security*. O'Reilly, 2005.

[KP05]   Michael Kruckenberg and Jay Pipes. *Pro MySQL*. Apress, 2005.

[LL02]   Ben Laurie and Peter Laurie. *Apache: The Definitive Guide*. O'Reilly, 2002. 3rd Edition.

[Luc06]   Michael W. Lucas. *PGP & GPG*. No Starch Press, 2006.

[McC04]   Bill McCarty. *SELinux: NSA's Open Source Security Enhanced Linux*. O'Reilly, 2004.

[MM00]   Dianna Mullet and Kevin Mullet. *Managing IMAP*. O'Reilly, 2000.

[Mob04]   Tony Mobily. *Hardening Apache*. Apress, 2004.

[MS05]   Neil Matthews and Rick Stones. *Beginning Databases with PostgreSQL: From Novice to Professional*. Apress, 2005. 2nd Edition.

[PHS03]   Josef Pieprzyk, Thomas Hardjono, and Jennifer Seberry. *Fundamentals of Computer Security*. Springer, 2003.

[Pre07]   W. Curtis Preston. *Backup & Recovery*. O'Reilly, 2007.

[Ran04]   Kyle Rankin. *Knoppix Hacks*. O'Reilly, 2004.

[ROC06]   Kyle Rankin, Jonathan Oxer, and Bill Childers. *Ubuntu Hacks: Tips & Tools for Exploring, Using, and Tuning Linux*. O'Reilly, 2006.

[Roo05]   Garrett Rooney. *Practical Subversion*. Apress, 2005.

[Ryb05]   Peter Rybaczyk. *Expert Network Time Protocol: An Experience in Time with NTP*. Apress, 2005.

[RYK02]   George Reese, Randy J. Yarger, and Tim King. *Managing & Using MySQL*. O'Reilly, 2002. 2nd Edition with Hugh E. Williams.

[SEL01]   Hal Stern, Mike Eisler, and Ricardo Labiaga. *Managing NFS and NIS*. O'Reilly, 2001. 2nd Edition.

[Shi05]   Chris Shiflett. *Essential PHP Security*. O'Reilly, 2005.

[Slo04]   Joseph D. Sloan. *High Performance Linux Clusters with OSCAR, Rocks, OpenMosix, and MPI*. O'Reilly, 2004.

[SMM05]   Jared Smith, Jim Van Meggelen, and Leif Madsen. *Asterisk: The Future of Telephony*. O'Reilly, 2005.

[ST05]   Michael Stahnke and John Traenkenschuh. *Pro OpenSSH*. Apress, 2005.

[TECB03]   Jay Ts, Robert Eckstein, and David Collier-Brown. *Using Samba*. O'Reilly, 2003. 2nd Edition.

[Ves03]   Jennifer Vesperman. *Essential CVS*. O'Reilly, 2003.

[VMC02]   John Viega, Matt Messier, and Pravir Chandra. *Network Security with OpenSSL: Cryptography for Secure Communications*. O'Reilly, 2002.

[vT05]   Henk C. A. van Tilborg, editor. *Encyclopedia of Cryptography and Security*. Springer, 2005.

[Wai04]   Peter Wainwright. *Pro Apache*. Apress, 2004. 3rd Edition.

[WD02]   John C. Worsley and Joshua D. Drake. *Practical PostgreSQL*. O'Reilly, 2002.

[WH05]   Chris Wolf and Erik M. Halter. *Virtualization*. Apress, 2005.

Web Resources

1. Adaptive Technology Resource Centre.
   Learning Content Management System.
   http://www.atutor.ca/.
2. Alexander Enzmann. Persistence of Vision Raytracer.
   http://www.povray.org/.
3. Amnon Barak. MOSIX Grid and Cluster Management.
   http://www.mosix.org/.
4. Apache Software Foundation. Apache HTTP Server.
   http://httpd.apache.org/.
5. Apache Software Foundation. SpamAssassin Spam Filter.
   http://spamassassin.apache.org/.
6. Apple Computer, Inc. Mac OS X Operating System.
   http://www.apple.com/macosx/.
7. Argonne National Laboratory. Message Passing Interface.
   http://www-unix.mcs.anl.gov/mpi/.
8. Argonne National Laboratory. MPI Implementation.
   http://www-unix.mcs.anl.gov/mpi/mpich/.
9. Canonical Ltd. Bazaar Distributed Version Control Software.
   http://bazaar-vcs.org/.
10. Canonical Ltd. Ubuntu Linux.
    http://www.ubuntu.com/.
11. Carnegie Mellon University. Project Cyrus.
    http://cyrusimap.web.cmu.edu/.
12. Carnegie Mellon University. Simple Authentication and Security Layer.
    http://asg.web.cmu.edu/sasl/.
13. Cellule Technique du CRU. Sympa Mailing List Manager.
    http://www.sympa.org/.
14. Christian Bricar and Rainer Link. A Mail Virus Scanner.
    http://www.amavis.org/.
15. CollabNet, Inc. Subversion Version Control System.
    http://subversion.tigris.org/.
16. Dan Bernstein. Qmail Mailer.
    http://www.qmail.org/.

17. Debian Project. Debian Linux.
    http://www.debian.org/.
18. Derek Martin. rssh restricted shell.
    http://www.pizzashack.org/rssh/.
19. Derek R. Price and Ximbiot and FSF, Inc. Concurrent Versions System.
    http://www.nongnu.org/cvs/.
20. Digium, Inc. Asterisk telephone system IP PBX in software.
    http://www.asterisk.org/.
21. Don Libes. Automating Interactive Applications.
    http://expect.nist.gov/.
22. Double Precision, Inc. Courier IMAP/POP server.
    http://www.courier-mta.org/.
23. Erich Stefan Boleyn. GNU GRand Unified Bootloader.
    http://www.gnu.org/software/grub/.
24. Ethan Galstad. Nagios host and service monitor.
    http://www.nagios.org/.
25. Francois Dupoux and Franck Ladurelle. Partition Image.
    http://www.partimage.org/.
26. Frank Burkhardt. InstantAFS (German).
    http://instantafs.cbs.mpg.de/.
27. Frédéric Giudicelli. Newpki PKI based on OpenSSL.
    http://www.newpki.org/.
28. Free Software Foundation, Inc. GNU arch Revision Control System.
    http://www.gnu.org/software/gnu-arch/.
29. Free Software Foundation, Inc. GNU Mailing List Manager.
    http://www.list.org/.
30. Free Software Foundation, Inc. GNU Privacy Guard.
    http://www.gnupg.org/.
31. Free Software Foundation, Inc. GNU Project.
    http://www.gnu.org/.
32. FreeBSD Project. FreeBSD Operating System.
    http://www.freebsd.org/.
33. FreeRADIUS Project. Remote Authentication Dial In User Service.
    http://www.freeradius.org/.
34. GBorg. Slony-I replication system for PostgreSQL.
    http://slony.info/.
35. Gentoo Foundation, Inc. Gentoo Linux.
    http://www.gentoo.org/.
36. H. Peter Anvin. SYSLINUX, PXELINUX, ISOLINUX.
    http://syslinux.zytor.com/.
37. High-Availability Linux Project. heartbeat.
    http://linux-ha.org/.
38. Horde Project. HORDE Web Application Framework.
    http://www.horde.org/.
39. ICANN. Internet Assigned Numbers Authority.
    http://www.iana.org/.
40. ICANN. Internet Corporation for Assigned Names and Numbers.
    http://www.icann.org/.
41. IETF. Web-based Distributed Authoring and Versioning.
    http://www.webdav.org/.

42. ILIAS Open Source. Web-based Learning Management System.
    http://www.ilias.de/.
43. International Business Machines. IBM Corporation.
    http://www.ibm.com/.
44. Internet Engineering Task Force. Request for Comments.
    http://www.ietf.org/rfc.html.
45. Internet Systems Consortium. Domain Name System.
    http://www.isc.org/sw/bind/.
46. Internet Systems Consortium. Dynamic Host Configuration Protocol.
    http://www.isc.org/sw/dhcp/.
47. Internet Systems Consortium. InterNetNews.
    http://www.isc.org/sw/inn/.
48. Internet Systems Consortium. Network Time Protocol.
    http://www.isc.org/sw/ntp/.
49. Internet Systems Consortium. NTP Public Services Project.
    http://ntp.isc.org/.
50. Jabber Software Foundation. Jabber streaming XML technology.
    http://www.jabber.org/.
51. John Andrews and Robert Shingledecker and others. Damn Small Linux.
    http://www.damnsmalllinux.org/.
52. John Coffman. LInux LOader.
    http://lilo.go.dyndns.org/.
53. John K. Ousterhout. Tool Command Language plus a Widget Toolkit.
    http://www.tcl.tk/.
54. Kent Robotti. Recovery Is Possible Linux.
    http://www.tux.org/pub/people/kent-robotti/looplinux/rip/.
55. Klaus Knopper. KNOPPIX Linux.
    http://www.knoppix.org/.
56. KTH - Royal Institute of Technology. Arla AFS client implementation.
    http://www.stacken.kth.se/project/arla/.
57. KTH - Royal Institute of Technology. Heimdal Kerberos V implementation.
    http://www.pdc.kth.se/heimdal/.
58. Linux Kernel Organization, Inc. Linux Kernel.
    http://www.kernel.org/.
59. Mandriva. Mandriva Linux.
    http://www.mandriva.com/.
60. Martin Dougiamas. Course Management System.
    http://moodle.org/.
61. Massachusetts Institute of Technology. MIT Kerberos.
    http://web.mit.edu/kerberos/.
62. Microsoft Corporation. Windows XP Operating System.
    http://www.microsoft.com/windowsxp/.
63. Moshe Bar. OpenMosix cluster project.
    http://openmosix.sourceforge.net/.
64. Mozilla Corporation. Firefox web browser and Thunderbird mail client.
    http://www.mozilla.com/.
65. Mozilla Foundation. SeaMonkey integrated web and mail application.
    http://www.mozilla.org/.
66. MySQL AB. MySQL Database.
    http://www.mysql.org/.

67. National Security Agency. Security-Enhanced Linux.
    http://www.nsa.gov/selinux/.
68. NetBSD Foundation. NetBSD Operating System.
    http://www.netbsd.org/.
69. Netfilter Project. Packet filtering framework.
    http://www.netfilter.org/.
70. Nexenta Systems, Inc. Nexenta Operating System.
    http://www.gnusolaris.org/.
71. Novell, Inc. Novell SuSE Linux.
    http://www.novell.com/linux/.
72. ntp.org. Network Time Protocol Project.
    http://www.ntp.org/.
73. Oak Ridge National Laboratory. Parallel Virtual Machine.
    http://www.csm.ornl.gov/pvm/.
74. Open Source Applications Foundation. CalDAV calendar access via WebDAV.
    http://ietf.osafoundation.org/caldav/.
75. Open Source Initiative Corporation. OSI.
    http://www.opensource.org/.
76. OpenAFS Project. OpenAFS Distributed Filesystem.
    http://www.openafs.org/.
77. OpenBSD. OpenSSH Secure Shell.
    http://www.openssh.org/.
78. OpenBSD Project. OpenBSD Operating System.
    http://www.openbsd.org/.
79. OpenCA PKI Research Labs. OpenCA PKI.
    http://pki.openca.org/.
80. OpenLDAP Foundation. Directory Service.
    http://www.openldap.org/.
81. OpenSSL Project. Secure Sockets Layer and Transport Layer Security.
    http://www.openssl.org/.
82. Opera Software ASA. Opera web browser.
    http://www.opera.com/.
83. Patrick Powell. LPRng print spooler.
    http://www.lprng.org/.
84. Perl Foundation. Perl Programming Language.
    http://www.perl.org/.
85. pGina Project. Pluggable Graphical Identification and Authentication.
    http://www.pgina.org/.
86. Philip Hazel. Exim Mailer.
    http://www.exim.org/.
87. PHP Group. PHP Extension and Application Repository.
    http://pear.php.net/.
88. PHP Group. PHP Scripting Language.
    http://www.php.net/.
89. phpMyAdmin Development Team. PHP based MySQL management.
    http://www.phpmyadmin.net/.
90. phpPgAdmin Project. PHP based PostgreSQL management.
    http://www.phppgadmin.org/.
91. PostgreSQL Global Development Group. PostgreSQL Database.
    http://www.postgresql.org/.

92. Python Software Foundation. Python Programming Language.
    http://www.python.net/.
93. R Project. R Programming Language for Statistics.
    http://www.r-project.org/.
94. Red Hat, Inc. RedHat Linux.
    http://www.redhat.com/.
95. Remi Lefebvre. Advanced TFTP.
    http://freshmeat.net/projects/atftp/.
96. Rob Braun. eXtended InterNET daemon.
    http://www.xinetd.org/.
97. root-servers.org. DNS root servers.
    http://www.root-servers.org/.
98. Samba Project. SMB/CIFS server.
    http://www.samba.org/.
99. Sebastian Marsching. suPHP restricting PHP script permissions.
    http://www.suphp.org/.
100. Sendmail, Inc. Sendmail Mailer.
    http://www.sendmail.org/.
101. Silicon Graphics, Inc. XFS Filesystem.
    http://oss.sgi.com/projects/xfs/.
102. Slackware Linux, Inc. Slackware Linux.
    http://www.slackware.org/.
103. Squid Project. Squid Web Proxy Cache.
    http://www.squid-cache.org/.
104. SquirrelMail Project. SquirrelMail webmail package without JavaScript.
    http://www.squirrelmail.org/.
105. Stephen R. Van Den Berg and Philip Guenther. Procmail Mail Processing.
    http://www.procmail.org/.
106. Sun Microsystems, Inc. Java Programming Language.
    http://java.sun.com/.
107. Sun Microsystems, Inc. Network Filesystem.
    http://nfs.sourceforge.net/.
108. Sun Microsystems, Inc. OpenSolaris Operating System.
    http://www.opensolaris.org/.
109. Sun Microsystems, Inc. Solaris Operating System.
    http://www.sun.com/software/solaris/.
110. Sun Microsystems, Inc. ZFS Filesystem.
    http://www.opensolaris.org/os/community/zfs/.
111. SWsoft, Inc. OpenVZ Virtualization.
    http://openvz.org/.
112. The Open Group. Distributed Computing Environment.
    http://www.opengroup.org/dce/.
113. Thomas Lange. Fully Automatic Installation.
    http://www.informatik.uni-koeln.de/fai/.
114. Tomasz Kojm. Clam AntiVirus.
    http://www.clamav.net/.
115. Trustees of Indiana University. Local Area Multicomputer.
    http://www.lam-mpi.org/.
116. UML Project. User-mode Linux.
    http://user-mode-linux.sourceforge.net/.

117. University of California.
     Berkeley Open Infrastructure for Network Computing.
     `http://boinc.berkeley.edu/`.
118. University of Maryland at College Park.
     Advanced Maryland Automatic Network Disk Archiver.
     `http://www.amanda.org/`.
119. University of Washington. IMAP Toolkit.
     `http://www.washington.edu/imap/`.
120. University of Wisconsin-Madison. Condor High Throughput Computing.
     `http://www.cs.wisc.edu/condor/`.
121. UnixODBC Project. Unix Open DataBase Connectivity.
     `http://www.unixodbc.org/`.
122. VeriSign, Inc. VeriSign commercial certificate provider.
     `http://www.verisign.com/`.
123. Volunteers. Debian Backports.
     `http://www.backports.org/`.
124. Wietse Venema. Postfix Mailer.
     `http://www.postfix.org/`.
125. Wikimedia Foundation. Wikipedia free encyclopedia.
     `http://en.wikipedia.org/`.
126. XenSource, Inc. Xen Virtualization.
     `http://www.xensource.com/`.

Index